STUDIES IN MODERN ART 4

The Museum of Modern Art
at Mid-Century

At Home and Abroad

THE MUSEUM OF MODERN ART, NEW YORK

Distributed by Harry N. Abrams, Inc., New York

Studies in Modern Art is prepared by the Research and Scholarly Publications Program of The Museum of Modern Art, which was initiated with the support of a grant from the Andrew W. Mellon Foundation. Publication is made possible by an endowment fund established by the Andrew W. Mellon Foundation, the Edward John Noble Foundation, Mr. and Mrs. Perry R. Bass, and the National Endowment for the Humanities' Challenge Grant Program.

Produced by the Department of Publications,
The Museum of Modern Art, New York
Osa Brown, Director of Publications
Edited by Barbara Ross Geiger and Lucy O'Brien
Design and typography by Jody Hanson and Michael Hentges
Production by Marc Sapir
Printed by Science Press, Ephrata, Pennsylvania
Bound by Acme Bookbinding Company, Inc., Charlestown, Massachusetts

Published annually by The Museum of Modern Art,
11 West 53 Street, New York, New York 10019

Distributed in the United States and Canada by
Harry N. Abrams, Inc., New York, A Times Mirror Company

Distributed outside the United States and Canada by
Thames and Hudson Ltd., London

Contents

Studies in Modern Art 5 will comprise a companion volume to this issue, with
additional articles on The Museum of Modern Art's activities at mid century.

Preface

This issue of *Studies in Modern Art* is devoted to national and international activities of The Museum of Modern Art in the period around mid-century, and mainly in the 1950s. Our first issue, published in 1991 and devoted to American art of the 1960s, included two contributions that dealt with the Museum's own programs; it had always been one of our aims to publish research on both the Museum's programs and the works of art in its collection. This present issue of *Studies,* however, comprises our first detailed examination of the Museum's history. The next issue will be a companion volume to this one, examining additional aspects of the Museum's activities in the same period.

We chose the period around mid-century as our subject because it was an especially crucial one for the Museum. In 1939, on the tenth anniversary of its founding, the Museum was able to look back with great pride on what it had achieved. It had established the only public collection devoted exclusively to the modern arts anywhere in the world, and its rate of acquisitions had increased steadily as it attracted ample purchase funds and important gifts and bequests. Pioneering exhibitions on major tendencies in the modern arts had successfully enlarged public awareness of the Museum's educative mission. And as its collections and programs had grown, a new building had been planned; it was opened in 1939, tripling the Museum's gallery space. It was inevitable that the Museum would want to reexamine its policies and priorities in the light of what had been achieved in that first decade.

Such reexamination was made more urgent, however, by changed circumstances during the years of World War II. Funding was drastically reduced with the entry of the United States into the war, and the Museum's original mission was diverted as it embarked upon war-related programs, ranging from organizing propagandist exhibitions for governmental agencies to providing leisure facilities for the Armed Forces. And the requirements of war service significantly affected both the staffing of the Museum and the membership of its Board of Trustees and other policymaking committees.

Moreover, in 1943 the Museum's Founding Director, Alfred H. Barr, Jr., was dismissed from that position and from his concurrent title of Curator of Painting and Sculpture, to assume a shadowy role in the institution until he was appointed Director of Museum Collections in 1947. Though Barr's dismissal was unquestionably affected by wartime shifts in power within the Museum's Board, it is ultimately attributable to the very growth of the institution under his direction and its increased public prestige and administrative complexity, both of which apparently required a different kind of director to Barr. Such a director was eventually appointed in 1949, in the person of René d'Harnoncourt.

However difficult these years were for Barr (and we know that he found them to be very difficult), it appears in retrospect that his altered status within the institution afforded him more time and energy to devote to acquisitions, scholarly writing, and broad rumination on the intentions of the Museum, including the extent to which its original intentions had been fulfilled. He did, however, remain active in the formulation of the Museum's policies; the reexamination of those policies in the period around mid-century was as much Barr's as anyone else's.

During the war years, this internal reappraisal involved seeking ways to maintain the Museum's fundamental purposes while responding to changed circumstances and needs. In the years after the war, the focus necessarily shifted: The Museum's aims had to be reconsidered within the context of a changed world. Increasing affluence and, most especially, the emergence of a middle-class consumer society in the United States created a much larger audience for the Museum's programs than hitherto. And it was a changed audience, not only by virtue of its size. In the 1950s, national debate about contemporary American values, their ideological foundations, and their perception abroad necessarily affected a museum in New York devoted to international modern art. The Cold War alone occasioned changes in the Museum's policies and programs. To choose two obvious examples: It was not fortuitous that the International Program of Circulating Exhibitions was founded in 1952, only to find itself in an ambivalent relationship to similar, governmental agencies; or that the Museum's Department of Education sought to expand its role in the 1950s, stressing ideals of personal creativity in what it perceived to be a highly conformist period.

It is not at all surprising, then, that the period around mid-century was critical for the Museum. Since the articles in the present volume, and those in the forthcoming companion volume, do not presume to examine everything at issue for the Museum in this complex period, we have chosen to reprint here, as an Appendix, those sections of Barr's "Chronicle of the Collection of Painting and Sculpture, 1929–1967" pertinent to the mid-century period. This "Chronicle," originally published in 1977 and too little known, provides essential background information to the specialized articles that deal with painting and sculpture. We have added to it, again for reference purposes, a listing of all loan exhibitions of paintings and sculptures in the years it covers, prepared by Museum Archivist Rona Roob.

Barr's "Chronicle" details many of the basic policy questions that were debated in this period. Of these, perhaps the most important concerned the Museum's role in the collection and exhibition of both modern and contemporary art. When the Museum was founded in 1929, the modern and the contemporary were effectively the same thing; the Museum dedicated itself to art made over the preceding fifty years. (The year 1880 remains the official starting point for its collections and programs, except in Photography and Film, where the entire history of these modern mediums is within its purview.) As time passed, however, and as the Museum succeeded in its mission of proseltyzing for modern art, a gap necessarily opened between the modern and the contemporary, and with it potentially conflicting priorities in the institution's programs. An article in the companion volume will examine the consequences of this debate.

It deserves mention here, however, that by 1953 the Museum had committed itself to a balance between the modern and the contemporary in its acquisitions. As the "Chronicle" reminds us, a remarkable number of modern works of great historical importance were added to the collection, at Barr's initiative, from the mid-1940s to the late 1950s. These included some twenty works each by Henri Matisse and Pablo Picasso, among them, the former's *The Red Studio* (1911) and *The Moroccans* (1916) and the latter's *Three Musicians* (1921) and *Night Fishing at Antibes* (1939), as well as many other works considered classics of the collection, from Auguste Rodin's *Monument to Balzac* (1897–98) and Henri Rousseau's *The Dream* (1910) to Marc Chagall's *I and the Village* (1911) and Francis Picabia's *I See Again in My Dreams My Dear Udnie* (1914). Additionally, the Museum established a list of "masterworks" that would comprise the nucleus of the permanent collection, and dedicated itself to place permanently on public view masterpieces of the modern movement, beginning with the latter half of the nineteenth century.

As for contemporary art, acquisitions continued apace in that area as well. Throughout the 1950s, works that are now also considered to be pivotal were added to the collection. Among them were Francis Bacon's *Dog* (1952), Arshile Gorky's *Agony* (1947), Jasper Johns's *Target with Four Faces* (1955), Willem de Kooning's *Woman I* (1950–52), Jackson Pollock's *Number I, 1948,* and Frank Stella's *The Marriage of Reason and Squalor* (1959), to mention only a half-dozen. Newly created works, however, were unlikely to find a regular place on the Museum's walls until they had achieved, or had begun to achieve, classic status. Temporary exhibitions were understood to be the place for untested art, and, of course, for the commemoration of proven achievements.

•

One important thread discernible in Barr's "Chronicle" is how, from the start, the Museum's understanding of modern art had focused on modern European art as being of greater quality and interest. Yet modern American art, as the "Chronicle" confirms, always occupied a significant place in the Museum's programs. For example, Barr's survey of its collection of paintings and sculptures in 1940 showed that almost half comprised works by American artists. It remains no secret, however, that Barr considered modern art in the United States to be less mature than that in Europe. Thus, when faced with protests by American artists at their neglect by the Museum, Barr was at pains to point out that the Museum's mandate was an international one, and that it was seriously concerned with other modern arts in addition to painting and sculpture; also, that three other New York museums were interested in American art to varying degrees: the Whitney Museum of American art, of course, and the Solomon R. Guggenheim Museum and The Metropolitan Museum of

Art. The formation of a "balanced" American collection was, therefore, unnecessary; what mattered was the balance of the Museum's collection as a whole.

In practice, this meant that the contrast between the modern and the contemporary in the Museum's programs was paralleled by a contrast between European and American. At mid-century, the two pairs of contrasts were made inseparable by the emergence of what became known as Abstract Expressionism. For the first time, the Museum found itself addressing a body of contemporary American art fully as ambitious as the modern European art that had dominated its earlier programs. The Museum's response to Abstract Expressionism is integral to the subjects of three articles in this publication.

The "Americans" exhibition series, organized by Dorothy C. Miller, Curator of Museum Collections from 1947 to 1967, was the Museum's best-known contemporary exhibitions program of the period under consideration. It is the subject of an article by Lynn Zelevansky, Curatorial Assistant in the Department of Painting and Sculpture and recently the curator of an exhibition devoted to contemporary women artists. Miller's series was by no means dominated by Abstract Expressionism; nevertheless, it was one of the principal domestic arenas where the Museum's response to that style was particularly evident. There were other exhibitions held at the Museum, and circulated by the Museum, in this period that included representation of various Abstract Expressionist artists, and important acquisitions and promised gifts were made of Abstract Expressionist works. This said, the "Americans" series, as the Museum's principal and very closely observed forum for exhibiting new art, assumed particular significance in its treatment of Abstract Expressionism. It is, therefore, of far more than parochial interest to have a detailed account of the exigencies under which these exhibitions were prepared: the problems of scheduling, funding, and so on, as well as of selecting the artists to be included.

Necessarily, the "Americans" series occasioned new discussion about the Museum's imbalanced treatment of European and American art. How this became a matter of public debate is considered in Zelevansky's article. So is Miller's broad role at the Museum: as Barr's right hand, with special responsibility for contemporary art; and as a woman at a time when it was exceptional for women to have important professional roles. Miller occupied (not necessarily unwillingly) a subservient role in the institution that may be interpreted as having paralleled the role accorded American art in the Museum's programs.

No exhibition at the Museum in the 1950s was devoted solely to the Abstract Expressionists—or to any other single group of contemporary artists, for that matter—until "The New American Painting" exhibition of 1959. This now-famous survey was shown only at the Museum, somewhat as an afterthought, at the end of the European tour for which it had been organized by the Museum's International Program of Circulating Exhibitions. This Program, founded in 1952 under the direction of Porter A. McCray, and its supporting organization, the International Council, are the subject of an article by Helen M. Franc, formerly on the Museum's staff in various positions, including an involvement with the International Program from 1954 to 1958.

As Franc makes clear, the Program was founded in the context of postwar governmental anxieties about international relations and the beginning of the Cold War. Its founders all had government associations, and the aims of the Program reflected, supported, and helped to articulate national attitudes towards the dissemination of American culture abroad. Nevertheless, the Program soon found itself in opposition to governmental policies concerning art interpretable as "Communistic"—both the work of Social Realist artists such as Ben Shahn and that of abstract artists of many persuasions. Franc discusses in detail the philosophies that guided the Program as well as the extent of its activities through the 1950s, including representative press reactions to the exhibitions it sent abroad. This eyewitness report reveals how the Program's objectives, and those of the Council, were periodically redefined, in part owing to the extraordinary growth of their activities and their increasing importance within the Museum's organizational structure as a result of that growth, which was to such an extent as eventually to cause dissension about the Program's precise role within the institution. And, being a first-hand report, Franc's article is itself a historical document, providing a participant's version of the myriad activities that preoccupied the Program and the Council in the early years.

The Museum's international activities in the 1950s, particularly their role in the popularization of Abstract Expressionism, have been the subject of considerable critical interest over the past twenty-or-so years. A pioneering study by Max Kozloff (1973), followed by an article by Eva Cockcroft (1974), opened to discussion the ideological, including specifically political, imperatives of the Museum's programs. The very existence of a now-considerable body of revisionist literature on the Museum was certainly one of the reasons why we decided to organize the present publication.

Since this literature began to appear, nothing had been published about the Museum by a member of its own staff—that is to say, by someone fully conversant with the complicated realities of its institutional life and, consequently, its archival documentation. This is not merely to say that some of the information that has been disseminated in various revisionist accounts is incorrect because not based on a sufficiently careful study of the Museum's various archives. This is certainly true, and each of the contributions to this volume, and those in the companion volume, will serve to correct or expand the record in one form or another. Just as important, however, previous accounts have been noticeably incomplete in their presumption of a monolithic institutional ideology. As the articles in this volume demonstrate, this was far from the reality of the situation. For anyone ever associated with a complex institution, this will not come as a surprise; what might, however, is the extent to which the policies of a cultural institution are continually being reshaped, and sometimes fought over, in its own corridors of power.

All this notwithstanding, it nevertheless seemed inappropriate to ask a member of the Museum's staff to undertake a review of literature broadly critical of the institution. Yet it was essential to include such a review here, since this literature comprises the first extended examination of the Museum at mid-century and asks important questions about the Museum's purposes that are not to be ignored. Michael Kimmelman, chief art critic of the *New York Times* and currently engaged in the preparation of a book on aspects of the Museum's history, agreed to undertake this project.

Kimmelman's review draws attention to some of the inconsistencies and errors in the earlier literature. His intention, though, is not to rebut entirely the revisionist arguments concerning such topics as the Museum's proseltyzing for modern, including American, art as part of its own and national concerns to promote abroad American cultural activities and ideals of free expression in the Cold War period. It is, rather, to suggest that finer lines be drawn within such topics in order to distinguish more carefully, for example, Museum and governmental policies, different curators' enthusiasms in contemporary art, and different emphases in the presentation of that art. Additionally, and importantly, he places revisionist literature in its own context, that of American anti-establishment activities of the 1960s and 1970s, thereby showing that these accounts of the Museum's ideological stances had their own ideological imperatives.

It was not, in fact, Abstract Expressionism that either dominated the Museum's international programs or received the most attention in the exhibitions it sent abroad. As Kimmelman observes (and Franc more fully documents), painting and sculpture as a whole were often less commented on than photography, film, and design; these were the arts in which, many Europeans believed, the United States had made its most distinctive contributions. Unquestionably, the most popular of all the exhibitions the Museum circulated abroad was a photography exhibition, "The Family of Man," organized in 1955 by Edward Steichen, Director of the Department of Photography. This exhibition is the subject of an article by Steichen's successor in that position, John Szarkowski, now Director Emeritus of the Department of Photography. Shown first at the Museum, "The Family of Man" subsequently traveled to eighty-eight venues in thirty-seven countries, and was seen by some eight million people by the time its tour ended in 1965. It was the most visited of any exhibition of its period and must be a candidate for the most visited of any time.

As Szarkowski points out, it was not an exhibition in the conventional sense of comprising a selection of works of art or other objects chosen for and installed to emphasize their individual interest. Rather, it was itself a work of art: The individual photographs were chosen and installed to compose an aesthetic and didactic whole. In this respect, Szarkowski argues, it was the climactic event of Steichen's life as a romantic and idealist artist, and not so much a photography exhibition as a photographic exhibition —that is to say, unashamedly polemical, its message being the celebration of the community of peoples after the divisive war years. As such, it was continuous with the Museum's wartime propagandist exhibitions—among them, Steichen's own "Power in the Pacific," of 1945—only conceived on a far grander scale.

It was also, we learn, an expression of the Museum's pragmatic efforts to find financial support for its Department of Photography, Steichen having been offered the directorship of that department on the understanding that his appointment would bring such support from the photography industry. The exhibition's extraordinary success unquestionably consolidated the place of photography within the Museum, just as it drew new international attention to the art of photography itself. At the same time, its violation of the traditional distinction between the work of artists and that of curators proved to be alarming to many in both camps, the benevolent message of Steichen's curatorial despotism notwithstanding.

The installation of "The Family of Man" may be compared to that of a sophisticated trade fair or an educational display. As such, it is of a piece with two other extremely popular, and populist, programs undertaken by the Museum in this period: The People's Art Center and associated educational initiatives of the 1950s, which will be studied in the companion volume; and the "Good Design" exhibitions held between 1950 and 1954, which are the subject of an article here by Terence Riley, Chief Curator of the Department of Architecture and Design, and Edward Eigen, a doctoral candidate in the department of architecture at the Massachusetts Institute of Technology.

The "Good Design" series was the brainchild of Edgar J. Kaufmann, Jr., Director of the Department of Industrial Design from 1946 until 1948, when that department was merged into a newly-created Department of Industrial Design and Architecture under the direction of Philip Johnson (until 1951), and subsequently, Arthur Drexler, under whom Kaufmann worked until resigning from the Museum in 1955. Since the Good Design program was conceived in implicit opposition to the conception of modern design promulgated by Johnson's "Machine Art" exhibition of 1934—the Museum's first exhibition to be devoted to industrially-made products— the foregoing record of Kauffman's employment is not irrelevant to the demise of his program. Its conception, as Riley and Eigen point out, is inseparable from Kaufmann's family connections with merchandising. Whereas Johnson posited an elitist notion of modern design as an extension of modernist architecture and fine arts, austere and purist, Kaufmann was an egalitarian for whom good modern design could include inexpensive, well-crafted objects of all kinds.

Kaufmann's program involved a collaboration between the Museum and The Merchandise Mart of Chicago, the nation's largest wholesale marketer, and comprised three annual exhibitions of utilitarian and decorative objects, most machine-made, displayed in specially commissioned settings. Two of these exhibitions were selected by jury and held in Chicago; a compilation of the best works in them, chosen by Kaufmann, was shown at the Museum at year's end. The program was very widely publicized in the print and broadcast media, including television.

Although the program was nonpolemical and non-ideological in the sense of assiduously avoiding giving a prescription for good design, it was of course more broadly polemical and ideological in seeking to influence the habits of American consumers and the selling practices of retailers. It sought to promote what Kaufmann and his fellow jurists considered good, modern taste, and to associate that with domestic pleasures denied to the ordinary American public during the war—both because this was intrinsically desirable and because it would make consumers more receptive to good, modern art. In this respect, there was a parallel with Johnson's aims; Kaufmann's, however, were pitched more broadly, which is to say, they were more democratic.

In effect, what we see in this mid-century period is the beginning of a shift of attitudes within the Museum toward appealing to a larger audience. It was a shift with momentous consequences, if only because the increase in audience meant larger and more expensive programs, which altered the structure of private funding with which the Museum had begun. This in turn meant securing the support and approval of a larger audience in order to attract support for the programs designed for its education. And it meant thinking more carefully about the Museum's public and educative mission. Further consequences of this will be examined in the companion volume.

As noted earlier, Barr was not the Museum's director throughout the mid-century period; that post had been assumed in 1949 by d'Harnoncourt (himself more of a populist than Barr). Barr subsequently devoted his time to acquisitions, to organizing exhibitions of painting and sculpture, and to writing; aspects of these activities will be examined in the companion volume. Barr, like the Museum he founded, also went through crisis and reexamination in the period around mid-century.

•

"The Museum of Modern Art at Mid-Century" is not an official history but an anthology of individual views on the Museum's past. Of course, the institutional allegiances of those authors who are staff members inevitably must bias their accounts, however subtly. This is not to say, however, that an author affiliated with the institution will necessarily be approving of its past programs; some are evidently very ambivalent about what they describe. The observant reader will have noticed that every article by a Museum staff member in this publication treats not only an aspect of the Museum's programs but also the individual responsible for it: Miller, McCray, Steichen, Kaufmann. The thoughtful reader will understand why.

And yet, this volume is issued by the Museum. For that reason, we have done our utmost to insure that what is presented here accurately records the Museum's history. Consequently, this has been an especially demanding publication to prepare. I am grateful to the authors for submitting to its demands as well as for the quality of their contributions. And I, and the authors, am deeply indebted to the anonymous readers, both inside and outside the Museum, who offered pertinent, useful criticism of the articles in draft form, which ranged from drawing to the attention of authors the complex and sometimes contradictory nature of evidence in the Museum's archives, to recommending revision and rethinking of broad issues as well as points of detail.

I and the authors also owe a particular debt of thanks to Beatrice Kernan, Executive Editor of *Studies in Modern Art,* who supervised all the detailed scholarly and editorial procedures in addition to reading and offering valuable commentaries on the articles in their various drafts. Our work was made easier by the administrative support of Sharon Dec, who assisted this effort in myriad ways, and by the secretarial support of Alexandra Ames and Holly Goetz. Rona Roob and her staff in the Museum's Archives, especially Leslie Heitzman and Apphia Loo, also deserve our deepest thanks; without the documentation that they made available, this publication could not have been written. Among those who provided research support on individual and sometimes several articles, we thank especially Christel Hollevoet; also Jill Carrick, Anne Dixon, Virginia Dodier, Jodi Hauptman, Rachel Posner, and Rachel Salzmann. Mikki Carpenter and Noelle Soper in the Department of Photographic Services and Permissions helped secure the many documentary photographs reproduced in this volume. And we are most grateful to the members of the Advisory and Editorial Committees of *Studies in Modern Art* for their advice and support.

The editorial work for this volume was especially complex. It was done principally by Barbara Ross Geiger and Lucy O'Brien, whose contributions were major and substantial. Mel Byars and Jessica Eber also participated in the editorial process. We thank them all most sincerely, as we do Jody Hanson, who designed this volume, and Marc Sapir, who supervised its production.

The purposes of *Studies in Modern Art* are described in my prefaces to previous issues, most completely in that to the first issue, in 1991. It seems unnecessary to repeat them here, except to say, broadly, that this series is devoted to the study of the Museum's collections and programs and is intended to encourage such study. My final words of thanks, then, should be for those individual and collective donors who have made it possible to initiate and maintain this series, and for those whose interest in it—not only its contributors, advisers, and editors but also its readers—encourages us to continue.

John Elderfield
Editor-in-Chief
Studies in Modern Art

Entrance to "The Family of Man," The Museum of Modern Art, New York, 1955. Photograph by Ezra Stoller

"The Family of Man"

John Szarkowski

"The Family of Man" was surely the most successful photography (or photographic) exhibition ever mounted. It opened at The Museum of Modern Art on January 26, 1955; during its 103-day run there it was seen by more than a quarter-million people, a total exceeded (slightly) in the Museum's previous history only by the "Italian Masters" exhibition of 1940.[1] Eventually, five copies of the exhibition were circulated, and were seen at eighty-eight venues in thirty-seven countries, on all of the continents except Antarctica. Circulation of the exhibition overseas was sponsored by the United States Information Agency (USIA), which estimated that when the last, battered copy was finally retired in 1965, the show had been seen by seven and a half million people, not counting those in the United States and Canada. If the USIA figures are to be trusted, this means that "The Family of Man" was seen by almost half again as many people as saw the Crystal Palace exhibition—"The Great Exhibition of the Works of Industry of All Nations"—a century earlier.[2]

"The Family of Man" consisted of 503 photographs made by 273 photographers from 68 countries. Almost all of the photographs were of people, and almost all of the people were ordinary, unknown people, engaged in unexceptional activities. The photographs were arranged to suggest that all peoples' goals and problems were fundamentally similar, and to recapitulate in broad strokes the life cycle of the species, beginning with love and proceeding through marriage, childbirth, family life, play, work, aspiration and religious feeling, and death, followed by a brief survey of the bad news—hunger, barbarity, and war—and then a final reprise to the magic of childhood. The penultimate gallery of the New York installation showed only a large color transparency of a hydrogen bomb explosion, warning that the cycle might be nearing its end, but the picture was not included in subsequent showings, perhaps because of technical difficulties but more likely because Edward Steichen, the exhibition's creator, found it in conflict with the central mood of the show.

The exhibition was designed to be an architectural as well as a pictorial experience, and the placement and the size of the photographs—which varied from 8 by 10 inches to 10 by 12 feet—were calculated not only to emphasize their intrinsic meanings but to contribute pace and drama to the story. A wide variety of exhibition techniques was used to free the pictures from their traditional dependence on the wall: They were hung from wires, fastened to poles, and mounted on clear Lucite panels; photographs of children playing ring-around-a-rosy were mounted on a freestanding, circular shelf that suggested playground furniture, and the section on childbirth was partially enclosed by a diaphanous white curtain. This section was sometimes called the nursery, but *Interiors* magazine called it "the pregnancy temple, a shimmering, white-curtained womb."[3]

Installation view of "The Family of Man," The Museum of Modern Art, New York, 1955. Photograph by Ezra Stoller

The groups of pictures were punctuated by brief quotations from the bible and the Bhagavad Gita and legends of the Sioux nation, and from Shakespeare and James Joyce and others. In the words of its maker, the exhibition was conceived "as a mirror of the essential oneness of mankind throughout the world . . . and created in a passionate spirit of devoted love and faith in man."[4] It was apparently accepted in that spirit by a very great majority of the general audience.

Critical response to the exhibition was less uniformly enthusiastic. This article will consider later a number of representative reviews; I mention here only one, which seems to me to define correctly the frame of reference within which the exhibition must be considered. Four days after the show's opening Jacob Deschin wrote in the *New York Times* that the exhibition was "essentially a picture story to support a concept . . . an editorial achievement rather than an exhibition of photography in the usual sense."[5] "The Family of Man" was, in other words, not a gathering together of a number of discrete, more-or-less successful works of art, but was itself a work of art. The beauty or quality of its component parts was not quite to the point, except as they served their role as threads in a grand tapestry. "The Family of Man" was the most ambitious work of art and the climactic event of Steichen's long life as an artist, and it is perhaps best to begin by considering the work in the context of the life.

Steichen began work on his great exhibition sometime after his seventieth birthday. His career in photography had already covered more than half a century—virtually half the life span of the medium—and he had been a superstar in each of the several branches of the field that he had put his hand to. Yet it would seem that he was not long content with any of those branches, or with any of the styles that he evolved to deal with them, and at least four times in his life he cut short highly successful photographic careers, and began again.[6]

In the first decade of this century he was the brightest and most inventive talent among the photographers who had gathered around Alfred Stieglitz. In 1908, when Steichen was twenty-nine, Auguste Rodin called him "a very great artist, and the leading, the greatest photographer of the time,"[7] but within a few years Steichen had broken with the heavily aestheticized symbolist manner that had earned him Rodin's high praise, and developed a style that was harder-edged in aspect and less obviously romantic in content. Steichen later explained the change as the expression of a new vision of photography that he had gained as an aerial photographer in World War I: "The wartime problem of making sharp, clear pictures from a vibrating, speeding airplane ten to twenty thousand feet in the air had brought me a new kind of technical interest in photography completely different from the pictorial interest I had had as a boy in Milwaukee and as a young man in Photo-Secession days."[8]

His experience with aerial photography was doubtless of great importance to Steichen's change in style, but it seems likely that other factors had already been at work. From 1906 until the outbreak of the war, Steichen had been Stieglitz's principal collaborator in defining the program of the gallery "291." The gallery had opened in 1905 as the Little Galleries of the Photo-Secession, but by its third season (1907–08) half of its exhibitions were nonphotographic, and included a show of Rodin drawings and one of works on paper (plus one oil) by Henri Matisse, both arranged by Steichen. Three years later the gallery presented the first exhibitions in this country of the work of Paul Cézanne and Pablo Picasso. In fact, for the last nine years of the gallery's twelve-year life photography exhibitions never reached parity with those of the older arts; in the last four seasons only one photography show was mounted—that of the young Paul Strand. For several years before World War I, Steichen devoted himself primarily to painting, and lived principally in France

Installation view of "The Family of Man," The Museum of Modern Art, New York, 1955. Photograph by Ezra Stoller

(although he seems to have been a frequent visitor to New York).[9] He was in immediate contact with advanced European art, and it is hardly credible that he failed to consider the profound difference in intention and manner that distinguished the work he was recommending to Stieglitz—work that was rigorous, economical, bright in tonality, and wide-awake—from the gloomy and lugubrious reveries that had characterized his photography during the previous decade.

It also seems certain that Steichen would have been deeply impressed—or perhaps shaken—by the radical new work done during the war years by two somewhat younger American photographers, Charles Sheeler and Strand. Strand's first mature work was published in 1916 in the last two issues of *Camera Work,* the quarterly that served almost as a catalogue for the exhibitions of "291." Sheeler's work of the same period was not published in *Camera Work,* but it was surely known to Steichen, for it would seem that even before he and Sheeler became friends, they shared the important and regular patronage of Mr. and Mrs. Eugene Meyer.[10] Sheeler's 1917 pictures of vernacular Pennsylvania architecture, and Strand's contemporary still lifes, architectural details, and unposed street portraits established for photography a new and profoundly photographic aesthetic—one that had been illustrated in passing throughout the prior eighty years of photography's history, especially in vernacular, instrumental work, but that had never been explicitly claimed as a fundamental principle of the medium. The radical new work of Sheeler and Strand proposed that the art of photography was built on specific, local facts, precisely described. This was in direct opposition to the work of photography's aging fine arts movement—and to Steichen's own work of the prewar period—which described grand, abstract issues vaguely.

The new work of the two young photography radicals had far-reaching effects; one might argue that the most important of these effects were those absorbed by the two dominant (and by this time rival) American photographers of the day: Stieglitz and Steichen.

It is a measure of the stature of Stieglitz and Steichen that they were both able—repeatedly—to learn from the example of younger artists. As an old man Steichen wrote of Stieglitz that his greatest gift to the world was his photographs, and that the greatest of these were those begun toward the end of the "291" days.[11] It seems to me that Steichen as a critic is here precisely right: Stieglitz had earlier learned much from the young Steichen, and doubtless something of value from Alvin Langdon Coburn (though he would have denied it), but what he learned from Strand gave him the new clue from which he produced his best and most original work.

Steichen also understood that the game had changed; after the war he largely abandoned painting, and, as he recalls it in his memoir, spent a year or more in a self-imposed apprenticeship, relearning photographic technique.[12] Beginning at this time he also made his first photographs with clearly modernist ambitions. These include not only the synthetic still lifes with the aggressively *avant* titles (*Time-Space Continuum, Harmonica Riddle, Diagram of Doom,* etc.) but the studies of plant forms (fruits, sunflowers, nasturtiums, etc.). Steichen was a serious gardener, and later became a famous amateur plant breeder; his plant pictures might be seen as the extension in photographic terms of a deep curiosity about the structure of the organic world.

Steichen's retreat into study and experiment was not unbroken; he made several trips to New York during these years, and one to Greece, in 1921, made on the spur of the moment with Isadora Duncan and her dance troupe. Six pictures made on the trip were shown in his 1961 exhibition "Steichen the Photographer," at The Museum of Modern Art, and four were included in his memoir; all of these include the famous Isadora, at a distance, or her toothsome adopted daughter, Thérèse, at close range. The splendid *Pillars of the Parthenon* was not chosen by Steichen for the exhibition or the book, although a superb large print of the period was then in his own collection, and although—to put the matter bluntly—it is surely the best picture of the group: best, meaning not most broadly accessible, or most entertaining, or most commercially valuable, but most useful to the subsequent exploration of photography's potentials. Steichen's rejection of the *Pillars* in favor of the six pictures of presumably broader appeal should not be taken as proof that he thought it a lesser work; on the contrary, I believe that he was confident that it was a superior work, in disinterested artistic terms, but one that would contribute less to the problem immediately at hand, as he saw it, which was to maintain the interest of a large audience. It would seem that Steichen was able throughout his career to live comfortably with a two-track value system—one relating to popular success and one to his private artistic standards. Perhaps in the retrospective examination of his own work, which had succeeded so conspicuously on both elite and popular grounds, it had become especially difficult for him to shift gracefully from one track to the other, or indeed to know with certainty which was which.

In 1923 Steichen returned to New York and negotiated a contract with Condé Nast that made him chief photographer of *Vanity Fair* and *Vogue,* and almost surely the best-paid photographer of the time. Steichen was brought to Condé Nast to do portraits and fashion photographs, and he was a brilliant success in both fields. He soon developed a highly original style based on the theatrical use of electric light. He was the first photographer to welcome and revel in the artificiality of the new light, and used it not only to heighten dramatic effect but also to construct pictures that gave the impression of dazzling brilliance and clarity, even when the magazine's reproduction quality was no better than adequate. He did this by designing his lighting to insure that important transitions of volume and space were defined by decisive tonal changes; the extraordinary intelligence of his craft is demonstrated by the fact that the essential lineaments of his magazine pictures survive even in photocopies. Moreover, this style was ideally matched to the fundamentally ritualistic nature of his subject matter: Surely it does not denigrate celebrity and high fashion to say that they are not well served by an excess of subtlety.

Shortly after going to Condé Nast Steichen also began doing advertising photography. He was a success in this field also, although his advertising pictures, like most advertising photography, perhaps remain interesting primarily for sociological reasons.

For more than a decade Steichen was the most famous and most admired figure in magazine photography. But by the late 1920s a new kind of magazine photography was gaining attention, first in Germany and France, and then in England.[13] In the preceding quarter-century the triumph of photomechanical reproduction (and the concomitant rise of picture agencies) had further advanced one of the broad historical changes in photography: the movement that progressively separated the function of making photographs from the function of defining their use. In 1934 Time, Inc., published a prospectus for a magazine provisionally called *The Show*

Edward Steichen. *Pillars of the Parthenon.* 1921. Platinum print. 19 3/16 x 13 1/2" (48.7 x 34.4 cm). The Museum of Modern Art, New York. Gift of the photographer

Book of the World, which would be published two years later as *Life.* The prospectus promised advertisers something new—"the mind guided camera," obviously referring to a mind other than that of the photographer. The new magazine would "edit pictures into a coherent story—to make an effective mosaic out of the fragmentary documents which pictures, past and present, are."[14]

The new photography was not done in studios, but in the outside world, and it attempted to catch the flavor of real happenings—both great events and the characteristic passages of ordinary life. The photographers who did such work did not direct the subject, but followed it, or contrived to make it seem so; technical quality and formal elegance were less important than a sense of immediacy and truthfulness. Brilliance was suspect. This new photographer used a small camera and made many more pictures than the studio photographer (though not nearly so many as he would later), and was seldom present when an editor selected those few that would form (or illustrate) the story. In Steichen's time with Condé Nast he was the editor's full collaborator; he was unsuited by experience and temperament to be merely a supplier of what the prospectus writer had called fragmentary documents. He was, however, a person of exceptional sensitivity to ground movements, and by the time *Life*—the most ambitious and the most costly of the new picture magazines—published its first issue late in 1936, he surely understood that photography's center of attention had shifted. In the same year he had his first one-person show at The Museum of Modern Art—not of his photographs, but of his hybrid delphiniums.

In 1938 Steichen closed his studio. He said, "I had lost interest because I no longer found the work challenging; it was too easy." He added, "For a long time, I had been envying some of my friends their use of the small 35-mm camera. I had been using the big, clumsy 8 x 10 studio camera."[15] Once rid of his studio he traveled to Mexico and photographed with a new miniature camera, a Contax, and with Kodachrome film, which had been introduced three years earlier, and which marked the beginning of the ascendancy of color photography. Steichen included three pictures from the trip in his 1963 memoir, but they proved not to be the beginning of a new career, and by the end of the thirties the world might have been forgiven for thinking that Steichen had retired as a photographer.

Steichen was apparently neither an active letter writer nor a diarist, and his own highly compacted comments on his life and work are generally retrospective; they do not give us his thoughts while they are still warm. His writings on photography are also scant, and are characteristically oracular rather than analytical. However, in the same year he closed his studio he wrote a review of what was the first exhibition of consequence of the work of the Farm Security Administration (FSA) photography unit.[16] His review was strongly positive; in the present context its importance lies in a sentence that documents Steichen's new interest in the possibility of using photographs as building blocks from which one might construct cumulative and coherent meanings: "It is not the individual pictures nor the work of the individual photographers that make these pictures so important, but it is the job as a whole as it has been produced by the photographers as a group that makes it such a unique and outstanding achievement."[17] In the same review Steichen provided an interesting definition of propaganda: "I do not look upon these photographs as propaganda. Pictures in themselves are very rarely propaganda. It is the use that is made of pictures that makes them propaganda. These prints are obviously charged with human dynamite and the dynamite must be set off to become propaganda; they are not propaganda—not yet."

Three years after he closed his studio, and a few weeks before the United States entered World War II, Steichen asked to be reactivated in the Air Corps, in hopes of creating a photographic record of the war, but was rejected because of his age— he was then sixty-two. Shortly after the bombing of Pearl Harbor, however, the United States Navy accepted Steichen's proposal that he command a small group of photographers to record the role of naval aviation in the war. It was the perfect job for Steichen at that moment. It allowed him to explore his new interest in reportage, and in the idea that patterns of photographs might contain an idea larger than the sum of their parts; it also allowed him to be both photographer and editor—an editor with military authority.

Steichen's Navy unit produced an extraordinary body of work, and Steichen himself contributed excellent pictures,[18] but he also found time during the war to pursue the idea of photographic assemblage in a civilian context. In the spring of 1942 he was guest director of the Museum of Modern Art exhibition "The Road to Victory,"[19] which used photographs from various government offices and picture agencies to produce a very effective patriotic collage, in service of the idea that the United States would win the war because of the justice of its cause and the vitality of its people. In January 1945 the Museum opened the second of Steichen's war exhibitions, "Power in the Pacific," which dealt with more purely military aspects of the war. These two exhibitions were well received and well attended, as was "Korea," Steichen's 1951 exhibition on the Korean War. In retrospect, however, he regarded these exhibitions as failures: "I had failed to accomplish my mission. I had not incited people into taking open and united action against war itself."[20] It seems that in Steichen's memory, his mission had shifted over the years that separated the events from their recollection in his memoir. Certainly with reference to the two exhibitions produced during the hostilities of World War II, an attempt to incite people to take open and united action against war itself would have been a serious offense even for a civilian, to say nothing of a uniformed officer of the armed forces. Steichen's formulation is nevertheless useful, for it makes it clear that in retrospect he thought of the three earlier theme exhibitions as efforts that preceded "The Family of Man," and his description of the earlier exhibitions as failures, in spite of its recklessness, gives a sense of how enormous his ambitions were for the major work of his life. In August 1952, after Steichen had been Director of the Museum's Department of Photography for five years, he first wrote to Dorothea Lange about the exhibition. He said, "I hope this will be the realization of the dream I had when I took over this job."[21]

•

Nevertheless, the evolution of the idea for "The Family of Man" had been slow and convoluted. In the end it was the expression not only of Steichen's romantic idealism and heroic ambition but also of the Museum's pragmatic efforts to find financial support for the Department of Photography. The department had been founded in 1940, and like the Museum as a whole, it found its means sadly incommensurate with its ambitions, with no obvious solution in sight. It was clear to the young Nelson A. Rockefeller, who became President of the Museum in 1939 at the age of thirty-one, that the Museum could not keep growing as it had in its first ten years, and fulfill the role that it had set for itself, if it continued to be seen as the special preserve of the Rockefeller family and its friends. Thus the policy was established that any expansion of the Museum's program must be supported by new funding sources.

Late in 1945 Tom Maloney, publisher of *U.S. Camera* and a friend and unqualified admirer of Steichen, proposed to the Museum that he could raise $100,000 from the photographic industry for the support of the Museum's photography program, on condition that the program was directed by Steichen.[22] Steichen was a giant in the field, and had, as guest director, already mounted two successful wartime shows at the Museum. Maloney's proposal was attractive, except for the fact that the department already had a head—Beaumont Newhall, who two months earlier had returned to his position as Curator of Photography after more than three years of service as a photo-interpreter with the Army Air Corps. During his absence his wife, Nancy Wynne Newhall, had served as Acting Curator, and had accomplished much of value during a very difficult period at the Museum, in spite of tribulations and bitter defeats. The most damaging of the latter was perhaps the loss of the department's Photography Center, which provided space for small informal exhibitions and a study room, as well as staff offices. The Center had opened in November 1943 in quarters across Fifty-fourth Street from the Museum garden, rented from Museum Trustee Philip L. Goodwin.[23] It closed a scant eight months later, when Goodwin decided to sell the building. No alternative space was found. The brevity of the Center's life was perhaps not unrelated to the only slightly longer tenure of Willard Morgan as the first Director of the Department of Photography. Morgan, known principally as a publisher of technical books on photography, had perhaps been offered the job because of his familiarity with the photographic industry, which was regarded as a natural source of financial support. He did secure support from the Eastman Kodak Company for the exhibition "The American Snapshot," in the spring of 1944. It was a show of remarkable banality, which missed all of the genuine virtues of the family album, and showed only its smug insularity. The show was recognized as a serious mistake by both populists and elitists; it undoubtedly damaged the reputation of the department, and muddied the distinction between administrative and curatorial responsibilities. Shortly after the show closed Morgan moved on to *Look* magazine, and was not replaced. By the end of 1944, however, a year before the Maloney memorandum, Nancy Newhall wrote to her husband and reported rumors that Steichen was being considered as director of the department.[24]

The Maloney proposal was debated with spirit; it was opposed by some who felt that Steichen was a free lance, who was uninterested in the program of the Museum as a whole, and by others who thought that an expanded photography program could only be achieved at the expense of other departments. Those in favor of the Maloney proposal believed that all departments needed additional funding, and that it was unrealistic to expect them all to find help simultaneously; they also believed, or perhaps hoped, that the Museum could have both Steichen and Newhall, the first perhaps responsible for vision and the future, the second for history and scholarship. Newhall did not find this view persuasive, and after a brief and unsuccessful effort to rally support to his cause submitted his resignation to Stephen C. Clark, then Chairman of the Board of Trustees, on March 7, 1946.

In the event, Steichen got the job—officially in July 1947, more than a year after Newhall's resignation, although his appointment was understood to be an accomplished fact some months earlier. Maloney, however, did not find the money, and the proposed expansion of the Department of Photography did not occur. The realities of the situation had been clearly spelled out by Henry Allen Moe, Chairman of the Trustees' photography committee, in a letter to Steichen dated March 20, 1946: "... if it is to succeed, the Department of Photography must attract to itself the type of support which enables the Museum as it is now to survive and develop. The Museum earns a large percentage of its budget; the balance is obtained by contributions. The situation in respect to the Department of Photography would be no different: it will have to *earn* its way [if] by 'earn' we mean, as we do, that it must attract to itself the financial support needed for survival and development. . . . Mr. Maloney, disinterestedly and high-mindedly, proposes both to contribute to and to raise funds to a total of $100,000. . . . [W]ithout these funds in hand the proposed development will be impossible."[25]

Moe's prediction was accurate; without the money that Maloney had promised, Steichen and the Department of Photography limped along without exhibition space, or storage space, or professional staff. Maloney's proposal had envisioned a wing of the Museum, or a separate building, devoted exclusively to photography; plus a greatly expanded schedule of traveling shows; plus a quarterly magazine of the quality of *Camera Work,* but with a much larger circulation; plus a publication program that (to begin with) would produce six to twelve books a year. It was not explained how all of this would be accomplished with $100,000, even in the late forties, but it turned out that explanations were unnecessary, since the money proved to be pie in the sky. In the years that followed, the department was approximately as poor under Steichen as it had been under Newhall; fund-raising efforts continued, but were not significantly successful.

In September 1949 Steichen wrote to Dorothea Lange: "I presume Wayne Miller[26] has told you about the tentative plans for a national exhibition revolving in some general way around the themes of Human Relations and Human Rights. It is all still in the research stage and as soon as I get . . . from the realm of probabilities to that of actual possibility, I shall begin work by coming out to talk to you and Paul Taylor"[27](September 19, 1949). If this was the germ of "The Family of Man," it seems not yet to have infected Steichen's imagination, perhaps because of the adjective "national." Ten months later René d'Harnoncourt, the Director of the Museum, wrote to Nelson Rockefeller, its President, in relation to a fund-raising proposal that involved a photographic competition cosponsored by the Museum and Ziff-Davis, publisher of *Popular Photography.* D'Harnoncourt strongly advised against the idea on the grounds of conflict of interests, and proposed that some new approach be tried:

. . . for example, a series of exhibitions of quality but on popular subjects that would be organized by us and shown all over the country. In such a venture we could use Steichen's talent for dramatization. Here is a sample idea:
    Self-portrait of America
    An exhibition of photographs on American life by American photographers, including both professionals and amateurs from all groups that make up this country. . . .[28]

Again the idea proposed is specifically American. Three months after "The Family of Man" opened Steichen told a seminar of USIA staff that during the long and unsuccessful effort to find funding for the exhibition "one important foundation was almost ready with the money—they tinkled it. . . . [But then] they said the idea was too big, to cover the whole world. Why not limit it to the Atlantic Pact nations? I cried about that."[29] Earlier, however, it had taken Steichen some time to come to the decision that the exhibition should be international in its reach.

In June 1950, even before the exhibition had a name, Monroe Wheeler (the Museum's Director of Exhibitions and Publications) had written to the Economic Cooperation Administration (ECA)—the American agency responsible for administering the policies popularly known as the Marshall Plan—in hopes that an exhibition on human rights, executed in a style something like that of "The Road to Victory," might be useful to the ECA.[30] In September, after an exchange of several letters, Hugh L. Latham of the ECA suggested to Wheeler that there were really three problems: preparation costs, distribution costs, and sponsorship; further, that financing of preparation might come from the Public Affairs Office of the State Department, distribution costs jointly from the ECA and the United States Information Service (USIS), and sponsorship by the United Nations Educational, Scientific, and Cultural Organization (UNESCO) or a private organization. The Paris secretariat of UNESCO may have suggested that they might be able to respond favorably if they were approached by the United States National Commission for UNESCO, which might be willing to do so if they were asked to do so by the State Department's office for UNESCO matters, and also by the Assistant Secretary for Public Affairs.[31] The almost imperturbable Wheeler responded in November: "I was very grateful for your letter explaining the rather circuitous route which you think should be travelled in order to obtain financing for this show, but so far we have not made much progress."[32]

The letter from the ECA did not lead to financing, but it may have influenced the conception of the show: "In regard to the exhibit itself, both Tyler and Schneider[33] feel very strongly that it should be prepared on an international rather than a purely American basis, for showing in all the free nations, and especially to the simpler laboring people in factories and market places." Among Wheeler's papers is a summary of a meeting attended by Steichen, d'Harnoncourt, presumably Wheeler, and perhaps others. The summary minutes are undated, but the meeting clearly followed the September letter from Latham. At the meeting the two alternative approaches to the show—as a picture of American life, or with international content—were discussed, and it was agreed that the international approach was best.[34]

It is true that Steichen sometimes played his cards close to his vest, and it is entirely possible that circumstances had made it easier for him to do what he was already determined to do. It was at the undated meeting that Steichen proposed the title "The Family of Man,"[35] which would hardly have been credible for an exhibition dealing with life in the United States. At the meeting Steichen offered no concrete ideas as to how the goal was to be achieved, but said that it should emphasize the dignity of Man, and he rejected the ECA proposal that the exhibition should concern itself with the historical development of liberty, with reference to the "French Republic, first women's vote in Denmark, the Iceland Parliament etc."; all the photographs should be contemporary, Steichen said.

At a meeting of the Museum's Coordination Committee on September 13, 1950, Wheeler read the Latham letter, and it was discussed. It was agreed that the theme of the exhibition should express the idea of a choice between two ideologies, and stress the idea that America had produced a new affirmation of the dignity of Man.[36] Steichen was not present; if this version of the idea was reported to him, he obviously ignored it.

Almost four years later the Museum was still trying to find funding for the show—now, for the second time, from the Ford Foundation—and it was still unsuccessful. By this time, however, news of the exhibition had been so widely broadcast that the Museum had little choice but to go ahead without outside subvention. Steichen seemed to think, in retrospect, that it was Nelson Rockefeller who finally bit the bullet and agreed to guarantee the exhibition's costs.[37] According to Wheeler, these expenses, at the time of the 1955 opening in New York, were approximately $100,000.[38] It is a suspiciously round number, and one might suspect exaggeration, but a year later Porter A. McCray, Director of the Museum's International Program, told the USIA that the costs had been $110,915. In any event, the estimates surely referred only to out-of-pocket costs, rather than to those plus an appropriate allocation of overhead expense—now the universal method of budgeting exhibitions. It was Steichen's understanding (correct or otherwise) that in the end no subvention was required because of increased ticket sales during the run of the extremely popular show.

It is possible that Steichen was not altogether disappointed when efforts to find an outside sponsor failed. In his August 1952 letter to Lange he wrote, "I believe we can do this exhibition with fullest freedom and that we are beholden to no one. For this reason it could not be done with the help of the State Department or the Ford Foundation. To the Museum's contributors of the funds for this purpose I have said there must be no trace of propaganda of any kind"[39] (August 25, 1952).

Steichen had committed himself to the show as a pure idea, with little or no idea as to how it might be made flesh, and he clung bravely to his indecision for many months while his friends and associates were crying for definitions, outlines, lists. In the letter to Lange quoted above he describes the general idea of the show's content: "The stress would be on the universal through the particular with an emphasis on fundamental periodless

Left:
Edward Steichen, Elizabeth Shaw, and René d'Harnoncourt in the Fifty-second Street loft, probably 1954. Photograph by Wayne Miller

Right:
Wayne Miller and Edward Steichen in the Fifty-second Street loft, probably 1954. Photograph by Homer Page

forces in human relations. So far I have tried to avoid thinking in any particular detail. The final sentence in Lewis Mumford's fine piece in [*The Arts in Renewal*], 'At the beginning of human culture stand the word and the dream, both ultimately expressions of human love; the love of lovers, the love of friends, and the love of parents and children; and in the last days, which may also become the first days, the word and the dream, uttered once more in passionate and devoted love, may yet save us,'[40] is pasted in my hat. The exhibition is scheduled for the spring or summer of 1954."

In January 1953 he wrote Lange again: "In my contacts with photographers here and in Europe, I have found the universal cry has been, 'Just what do you want from us and what are the specific details involved in the exhibition'; therefore I believe a brief circular must be produced immediately about the general over-all plan of the show, and above all they will want a list of themes and subjects. . . . It is along this line that I do hope both you and your good husband can give us some thoughts (and as soon as possible, please)" (January 9, 1953).

Lange had suggested the previous month that an ambitious meeting be held the next September, at which serious photographers and heavy thinkers would discuss the concept and the execution of the exhibition. In the letter quoted above, Steichen sidestepped the idea by pointing out that according to the then-current production schedule he was supposed to have all pictures in hand by the following September. He also emphasized that it was *her* help that he wanted, and that her earlier promise to "'fight for liberty and time to do this project' has been duly accepted and recorded in our hearts here."

A week after Steichen's request for themes and subjects for a "circular," Lange sent three drafts of an announcement, one by her, one by her husband, Paul Taylor, and one by their (and Steichen's) young friend, the photographer Wayne Miller. To her own contribution she appended a list of thirty-three words that she hoped might be edited down to something that would stimulate the imaginations of the photographers:

Man	*Friends*	*Government*
Universal	*Work*	*Competition*
Timeless	*Home*	*Invention*
Love	*Worship*	*Beauty*
Create	*Peace*	*Migration*
Birth	*Conflict*	*Fear*
Death	*Abode*	*Hope*
Family	*Hunger*	*Cooperation*
Word	*Pestilence*	*Dream*
Father	*Communication*	*Woman*
Mother	*Ancesters* [sic]	*Descendents* [sic]

Lange titled her announcement "A SUMMONS TO PHOTOGRAPHERS ALL OVER THE WORLD to participate in an exhibit under the title *THE FAMILY OF MAN*." Its first paragraph says:

Under this simple universal theme we propose to show Man to Man across the world. Here we hope to reveal by visual images Man's dreams and aspirations, his strength, his despair under evil. If photography can bring these things to life, this exhibition will be created in a spirit of passionate and devoted faith in Man. Nothing short of that will do (January 16, 1953).

It was not until a year later—only a year before this extraordinarily ambitious exhibition would open, and after a hundred sketches and tortuous revisions—that Steichen managed to produce a statement of the idea of the exhibition, including an invitation to photographers who might wish to submit work. This first official release on the exhibition incorporated most of the first paragraph of Lange's statement, only slightly revised. One interesting change was the revision of Lange's phrase "man's . . . despair under evil" to Steichen's "the corrosive evil inherent in the lie."[41] Steichen was uncomfortable with the idea of evil, but could accept it, reluctantly, if it were identified as a falsehood.

From time to time during preparation of the exhibition Steichen held meetings with various handpicked groups from the photography and journalism worlds. It is possible that Steichen thought that he might get useful ideas from these groups; it is certain that he understood the value of asking people to advise him. One such meeting, of editors and photographers (especially photographers who had the ear of editors), took place on February 27, 1953.[42] The surviving two-and-a-half-page summary of the meeting is doubtless too condensed to do justice to the intellectual quality of the exchange.

Steichen's most important assistance on the project did not come from all-star panels, but from two tested friends. His principal lieutenant in the selection of the show was Wayne Miller, but the role of Dorothea Lange was also substantial. Miller had been one of the photographers in Steichen's Navy unit, and their mutual affection had survived both the war and demobilization. In the last week of 1952 he wrote Steichen to say that he wished he were doing something more socially useful than the work he was doing for *Life,* and that he would like to work on Steichen's new project, if he could make a real contribution. The suggestion was accepted, and he and his family moved from California to New York early in the summer of 1953. In May, Miller wrote Steichen: ". . . the kids . . . all asked about you. They are so pleased that you have asked for their chickens, pups, bird, cats and turtle. Joan and I are pleased too because until you made your offer we were worried about their disposition."[43] Miller recalls the following eighteen months as being totally filled with work on the exhibition.[44] The work space was a dirty loft on Fifty-second Street, over a striptease bar. The editing and arguing and designing went on there until late at night, every night, to the accompaniment of bump-and-grind music from the floor below, until Steichen and the Millers would return to the Millers' apartment for sleep. On weekends they and the problem would move to Steichen's place in rural Connecticut, where the discussion would continue. As Miller remembered it later, no matter how long the work went on Steichen was never anything but hungry for more.

Miller may have known better than anyone else which pictures Steichen would want to look at twice; or if he did not know this when he began work on the big exhibition, he surely did after looking at perhaps as many as four million photographs in the files of *Life* magazine and in other archives.[45] He could also argue with Steichen, passionately and sincerely, about how the edifice should be constructed, without challenging its basic conception.

Meeting of San Francisco Bay photographers at Orinda, California, March 28, 1953. Dorothea Lange (center, in white dress) is on Steichen's right, Joan Miller on his left. Wayne Miller (with glasses) is standing behind his wife, and Paul Taylor behind his wife, Lange. Imogen Cunningham and Minor White are visible on the balcony. Photograph by Fred Lyon

It is impossible to know how large an influence Dorothea Lange had on "The Family of Man," but it might have been great—not, perhaps, by virtue of her specific suggestions, but by holding Steichen's feet to the fire, by insisting that he settle for nothing less than a work of vaulting ambition. It was Lange, not Steichen, who had written that the exhibition should reveal "Man's dreams and aspirations, his strength, his despair under evil. . . . Nothing short of that will do."

Lange first learned of the exhibition in June 1952, when Betty Chamberlain, then head of Public Information at the Museum, visited her in California. Lange wrote, "Dear Steichen: Betty C has just been here and has told me something of your latest undertaking. This sounds to me like the real thing, going into the heart of the matter. I want to help. So call on me and count on me for whatever. Dorothea" (July 1, 1952). From the period of the next fifteen months, twenty-three letters and three postcards from her to Steichen have survived.[46] Addressed sometimes to "Dear Steichen" and sometimes to "Beloved Steichen," their characteristic tone is encouraging, impatient, hortatory, insistent: "Ask me to do anything, including the improbable and the impossible, also the unreasonable. Write me when you can, and your thoughts need not be logical. Scold, and be in bad temper, if you feel that way. I shall do all that I can to give answer and support. . . . We are planning a gathering of photographers to see where we stand and what we can stir up. . . . Wayne [Miller] and I may decide to make a week-end affair, etc. A small Aspen [conference], using his home and my home for a long series of meetings" (January 14, 1953); and three weeks later, "I am needing to hear from you, particularly in regard to my idea for a Photographers 2 day conference. This calls for definite plans to be made very soon, and writing, and telephoning, and a time-table, and a framework of procedure. So that, if it all comes off—photographs will be produced, and persons become truly involved. Shall I try to do this? Perhaps you are not enthusiastic. Perhaps you are even not approving. I need to know, or I am working in the dark and not certain of my ground" (February 4, 1953). Steichen evidently approved, and Lange apparently organized two conferences for photographers of Northern California, and another in Los Angeles. Steichen attended the first,[47] and on the occasion of the second telephoned at "just the right moment" and apparently said just the right thing. "The support which you feel you are receiving from us here is a small part of what you have earned. A token only" (April 26, 1953).

Two weeks later Miller wrote: "Dear Captain, . . . I don't know if you fully realize how completely [Lange] has thrown herself into this show. She is not one to be able to do something with ease and moderation. . . . She is planning another meeting of this group the first weekend in June which she wants me to attend. At this time she will present your outline. The outline will be the reason for the meeting. She went on like this for a half an hour and I must admit that she got way ahead of me. . . . If you are thinking that she has been giving her interest on only a part time basis you should realize that she is an all or nothing girl. She really throws herself completely into whatever she tackles. If you don't utilize her time and interests fully at this time, you will be having an unhappy Dorothea on your hands."[48]

Miller's letter is interesting for (among other reasons) the remarkable similarity of its appraisal of Lange to one made fourteen years earlier. In 1939 Jonathan Garst of the Department of Agriculture had written to Roy Stryker, head of the photography unit of the Farm Security Administration, in an unsuccessful effort to persuade Stryker to reconsider his firing of Lange. He said, "Dorothea Lange has been whole-souled in this enterprise. She has that sort of nature wherein she can only go pell-mell into something. . . ."[49]

Steichen, however, was deeply fond of Lange, and admired her work greatly. He also understood that Lange's passion and intuition more than compensated for her occasional hubris. She in turn understood that he loved her and her work, and therefore would forgive him almost anything.[50]

In addition to Miller and Lange, Steichen enlisted two other old friends, and the young architect Paul Rudolph, to help give shape to his idea. Rudolph had never designed a photographic exhibition before, and in his first tries it seemed to Miller that he treated the pictures as if they were abstract shapes, without regard for their content, but he soon got the hang of it. Steichen and his brother-in-law Carl Sandburg had been through many campaigns together, and it was perhaps inevitable that the poet and Lincoln biographer be asked to write a prologue for the exhibition. Sandburg was only a year older than Steichen, but seemed older, and his contribution, written in a vaguely Old Testament style, was perhaps not his best effort.[51] The more important texts were the quotations placed throughout the exhibition, chosen by Dorothy Norman from a wide range of the world's literature. Much of the meaning that English-reading audiences ascribed to the photographs were without doubt produced by the juxtaposition of the pictures with texts of great beauty and poetic compaction.

At the end of 1952, more than two years after he had given the show its name, Steichen was still not sure that it could be done. On December 14 the *New York Times* reported that after completing his tour of nineteen cities in eleven countries

"Edward Steichen was now optimistic about the plan's chance of succeeding."[52] When Steichen wrote Lange the next day, he was a good deal less sanguine. "It will be another month or so before all the things arrive in New York; and then I will have to study it all very carefully and weigh against the visible or known potentialities to decide whether it is at all possible" (December 15, 1952). It was almost a year later before he expressed confidence to her: "I am now wholly convinced that the exhibition is not only realizable but that we are on the way and every added day we are learning and clarifying" (October 20, 1953).

Lange, in contrast, seemed to have harbored no doubts about the possibility of success; if Steichen would just tell her what he needed she would help him find it, or harangue the photographers into producing it. Seventy-five California photographers were invited to one of the weekend meetings that she organized; from pictures that they submitted she and Miller made a preliminary selection, and sent them on to Steichen. By May 1953 she had sent two packages of photographs. "You may be dismayed by the narrow range which I have thus far been able to send you. . . . There are more photographs of fear than there are of courage. There are few photographs of love, or a sense of belonging. etc etc etc.

Porter McCray, Monroe Wheeler, and Paul Rudolph in the Fifty-second Street loft, probably 1954. Photograph by Wayne Miller

"But the people are keen, and they will work, if we could encourage and stimulate them to go out with their cameras on a search, a crusade, for the *really important values* in their many worlds, instead of taking the role of lonely critical observers of the passing show. Then we may see something spontaneously happening. This, as I see it, is the next step. Am I right? Answer, please. Love Dorothea" (May 13, 1953). Presumably Steichen did not tell her that she was wrong, but he surely realized that his show could not wait until he had reformed photographers' habits of thinking. He did write a 300-word response to the California submission—perhaps the only written response to work submitted—which is gracious, grateful, and ultimately evasive. He could not of course tell the photographers what he wanted, because he would not know it until he saw it. He would not in fact know even then; he would only recognize it as a possibly usable part, depending on the shape of the whole, which (a snake with its tail in its mouth) depended in turn on a whole field of parts. In the event, five of the seventy-five photographers whom Lange invited to the meeting had photographs included in the exhibition. It is impossible to know whether they were represented by pictures that they had submitted to Lange, or by pictures that were selected in New York, from picture files or from Steichen's capacious memory.

Dorothy Norman and Edward Steichen in the Fifty-second Street loft, probably 1954. Photograph by Wayne Miller

Steichen did "The Family of Man" like a photographer at work: not a photographer on assignment, but one working freely, for whom no part of the world is proscribed in advance, and for whom no part is irredeemably uninteresting or irrelevant, if it fits perfectly with every other part within the frame to make a coherent idea. But Steichen was like a photographer working not from the real world but from a pile of several million photographs. In the entire pile there was no single picture so good, so central to the core of the exhibition's intuited, hoped-for meaning, that it deserved inclusion. It did not deserve inclusion unless it fit, and—like one stone in a good masonry wall—the place where it might fit could only be determined in reference to all the parts that surrounded it.

Steichen had understood from the beginning that the exhibition he wanted to make would not be a collection of the best photographs of sociological subject matter, and he made no attempt to keep the fact secret—certainly not from Lange. After returning from his European research trip, he wrote to Lange that he had seen "considerable material of a secondary nature which would be of interest to the 'Family of Man' project, but very little major or basic photography" (December 15, 1952).

Miller explained to Margaretta Mitchell some twenty years later the process of creating the exhibition, and in doing so amplified the point that Steichen had made to Lange: "We didn't take the best pictures, that wasn't the criterion. The decision point was 'what says it best.' As we all know you don't know what a white is, until you put a black against it. . . . So we worked on this in fact almost like music. It had to have peaks, it had to build up and drop down, and build up higher and drop down a little bit . . . Steichen was a master at this . . . intuitively, he'd say this doesn't feel right, let's play it down some more, or what have we got here, find it, gee this doesn't quite go, how about trying something entirely different, let's try something over here—wow, that was it! So it was the [relative] positions that created electricity, as well as individual photographs."[53]

Carl Sandburg and Edward Steichen in the Fifty-second Street loft, probably 1954. Photograph by Wayne Miller

Miller's excellent evocation of the way in which the exhibition was made suggests that here, as with art generally, the idea of the work is continually reformed by the process of working. When a felicitous rhyme or rhythm, or a beautiful series of sounds, or a surprising metaphor presents itself to a poet it will change a little the poet's idea of what the subject is. This is the difference, in the visual arts, between illustration and what we think of as the artist's higher functions, for in illustration the idea is (in theory) secure before the picture is begun.

In this real sense Steichen did not "know what he was doing" when he was forming "The Family of Man"; the shape and meaning of the work may have devolved from an accident, such as the discovery that many photographs existed of children dancing ring-around-a-rosy, in many countries of the world.

It is a measure of Steichen's success that it is now difficult to imagine the exhibition as other than it was. Neither those who applauded it nor those who regretted it argued with details; all agreed, tacitly, that it was cut from one piece of cloth. But it seemed inevitable only in retrospect; no one, including Steichen, knew in advance what the character or vocabulary of the exhibition would be. Early in 1953 Lange wrote:

I carry a mental image for the 1954 Family of Man Show. . . . These photographs are . . . in 3 groups, of 2 companion photographs each. These photographs are huge, more than life size. They are of the utmost simplicity and economy of statement. These should feel like a simple declaration.

The first is of a full-length man's figure and a full-length woman's figure. Caucasians, very white against a background very black. They are naked[.]

The second group is again full-length man's and woman's figures. Negroes, very black, background white. Naked.

The third group is again full-length figures, man and woman, naked. [Asian] race, photographed as grey figures, against grey background, or indeterminate tone, against indeterminate background, the whole panels being colored, or toned yellow.

These are not idealized figures. They are working peoples' bodies. Strong, medium-aged. The job would require enormous photographic skill to execute, along with taste and delicacy. These groups could be the key panels of the Family of Man show (January 7, 1953).

Perhaps it was at this point that Steichen decided that the exhibition would be produced entirely from photographs that already existed. Nevertheless, we must grant, I think, that there is nothing intrinsically ludicrous about Lange's idea. It might even have been made to work, in the context of a different formal conception and a different vocabulary. It seems wildly inappropriate to us now because Steichen's solution persuaded us that it was natural, even unavoidable.

Wayne Miller's description of how the exhibition was edited gives a sense of how complex the formal problem was; it perhaps also suggests a partial answer to the question of why the exhibition's message was so very simple. If the problem is how to make 500 photographs speak with one voice, they should not be asked to say anything subtle. This was the historic problem of the photo-story of the magazines. One might think the problem would have been easier when only one or two dozen photographs were involved, but the problem was still unsolved when the magazines abandoned the field to television. The magazine photo-stories that are remembered most fondly for their artistic success were often more limited in their intellectual content than "The Family of Man." Consider, for example, W. Eugene Smith's greatly admired "Spanish Village" (1951): a story without a story, and one that touches only half the thematic issues of the Steichen exhibition, sharing with the latter references to work, ritual, death, and a hint of evil, but lacking romantic love, children's play, parenthood, and parties.[54]

Edward Steichen, Nelson A. Rockefeller, and Carl Sandburg at the opening of "The Family of Man" in New York, January 24, 1955. Photographer unknown

The photography *book* has on occasion achieved greater complexity and subtlety of meaning, perhaps because it has not attempted so total a unity. Characteristically, its pace has been discursive, and its unity relative and provisional, as in an essay, rather than totalitarian, as with opera and film. Walker Evans's *American Photographs* (1938), perhaps the most influential of photographers' books, is a carefully structured whole, with a lifeline and development, but it does not aim at perfect aesthetic unity, for that could only be achieved by sacrificing the independent meanings of particular pictures.

In the traditional art exhibition also, the integrity of the individual work is more important than its role as evidence in service of the idea of the exhibition as a whole. "The Family of Man" reverses this order of priorities, and sacrifices the part to the whole. Traditionally, this is what artists do, not curators.

Before "The Family of Man," and afterwards, most museums dealt with photography (if at all) much as they dealt with the traditional arts: by means of one-person shows, group shows, surveys based on style, technique, period, or region, and (occasionally) investigations of what were felt to be fundamental formal issues. In spite of its phenomenal popular success, it would not seem that "The Family of Man" had much effect on museums' views of their relationship to photography. Nor was Steichen's example of the curator as *auteur* widely followed, at least not in the field of photography.[55] The 1970s did see a rise in curatorial activism, and in exhibitions in which the curator and the artist became collaborators in realizing works of art that did not exist, except perhaps in broad concept, at the time that the exhibition space and budget were approved. It would be adventurous, however, to propose that these exhibitions were influenced by "The Family of Man."

A decade later an exhibition titled "The Family of Man: 1955–1984"[56] appropriated, half-heartedly, much of the formal strategy of the original show to demonstrate a similar point: Mankind in 1984 still seemed to hold in common the same

Installation view of "The Family of Man," The Museum of Modern Art, 1955. Photograph by Ezra Stoller

goals and problems, but the goals and problems now seemed trivial. It was in fact the triviality of values celebrated, and the triviality of the photographs that described them, that the exhibition found worthy of appreciation. An interesting reversal had taken place. Steichen's show had in the beginning been appreciated for the thrust of its moral intuition, and occasionally deplored for the vulgarity of its means. A short generation later, after the popularization of camp, that verdict was neatly inverted.

Among museums, the sense that the exhibition was a special case, something of a biological sport, was reinforced by the fact that the prints in the show were frankly expendable; like the print of a movie, the physical object had no status. When it wore out, one ordered a new one. It would of course have been a gross aesthetic mistake to frame and glaze the pictures in "The Family of Man." Such treatment would call attention to their discreteness and their physicality; ideally one would want instead wholly disembodied images, floating in space. The exhibition's actual presentation technique was not quite ideal, but it served: In most cases the photograph was mounted to a Masonite panel, which was trimmed flush with the image and painted black on its edges. This simple solution came close to producing a dematerialized image (until it became beaten and bruised by the world, and yellowed by the Masonite), but of course no one would do such a thing to a photograph that was irreplaceable, meaning most of the photographs that a museum would most cherish.

In terms of its influence on subsequent photography exhibitions, it would seem that "The Family of Man" was the last word on an idea, not the first. Formally it was perhaps the last and best photo-story, although done on a different scale, and by a genius. After the last copy of the exhibition was retired in the mid-sixties, periodic attempts were made to capitalize on its success with look-alike shows, but all these sank like stones, without ruffling the water. The most egregious of the sequels was probably "The Family of Children," which skipped the exhibition and imitated the book only. Produced by Jerry Mason, the original publisher of the book *The Family of Man,* it serves the function of demonstrating how good the original was.

(The book titled *The Family of Man* was perhaps even more successful than the exhibition. It is still in print, and has sold more than three million copies, from more than thirty printings, although the records on this are a little vague. It was, remarkably, something of an afterthought; two months before the opening of the show Pocket Books wrote Monroe Wheeler that they did not think a paperback was economically practical; Wheeler responded that he still hoped that a large-format edition might be possible,[57] but it seems that nothing was done to produce a book until the exhibition proved an immense success; even then, the crucial deal seems to have been struck not by the Museum's Department of Publications, but by Steichen and Mason, a fellow commuter on the Connecticut train and the publisher of the men's magazine *Argosy.* When Mason volunteered to do a large-format paperback to sell for one dollar, the Museum became serious, and the first copies were in the stores by May 1955, four months after the opening of the exhibition and a month before the book's official publication date. By early June it was in third place on the *New York Times* nonfiction bestseller list, after Anne Morrow Lindbergh's *Gift from the Sea* and Norman Vincent Peale's *The Power of Positive Thinking.* The book, however, is another story.)

Steichen's only subsequent venture with the theme exhibition was "The Bitter Years," his 1962 show selected from the work of the FSA photography unit. That work was of course much narrower in its range than the material from which "The Family of Man" had been selected, and Steichen narrowed it further by concentrating on the bleakest stratum of the file. The result was perhaps too consistently desolate for tragedy; the show did not achieve the drama and drive that Miller described as Steichen's aim in the shaping of the earlier show.

Critical response to "The Family of Man" would in itself provide the material for an interesting and difficult study, for the exhibition confronted critics with a wide range of aesthetic, intellectual, and political questions that lay outside their habitually traveled routes. It is beyond the scope of this essay to review the extensive critical comment that the exhibition has inspired over the past generation, but it may be useful to consider the response of some of those who wrote while the exhibition was still new. A few of those surrendered unconditionally, gratefully letting the exhibition wash over them like a great warm wave. At least one, perhaps embarrassed by the homely emotionalism of the show, pretended to analyze it as an exercise of primitive magic, designed to propitiate gods that are not only unpredictable but not very bright.[58] It was a nice conceit, but the joke does not work as well as one would have expected, perhaps because we have not totally shaken the belief that art *is* something like magic, and dangerous to make fun of.

Aline Saarinen, in the *New York Times,* did not precisely address the exhibition, but was moved by it to ask the question, ". . . has photography replaced painting as the great visual art of our time?," and to answer, with stunning precision, that photography was not as important as the work of the ten greatest modern painters, but more important than that of the rest of them.[59]

In a thoughtful and generous consideration of the exhibition Dorothy Norman said that "the one thing that cannot be held against the Steichen exhibition is that it is not in the 'purist' tradition of Stieglitz. It does not pretend to be. It must be judged according to its own merits; for its own lacunae. It cannot be judged for what it is not."[60]

This is a caution often delivered and almost never heeded. Perhaps it need not be heeded. Perhaps it is only democratic sentiment that makes us think an author is free to write any book he (she) chooses, rather than one that is needed; in any case, the rest of us are surely free to disapprove the choice. If we have this right toward an artist who is the sole proprietor, so to speak, of his artistic ambition, it is all the more clearly our right to criticize the conductor of an orchestra, for example, for the program he chooses, as well as the quality of the performance, or to criticize a curator for his definition of his role and responsibility.

I believe that many serious photographers were deeply ambivalent toward "The Family of Man." Although grateful for the attention that it brought their art, in a generalized way, they were distressed to have that art characterized in a way that seemed to allow little room for the stylistic intuitions and moral certainties of individual photographers. Most of those whose work was included in the exhibition were pleased to have their photographs used to form part of a new work by an aging artist who had earned their respect; at the same time they regretted that the meanings of their pictures had been subsumed into another artist's grand pattern. Professional photographers, especially journalists, were of course thoroughly familiar with the process, and were in varying degrees resigned to it in their professional lives; but many of them regarded The Museum of Modern Art as a place where a different standard prevailed, and where their work was judged not as raw material, but as something finished.

Viewed in this light, Steichen's great exhibition violated the traditional museum principle that the work of the artist and that of the curator are discrete, and should not be confused.[61] Nevertheless, once the principle was broken, the question was not whether the play was legal, but whether it was useful.

"The Family of Man" produced unlikely bedfellows. Hilton Kramer, in *Commentary,* and Roland Barthes, in his essay "The Great Family of Man," approached the exhibition from different vantage points but rejected it in surprisingly similar terms: Kramer said that the exhibition was colored by "a distinct ideological cast . . . which embodies all that is most facile, abstract, sentimental, and rhetorical in liberal ideology." Barthes said the exhibition existed in "the realm of gnomic truths, the meeting of all the ages of humanity at the most neutral point of their nature, the point where the obviousness of the truism has no longer any value except in the realm of a purely poetic language." Barthes continued to argue (or state) that the false unity ("identity") among men postulated by the exhibition is a device with a political motive: "We are held back at the surface of an identity, prevented precisely by sentimentality from penetrating into this ulterior zone of human behavior where historical alienation introduces some 'differences' which we shall here quite simply call 'injustices.' . . ." He concluded that "the final justification of all this Adamism is to give to the immobility of the world the alibi of a 'wisdom' and a 'lyricism' which only make the gestures of man look eternal the better to defuse them."[62] Kramer said that "pieties about 'the universal elements . . . in the everydayness of life' are revealed for what they are: a self-congratulatory means for obscuring the urgency of real problems under a blanket of ideology which takes for granted the essential goodness, innocence, and moral superiority of the international 'little man,' 'the man on the street,' the abstract, disembodied hero of a world view which regards itself as superior to mere politics."[63]

Kramer and Barthes condemned "The Family of Man" for serving a political

Edward Steichen at "The Family of Man," Sokolniki Park, Moscow, 1959. Photograph by Elliott Erwitt

sentiment while rejecting disciplined political thought. That is, the exhibition proposed no solutions to the world's terrible problems, and refused even to choose among solutions already proposed. It took the side of Mankind, and perhaps also the side of Nature, but it did not identify the opposition—the villain. Perhaps by implication, or by elimination, the villain was government. To the degree that the exhibition reflected a coherent philosophy it was a kind of homemade Rousseauism that saw individuals as good and governments as bad, except for village governments, and perhaps sometime in the future, world governments. Of the thirty-three words on Lange's list, perhaps the one treated most perfunctorily and least persuasively was the word "Government," which is understandable not only because government (especially limited government) is hard to photograph, but because the idea of government was not really relevant to the idea of the exhibition, which was that people were born friends, and could be friends again if they closed their ears to argument and embraced.

Jacques Barzun accused the exhibition of being not only sentimental but anti-intellectual.[64] It was in fact even anti-technological. Its primitivism was insistent: Among the 500 pictures, none showed an airplane, or a railroad train, or a telephone; there was one automobile—a racing jalopy full of teenagers, in full flight from reason. Science and technology were represented most memorably by the huge color transparency of a hydrogen bomb explosion, and by a picture of a man dressed rather like a space traveler, holding a white mouse in his asbestos glove.

It is difficult to argue with the logic of Kramer's and Barthes's and Barzun's complaints, but one might suggest that they could with equal justice be directed toward much of the world's art—to those works that do not propose or endorse solutions, or explain or exhort, but merely offer comfort, or diffuse anger, or hold despair at bay. Augusta Strong, in the *Daily Worker* (in a review that one hopes Barthes was spared), said that "you are catapulted into a world completely beyond your worries and concerns of the moment."[65]

It seems likely that the great international success of Steichen's exhibition was due to the fact that its biases and intuitions matched those of the people who saw it, who were sick to the teeth of contention and brinkmanship, of tortuous political arguments, of being told that half the world was their enemy; and sick also of scientific sorcerers, and perhaps of their own pompous and self-satisfied governments. It seems to me not inconceivable that the millions (however many millions) who stood patiently in line to see an exhibition that showed them what they were ready to be shown—that they were not unlike the others—were buoyed up and strengthened a little by the exhibition, at least temporarily.

In 1958 Lange wrote Steichen from Saigon: "I feel impelled to quickly take a piece of paper out of my notebook to speak to you, for I do so often *think* of you here in Asia, and what was said to the world, through you, in Family of Man. . . . If you have not already heard it too many times I would recount to you what impact the F. of M. made. I hear it all over, and in unexpected places—for instance, in a tiny Chinese fishing village, 10 miles from Hong Kong, only accessible by a junk. Also in a Philippine barrio in a muddy swamp. I think that if ever you were to visit the Philippines, and they heard of it, you would receive a Hero's Welcome. . ." (September 25, 1958).

"The Family of Man" was the most successful photography (or photographic) exhibition ever mounted; and if it was also in some ways a failure, the end of its line, it was a heroic failure, and the work of an artist of noble ambitions. At the seminar for staff of the USIA, Steichen tried to explain the exhibition that they had decided to circulate. He said: "I spent a good thirty-five years and all the money I made in the photographic business in financing a plant breeding experiment—breeding delphinium—a study of genetics. That backed me up in my observation of people—that essentially we were all alike, and if we could see that alikeness in each other, we might become friends."[66]

Author's Note

During much of 1954 and all of 1955 I was wholly absorbed in the task of finishing (and then finding a publisher for) a long photographic essay on the work of the architect Louis Sullivan. This absorption largely insulated me from what else was happening in photography at the time, and in consequence I did not see the original "Family of Man" exhibition at any of its venues.

If memory serves me well, I was until the summer of 1955 only peripherally aware that the exhibition existed, and knew nothing of the critical controversy that it had engendered. That summer my father visited Minneapolis on business, and while there saw the exhibition at the Minneapolis Institute of Arts. He returned full of praise for the show, and with a copy of the book for me. He said that he understood much better now what I was trying to do with my own photography. Although he had been consistently and unquestioningly supportive of my ambitions as a photographer, it had never occurred to me to try to explain to him what they were. As I looked at the book that he had brought I considered for a moment trying to explain that it did not seem to express my own idea precisely, but rejected the impulse. Steichen's show had brought my father into photography's great tent, which I had not done. I was (and remain) grateful for that, and under the circumstances it seemed small-minded to quibble about details.

Notes

I would like to thank Wayne Miller for his invaluable advice, and for his cogent and generous comments on the manuscript of this essay. I am also indebted to Virginia Dodier, Supervisor of the Study Center of the Museum's Department of Photography, for her essential and effective assistance with the research on which this essay is based.

1. "Italian Masters" was perhaps an even more atypical exhibition for the Museum than "The Family of Man." The show consisted of twenty-eight paintings and sculptures, ranging in time from the early fifteenth century to the late Baroque, which had been shown at the San Francisco World's Fair of 1939. When it was decided that they could be shown in New York on their way home, the logical venue—the Metropolitan Museum of Art—found the conditions imposed by the Italian government unacceptable, and the exhibition ended up in The Museum of Modern Art, to the amazement of all and the consternation of many. See Russell Lynes, *Good Old Modern: An Intimate Portrait of the Museum of Modern Art* (New York: Atheneum, 1973), pp. 227–29.

2. George Collins Levey writes in the article "Exhibition," in the 11th edition of *The Encyclopædia Britannica* (1910), that 6,039,195 people saw the Crystal Palace exhibition in London during a period of five months, fifteen days, in 1851. Since visitors paid an entrance fee, the figure is presumably reasonably accurate. The attendance of "The Family of Man" in the United States and Canada is recorded as a round 1,200,000, bringing the total to 8,700,000. I know of no way to assess the accuracy of the USIA estimate.

3. "The Family of Man," *Interiors* 114 (April 1955), p. 117.

4. Edward Steichen, Introduction to *The Family of Man* (New York: Maco Magazine Corporation for The Museum of Modern Art, 1955), pp. 4–5.

5. Jacob Deschin, "Panoramic Show at the Museum of Modern Art," *New York Times,* January 30, 1955.

6. During World War I Steichen put aside his artistic ambitions to become head of aerial photography for the American Expeditionary Force; in the early twenties he abandoned painting to rededicate himself to photography; in 1936 he retired from an enormously successful career as a commercial photographer to breed delphiniums; at the end of World War II, after a brief but brilliant career as the leader of a documentary unit that recorded the naval war in the Pacific, he became Director of the Department of Photography at The Museum of Modern Art.

7. George Besson, "Pictorial Photography: A Series of Interviews," *Camera Work,* no. 24 (October 1908), p. 14.

8. Edward Steichen, *A Life in Photography,* (Garden City, N.Y.: Doubleday, 1963), n.p. (4 pp. after pl. 62).

9. In spite of Steichen's great fame, many biographical details of his long life are missing, or are sketched in broadly according to his own later memory. In *A Life in Photography* only 8 pictures (out of 239 in the book) are dated between 1910 and 1920, and it seems clear that his principal energies in that decade were devoted to painting.

10. Agnes Meyer had for whatever reason argued with Stieglitz by about 1915, and had advised Marius de Zayas to have nothing to do with him. The break may have colored the relationships between Stieglitz and both Steichen and Sheeler. See Theodore E. Stebbins, Jr., and Norman Keyes, Jr., *Charles Sheeler: The Photographs* (Boston: Museum of Fine Arts, 1987), p. 12; p. 4, n. 30.

11. Steichen, *A Life in Photography,* n.p. (p. before pl. 44).

12. Carl Sandburg, in *Steichen the Photographer* (New York: Harcourt Brace, 1929), refers specifically to a "one year apprenticeship" (p. 38), but in *A Life in Photography* Steichen seems to regard the period of 1919 through 1921 as a time of re-evaluation and re-education.

13. The *Berliner Illustrierte Zeitung* had existed since 1890, but in the twenties reformed itself to exploit the potentials of photojournalism. The *Munchner Illustrierte Presse* and *AIZ (Arbeiter Illustrierte Zeitung)* were founded in the early twenties. All three magazines were suppressed in 1933 when Hitler came to power.

14. "A Prospectus for a New Magazine," 1934. Courtesy Time, Inc., archives.

15. Steichen, *A Life in Photography,* n.p. (p. after pl. 209).

16. The Farm Security Administration (originally the Resettlement Administration) photography unit was formed in 1935 to document the plight of American farmers. The exhibition that Steichen wrote about was part of the larger "First International Photographic Exhibition," organized by Willard D. Morgan and held at the Grand Central Palace in New York for one week in April 1938. The FSA component of the exhibition was evidently selected by Roy Stryker, the chief of the group.

17. Edward Steichen, "The F.S.A. Photographers," *U.S. Camera Annual for 1939* (New York: William Morrow, 1939), p. 45.

18. Especially during November and December 1943, during the Gilbert and Marshall Islands Operation. Biographical outline by Grace M. Mayer in *A Life in Photography,* n.p.

19. This exhibition was apparently the final product of an idea first proposed by David H. McAlpin during the autumn of 1941 under the title "The Arsenal of Democracy." McAlpin was a Trustee of the Museum and the first Chairman of its Department of Photography.

20. Steichen, *A Life in Photography,* n.p. (3 pp. after pl. 225).

21. Steichen to Dorothea Lange, August 25, 1952. All Steichen–Lange correspondence quoted in this essay is from the Department of Photography files, The Museum of Modern Art. Subsequent quo-

tations are identified by date only within the text.

22. A memorandum of December 10, 1945, from Maloney to someone unspecified (or, more probably, a retyped copy of that memorandum), exists in The Museum of Modern Art Archives: James Thrall Soby Papers, III.55.2. Soby, who would later become Director of the Museum's Department of Painting and Sculpture, was a longtime member of the Trustee Committee on Photography. He is known to have been the committee member most consistently opposed to the changes implicitly proposed by Maloney's memorandum.

23. Numbers 9 and 11 West Fifty-fourth Street were owned by architect and Museum Trustee Philip L. Goodwin and his brother, James. The Photography Center, which occupied a continuous floor in both buildings, was forced to move when the Goodwin brothers decided to sell the buildings to Nelson Rockefeller. The buildings were demolished to make way for apartments.

24. Nancy Newhall to Beaumont Newhall, October 29, 1944. Quoted in Beaumont Newhall, *Focus: Memoirs of a Life in Photography* (Boston: Little, Brown, 1993), pp. 127–28.

25. Henry Allen Moe to Steichen, March 20, 1946. The Museum of Modern Art Archives: James Thrall Soby Papers, III.55.2.

26. Wayne Miller had been a member of Steichen's photography unit in the Navy. In 1947 he was included in the Museum exhibition "Three Young Photographers," with Homer Page and Leonard McCombe. At the time of Steichen's letter to Lange, Miller was living in Northern California and working for *Life* magazine.

27. Paul Taylor was Lange's husband. They had met in 1935, when Taylor hired Lange to photograph migrant workers for the California Rural Rehabilitation Administration, of which he was then director. They subsequently collaborated on documentary projects for the FSA under Stryker.

28. René d'Harnoncourt to Nelson Rockefeller, July 7, 1950. The Museum of Modern Art Archives: René d'Harnoncourt Papers [AAA: 2930; 441].

29. "Transcript of U.S.I.A. Seminar with Steichen 4/27/55," p. 3. Edward Steichen Archive, Department of Photography, The Museum of Modern Art.

30. Monroe Wheeler to Hugh L. Latham, June 1, 1950. The Museum of Modern Art Archives: Monroe Wheeler Papers, Exhibitions and Publications series, *Family of Man.*

31. Latham to Wheeler, September 5, 1950. The Museum of Modern Art Archives: Wheeler Papers, Exhibitions and Publications series, *Family of Man.*

32. Wheeler to Latham, November 13, 1950. The Museum of Modern Art Archives: Wheeler Papers, Exhibitions and Publications series, *Family of Man.*

33. William Tyler was a chief of the USIS for France; Douglas Schneider was Information Chief for UNESCO in Paris.

34. Summary minutes titled "ECA Photography Show," [c. October 1950]. The Museum of Modern Art Archives: Wheeler Papers, Exhibitions and Publications

Publications series, *Family of Man.*

35.   Much later, when Steichen was eighty-seven, he wrote to Alfred H. Barr, Jr., apparently in answer to Barr's question, that he had found the phrase in one of Lincoln's speeches, "after completing the selection and organization of the exhibition" (October 3, 1966). The Museum of Modern Art Archives: Alfred H. Barr, Jr., Papers [AAA: 2193; 1022]. Steichen's memory was playing tricks on him, however, since the name was in place years before the selection of the exhibition was well begun.

36.   Minutes of the Meeting of the Coordination Committee of The Museum of Modern Art held on Wednesday, September 13, 1950. The Museum of Modern Art Archives: Coordination Committee Minutes, Box 1.

37.   Steichen to Barr, October 3, 1966. The Museum of Modern Art Archives: Barr Papers [AAA: 2193; 1022].

38.   Wheeler to Howard D. Fletcher, of Fletcher Film Productions, Toronto, September 19, 1957. The Museum of Modern Art Archives: Wheeler Papers, Exhibitions and Publications series, *Family of Man.* Fletcher had asked for advice on his project, "The Face of Canada."

39.   This apparently refers to a first effort to interest the Ford Foundation in the exhibition. A second effort was made in 1954. It is not clear what Steichen means by the phrase "the Museum's contributors of the funds for this purpose." He may have been referring to potential contributors, or perhaps some small contribution had been made for preliminary planning costs.

40.   Lewis Mumford, "From Revolt to Renewal," in Mumford et al., *The Arts in Renewal,* The Benjamin Franklin Lectures of the University of Pennsylvania, Series 3 (Philadelphia: University of Pennsylvania Press, 1951), pp. 1–31; the quotation appears on p. 31.

41.   "Museum of Modern Art Plans International Photography Exhibition," MoMA press release no. 11, January 31, 1954. Department of Public Information, The Museum of Modern Art.

42.   The meeting was attended by Jerry Mason (Editor of *Argosy*), John Morris (Director of Magnum Photos), Bernard Quint (Art Director of *Life*), Arthur Rothstein (Chief Photographer of *Look*), Walker Evans (photographer and Assistant to the Managing Editor at *Fortune*), and the photographers Eliot Elisofon, Philippe Halsmann, Gordon Parks, and W. Eugene Smith, all of whom were strongly identified with *Life* magazine. Department of Photography files, The Museum of Modern Art.

43.   Miller to Steichen, May 12, 1953. Department of Photography files, The Museum of Modern Art. The reference to the long list of pets was evidently a joke in response to the open-ended character of Steichen's invitation.

44.   The following information comes from an incomplete and undated transcript of an interview between Miller and an unidentified interviewer, perhaps Margaretta Mitchell. The interview apparently dates from the seventies. Department of Photography files, The Museum of Modern Art.

45.   It has generally been reported that Miller saw about two million pictures, but he has written recently that he looked through "every box and file drawer" of the Time-Life photo files, which then contained three million photographs, plus a million more in other archives (see Wayne Miller, "1953–1955," in Jean Back and Gabriel Bauret, eds., *The Family of Man: Témoignoges et documents* [Dudelange, Clervaux (Grand Duché du Luxembourg): Editions Artevents, Ministère des Affaires Culturelles, 1944], pp. 45–54). When Steichen asked Miller how many pictures he had looked at, Miller said about four million; Steichen replied, "No one will believe those numbers; let's say two million" (Miller in conversation with the author).

A reconstituted copy of "The Family of Man" was opened in June 1994 as a permanent installation at the Chateau du Clervaux, Luxembourg. The opening was accompanied by the book *The Family of Man: Témoignoges et documents,* which contains numerous essays and interviews, including a text by Joanna Steichen, Steichen's widow.

46.   These letters are in the Department of Photography files, The Museum of Modern Art. I do not know why the files contain no letters from Lange from the final year of the exhibition's preparation. After Miller moved to New York Lange may have felt less close to the project. On October 10, 1953, she wrote and asked "whether you agree that I could be more effective in helping you if I could be with you for a little while." Steichen answered promptly and said that it would be great if she could come out, but he does not say he needs her. If later letters were sent to the temporary work space in the Fifty-second Street loft, rather than to the Museum, they might easily have been lost.

47.   The surviving Steichen–Lange correspondence does not seem to refer to Steichen's attendance at any of the California meetings, but the photograph reproduced on page 26 shows those in attendance at a meeting at Miller's house on March 28, 1953.

48.   Miller to Steichen, May 12, 1955. Department of Photography files, The Museum of Modern Art.

49.   Garst to Stryker, November 21, 1939. Roy Stryker Papers, 1912–1972, University of Louisville Photographic Archive, Louisville, Kentucky.

50.   In the fall of 1962 it fell to me to escort Lange through Steichen's last exhibition, "The Bitter Years," on the morning of the opening, while Steichen was still directing last-minute changes. On entering one gallery we saw to our mutual astonishment a large blow-up of one of Lange's FSA photographs—a picture that had until then shown a woman and two men sitting on the buckboard of a wagon—in which the two men had been airbrushed out. Lange's response, as I remember it, began with a gasp, then a stamped foot, a quiet groan, the rolling of eyes, the slapping of her knee, frantic laughter, and then the comment, "That astonishing rascal!" or something similar.

51.   For example: "Here are set forth babies arriving, suckling, growing into youths restless and questioning. Then as grownups they seek and hope. They mate, toil, fish, quarrel, sing, fight, pray, on all parallels and meridians having likeness."

52.   Jacob Deschin, "Steichen Reports: After European Trip, He Sees Success for Museum's 'Family of Man' Project," *New York Times,* December 14, 1952.

53.   Incomplete transcript of interview of Wayne Miller by Margaretta Mitchell, n.d., pp. 10–11. Department of Photography files, The Museum of Modern Art.

54.   W. Eugene Smith, "Spanish Village," *Life,* April 9, 1951, pp. 120–29.

55.   An exception to this general observation is the series of four large theme exhibitions done between 1968 and 1974 by Minor White for the Hayden Gallery of The Massachusetts Institute of Technology: "Light," "Being Without Clothes," "Octave of Prayer," and "Celebrations." These exhibitions used pictures selected from those submitted by many photographers to illustrate White's understanding of large philosophical and aesthetic issues.

56.   "The Family of Man: 1955–1984" was directed by Marvin Heiferman and shown at P.S. 1, Long Island City, N.Y., January 22–March 18, 1984.

57.   Freeman Lewis to Wheeler, November 17, 1954; Wheeler to Lewis, November 18, 1954. Steichen Archive, Department of Photography, The Museum of Modern Art.

58.   Phoebe Lou Adams, "Through a Lens Darkly: Steichen," *The Atlantic* 195 (April 1955), pp. 69–73.

59.   Aline B. Saarinen, "The Camera Versus the Artist," *New York Times,* February 6, 1955.

60.   Dorothy Norman, "The Controversial Family of Man," *Aperture* 3 (1955), pp. 8–27.

61.   Twenty years later it was not uncommon to see museum exhibitions in which the curator was in effect the patron, defining commissions to be executed for the show, but I do not think that this practice was known in the fifties.

62.   Roland Barthes, "The Great Family of Man," originally published in *Les Lettres nouvelles*; reprinted in *Mythologies,* selected and translated by Annette Lavers (Frogmore [St. Albans]: Paladin Books, 1973), pp. 101–02.

63.   Hilton Kramer, "Exhibiting The Family of Man: The World's Most Talked About Photographs," *Commentary* 20 (October 1955) pp. 366–67.

64.   Jacques Barzun, "The Three Enemies of Intellect," in Barzun, *The House of Intellect* (New York: Harper, 1959), pp. 28, 29.

65.   Quoted in Kramer, "Exhibiting the Family of Man," p. 367.

66.   "Transcript of U.S.I.A. seminar with Steichen 4/27/55," p. 4. Steichen Archive, Department of Photography, The Museum of Modern Art.

1. Installation view of "12 Modern American Painters and Sculptors," Musée National d'Art Moderne, Paris, 1953

Revisiting the Revisionists: The Modern, Its Critics, and the Cold War

Michael Kimmelman

On Tuesday afternoon, November 18, 1969, two men and two women entered The Museum of Modern Art and began to wrestle on the lobby floor. They continued until all four of them were writhing and moaning in a pool of blood, and then, as suddenly as they had appeared, they got up, exited through the revolving doors, and hailed a cab, leaving behind leaflets identifying them as members of the Guerrilla Art Action Group. The group called for "the immediate resignation of all the Rockefellers from the Board of Trustees of The Museum of Modern Art," because the Rockefellers, it claimed, used "art as a disguise, a cover for their brutal involvement in all spheres of the war machine."[1]

•

Since the late 1960s, revisionist historians and critics have worked to shift the discussion of postwar American art away from the formalism of Alfred H. Barr, Jr., Michael Fried, Clement Greenberg, William Rubin, and others.[2] Critical of the notion of art as a hermetic practice, the revisionists have directed attention to the political, economic, and social circumstances in which this art was produced. In so doing, they have linked the critical reception and promotion of postwar American art to political ideology, relating the promotion of American art abroad to the Marshall Plan, for instance, or Greenberg's writings on Abstract Expressionism to Arthur Schlesinger, Jr.'s manifesto of anti-Communist and antifascist liberalism, *The Vital Center* (1949).[3]

If a single text signaled this shift in critical practice it was Max Kozloff's "American Painting During the Cold War," originally an introduction to an exhibition catalogue,[4] and published in a revised version in the May 1973 issue of *Artforum*, of which Kozloff was an editor. What, Kozloff asked, "can be said of American painting since 1945 in the context of American political ideology, national self-images, and even the history of the country? Such a question has not been seriously raised by our criticism. . . ."[5] Kozloff supplied his own answer, in the form of a mea culpa: "Never for one moment did American art become a conscious mouthpiece for any agency as was, say, the Voice of America. But it did lend itself to be treated as a form of benevolent propaganda for foreign intelligentsia. Many critics, including this one, had a significant hand in that treatment. How fresh in memory even now is the belief that American art is the sole trustee of the avant-garde 'spirit,' a belief so reminiscent of the U.S. government's notion of itself as the lone guarantor of capitalist liberty."[6]

After Kozloff's article, *Artforum* published other articles that addressed his question in different ways. The first was William Hauptman's "The Suppression of Art in the McCarthy Decade," in October 1973.[7] The second was Eva Cockroft's "Abstract Expressionism, Weapon of the Cold War," in June 1974.[8]

Kozloff touched only briefly on The Museum of Modern Art in "American Painting," asserting that the United States Information Agency (USIA), which was in charge of exporting American culture abroad, and which "had earlier capitulated to furious reaction from right-wing groups when attempting exhibitions of non-representational art or work by 'communist tinged' painters," was by the late 1950s "able to mount, without interference, a number of successful programs abetted and amplified by the International Council of the Museum of Modern Art."[9]

That was his sole reference to the Museum. But in a sense, this ideology was rooted in an implicit criticism of the Modern, as Kozloff and his colleagues positioned their own writings in opposition to those by Barr, Andrew Carnduff Ritchie, Rubin, James Thrall Soby, and others published by the Museum. The success of the Museum in conceiving and promulgating a notion of modernism—a formalist history culminating in Abstract Expressionism—made it a prime target of revisionists: "The Modern," in a sense, equaled "modernism." So embedded was the institution in revisionist arguments that its role sometimes went without saying. Indeed, the last twenty years have witnessed the accumulation of a significant body of writing on postwar art in which opposition to the Modern is inherent.

Kozloff prepared the way for an analysis of the Modern's activities during the fifties, but it was Cockroft who did the job. In "Abstract Expressionism, Weapon of the Cold War" she focused particularly on the International Council and on Nelson A. Rockefeller, concluding that "Rockefeller, through Barr and others at the Museum his mother founded and family controlled, consciously used Abstract Expressionism, 'the symbol of political freedom,' for political ends."[10]

"Throughout the early 1940's," Cockroft wrote, "MOMA engaged in a number of war-related programs which set the pattern for its later activities as a key institution in the cold war."[11] Several high-placed officials at the Modern were, in Cockroft's view, government operatives who used the Museum to further their own agendas: They included Thomas W. Braden, who had served as Executive Secretary of the Modern in the late forties, before joining the Central Intelligence Agency (CIA) in 1950 to direct its cultural activities; René d'Harnoncourt, who had been head of the art section of Nelson Rockefeller's Office of the Coordinator of Inter-American Affairs (CIAA) in 1943, before joining the Museum in 1944; Porter McCray, who also had worked in the Coordinator's office, before becoming the Museum's Director of Circulating Exhibitions in 1947, and subsequently, its International Program; and, of course, Rockefeller himself.

"Freed from the kinds of pressure of unsubtle red-baiting and super-jingoism [that were] applied to official governmental agencies like the United States Information Agency," Cockroft argues, "CIA and MOMA cultural projects could provide the well-funded and more persuasive arguments and exhibits needed to sell the rest of the world on the benefits of life and art under capitalism. In the world of art, Abstract Expressionism constituted the ideal style for these propaganda activities."[12] To this end, "Willem de Kooning's work was included in the U.S. representation at the Venice Biennale as early as 1948. By 1950, he was joined by Arshile Gorky and Pollock. The U.S. representation at the Biennales [sic] in São Paulo beginning in 1951 averaged three Abstract Expressionists per show. They were also represented at international shows in Venezuela, India, Japan, etc. By 1956, a MOMA show called 'Modern Art in the U.S.,' including works by 12 Abstract Expressionists (Baziotes, Gorky, Guston, Hartigan, de Kooning, Kline, Motherwell, Pollock, Rothko, Stamos, Still, and Walker Tomlin) toured eight European cities, including Vienna and Belgrade."[13] And so on, she wrote, culminating in the International Council's "The New American Painting" of 1958–59, directed by Dorothy C. Miller and with a catalogue essay by Barr. An "enlightened cold warrior," like Braden and McCray, Barr became an enthusiast for the Abstract Expressionists, Cockroft proposes, because he grasped their political value (or, more precisely, the value of their apolitical stance, which she feels allowed their work to be more easily molded to fit a Cold War cause).[14]

Revisionist historians after Cockroft have essentially accepted her conclusion about the Modern and restated it in one form or another. David and Cecile Shapiro were among the first to follow her lead, in "Abstract Expressionism: The Politics of Apolitical Painting," published in the journal *Prospects* in 1977.[15] The rise of Abstract Expressionism, they hypothesize, must have come as a kind of salvation to officials at the Modern: The Museum "may now have been relieved to be helped off a hot spot, for it should not be forgotten that MOMA, like most American museums, was founded and funded by extremely rich private collectors, and MOMA was still actively supported by the Rockefellers, a clan as refulgent with money and power as American capitalism has produced."[16] Thus, they contend, the Modern early on supported Abstract Expressionism: Witness its acquisition of Jackson Pollock's *She-Wolf* (1943) in 1944; its inclusion of Pollock in the 1944 national circulating show "Twelve Contemporary American Painters," and of Gorky and Robert Motherwell in the 1946 "Fourteen Americans."[17] True, the Shapiros concede, the Modern also organized a retrospective of Ben Shahn in 1946 (the exhibition actually took place in 1947–48), but they imagine it did so reluctantly: The Museum never felt comfortable with Social Realism because that movement was "programmatically critical of capitalism."[18]

Serge Guilbaut has taken a similar tack in several of his writings. He delivered a first, glancing blow to the Museum in 1980, in an article for the journal *October*, "The New Adventures of the Avant-Garde in America," in which he blasts "the imperialist machine of the Museum of Modern Art."[19] Next came Guilbaut's book, *How New York Stole the Idea of Modern Art* (1983), which acknowledges Kozloff, Cockroft, and the Shapiros. Here, Guilbaut addressed the connections between Cold War rhetoric and the rhetoric surrounding the Abstract Expressionists in the years leading up to 1952. He contradicts himself in his descriptions of precisely what role the artists themselves played in making these connections, at one point writing that the Abstract Expressionist group "forged an 'American' image for itself, something that was becoming increasingly necessary for selling art in the United States."[20] At other points he implies that the artists were passive and that the sheer ambiguity of Abstract Expressionist art allowed it to be easily appropriated by powerful forces: "the avant-garde artist who categorically refused to participate in political discourse and tried to isolate himself by accentuating his individuality was coopted by liberalism, which viewed the artist's individualism as an excellent weapon with which to combat Soviet authoritarianism."[21]

About the Modern itself, he reasserts the alliance Kozloff and others had drawn between the Museum and the USIA, and he points out, as did Cockroft, that during World War II the Modern "served as a recreation center for soldiers, a symbol of free expression and a place to mount military exhibitions for propaganda purposes."[22]

That is the extent of it for the Modern in *How New York Stole the Idea of Modern Art.* But in "Postwar Painting Games: The Rough and the Slick," an article he published in the 1990 anthology *Reconstructing Modernism,* which he also edited, Guilbaut elaborates.[23] He maintains that there was an "important and successful push by the Museum of Modern Art between 1948 and 1950 to impose Abstract Expressionism as the most advanced and significant modern art in America. . . ."[24] And he cites Barr's appeal in a letter to *Life* magazine's Henry Luce that Luce embrace Abstract Expressionism (Barr called the movement "artistic free enterprise"), as well as Barr's 1952 article "Is Modern Art Communistic?" in *The New York Times Magazine.*[25] Guilbaut connects Barr with Nelson Rockefeller, to whom he pays a compliment of sorts: He points out that Rockefeller, like Barr, objected to attacks against modernism from the right wing and compared them to those by the Nazis.[26]

Guilbaut concludes: "Since 1950, one knew, thanks to the strenuous efforts of Alfred Barr, Nelson Rockefeller, and Thomas Hess, director [sic] of *Art News,* that modern art was in no way a Communist plot to destroy Western values. They had also done well in convincing most Americans that it was, in fact, a sign of freedom."[27]

Guilbaut's assessment has become the standard view, recapitulated often. It appears, for example, in a catalogue for "Constructing American Identity," a 1991 exhibition organized by the Whitney Museum of American Art's Independent Study Program. The catalogue refers to the coordinated "propaganda effort" involving "The International Council at the Museum of Modern Art and the United States Information Agency's sponsorship of traveling exhibitions of Abstract Expressionism. The most notable [example] was 'The New American Painting'. . . ."[28] The introduction to the Whitney catalogue claims that the show was "organized by The International Council . . . and sent abroad under the auspices of the . . . USIA."[29]

•

Context is essential to revisionist historians and critics. And their critique of the Modern has a context as well, namely the late 1960s and early 1970s, the era of the Vietnam War and domestic social upheaval.

It is worth recalling the Guerrilla Art Action Group. A "communiqué" from it, dated that November afternoon in 1969, was signed by four artists: Jon Hendricks, Jean Toche, Poppy Johnson, and a woman who identified herself as Silvianna.[30] Four days earlier, in another performance, Toche and Hendricks had tossed red powder across the lobby of the Whitney, shouting "We have to clean this place up, it is dirty from the war."[31]

The Modern was the group's main target, as it was also the target of another, better-known group, the Art Workers Coalition, to which Toche and Hendricks were also linked.[32] Formed in January 1969, the Coalition was a "loose-knit group of museophobic artists, writers, filmmakers and ephemeralists, who [sought]—without the aid of foundation money—to reform the art world structure," as the *New*

York Times put it in late January 1970, following a series of protests by the Coalition.[33] One of its protests, staged in front of *Guernica* (then on extended loan to The Museum of Modern Art), was provoked when William S. Paley, President of the Modern's Board of Trustees, reneged on a plan for the Museum to publish an antiwar poster that had been conceived by artists from the Coalition and agreed to by curators at the Modern. The Museum's Trustees, said Paley, could not permit the Museum to take "a position on any matter not directly related to a specific function of the Museum."[34] He insisted that politics and war were not the Modern's business.

In June 1970, another group, New York Art Strike Against Racism, Sexism, Repression and War, accosted Nelson Rockefeller after a speech he gave at the American Association of Museums convention, demanding his resignation from the Modern's Board and citing Rockefeller business links to the manufacture of war matériel. It didn't help that Rockefeller responded by asking, "What's sexism? And what does it have to do with art?"[35]

Among the active Art Strike members were Poppy Johnson, Max Kozloff, and Robert Morris. Perhaps their most public battle was waged against the USIA: The strikers called for artists to withdraw from the forthcoming 1970 Venice Biennale to protest the Vietnam War. Several artists did so. The USIA chose replacements and tried to keep their names secret. No one, it seems, trusted anyone.[36]

Art Strike had common cause with the Art Workers Coalition, which had been modeled after the civil-rights and antiwar movements of the sixties. The seeds of the Coalition had been planted by 1966, when some 300 artists, united in opposition to the war, created the 58-foot-high California Peace Tower, consisting of works by dozens of artists, that stood for several weeks on an empty lot along the Sunset Strip in Hollywood. Other events helped prepare the way: the Angry Arts Week in 1967, a series of meetings and exhibitions that took place in New York, Boston, and Philadelphia; the artists' boycott of Chicago galleries and museums, held in response to Mayor Richard J. Daley's crackdown on protesters at the 1968 Democratic Convention; and exhibitions like the one in October 1968 at the Paula Cooper Gallery, in New York, to benefit the Student Mobilization Committee to End the War in Vietnam.

Also preparing the way was a protest in March 1968 by about 300 people, at the black-tie opening of the Modern's "Dada, Surrealism and Their Heritage." The protesters opposed what they considered the co-opting of an anti-establishment movement, Dada, by an establishment like The Museum of Modern Art (the Modern's groundbreaking 1936 show, "Fantastic Art, Dada, Surrealism," organized by Barr, seems to have been forgotten). Among them were future leaders of the Art Workers Coalition, including John Perreault and Gregory Battcock.[37]

In January 1969, the artist Takis, along with several friends, removed his *Tele-Sculpture* from a show at the Modern called "The Machine as Seen at the End of the Mechanical Age," venting his frustration that the work had been included without his consent. Takis and friends presented Bates Lowry, the Museum's apparently startled Director, with a list of four demands relating to artists' rights over the use of their works. Lowry agreed to meet the group under calmer circumstances. By the end of the month, Takis's troop had swollen to fifty and their demands to thirteen. Among the new demands: that the Modern should devote a section of the Museum to the work of black artists and allow black artists to run it; that the Modern should extend its activities into African American and Hispanic neighborhoods; and that the Modern should be altogether more responsive to living artists—providing exhibition space for those without galleries, paying fees to those whose works were exhibited in the Museum, letting artists curate. The Art Workers Coalition was born.

The Coalition's basic goals were to have museums run more from the bottom up than the top down, and it was the Trustees at the very top whom the Coalition principally targeted. Over the months, its demands came to include a Martin Luther King, Jr., Study Center for Puerto Rican and Black Culture, and—almost as an afterthought—a higher representation in the Modern of work by women artists.[38] (Lowry responded that the Museum must select art "without regard to the artist's religion, race, political affiliation or the country in which he was born."[39]) Coalition members also asked that the Modern stop lending art to United States embassies for the duration of the war; Museum officials—who had instituted the loan program years earlier hoping to spur the government to initiate its own embassies loan program—sympathized with this request.[40] A call to make admission free resulted in the most tangible response: Mondays were made free, for a time.[41]

Some protesters even called for the Museum to close altogether until the war ended.[42] During a "speak-out" organized by the Coalition in April 1969, at the School of Visual Arts, Battcock reflected the escalating fever of the fractious group's demands when he suggested that the Modern pay Black Panther Huey Newton's bail bond. "The simple fact is that those who control the museum—whatever museum you care to consider—are the super-rich who control ALL legitimate communicative agencies," he said. "The Trustees of the museums direct NBC and CBS, the *New York Times* and the Associated Press, as well as that greatest cultural travesty of modern times—the Lincoln Center."[43]

As the Coalition explained in a letter to the *Times,* The Museum of Modern Art was "the establishment of establishments," at least for living artists.[44] More than The Metropolitan Museum of Art, or the Whitney Museum of American Art, or the Solomon R. Guggenheim Museum, it was the institution whose imprimatur they sought, and yet also the one whose influence they most deeply resented. It was the institution they felt had been largely responsible for putting Abstract Expressionism, and therefore American art, on the international map, but it was also an institution wary of sixties art movements—to which many Coalition members belonged and, most importantly, which rebelled against the principles and values of Abstract Expressionism.

To Coalition members it made little difference that seventy-nine percent of the purchases by the Museum between the middle of 1967 and the middle of 1969 were of works by living artists, and that forty percent of those were by artists under forty-five years old, as the Modern pleaded in a 1969 press release. The perception was that the Modern was out of touch. As Therese Schwartz observed in the last of a series of four articles in *Art in America* called "The Politicalization of the Avant-Garde" (1974), there arose "a sense of solidarity in the artistic community" about "the demise of the Museum of Modern Art—the cathedral of the American avant-garde—as an active and sympathetic force in the evolution of new art."[45]

Revisionists perceived abuses of power and discrimination by institutions that were similar to those being protested by the civil-rights and antiwar movements.

These perceived abuses were eventually articulated in such criticism of the Modern's permanent installation and collection as "Museum of Modern Art as Late Capitalist Ritual: An Iconographic Analysis," by Carol Duncan and Alan Wallach, in *Marxist Perspectives* (Winter 1978),[46] and the duo's "MOMA: Ordeal and Triumph on 53rd Street," in *Studio International* (January 1978).[47]

Perhaps inevitably, the historical Modern was in for the same scrutiny. And the fifties was an obvious place to start. It was the decade when the Museum not only assumed the mantle of international authority but also committed itself, once and for all, to a permanent collection[48]—when, that is to say, the modernist canon became physically enshrined in the Modern. During the fifties, the Museum's account of twentieth-century art took on the authority of scripture, to use the clichéd religious metaphor, and it was this account—and this authority—that the new historians and critics called into question.

•

Were critics such as Cockroft accurate in their accounts of the Museum's activities? Contrary to what she wrote, de Kooning was not included in the 1948 Venice Biennale.[49] In 1950, he was represented in the Biennale by four works in a show of six artists that was ancillary to a John Marin retrospective comprising eighty-one works. Four years later, de Kooning was given a retrospective at the Biennale, as was Shahn.[50] The Modern did not, as Cockroft contended, take sole responsibility for the U.S. representation at the Biennales from 1954 through 1962: It ceded that task twice   to The Art Institute of Chicago (in 1956) and to The Baltimore Museum of Art (1960).[51] As for the São Paulo Bienal, the Modern put together only three of the U.S. exhibitions between 1953 and 1965 (in 1953, 1957, and 1961); others were organized by the San Francisco Museum of Modern Art (1955), the Walker Art Center (1963), the Minneapolis Institute (1959), and the Pasadena Art Museum (1965).[52] Abstract Expressionists were represented in the Bienal exhibitions organized by the Modern, but it is not at all self-evident that they were dominant. At the 1953 Bienal, for example, Alexander Calder was the main representative. And the 1955–56 "Modern Art in the United States," which Cockroft claimed included a dozen Abstract Expressionists, had works by 112 artists in all.[53]

How is one to judge the meaning of such statistics, in any case? Is the number of participants or pictures a reliable guide to the character of an exhibition? What about the placement and size of the pictures? What about the language of the exhibition's promotional and educational materials? What about the extent to which the art may, or may not, have been selected and analyzed in ways indebted to Abstract Expressionist values?

One needs to know more about the big survey of 112 artists organized by Dorothy Miller, for example, which Cockroft cited. Did the Abstract Expressionists culminate a chronological progression, or did they constitute a critical mass that outnumbered any other cluster of artists? The evidence is ambiguous. In the catalogue for the exhibition's presentation in London, ten of the twenty-nine plates reproducing paintings are devoted to Abstract Expressionist works. Holger Cahill's text for the painting section is organized according to the following sequence of categories: The Eight; Early Moderns; The Armory Show; Americans Abroad; The Return to the Object; Precisionism and the Industrial Theme; Painters of Social Content; The Second Wave of Abstraction; Realists, Romantics and Pure Painters; Geometric

2. Entrance to "Modern Art in the United States: A Selection from the Collections of the Museum of Modern Art, New York," The Tate Gallery, London, 1956, with a painting by John Kane (left) and a sculpture by William Zorach (right)

3–8. Installation views of "Modern Art in the United States: A Selection from the Collections of the Museum of Modern Art, New York," The Tate Gallery, London, 1956

3. In the foreground, paintings by Niles Spencer; in the background, paintings by Joseph Stella (left) and Man Ray (right)

5. Paintings by (left to right) Louis Michel Eilshemius, Herman Rose, and Ben Shahn (four)

4. Paintings by (left to right) John Marin, Florine Stettheimer, and Yasuo Kuniyoshi (two); sculpture by Gaston Lachaise

6. Sculptures by (left to right) William Zorach, Gaston Lachaise, and Elie Nadelman (four)

7. On wall, a painting by Franz Kline; in the foreground, sculptures by (left to right) Herbert Ferber, David Hare, and Alexander Calder (two)

Below:

9–10. Installation views of "50 Ans d'Art aux Etats-Unis: Collections du Museum of Modern Art de New York," Musée National d'Art Moderne, Paris, 1955. (Portions of the exhibition subsequently toured as "Modern Art in the United States: A Selection from the Collections of the Museum of Modern Art, New York)

9. Partial view of the architecture section. In the foreground, photographic enlargement and model of building by Ludwig Mies van der Rohe; in the background, photographic enlargements of buildings by Lloyd Wright (center) and Eric Mendelsohn (far right)

8. Paintings by (left to right) Jackson Pollock (two), Robert Motherwell, and Clyfford Still

10. Partial view of the photography section, with photographs by (left to right) Dan Weiner, Alfred Stieglitz (four), Dmitri Kessel, and Man Ray (three)

Abstraction; Abstract Expressionism (which included not twelve but fourteen artists—those mentioned by Cockroft, plus Richard Pousette-Dart and Mark Tobey); and as the culminating category, Folk Art (which included Patrocino Barela, Louis Michel Eilshemius, Morris Hirshfield, John Kane, José Dolores Lopez, Joseph Pickett, and Clara McDonald Williamson).

But photographs of the installation in London (figs. 2–8) tell a somewhat different story from the catalogue. The painting section was divided into five parts, with modern "primitives," meaning folk artists, first, and contemporary abstraction last. It was succeeded by sections devoted to sculpture and then prints (which consisted mostly of works by now-forgotten figures like Walter Rogalski, Leona Pierce, and Misch Kohn). And the show's overall effect was to stress diversity in twentieth-century American art.

The reception of the show in London was described in an analysis by the Modern of the press reaction: "Although abstract expressionism was certainly the most frequently discussed and controversial section of the exhibition, there was an overwhelming preference for the more realistic canvases."[54] The analysis goes on: "'Christina's World' was undoubtedly the most popular painting in the exhibition among critics and public alike," and there was considerable response, according to the Modern's analysis, to the social commentary in such major works in the show as Shahn's *Bartolomeo Vanzetti and Nicola Sacco* (1931–32), Blume's *The Eternal City* (1934–37), Levine's *The Feast of Pure Reason* (1937), and several of Hopper's paintings.

The reception of the inaugural version of the show in Paris, which had included works in even more mediums than would London's, was very different. Critics focused above all on the architecture section, which was regarded as "the most original and esthetically satisfying form of art produced by the United States, and the one which dominated the other mediums"[55] (fig. 9). It was also the opening section of the exhibition. Photography (fig. 10) and film were picked out for praise, too, and to a lesser degree, industrial design. Prints were written about more favorably than was either painting or sculpture, which were treated most dismissively. Some critics noted, unfavorably, that the painting section was weighted toward abstraction. Clearly, this exhibition did not have the effect of elevating American abstraction in the eyes of French critics. To the contrary: The "primitives" were given sympathetic treatment among the painters, and between painting and sculpture, the latter was preferred. The spirit of the coverage was altogether against Abstract Expressionism and toward other forms of American culture. André Chastel summed it up in his review in *Le Monde* (January 17, 1959): "It becomes apparent that the two arts in which the United States reveals itself most forcefully are architecture and photography, and after that, of course, film."[56]

How, then, is one to judge, from the evidence of this exhibition, the extent to which the Modern pushed Abstract Expressionism?

And who were the Abstract Expressionists? Not all of those listed as Abstract Expressionists in the Miller show would now be regarded as such. Would the inclusion of Bradley Walker Tomlin make Calder or Stuart Davis look more like one of them? Throughout the forties, there was little agreement about whether a new school of painting had come into existence, much less what constituted membership in it. As Michael Leja has pointed out, the problem for critics and dealers was "to articulate for the purported group a platform that was powerful and specific and yet managed to conceal ideological and aesthetic diversity. For their part, the artists refused to accept the distortions involved in the process of producing a common denominator."[57] A consensus began to form by the fifties, but it remained contested by artists and critics alike, and it would not have been obvious to everyone precisely who was an Abstract Expressionist.[58]

Finally, there is the issue of the institutional character of a museum which, like every such big organization, has multiple, often competing viewpoints among its curators. How were individual choices politically and bureaucratically conditioned? What is clear is that the artists selected for the Modern's circulating shows varied with the curator in charge: Ritchie and Miller—along with Robert Beverly Hale of the Metropolitan, Lloyd Goodrich of the Whitney, and John I.H. Baur of The Brooklyn Museum—selected the works for the painting and sculpture section of the first Bienal in São Paulo in 1951; their list included thirty-two painters and sixteen sculptors (of whom six painters and three sculptors are today widely considered to be Abstract Expressionists[59]). Ritchie's 1955 "International Exhibition of Painters Under 35," which toured Europe, included Richard Diebenkorn, Seymour Drumlevitch, Joseph Glasco, John Hultberg, Irving Kreisberg, and Theodoros Stamos. Frank O'Hara's choice for the 1957 São Paulo Bienal comprised paintings by James Brooks, Philip Guston, Grace Hartigan, Franz Kline, and Larry Rivers; sculpture by David Hare, Ibram Lassaw, and Seymour Lipton; and a Pollock retrospective.

The story of the inspiration for "The New American Painting," of 1958–59, needs elucidating. The International Program was established in 1952; the next year it sent to Europe "12 Modern American Painters and Sculptors," which included a mix of artists (chosen by Ritchie; see fig. 1): Ivan Le Lorraine Albright, Calder, Davis, Gorky, Morris Graves, Hopper, Kane, Marin, Pollock, Theodore Roszak, Shahn, and David Smith. Along with "Modern Art in the United States," it prompted museum officials in Amsterdam, Berlin, Brussels, and Milan to request that the Modern organize a show specifically devoted to "our most avant-garde American painters and sculptors," as Porter McCray wrote in a 1956 confidential memorandum to René d'Harnoncourt.[60] McCray continues: "Especially in view of the USIA's present orientation and the probability that exhibitions assembled under its auspices may become increasingly conservative, it seems that The Museum of Modern Art is the only institution likely to organize this kind of representation for showing abroad and our obligation to do so is thereby all the greater." D'Harnoncourt's foreword to the American catalogue reiterates McCray's memorandum: "*The New American Painting* was organized at the request of European institutions. . . ."[61]

Whether or not individuals at the USIA privately wanted to push Abstract Expressionism, the reality of the McCarthy era was that the agency could not co-organize an exhibition of such vanguard art, although in certain European cities the offices of the United States Information Service (USIS, a division of the USIA) could assist with local publicity and transportation costs. In fact, the only time the USIS is mentioned in a catalogue for "The New American Painting" is in that for the London showing, where it is credited with a donation towards British catalogue costs. Shows like "The Family of Man" and "Built in the U.S.A.—Postwar Architecture" were something else: The USIA shared responsibility for the circulation of these exhibitions abroad. But to link as one the USIA and the International Council, as some have done, is a generalization that simplifies the byzantine cultural politics of the era.

Clearly, exhibitions sent abroad, like "The New American Painting," participated in a cultural campaign to fight Communism. D'Harnoncourt was entirely open about aiding this campaign, as were virtually all museum directors at the time. From the perspective of the early seventies, in the midst of the Vietnam War, such a campaign may have seemed to critics like Kozloff and Cockroft to be as objectionable as the covert bombing of Cambodia. But during the fifties, d'Harnoncourt was one museum official among dozens who openly lobbied Congress to finance this campaign.

During the late forties, requests by foreign institutions for shows of contemporary American art and architecture were regularly presented to the Modern via the State Department.[62] D'Harnoncourt, Ritchie, and others served on a committee in 1948 that recommended more government involvement to promote shows abroad, a plan endorsed by numerous U.S. museums. In 1951, officials from The Brooklyn Museum, The Cooper Union for the Advancement of Science and Art, the Morgan Library, the New-York Historical Society, the American Museum of Natural History, and other New York institutions convened at the Modern to discuss joint projects with the United Nations Educational, Scientific, and Cultural Organization (UNESCO).[63]

A series of bills was presented to Congress during the fifties, like the one that representative Frank Thompson of New Jersey proposed in 1955 "to establish a program of cultural interchanges with foreign countries to meet the challenge of competitive coexistence with communism."[64] Thompson wrote to d'Harnoncourt: "The ultimate outcome of the struggle between the totalitarian and free worlds will be decided by ideas."[65] D'Harnoncourt's abiding concern, however, was that in undertaking cultural interchanges, the U.S. government not censor its own artists, as it had been doing to suspected Communist sympathizers, under pressure from redbaiting representatives like Representative George A. Dondero of Michigan[66] and others. (D'Harnoncourt joined the Advisory Panel of the National Council on Freedom from Censorship in 1956 to protest the exclusion of Yasuo Kuniyoshi, Shahn, and others from the USIA exhibition "Sport in Art" because of the supposed political leanings of these artists.[67])

The leap that The Museum of Modern Art's critics have taken is to link the anti-Communist cultural campaign with an embrace by the Museum of Abstract Expressionism. The Museum's acquisitions and roster of exhibitions during the fifties suggest at the least a more complex story. In fact, the Modern would seem to have been slow to take up Abstract Expressionism's cause. Its circulating shows stressed European masters, as did shows at the Museum. Take, for example, 1950. The Modern presented nine loan exhibitions of painting and sculpture: one on the Percival Goodman War Memorial Model; others on Charles Demuth, Edvard Munch, Chaim Soutine, and Franklin C. Watkins; two New Talent surveys in the penthouse that included the work of Louis Bunce, Drumlevitch, Ynez Johnston, William D. King, Ernest Mundt, and Raymond Parker; and two group shows, one a historical survey of works from Art Nouveau through organic abstraction, the other a selection of recent sculpture that included eleven artists, of whom only three—Hare, Roszak, and Smith—could even distantly be linked with Abstract Expressionism. In 1954, the exhibition roster was "Ancient Arts of the Andes," "Japanese Calligraphy," and exhibitions of works by Jacques Lipchitz, Niles Spencer, and Edouard Vuillard.[68]

Occasionally, there were exhibitions that included Abstract Expressionists, like

Ritchie's 1951 show and Miller's 1952 "15 Americans," which included Pollock. But not until 1956–57 did the Modern organize in New York a one-person retrospective of an Abstract Expressionist, a posthumous one for Pollock, organized by Sam Hunter. With the exception of this and another show organized by Hunter in 1957, devoted to David Smith, the only other specifically New York School exhibition in New York was "The New American Painting" (subtitled "As Shown in 8 European Countries 1958–59; see pp. 88–89, figs. 20–21; p. 89, fig. 21; p. 91, fig. 23) in 1959. This raises a point that historians and critics have minimized: The Modern's exhibitions of Abstract Expressionism, more so at home but also abroad, came on the whole only during the later fifties, by which time the movement's first generation had already been followed by a second (by 1958, Jasper Johns was in the Venice Biennale). The Museum's promotion of its 1958–59 touring Pollock retrospective and "The New American Painting" (see pp. 134–35, figs. 15–17) was skillful and effective, though hardly flawless, in persuading Europeans to take the Abstract Expressionists seriously. But these were relatively isolated shows and late undertakings in a wide-ranging program of exhibitions that had been conspicuous, if for anything, for its reticence toward the New York School.

So it seemed at the time, at least. Thomas Hess complained in a 1954 editorial in *Art News,* where he was executive editor, about the Museum's "baffling lack of recognition of postwar American abstract painting and sculpture," a failing "prevented from becoming a scandal" only by "Dorothy Miller's exhibitions of American artists in 1946 and 1952."[69] In a 1957 editorial in the magazine's fifty-fifth anniversary issue, he wrote that matters had improved, but only somewhat since 1952,[70] provoking a response from Barr in the form of a letter to the editor.[71] Barr took issue with *Art News*'s own record of support for the Abstract Expressionists. He pointed out that before 1952 the Modern had exhibited examples of Gorky's art in 1930, 1936, 1938, and 1946 (ten works in "Fourteen Americans"), and had bought paintings of his in 1941, 1942, and 1950. He noted that an *Art News* critic had dismissed the works in "Fourteen Americans" as "decorative meanderings." By 1952, "at least sixteen paintings by Tomlin, Motherwell, Pollock, Baziotes, Gorky and de Kooning had been acquired by four trustees of the Museum," Barr wrote. He cited a 1949 show of the Modern's American painting collection that grouped William Baziotes, Gorky, de Kooning, Motherwell, Pollock, and several others "as the climax of the exhibition, a gesture made with enthusiasm and conviction. . . ."[72] Again taking a swipe at *Art News,* Barr added that the magazine had failed to mention Pollock's *Number 1, 1948* and Gorky's *Agony* (1947), both owned by the Modern, in its deliberations on the most important modern American paintings acquired by an American public collection in 1950. Instead, it cited a Shahn. That same year, the magazine had named Shahn, Balthus, Blume, Lee Gatch, and Jean Arp as the five artists with the best one-person shows of the year.

He concluded: "The Museum's record is far from perfect. Sometimes it was handicapped by lack of money, always by lack of time and space; occasionally it was retarded by differences of opinion, more often, I know, by lack of vision. Furthermore—*pace* the partisans—the Museum has not, and I hope will not, commit itself entirely to one faction. . . . Some of the Museum's friends have questioned this policy, urging that the Museum align itself exclusively with the current avant-garde. Its bitterest enemies insist that the Museum has already done exactly that."[73]

•

Clearly, the Modern's record regarding the Abstract Expressionists was a matter of lively debate during the fifties. The figures regarding acquisitions and exhibitions do not, in any case, simply speak for themselves, as Barr implied. If the Modern was early in buying works of Pollock, and if it did buy a de Kooning as early as 1948—which Barr pointed out—and if it did show Baziotes, Gorky, de Kooning, Motherwell, and Pollock, in 1949, a perusal of the dates of acquisition in Barr's *Painting and Sculpture in The Museum of Modern Art, 1929–1967* reveals that it acquired as many works by Lucian Freud as by de Kooning throughout the fifties; as many by Eduardo Paolozzi as by Smith; and as many by Reg Butler as by Baziotes, Kline, Barnett Newman, and Tobey combined.

When the Museum ultimately tried to make up for what it had come to feel were lost opportunities in building its Abstract Expressionist collection (for example, its lack of one of the largest Pollocks or a big Newman), it provoked the Art Workers Coalition—not, as it happened, because of any opposition to the art but because of the reverse, in a sense: The Coalition had become the self-appointed champion of Abstract Expressionist artists' rights. For "The New American Painting and Sculpture: The First Generation," of 1969, the Modern asked participating artists, or their estates, to contribute works to the Museum's collection. This show—like "The 1960's" (1967), "Word and Image" (1968), and "Jean Dubuffet" (1968)—was to consist only of things owned by or promised to the Modern. The Coalition issued a statement that, paradoxically, is a partial rebuttal to the historians who are the Coalition's ideological allies and heirs: To create "the world's major collection" of Abstract Expressionism, it stated, the Modern had asked artists to donate works that "could have been but were *not* purchased by the Museum when they were relatively undesirable and inexpensive."[74]

About the eventual embrace of Abstract Expressionism by the Modern, self-evident by the time the revisionists began to write, there can be no doubt. In the general sense that there developed a link between the fortunes of that art and those of the institution, the revisionist argument is clear. But many of the particulars of that argument—and the statistical and historical assumptions underlying it—simply do not bear up under the weight of the historical evidence.[75]

Notes

I am indebted to Amy Zorn for collaborating with me on the research and preparation of this article, and to the anonymous reader. I hope to have addressed, and in some cases incorporated, a few of his or her concerns.

1. Guerrilla Art Action Group "Communiqué," November 18, 1969; see also the memorandum from J. M. Chapman to Walter Bareiss, Richard H. Koch, and Wilder Green, November 19, 1969. The Museum of Modern Art Archives: John B. Hightower Papers, III.1.11.b. The blood was cow's blood, sealed in plastic packets beneath their clothes.

2. The publication in 1970 of Irving Sandler's *The Triumph of American Painting: A History of Abstract Expressionism* (New York: Harper & Row; Praeger, 1970) was perhaps the single publishing event that most galvanized the revisionists.

3. Arthur Schlesinger, Jr., *The Vital Center: The Politics of Freedom* (1949; Cambridge, Mass.: Riverside Press, 1962; rpt. New York: Da Capo Press, 1988).

4. "Twenty-five Years of American Painting 1948–1973," organized by James T. Demetrion for the Des Moines Art Center, March 6–April 22, 1973.

5. Max Kozloff, "American Painting During the Cold War," *Artforum* 11 (May 1973), pp. 43–54. The quotation appears on p. 43. Reprinted in Francis Frascina, ed., *Pollock and After: The Critical Debate* (New York: Harper & Row, 1985), pp. 107–23.

6. Ibid., p. 44.

7. William Hauptman, "The Suppression of Art in the McCarthy Decade," *Artforum* 12 (October 1973), pp. 48–52.

8. Eva Cockroft, "Abstract Expressionism, Weapon of the Cold War," *Artforum* 12 (June 1974), pp. 39–41. Reprinted in Frascina, ed., *Pollock and After*, pp. 125–33.

9. Kozloff, "American Painting During the Cold War," p. 49.

10. Cockroft, "Abstract Expressionism, Weapon of the Cold War," p. 41.

11. Ibid., p. 39.

12. Ibid., p. 40.

13. Ibid. An extended discussion of "Modern Art in the United States," organized by Dorothy C. Miller, follows in the body of this article; see pp. 45–48.

14. Ibid., p. 41.

15. David and Cecile Shapiro, "Abstract Expressionism: The Politics of Apolitical Painting," *Prospects*, no. 3 (1977), pp. 175–214. Reprinted in Frascina, ed., *Pollock and After*, pp. 135–51. Frascina provides an excellent, sanguine introduction (pp. 91–106) to this as well as to Kozloff's and Cockroft's articles, and to the entire shift in critical practice that occurred around 1970.

16. Frascina, ed., *Pollock and After*, p. 147. The "hot spot" the Shapiros referred to was evidently the necessity of supporting openly left-wing artists like Ben Shahn in order to endorse leading-edge art.

17. Ibid., p. 142.

18. Ibid., p. 147.

19. Serge Guilbaut, "The New Adventures of the Avant-Garde in America," *October*, no. 15 (Winter 1980), pp. 61–78. The quotation appears on p. 77.

20. Serge Guilbaut, *How New York Stole the Idea of Modern Art: Abstract Expressionism, Freedom, and the Cold War* (Chicago and London: University of Chicago Press, 1983), p. 121.

21. Ibid., p. 143.

22. Ibid., p. 88. The Modern held a poster competition, "Posters for National Defense," in the spring of 1941, around the same time it presented an exhibition called "Britain at War." After the bombing of Pearl Harbor in December 1941, the Museum stepped up its war-related activities considerably. It began, under the leadership of James Thrall Soby, the Armed Services Program, which Russell Lynes described as "partly therapy, partly exhibitions, partly morale-sustaining, and partly making the Museum's facilities and talents available to Nelson Rockefeller and his Office of Inter-American Affairs." In addition to organizing numerous exhibitions related to the war (many sent by Rockefeller's office to Latin America), the Museum supplied art materials to military camps. It held garden parties for soldiers and sailors, and a canteen was installed in the garden, where, under the aegis of the Salvation Army, women from the Junior League sold coffee, sandwiches, and doughnuts to servicemen and their friends (the canteen was not open to the public). See Russell Lynes, *Good Old Modern: An Intimate Portrait of the Museum of Modern Art* (New York: Atheneum, 1973), pp. 133–38.

23. Serge Guilbaut, "Postwar Painting Games: The Rough and the Slick," in Guilbaut, ed., *Reconstructing Modernism: Art in New York, Paris, and Montreal 1945–1964* (London and Cambridge, Mass.: MIT Press, 1990), pp. 30–84.

24. Ibid., p. 32.

25. Ibid., p. 35. Barr's article (published in *The New York Times Magazine* of December 14, 1952) is mentioned on p. 75, n. 8. It is reprinted in *Defining Modern Art: Selected Writings of Alfred H. Barr, Jr.*, ed. Irving Sandler and Amy Newman (New York: Abrams, 1986), pp. 214–19. The article was written in response to an assertion by Harry S. Truman that modern art was, in fact, "Communistic." See also Lynn Zelevansky, "Dorothy Miller's 'Americans,' 1942–1963," pp. 86–91 of the present volume.

26. Ibid., p. 34.

27. Ibid., p. 67.

28. Elizabeth Bigham and Andrew Perchuk, "American Identity/American Art," in *Constructing American Identity* (New York: Whitney Museum of American Art, 1991), p. 11.

29. Eric Miles, Introduction to *Constructing American Identity*, p. 2. A clarification of the USIS's involvement in "The New American Painting" follows in the body of this article; see p. 49.

30. Guerrilla Art Action Group "Communiqué," November 18, 1969. The Museum of Modern Art Archives: Hightower Papers, III.1.11.

31. Guerrilla Art Action Group leaflet titled "Guerrilla Art Action at the Whitney Museum of American Art," November 14, 1969. The Museum of Modern Art Archives: Hightower Papers, III.1.11.b.

32. At the time, there were many similarly constituted groups with like aims and overlapping memberships. In a Museum memorandum from Richard Koch to Richard Dana, November 11, 1969, Koch refers to Hendricks and Toche as "a splinter group of the Art Workers Coalition" and goes on to write: "Lucy Lippard, one of the more responsible members of the Art Workers Coalition, tells us that Messrs. Hendricks and Toche do not represent the views of the majority of the group, and I gather that the coalition is embarrassed by their use of its name." The Museum of Modern Art Archives: Hightower Papers, III.1.11.b.

33. Grace Glueck, "Yanking the Rug from Under," *New York Times*, January 25, 1970.

34. "Ars Gratia Artis?," *Newsweek*, February 9, 1970, p. 80.

35. Grace Glueck, "Dissidents Confront Rockefeller After Speech to Museum Group," *New York Times*, June 4, 1970.

36. Barbara Rose, "Out of the Studios, on to the Barricades," *New York Magazine*, August 10, 1970, p. 56.

37. Therese Schwartz, "The Politicization of the Avant-Garde," *Art in America* 59 (November–December 1971), p. 100.

38. Synopsis of the dialogue between the Museum and the Art Workers Coalition, February 24, 1970 (rev. April 18, 1970). The Museum of Modern Art Archives: Hightower Papers, III.1.11.a.

39. See, for example, the memorandum from Betsy Jones to John Szarkowski regarding "Meeting with the Women Artist Revolutionaries," January 20, 1970; Szarkowski and Jones, "Report on Meeting," memorandum to The Museum of Modern Art Executive Committee, n.d.; and recommendations by Szarkowski and Jones "Concerning the Relationship of the Museum to Women Artists," n.d. The Museum of Modern Art Archives: Hightower Papers, III.1.11.a.

40. Kozloff, along with Robert Morris and Irving Petlin, signed a letter from the Emergency Cultural Government to the International Program of the Modern, about loans to embassies. Waldo Rasmussen, Director of the Program, stated in his reply of June 4, 1970: "As I am sure you know, the Museum is strongly in sympathy with the desires of the artists to respond to national crises, and we will look forward to any comments you would care to make on the Embassy program." The Museum of Modern Art Archives: Hightower Papers, II.1.1.

The Art in Embassies program, which had been founded in 1959 as a pilot project, was discontinued in 1970. It was felt to have become redundant since the State Department had established a similar program; it had also become increasingly difficult, and administratively demanding, to obtain loans to send to embassies (Rasmussen in interview with the author, October 19, 1993).

41. See Lawrence Alloway, "Art," *The Nation*, February 23, 1970, p. 221.

42. Guerrilla Art Action Group and Art Workers Coalition "Manifesto for the Guerrilla Art Action Group," October 30, 1969. The Museum of Modern Art Archives: Hightower Papers, III.1.11.b. The manifesto demanded "that the Museum of Modern Art be closed until the end of the war in Vietnam."

43. Gregory Battcock, "Text of Remarks Read at Art Workers Open Hearing at School of Visual Arts," April 10, 1969. The Museum of Modern Art Library Subject File: Art and Politics.

44. Letter signed by Lucy Lippard, Hans Haacke, and Frazer Doughtery, published in the *New York Times*, January 22, 1970.

45. Therese Schwartz, "The Politicization of the Avant-Garde IV," *Art in America* 62 (January–February, 1974), p. 82.

46. Carol Duncan and Alan Wallach, "The Museum of Modern Art as Late Capitalist Ritual: An Iconographic Analysis," *Marxist Perspectives* 1 (Winter 1978), pp. 28–51.

47. Carol Duncan and Alan Wallach, "MOMA: Ordeal and Triumph on 53rd Street," *Studio International* 194 (January 1978), pp. 48–57.

48. The tortuous and fascinating history of the Modern's policy toward its collection is beyond the scope of this article. At its heart was a debate, still central to the question of the museum's purpose, about how to remain a modern museum and at the same time become a historical respository. Barr's metaphor was of the Modern as a torpedo moving through time, ". . . its nose the ever advancing present, its tail the ever receding past of fifty to a hundred years ago. If painting is taken as an example, the bulk of the collection . . . would be concentrated in the early years of the twentieth century, tapering off into the nineteenth with a propeller representing 'Background' collections." A remark supposedly made by Gertrude Stein about the Modern was often cited: "A museum can either be a museum or it can be modern, but it cannot be both." On-again, off-again relationships with the Metropolitan and the Whitney involved plans to periodically purge the Modern of its historical holdings. In 1943, the three museums arrived at an agreement to collaborate on acquisitions. But by the fifties these plans were finally scotched—in part because the escalating value of modern art had made it financially irresponsible for the Modern simply to give away such valuable assets—and a commitment to the permanent collection was made. See Lynes, *Good Old Modern*, pp. 286 ff.

49. Cockroft, "Abstract Expressionism, Weapon of the Cold War," p. 40. Cockroft may have made this mistake by copying it from the Modern's catalogue for "The New American Painting." The exhibition history for de Kooning (p. 92 of the catalogue for the version of the show installed at the Modern, a reprint of the catalogue used for The Tate Gallery's presentation) lists the 1948 Venice Biennale under group shows. For the correct information, see Philip Rylands and Enzo di Martino, *Flying the Flag for Art: The United States and The Venice Biennale, 1895–1991* (Richmond, Va.: Wyldbore Wolferstan, 1993), pp. 277–79. See also Paolo Rizzi and Enzo di Martino, *Storia della Biennale: 1895–1982* (Milan: Electa, 1982), p. 97.

50. See Frances K. Pohl, "An American in Venice: Ben Shahn and United States Foreign Policy at the 1954 Venice Biennale," *Art History* 4 (March 1981), pp. 80–113.

51. In 1954, the Modern, with the support of the International Program and a grant from the Rockefeller Brothers Fund, bought the U.S. Pavilion from the Grand Central Art Galleries, which had built it in 1930. It was the only pavilion not owned by its nation's government. While it meant that the Modern paid the bills for upkeep, it did not mean that the Museum took control of all the shows installed in the pavilion. Beforehand, the Modern had been involved in the 1950 show, jointly organizing it with The Cleveland Museum of Art. In 1952, David E. Finley, Director of the National Gallery of Art and Chairman of the National Commission of Fine Arts, asked the American Federation of Arts to select the artists and arrange the exhibition. In 1954, the first year of the Modern's ownership, the Museum took sole responsibility and organized the Shahn and de Kooning twin bill. In 1956, The Art Institute of Chicago assumed control of the exhibition. In 1958, control reverted to the Modern. In 1960, it was Baltimore. In 1962, it was again the Modern. And after that, the Museum gave over responsibility to the USIA, which in 1964 asked The Jewish Museum to organize the show featuring Robert Rauschenberg that would become perhaps the most famous American presentation ever at the Biennale. See Rylands and di Martino, *Flying the Flag for Art*, pp. 101–45.

52. In November 1950, the Modern signed an agreement of cooperation with the Museu de Art Moderna of São Paulo, under which the Modern organized the United States' entries to the Bienal in 1951, 1953, and 1957 and helped provide support for the other museums that oversaw the U.S. representation at the Bienal during the mid- and late fifties. Ibid., p. 109. The selection of the U.S. representation at the 1951 and 1957 Bienals is discussed on p. 49 of this essay.

53. Cockroft, "Abstract Expressionism, Weapon of the Cold War," p. 40 (writing about "Modern Art in the United States"). Cockroft does not provide sources for any of her figures. The show began at the Musée National d'Art Moderne, Paris, in 1955, as "50 Ans d'Art aux Etats-Unis: Collections du Museum of Modern Art de New York," a survey of several hundred paintings, sculptures, prints, photographs, films, industrial design objects, and architectural models. The painting and sculpture sections (selected by Dorothy Miller) and the print section (selected by William S. Lieberman) were shown in seven other European cities in 1955–56 as "Modern Art in the United States: A Selection from the Collections of the Museum of Modern Art," and consisted of a total of 112 artists, including Charles Burchfield, Charles Demuth, Arthur Dove, Lyonel Feininger, Marsden Hartley, Edward Hopper, Jack Levine, Maurice Prendergast, Ben Shahn, Joseph Stella, Florine Stettheimer, Max Weber, and Andrew Wyeth, among many others. At several of these venues, one or more additional curatorial departments were represented as well. A more detailed discussion of the show immediately follows in the body of this essay.

54. "Press Analysis" of "Modern Art in the United States: London," May 1, 1956, p. 10. The Museum of Modern Art Archives: International Council/International Program Exhibition Records (ICE-F-24-54; London): Box 11.1. The analysis, like the accompanying one for the showing in Paris (see n. 56 below), contains numerous and extended excerpts from many articles written about the exhibition.

55. "Press Analysis" of "50 Ans d'Art aux Etats-Unis," May 1, 1956, p. 11. The Museum of Modern Art Archives: IC/IP Exh. Records (ICE-F-24-54; Paris): Box 11.1.

56. Ibid., p. 10.

57. Michael Leja, *Reframing Abstract Expressionism: Subjectivity and Painting in the 1940s* (New Haven, Conn.: Yale University Press, 1993), p. 47.

58. As with all of the questions posed in these paragraphs, the point is not to rebut specifically the revisionist argument—in this case the membership of certain artists in this school as Cockroft and others might have defined it—but to suggest that an analysis of the school's identity more subtle than any that has yet been put forward may yield a more complex understanding of the Modern's role in promoting that school.

59. The painters were William Baziotes, Willem de Kooning, Jackson Pollock, Mark Rothko, Mark Tobey, and Bradley Walker Tomlin. Sculptors were David Hare, Theodore Roszak, and David Smith. MoMA press release no. 21, March 25, 1955. Department of Public Information, The Museum of Modern Art.

60. McCray's June 11, 1956, memorandum cites specific requests "from Berlin, . . . the Stedelijk Museum at Amsterdam, . . . the Palais des Beaux Arts at Brussels, . . . and the Galleria d'Arte Moderna at Milan. . . ." The Museum of Modern Art Archives: Dorothy C. Miller Papers, I.14.f.

In 1957, Arnold Rüdlinger, of the Kunsthalle, Basel, traveled to the United States with a proposal for a similar exhibition, which he had previously discussed with directors of various European museums, including the Palais des Beaux-Arts, Brussels. On learning of the Modern's plans, he deferred to its initiative. See Robert Giron, letter to McCray, April 2, 1957. The Museum of Modern Art Archives: IC/IP Exh. Records (ICE-F-36-57; Brussels): Box 23.11.

61. *The New American Painting: As Shown in 8 European Countries, 1958–1959* (New York: The Museum of Modern Art, 1959), p. 5.

62. The Museum of Modern Art Archives: René d'Harnoncourt Papers [AAA: 2928, 250f; 2928, 147f].

63. The Museum of Modern Art Archives: D'Harnoncourt Papers [AAA: 2924; 1107].

64. House of Representatives Bill No. 6874; see also bills regarding cultural freedom of expression and foreign competitiveness through cultural programs: H. R. Bill Nos. 4913, 5756, 6713, 5040.

65. Thompson to d'Harnoncourt, November 7, 1955. The Museum of Modern Art Archives: D'Harnoncourt Papers [AAA: 2924; 974].

66. Representative George A. Dondero of Michigan in a speech before the House of Representatives, August 16, 1949: "Modern Art Shackled to Communism," in *Congressional Record: Proceedings and Debates of the 81st Congress, First Session* (4 pp.).

67. The Museum of Modern Art Archives: D'Harnoncourt Papers [AAA: 2924; 234–36]. D'Harnoncourt's support of Shahn and Kuniyoshi on political grounds, like the sponsorship of Shahn at the 1954 Venice Biennale, is obviously contrary to the assertion by the Shapiros that the Modern was reluctant to throw its weight behind such artists. If anything, it suggests, as Barr often contended, that the Museum wished above all to be an institution of catholic taste, unallied to any one particular school of art. A press release concerning the 1956 Venice Biennale refers to the 1954 show in a way that implies this posture of equanimity: "At the XXVII Biennale in 1954, the Museum presented an exhibition of work by 2 painters of widely contrasting tendencies, Willem de Kooning and Ben Shahn. Three sculptors, Gaston Lachaise, Ibram Lassaw and David Smith, were each represented by a major work. Ben Shahn won the highest purchase prize awarded by the international jury" (July 8, 1956).

68. One more example: In 1955, the loan shows of painting and sculpture included an exhibition of nineteenth-century paintings from France; a New Talent show featuring Tom Benrimo, Hugh Townley, and Richard O. Tyler; "The New Decade: 22 European Painters and Sculptors," a show of paintings from private collections; exhibitions of Giorgio de Chirico and Yves Tanguy; and a second New Talent show, with works by Martin Craig, Leander Fornas, and Nora Speyer.

69. Thomas B. Hess, "Eros and Agape Midtown," *Art News* 53 (November 1954), p. 17. This quotation appears in Barr's letter to the editor, *Art News* 56 (September 1957), p. 6 (see n. 71 below).

70. Thomas B. Hess, "Fifty-fifth Anniversary," *Art News* 56 (Summer 1957), p. 27.

71. Alfred H. Barr, Jr., letter to the editor, *Art News* 56 (September 1957), p. 6, 57. Reprinted as "The Museum of Modern Art's Record on American Artists," in *Defining Modern Art*, ed. Sandler and Newman, pp. 226–29.

72. Ibid., p. 228.

73. Ibid., p. 229.

74. "Errata," issued by the Art Workers Coalition, June 15, 1969. Department of Public Information, The Museum of Modern Art.

The AWC statement, although dated June 15, 1969, was postmarked June 9, before the installation of the exhibition. Presumably, the AWC based its accusations on information contained in an advance copy of MoMA press release no. 79, which concerns the press preview planned for June 13. On June 11, the Museum's Department of Public Information issued a statement refuting the AWC's accusations, "particularly in regard to the Museum's intent," which was not "'to build for The Museum of Modern Art the world's major collection of art of that period.' The Museum has had for some time the world's major collection of painting and sculpture of this generation, though it is always concerned with further enriching its collection in this as in all other phases of modern art." The statement continues, "The project of realizing the fullest possible collection of post–World War II art is a collaborative endeavor, in which many collectors, friends and Trustees of the Museum participate, along with the artists, in making important gifts." On the same date, a letter signed by Herbert Ferber, Adolph Gottlieb, Peter Grippe, Philip Guston, Seymour Lipton, Robert Motherwell, Theodore Roszak, Mark Rothko, and Mrs. Ad Reinhardt on behalf of her husband—artists who had made gifts or promised gifts to the Museum in connection with this exhibition program—was sent to William Rubin, co-curator of the exhibition with William C. Agee, stating that they would like "to make clear that the various allegations and innuendoes [made by the AWC] to the effect that we have been pressured or coerced into donating our works is false." In addition, Louise Bourgeois, David Hare, and Richard Pousette-Dart issued individual statements to the same effect. Department of Publication Information, The Museum of Modern Art.

75. This is to take issue with T. J. Clark's remark in a recent issue of *October* about the certitude of the revisionist argument, if not with the gist of his feeling about "an impasse": "There has been a feeling in the air for some time now that writing on Abstract Expressionism has reached an impasse. The various research programs that only yesterday seemed on the verge of delivering new and strong accounts of it, and speaking to its place (maybe even its function) in the world fiction called America, have run into the sand. Those who believed that the answer to the latter kind of question would emerge from a history of Abstract Expressionism's belonging to a certain Cold War polity, with patrons and art world institutions to match, have proved their point and offended all the right people. But the story, though good and necessary, [has] turned out not to have the sort of upshot for interpretation that the storytellers had been hoping for" (Clark, "In Defense of Abstract Expressionism," *October*, no. 69 [Summer 1994], pp. 23–48; the quotation appears on p. 26).

1. "The New American Painting," 1959. *Back row:* Theodoros Stamos, James Brooks, Philip Guston, Dorothy Miller, Franz Kline, William Baziotes. *Front row:* Jack Tworkov, Barnett Newman, Sam Francis. *Not photographed:* Arshile Gorky, Adolph Gottlieb, Grace Hartigan, Willem de Kooning, Robert Motherwell, Jackson Pollock, Mark Rothko, Clyfford Still, Bradley Walker Tomlin. Photograph by Irving Penn

Dorothy Miller's "Americans," 1942–63

Lynn Zelevansky

Between 1942 and 1963, The Museum of Modern Art presented a series of six exhibitions of contemporary painting and sculpture from the United States.[1] Each was titled by the number of artists included or by the year it was on view (for example, "15 Americans" or "Americans 1963") and was directed by Dorothy C. Miller, a curator at the Museum and Alfred H. Barr, Jr.'s trusted right hand. Pluralistic in conception, the "Americans" shows attempted to assess the broad state of visual art in this country by mixing the work of older, better-known painters and sculptors, whom Miller felt deserved greater recognition, with that of newly discovered talents. So as not to endorse a particular movement or style, the exhibitions included artists working in a variety of modes, from naturalistic to expressionistic, and from representational to more purely abstract. In all of these exhibitions, each participant was given his or her own gallery, so that the art could be appreciated in depth. Many of the works were offered for sale by the Museum.[2]

The form of the "Americans" exhibitions provided an alternative to the annual salons mounted by other national institutions. As Miller recalled in 1957:

Well, the first one I did . . . was called "Americans 1942." However, I didn't invent that type of show. Like practically everything good at The Museum of Modern Art, it was invented by Alfred Barr, way back in 1929–30—the first American survey the Museum did, "[Paintings by] Nineteen Living Americans." In that show they had a limited number of artists, instead of a hundred or two hundred . . . and each one was represented with a whole group of work, four to six or even more paintings by each, so you could really see what the man was like, as you can't in one example. . . . My name became associated with that type of show.[3]

The format of the "Americans" catalogues, established with the 1942 exhibition, included a brief introduction, written by Miller, that changed little from publication to publication. It described the series and usually traced the form of the shows back to "Paintings by Nineteen Living Americans," underscoring the Modern's long-term commitment to the art of its compatriots. It also gave the rationale for the mix of styles presented. The 1952 publication, in which individuality was especially emphasized, is a good example of the organizational logic that pertained from the beginning of the series:

Fifteen Americans . . . *again brings together a group of distinguished artists of marked individuality and widely differing aims. Their achievements may indicate trends in our art today, but to discover and illustrate such trends was not the primary intention behind the exhibition. The purpose was rather to give each artist an opportunity to speak to the Museum's public, in clear and individual terms, through a strong presentation of his work.*[4]

In the early 1940s, when the "Americans" exhibitions began, New York was culturally provincial, but by their conclusion two decades later, the city had become a capital of the international art world. Chronologically, the series paralleled the development of Abstract Expressionism in the United States; first-generation New York School artists figured in four of the six exhibitions and dominated two of them. This essay will examine the "Americans" shows as a means of better understanding the Museum's evolving relationship to art from the United States in general, and to the New York School in particular. It will also consider Dorothy Miller's role in the creation and realization of these exhibitions.

"Americans 1942: 18 Artists from 9 States" and Some Early History of the Museum

"Americans 1942: 18 Artists from 9 States" (fig. 2) was limited to artists living outside New York City. Almost all of its eighteen painters and sculptors worked in a figurative mode,[5] with Surrealist-like magic realism and various forms of Social Realism predominating. The artists were Darrel Austin, Hyman Bloom, Raymond Breinin, Samuel Cashwan, Francis Chapin, Emma Lu Davis, Morris Graves, Joseph Hirsch, Donal Hord, Charles Howard, Rico Lebrun, Jack Levine, Helen Lundeberg, Fletcher Martin, Octavio Medellin, Knud Merrild, Mitchell Siporin, and Everett Spruce.

To select works for the show, Miller traveled the country looking at art and was most enthusiastic about what she found in Seattle. Although she recognized that abstract artist Mark Tobey was the "old master" of the area, she bypassed him until 1946, when she included him in the exhibition "Fourteen Americans." Morris Graves was the discovery that preoccupied her in 1942.[6] Graves was initially reluctant to exhibit;[7] he was, however, like many artists of the time, in dire need of funds, and Miller convinced him to send his works to the Museum with the promise that she would sell them.[8] This was a realistic commitment, since Barr and Miller routinely counseled the Museum's patrons on art purchases, with an eye to the works' eventual entry into the Modern's collection. Museum staff members also often bought contemporary works. According to Miller, Graves's art elicited considerable excitement among Trustees as well as staff when it arrived.[9] The artist's ultimate participation in the exhibition in fact marked a turning point in his career.

Like Graves, Hyman Bloom was not eager to show. Miller enlisted the help of a friend who knew Bloom through his involvement with the Works Progress Administration (WPA) Federal Art Project, to take her to the artist's Boston studio on a Sunday morning. Since Bloom had no telephone, he was unprepared for their visit and they were uncertain as to whether he would welcome it. He allowed them in and gradually warmed to Miller, to the point where he was willing to consider taking part in the 1942 exhibition. Miller, disinclined to let his mind percolate too long on the matter, sent their mutual friend back the next day with a station wagon and instructions to bring Bloom's paintings to the Museum.[10]

Neither Graves nor Bloom had exhibited in New York before, and after the show many dealers were eager to represent them.[11] Indeed, works by the two artists, as well as by nine or ten others, were sold from "Americans 1942" to purchasers from around the country and to the Modern; buyers included those close to the Museum, like Trustees, as well as outsiders with no evident ties to the institution.[12] The press reaction to the exhibition, on the other hand, was mixed. Emily Genauer, writing in the *New York World Telegram,* called it "another half-hearted gesture of support-ing living Americans" and "the clearest evidence yet of uncertainty and even down-right ignorance." She claimed that of the eighteen artists included in the exhibition, eight had been shown in New York repeatedly; one had had three one-person shows during the ten-year period preceding the exhibition; a second had had a one-person show five years before and was represented in the collection of the Whitney Museum; and a third had had one-person shows in 1937 and 1939.[13] But Genauer was always critical of the Museum. Even by the standards of the time, what she describes could hardly have constituted overexposure.

Edward Alden Jewell, in the first of his two reviews in the *New York Times,*[14] was generally positive: "This highly interesting, frequently fresh and sometimes really vital display was organized and installed by Dorothy C. Miller of the museum staff. . . . One's impression of the show . . . is that it reflects newer [and] often decid-edly radical trends. There is perhaps not a single work that would be classified as right-wing academism." However, a few days later, Jewell was less enthusiastic, claiming that "this survey as a whole may be said to represent the general 'type' of art toward which the museum sponsoring it is wont to extend the most sympathetic encour-agement. Here is . . . art that shuns the platitudes of right-wing academism, even though in some instances it evinces on the part of contributing artists a failure to real-ize that academism can, quite as truly, be of left-wing persuasion." *Art digest* called the show "a worthwhile experiment,"[15] while *The Daily Worker* ran its article under the headline "Modern Museum Show Proves Great Democratic Possibilities of Art."[16]

Because it was restricted to work from outside New York, the 1942 exhibition engendered resentment and controversy within the local art community. The Federation of Modern Painters and Sculptors protested that the show reduced U.S. art "to a demonstration of geography."[17] To make matters worse, in previews of the coming season the newspapers identified the exhibition as "New American Leaders." As a result, the painter Gerome Kamrowski sent an agitated letter to Monroe Wheeler, then the Museum's Director of Publications:[18] "Could you please tell me how it is possible to have an exhibition called 'New Leaders in American Art' with-out including the younger New York painters? Perhaps if the Museum of Modern Art is unaware of the 'new leaders' in American art, I would be glad to suggest the names myself. . . . Or could New York not be American?"[19] Miller blamed the press for pub-lishing the incorrect title, thereby giving an erroneous impression of the exhibition's premises;[20] however, the papers evidently took the name from a Museum of Modern Art press release, which announced "New American Leaders, an exhibition of the work of artists living outside New York City. . . ."[21]

Miller always took the position that it was the Museum's decision, not her own, to exclude New Yorkers: "Then, about 1942, the Museum's exhibition com-mittee decided to have an all-American show that would exclude New York artists. We all knew the New Yorkers . . . but we didn't know about the people who had developed out of the WPA art projects elsewhere."[22] In fact, she fought for the right to organize the show in that way. Barr supported her, writing on July 1, 1941, to Trustee and former Museum President A. Conger Goodyear to protest the recommendation of Wheeler that for financial reasons the 1942 exhibition should focus on New York artists almost exclusively:

Dorothy's plan would, however, put into effect our frequently recorded determination to do something about American art outside of New York—a policy also recommended by the Advisory Committee.[23] My principal point is this: this exhibition is one of next year's four or five major shows. If it were a European show or a Mexican show we would not hesitate, if conditions permitted, to send one or more people abroad in order to study and collect the material . . . it seems to me that, in an exhibition budget of between $30,000 and $40,000, a $1,000 item for travelling expenses for the American show would not be excessive, especially as this exploration would add greatly to our knowledge of the art resources of the West. I realize how extremely difficult our budget situation is, but proportionally, the American show seems to me very moderate in cost.[24]

Installation photographs of the 1942 exhibition lend credence to the idea, common among artists and their supporters at the time, that the Museum treated U. S. art less seriously than its European counterpart (figs. 2, 3). Works were hung close together in varied frames, often of old-fashioned design. This is in stark contrast to the exhibition "Miró/Dalí," for example, which closed only ten days before the opening of "Americans 1942," on January 21. Documentary photographs reveal that the earlier exhibition, which must have had a considerably larger budget, was far more elegantly presented (fig. 4). Framing was sleeker and relatively uniform, and works were hung with greater space between them.

It is difficult to reclaim the social and intellectual context within which "Americans 1942" would have made sense. It was almost certainly Miller's tribute to the Works Progress Administration (WPA), the New Deal agency that brought relief to artists of all kinds during the Depression, and for which Holger Cahill, Miller's husband, had been Art Project Director.[25] Cahill, a follower of the American philosopher John Dewey, believed in the primacy of the act of making art over the resulting product. For him, cultural democracy—a notion that had great currency at the time—meant accessibility for the public, a place for the artist within society, and the creation of a new national art. His substantial achievement during the New Deal was the establishment of more than a hundred community art centers in thirty-eight states, intended to foster growth in the arts at the local level.[26] In 1933, when he was Acting Director of the Museum during Alfred Barr's year of absence,[27] Miller assisted Cahill on his "American Painting and Sculpture 1862–1932," and "American Sources of Modern Art (Aztec, Mayan, Incan)." During the following year she helped him organize the "First Municipal Art Exhibition of New York City," which was shown in a large gallery in the RCA Building in Rockefeller Center.[28] Later, she accompanied him around the country, visiting the regional art centers he was developing and seeing the local art. Nine states were represented in her 1942 show, and twelve of its eighteen artists had found employment on the art projects of the WPA.[29]

Today, Miller's desire to promote her husband's accomplishments might appear suspect, but in that smaller art world, in which individuals often played mul-

2. Installation view of "Americans 1942: 18 Artists from 9 States," The Museum of Modern Art, New York, 1942, with sculpture by Donal Hord in the foreground and paintings by Mitchell Siporin in the background

tiple roles, mores were different.[30] In fact, given her training and predispositions, one presumes that Miller would have been an avid supporter of the WPA even if her husband had not been affiliated with it. In addition, the WPA—crucial to the development of modern art in the United States—had benefitted so many that it is not surprising that she was not criticized for celebrating it. Nonetheless, by defining the show in the way she did, Miller included in it many artists whose work has little relation to the dominant aesthetic concerns of the present. Others, like Stuart Davis and John Graham, who as New Yorkers were ineligible for the exhibition, have had broader and more lasting influence.

•

If it was hoped that one result of the "Americans" series would be to quell criticism of the Museum in relation to contemporary U.S. art, the project had an inauspicious beginning. The Museum had in fact signaled its interest in art from the United States in 1929, its inaugural year: "Paintings by Nineteen Living Americans" immediately followed the opening exhibition, "Cézanne, Gauguin, Seurat, van Gogh," and together the two shows framed the institution's concerns. However, by 1940, the Modern had mounted many more one-person exhibitions of foreign artists;[31] and group shows of U.S. art had most often been presented, some critics claimed, in intellectually unfocused surveys of contemporary activity.[32] In addition, United States representation in important exhibitions organized around ideas and movements could be extremely meager. For example, Alexander Calder, Lionel Feininger, and Man Ray, all living abroad, were the only U.S. nationals included in "Cubism and Abstract Art," of 1936.[33]

The problem was not only that the 1942 show excluded New York artists but that it also emphasized figuration over abstraction. Indeed, the Museum had demonstrated a marked preference, in regard to contemporary work from its own shores, for relatively conservative, figurative art. Of the seven U.S. artists who had one-person shows at the Museum between 1929 and 1940, four were formally more traditional than revolutionary: Charles Burchfield (in 1930), Maurice Sterne (1933),

Left:
3. Installation view of "Americans 1942: 18 Artists from 9 States," The Museum of Modern Art, New York, 1942, with paintings by Darrel Austin

Right:
4. Installation view of "Miró/Dali," The Museum of Modern Art, New York, 1941, with paintings by Joan Miró

Edward Hopper (1933), and—his Precisionist associations notwithstanding—Charles Sheeler (1939).[34] The others were the painter James MacNeill Whistler (1934), who was no longer considered avant-garde,[35] Gaston Lachaise (1935), and John Marin (1936).

From its inception the Museum had defined its relationship to European modernism differently from that to art from its own country. Barr felt from the outset that painting and sculpture in the United States had not yet approached the level of invention or sophistication found in the work of leading modernists in France, Germany, Italy, the Netherlands, the Soviet Union, and Mexico.[36] But the political realities of the art world at that time—for example, U.S. artists' profound resentment of the hegemony of Paris—combined with the general cultural environment in the United States, which was extremely nationalistic and, at best, unreceptive to the Museum's project, mitigated against a straightforward acknowledgment of this fact. The result was a two-pronged policy that, for reasons of tact and diplomacy, was never acknowledged, but was manifested especially in the Museum's exhibition program.

The Modern's early supporters were patriotic and community-oriented. If they saw a discrepancy between the quality of foreign and U.S. modernism, they also felt it was their responsibility to promote the arts of their own country. In 1935, Abby Aldrich Rockefeller, one of the institution's three founders,[37] gave the Museum 36 oils and 105 watercolors and pastels from her collection, most of them works by living U.S. artists.[38] And it was not by chance that the first painting to enter the Modern's collection was Edward Hopper's *House by the Railroad* (1925), bought by Trustee Stephen C. Clark from "Paintings by Nineteen Living Americans." In addition, it has always been the Modern's practice that no work by a living artist from the United States or Latin America could be sold unless it was to buy another, presumably superior, work by the same artist. This has never applied to Europeans.[39]

The Museum's policy toward contemporary U.S. art was established in July 1929, when Goodyear, appointed the first President of the Board of Trustees, sent Lillie P. Bliss, another of the Museum's three founders, a statement of purpose for the Museum. It was intended for the press in preparation for the opening of the institution. While she expressed "profound satisfaction and gratitude" in response to Goodyear's efforts, Bliss also thought, sagely, that "it might be wise to emphasize the fact that the exhibitions will be of American as well as foreign art." She worried that, "Otherwise we might lose the interest of some pretty helpful people." The finished statement proclaims that it was the intention of the Museum to "hold a series of exhibitions during the next two years which shall include as complete a representation as may be possible of the great modern masters—American and European—from Cézanne to the present day."[40]

In fact, the depth of the Modern's commitment to art from the United States remained, at least for a time, in question. In a 1933 Director's report prepared for the Trustees, in a section headed, "The Problem of our American Collection," Barr questioned the advisability of the Museum's continuing to collect U.S. art. While The Museum of Modern Art was the only one of Manhattan's major museums showing contemporary foreign work, both the Whitney Museum of American Art and The Metropolitan Museum of Art exhibited and collected contemporary art from the United States, and together they had the ability to spend $25,000 a year in this field. The Modern had no such capability. Barr did note that, if the Modern were to continue to collect U.S. art, "the presence of first-rate contemporary foreign pictures in the same building or even on the same wall would be an advantage as well as competition for American works."[41]

By 1940, in its November *Bulletin,* subtitled "American Art and the Museum," the Modern was able to demonstrate that works in the collection by U.S. artists outweighed those from other individual countries, including France and Germany.[42] This publication was a means of countering arguments made by artists during a demonstration, held the previous April in front of the Museum, that had elicited press coverage. The artists had protested the Modern's exhibition policies on the heels of "Italian Masters," a show of Renaissance art that originally had been scheduled to be installed at the Metropolitan following its showing at the San Francisco World's Fair; when the Metropolitan found the terms of the Italian government to be unacceptable, the Modern took the exhibition. The Museum tried to make up for this anomaly within its program by mounting a concurrent "Modern Masters" exhibition, but this did not sufficiently defuse the problem. The protest that ensued was organized by the American Abstract Artists group, which felt that, in its representation of art from its own country, the Museum was biased against abstraction. They distributed a leaflet, written by the painter Ad Reinhardt, headed "How Modern Is the Museum of Modern Art?" The leaflet, which was signed by fifty-two people, also lambasted the 1939 interdepartmental exhibition "Art in Our Time," of which Barr was coordinator: "Whose time? Sargent, Homer, LeFarge, Harnett [sic]? Or Picasso, Braque, Léger, and Mondrian? Which time? . . . And *Modern Masters* Eakins, Homer, Ryder, Whistler—died 1916, 1910, 1917, 1903. Those are the only Americans included."[43]

The April 1940 demonstration was followed by others in January 1942 (in response to Miller's show), 1943, and 1944 by the Federation of Modern Painters and Sculptors.[44] Barr expressed his sentiments on the issue in a private memorandum to Miller, written on October 10, 1940, as he was planning the *Bulletin* that would appear that November:

This is the background of our problem:
The Museum was founded for the presentation and study of the modern arts without any nationalistic biases or prejudices. It was an implicit part of our policy to choose the best from all over the world. This did not mean, of course, that our product was unimportant. I think statistics will show that we have been more concerned with American art than with the art of all foreign countries combined. In spite of this fact, there has certainly been some feeling, especially on the part of certain American artists and dealers, that the Museum was primarily concerned with "foreign art." This impression has been caused in part by the character and reputation of the Trustees' collections, partly by the success of certain foreign exhibitions, and partly by the fact that in New York, of the three principle museums concerned with modern art, only The Museum of Modern Art deals with foreign art, whereas the Whitney and the Metropolitan confine themselves in the 20th century exclusively to American art.
Still another important factor is the tendency on the part of the public to identify art with painting and sculpture, two fields in which America is not yet, I am afraid, quite the equal of France; but in other fields—the film, architecture and photography, for instance—the United States would seem to be the equal or superior of any other country.

If, then, we can in this Bulletin assemble our record in American art in all fields I am convinced that we will have a very strong case for [the claim that] no other Museum in the country has done as much to further the interest of American photography, American films, American architecture and American industrial design—nor when the facts are in do I think that painting and sculpture will be far behind.[45]

The information on the composition of the collection published in the November 1940 *Bulletin* was updated for the 1942 publication *Painting and Sculpture in the Museum of Modern Art*. In his foreword to this catalogue, Museum President John Hay Whitney represented the institutional position in regard to its collections:

. . . It is natural and proper that American artists should be included in greater numbers than those of any other country. But it is equally important in a period when Hitler has made a lurid fetish of nationalism that no fewer than twenty-four nations other than our own should also be represented in the Museum Collection.[46]

In the June 15, 1944, issue of *Museum News*, James Thrall Soby, then Director of the Department of Painting and Sculpture, defended the Museum's relation to U.S. art:

In recent years the museum has sometimes been berated for not buying more painting and sculpture by American abstract and Expressionist artists. . . .

But it should be remembered that the museum does not exist for the direct benefit and patronage of artists. . . .

. . . To quote a previous article on the subject, we try to buy "good examples of the work of those . . . artists who . . . have contributed to the evolution of a recognizable contemporary art. Standards of selection have been purposefully broad, and bias in favor of any one school has been disabled—always admitting that prejudice cannot be totally avoided by any force of detachment." . . . We do not consider it our job to force contemporary art in one direction or another . . . it is not our job to lead artists, but to follow them—at a close yet respectful distance.[47]

•

This was the environment in which the "Americans" series was conceived. Originally, these shows were to be yearly events. Following the 1942 exhibition, Miller organized "Americans 1943: American Realists and Magic Realists." The introduction to its catalogue states that the publication "records the Museum's annual exhibition of contemporary American art and illustrates a recent trend in that field."[48] However, the 1943 show differed from the others not only in that it concentrated on a particular manifestation of contemporary art, but also in that it contained a historical section.[49] Ultimately, Miller did not consider the exhibition to be part of the series. The words "Americans 1943" were dropped from the title of the catalogue, and the catalogue was not included in the volume, edited by Miller, consisting of reprints of the books for the six other "Americans" shows.[50]

"Fourteen Americans"

At one point, the 1943 exhibition was intended to contrast figuration and abstraction. Notes in the exhibition files show Miller attempting to compose a preface for the catalogue linking the two modes. However, the word "out" appears next to the names of several artists on her list who would take part in the exhibition "Fourteen Americans" in 1946:

In 1943 The Museum of Modern Art planned an Abstract American exhibition, and I invited Arshile Gorky, Theodore Roszak, and Irene [Rice] Pereira [to participate]. . . . It was supposed to be a contrast between realistic painting and sculpture and abstract, and the Museum decided that it was too much for one show and they would simply do the realists first, so I had to tell these three artists that it was postponed. I showed them all in 1946 instead.[51]

Informing these artists that they were to be dropped from the 1943 exhibition must have been ticklish. While Miller claimed that "the Museum" was responsible,[52] it is in fact impossible to know whose decision this actually was. It could easily have been her own.

"Fourteen Americans" actually included fifteen artists: David Aronson, Ben L. Culwell, Gorky, David Hare, Loren MacIver, Robert Motherwell, Isamu Noguchi, Pereira, Alton Pickens, C. S. Price, Roszak, Honoré Sharrer, Saul Steinberg, and Mark Tobey; George Tooker was added at the last minute, after the deadline for inclusion in the catalogue.[53] Seven of the fifteen painted or sculpted in an abstract mode: Gorky, Hare, Motherwell, Noguchi, Pereira, Roszak, and Tobey. The rest—with the exception of Saul Steinberg, who already had a caricatural drawing style—either worked with expressionist figuration, produced a kind of realism that bordered on the surreal, or did genre painting. Only four came from outside New York.

A list of artists Miller was considering as she planned the exhibition includes Adolph Gottlieb, Jackson Pollock, and Mark Rothko. The presence in the files of an announcement for a Louise Bourgeois exhibition suggests that Miller was thinking of her, as well. But at the time Miller felt that it was too early to show the first generation of the New York School in any depth:

[Around 1945 or 1946] we began to get excited about Motherwell. I put Motherwell in my 1946 show, "Fourteen Americans." And that was too early. You see, I was always either too early or too late with those shows. We didn't have them often enough. Those shows would have been awfully good if they had been at stated intervals like every three years. But some of them were six years apart and the others were four years apart. . . . Peggy Guggenheim never forgave me for the fact that I didn't put Pollock in that show in 1946. I looked at all those things she owned—she owned practically everything he'd done—and I loved about three or four of them. . . . And the rest I just didn't think were very good paintings. And I still don't. . . . Maybe I was wrong. . . . But when I did put him in it was already six years later. It should have been three years later. Then [it] would have meant something. Of course he'd done all his greatest work by 1952 when I finally was given a chance to have another show.[54]

Sales from the 1946 exhibition appear to have been mostly to staff, Trustees, and friends of the Museum, to the Museum collection, and to other institutions.[55] The press coverage was not as negative in 1946 as it would be for subsequent exhibitions. Nevertheless, in the *New York World Telegram,* Genauer complained that the Museum "should have elected for its initial and major event of the season to show

Left:
5. Installation view of the Isamu Noguchi gallery, "Fourteen Americans," The Museum of Modern Art, New York, 1946

Right:
6. Installation view of the Arshile Gorky gallery, "Fourteen Americans"

15 artists of whom two-thirds have either been familiar to gallery goers for well over a decade (Noguchi, I. Rice Pereira, Arshile Gorky, Theodore Roszak) or else become hardy 57th St. perennials in recent years (Loren MacIver, David Aronson, C. S. Price, David Hare, Mark Tobey, Robert Motherwell)."[56] And in *The New Republic*, Manny Farber identified Steinberg as "the one robust artist" in the show; he disliked almost everything else, but found Motherwell more bearable than most.[57]

There is the sense that with this exhibition Miller was beginning to hit her stride. She had a very good eye, and a talent for picking the best of what an artist had done. Many of the works from her shows would enter the collection and become icons of the New York School.[58] While the emphasis on figuration and the American scene that characterized the 1942 exhibition survived into the 1946 show in works by Aronson, Pickens, and Sharrer, and even in some paintings by MacIver, photographs of Gorky's gallery, for example, show not only the representational *The Artist and His Mother* (1926–29) but also fine abstract works, such as the 1941 *Garden in Sochi*, already in the Museum's collection, and *The Diary of a Seducer* (1945), which would come to the Museum in 1985 as a gift of Trustee William A.M. Burden. The three-dimensional forms in Hare's Surrealist sculpture *Magician's Game* (1944) clearly complemented Gorky's in two dimensions. (Miller showed the plaster for the Hare; a bronze casting of it would enter the Museum's collection in 1969.) In addition to oils and watercolors by Motherwell, the exhibition presented six of his early collages, including *Pancho Villa, Dead and Alive* (1943), which already belonged to the Museum. Moreover, the installation photographs indicate that in the consistent framing of the works and the relatively spacious distances between pictures, the exhibition resembled "Miró/Dalí" more than "Americans 1942" (figs. 5, 6).

Miller showed some earlier, representational works by Tobey and some of his less radical forms of abstract painting, along with examples of the allover abstraction for which he is best known today, providing a sense of the artist's development. Culwell, who, according to William S. Lieberman, was well respected by both Barr and Miller,[59] had in common with Tobey the movement from representation toward a calligraphic form of abstraction. But his paintings, executed onboard a ship under siege in the South Pacific during World War II, are at the other end of the emotional spectrum. Culwell's work is violent, reminiscent in its depictions of monsters of Dubuffet and art brut, but wholly different in its vivid coloration.[60]

In *The Nation,* Clement Greenberg stated that half the artists in the 1946 show constituted those among whom "the fate of American art depends at the moment." He cited Gorky, Hare, MacIver, Price, Roszak, Tobey, and, with some reservations, Motherwell, but felt that the inclusion of others blunted the point: "The net impression left by the *14 Americans* show is of a kind of shabbiness, half-bakedness, a lack of seriousness and independence and energy, the fault of which lies more with the person who selected and arranged the show than with the artists shown," adding, "Whoever he was, he seems altogether devoid of personal taste—more reliant on tips than on his own judgment."[61] It is incredible that in 1946, after Miller had been at the Museum for over twelve years and had organized related exhibitions, Greenberg had no idea who she was and felt no responsibility to find out.

Dorothy Miller

Greenberg's dismissal notwithstanding, by 1946, Dorothy Miller (fig. 7) was better prepared than most curators to act as a specialist in the emergent field of U.S. art.[62] When she came to the Modern as a permanent employee in the autumn of 1934, she was thirty years old and already had nine years of on-the-job experience. Her parents had wanted her to be an artist. Envisioning any vocation for a girl born in 1904 was unusual, and this encouragement may have given Miller license to pursue a profession when most women did not. Her father, an architect and engineer, researched women's colleges in the Eastern United States and chose Smith College for his daughter, believing that it provided the best art education. Miller soon realized that she would not be an artist, but she knew that she wanted to work with painting and sculpture and took art history courses along with her studio classes.[63]

She began her career at The Newark Museum, first training under, and then working for, the pioneering Americanist John Cotton Dana.[64] There she met her future husband, Holger Cahill, who was assisting Dana with the museum training program at Newark. As mentioned above, her first affiliation with The Museum of Modern Art occurred during Alfred Barr's absence in 1932 and 1933. In 1934, after he had returned and she was free of other commitments, Barr hired Miller on a full-time basis and gave her the role of liaison with the artists,[65] tantamount to handing her the field of contemporary art in the United States. By 1942, when the "Americans" series began, she knew many of the most prominent and promising artists working around the country.[66]

Miller was Barr's most trusted confidante. There was a remarkable seamlessness to their relationship, so that even today it is virtually impossible to tell where his ideas ended and hers began. Undoubtedly because of his stature, and also because Miller rarely wrote for publication,[67] there has been a tendency to give Barr credit for what she accomplished in the "Americans" shows. But there is no substantiation for claims like the one made by Milton W. Brown: ". . . since [Miller] was never actually director of painting and sculpture, and since Barr had his finger in everything, she obviously was not calling the shots."[68] On the contrary, while Barr in some cases may have influenced selections for the "Americans" exhibitions (although there is no documentary proof of this), Miller unquestionably had opinions of her own, and even in an arrangement as guarded as theirs, there is evidence that he depended on her judgment in the formulation of his opinions regarding contemporary U.S. art.[69]

In 1942, when the Museum was still small, before Barr was relieved of his duties as Museum Director and before the Department of Painting and Sculpture had others at the helm,[70] Miller was the obvious person to organize the series. Barr, a hands-on administrator, maintained a degree of control over any responsibility he relinquished. Miller, who was devoted to him and ambitious only for the institution, was trusted to share insights and keep him informed of her activities. In addition, some at the Museum may have felt that, in the midst of artists' demonstrations and expressed hostility toward the institution, a commitment to the regular exhibition of contemporary U.S. art would deflect criticism. At the same time, Barr, who was wholly identified with the Modern, would be insulated by Miller from controversies that the exhibitions would inevitably generate.

Her interest and experience and her relationship with Barr notwithstanding, the choice of Miller to direct the "Americans" series supports the notion that for the Museum's Director and Trustees, art from the United States played a subordinate role. First, in an area that was of abiding concern to him, Barr would not have relinquished authority to anyone else; and second, it is unlikely that an enterprise of great importance to the institution would have been directed by a woman. Historically, U.S. museums in large part have been populated by women and dominated by men.[71] Although founded by three powerful women, The Museum of Modern Art has been no exception. Having had a male director from the beginning, the Modern's most influential curators have also been men. It is telling that Miller was never asked to organize a major exhibition in the field with which the Museum has been most associated, that of modern European painting and sculpture. After all, from 1947 to 1967 she was Curator of Museum Collections. Presumably, the broad-based knowledge of modernism that allowed her to do that job would have permitted her to tackle a wide variety of other art-historical and art-critical problems as well.

Certainly, gender played a part in determining the trajectory of Miller's career, shaping the way she and others saw her role. A very attractive, and stylish woman, her feminine appeal probably worked both for and against her. William Rubin, who first came to the Museum in the mid-1960s as a guest curator in the Department of Painting and Sculpture,[72] recalls that Miller was "extremely beautiful and extremely feminine," and that for her generation, being feminine often implied "not being the boss."[73] The self-effacing aspects of her nature, which may have made her companionable and unthreatening in the short run, hurt her reputation over time. The fact that she wrote little for publication during her tenure rendered her virtually mute to the future, leaving us to piece together her actual contribution. Although she appeared commanding to artists on the outside,[74] and could be so inside the institution,[75] in the thirty-four years that she worked at the Museum she developed no power base of her own; hers was largely a reflected light.[76] Around 1981, long after her retirement, when asked if she would have liked to have advanced further within the Museum's hierarchy, Miller gave a predictably politic reply, signaling an acceptance of the limitations imposed upon her: "The idea of going any higher on the ladder at the Museum did not occur to me. I always felt it a great privilege to work with Alfred Barr and the other brilliant people there. . . . I was also lucky because I worked with two people who had the best eyes for art that I have ever known, Cahill and Barr."[77] And she defined her role in the following way: "In general, my work at the Museum always just was working with Barr on exhibitions, on acquisitions, on publications; first smaller ones and then bigger ones and so on[.] . . . I think I was rather lucky that these two brains, Cahill and Barr, really taught me everything I know."[78]

Despite these self-deprecating remarks, Miller's achievements were extremely impressive. At a time when most upper- and middle-class women were not working outside the home, she was organizing large-scale exhibitions for one of the world's premier art museums and was, for a time, responsible for its most public statements regarding contemporary U.S. art. Had she been a man, it probably would have gone unquestioned that her exhibitions embodied her own ideas; that she published little, for example, would have had less impact on subsequent appraisals of her accomplishments. But she was caught in a double bind: As a woman, she needed to do more than the men around her to secure the professional position that she had worked so hard to attain; at the same time, to manifest too much personal ambition might have threatened the position she did have. The sad irony is that the mechanisms that Miller developed, presumably unconsciously, to survive in a world hostile to career women, also made her compliant in camouflaging her own achievement. And if her reticence hid her contribution from her peers and from the future, then her readiness to credit the powerful men in her life (Barr and Cahill) with her own accomplishments, to blame the Museum for the tough decisions she made (many professionals tend to do this, but she carried it to an extreme), and to take a subservient role helped insure that she would, indeed, occupy a subordinate position.

Nevertheless, it was not only because of her own complicity that Miller's description of herself as primarily Barr's assistant was, ultimately, accurate. After his dismissal as Director of the Modern in late 1943, Barr, who never lost his august position within the art world, would eventually regain it within the institution as well; but Miller, whose projects he was apparently unable to sponsor in the way he previously had, would never attain the role toward which she had appeared headed earlier in her career. Between 1940 and 1946, she directed ten exhibitions at the Museum, but in the sixteen years between 1947 and 1963, only seven of her shows were presented in New York.[80] By 1946, Miller had been at the Museum for twelve years and had almost twenty-two years of experience. She had worked on many exhibitions and had organized two of the "Americans" shows, along with "American Realists and Magic Realists" and "Romantic Painting in America" in 1943.[80] On September 9, 1946, she wrote Soby from her house in Chatham, Massachusetts, apparently in answer to a letter from him asking her to work on his upcoming Ben Shahn exhibition:

7. Dorothy Miller, 1955. Photograph by Man Ray

I am thrilled and flattered out of my life that you think I might help with the Shahn show. It would be wonderful for me and I would love it, and so far as the Dep[artmen]t goes I am sure there is nothing ahead for me except a long barren period of nothing but routine work. I never expect to be allowed to do another show and I rather doubt that JJS [James Johnson Sweeney] will ask my help on any of his shows. . . . Anyway do do ask the powers if I may help you with Shahn.[81]

About the installation of her exhibitions she added, in characteristically self-effacing terms, "I have tried very hard to imitate Alfred in every way possible, and it is frustrating to find that at the end of all these years I am still just as far away as ever from achieving the first part of what he does." In the catalogue for the Shahn exhibition she is named "assistant director" of a show that, given her record, she easily might have organized herself.[82]

During this period Miller indeed may have been working under especially difficult circumstances. After "Fourteen Americans" in 1946, she did not organize another exhibition at the Museum until the 1952 installment of the series. In the mid-1950s, when the institution began to mount monographic exhibitions of artists associated with the New York School, some of whom Miller had included in her shows, she was not the one to direct them; as prestige increasingly accrued to the work in question, the role of the Museum's "expert" on U.S. art fell to a series of male curators.[83]

When Miller has talked about her "Americans" exhibitions, it is always in terms of the Modern "allowing" her to do them. For example: "The Museum let me do another American show in 1946 and then one in 1952."[84] She once commented plaintively, "I did only six of those American shows . . . because . . . there was so much else we had to exhibit."[85] As revealed before in relation to Pollock, Miller was frustrated by the fact that the shows were, to her way of thinking, too far apart. She believed that the Museum appeared late in its support of Abstract Expressionism because from 1946 to 1952 there was no installment in the "Americans" series. Most of the artists had found their mature styles by 1950, and by 1952, when she included a number of them in "15 Americans," their accomplishments were well-known within the art world.[86] Nevertheless, for the general public this work was new and radical.

"15 Americans"

"15 Americans" was the most controversial exhibition of the series, not only because abstraction dominated but also because eight of the artists—William Baziotes, Herbert Ferber, Frederick J. Kiesler, Richard Lippold, Jackson Pollock, Mark Rothko, Clyfford Still, and Bradley Walker Tomlin—produced large, formally radical work.[87] The show also included abstractionists Edward Corbett and Thomas Wilfrid. Only five of those shown—Edwin Dickinson, Joseph Glasco, Herbert Katzman, Irving Kriesberg, and Herman Rose—used figuration in a manner familiar to the Museum's general audience; they worked in an expressionistic or genre style. Miller later remarked that "that show made, I think, the biggest splash of any of them. . . . Oh, it made no splash with the critics. It was beyond them. That's one way I knew it was a success. . . ."[88]

Notes in her files indicate that Miller intended to include Willem de Kooning in her 1952 exhibition,[89] and in a 1985 interview she confirmed that she asked him to participate. He accepted, and Miller had already chosen works for the show when he suddenly withdrew without explanation, before the catalogue went to press. "I've often realized that people must wonder why de Kooning wasn't in that show that he was asked to be in. But there was no way for me to make a statement saying . . . he was asked but he withdrew."[90]

Miller had to contend with a host of temperamental personalities. Still was especially cantankerous and she handled him carefully: "Clyfford Still . . . was a very strange and difficult man. At the time he was with Betty Parsons Gallery[,] where he'd had three shows by 1950."[91] Miller attended the second Still show at the Parsons Gallery with Cahill, who called her at the Museum and implored her to "come over here quickly. . . ." She "had a feeling of being disturbed by those paintings and not knowing why: "It took me quite a long time to get it."[92] When she was organizing the 1952 exhibition, she was afraid Still would refuse to participate, since he wasn't allowing people to visit his studio and he was against showing in New York.[93] Nevertheless, one day she asked him: "I said, 'Would you consider being in this show?' He said[,] "Well, tell me the conditions.' I said, 'You'll have a gallery to your-self, as big a one as I can give you. We'll choose the paintings. . . .'"[94] She promised that he could write whatever he wanted for the catalogue, so long as it wasn't obscene, explaining that they needed to send the publication through the mail. He thought about it overnight and then agreed.[95] However, he refused to attend the opening: Miller escorted him to the event and through the receiving line. Then, she later reported, it was as if he evaporated.[96]

Rothko proved to be the most mercurial of the artists.[97] At his studio, located in an old stained-glass factory on Fifty-fourth Street and Sixth Avenue, Miller had chosen fifteen or twenty works to be brought to the Museum.[98] However, when the paintings arrived, she discovered that he had changed the selection drastically: "I couldn't get anywhere with him."[99] He wanted to install the paintings, with their edges touching, around the four walls of the gallery under blazing light. Miller asked Barr and then Museum Director René d'Harnoncourt to speak with Rothko and, in the end, there was a compromise: "I wasn't happy with the gallery, but I was almost happy with it."[100]

Rothko and Still, friends at the time,[101] were nonetheless extremely competitive. Miller saw Rothko's desire to use twice the usual illumination in each fixture, as well as his gallery's overhead lights, as an expression of the fear that he would literally be outshined by Still.[102] She had carefully planned a presentation of the abstract artists that would start "with a Baziotes piece and then [work] up to a crescendo of Still and Rothko . . . and going into abstract sculpture from there."[103] However, Rothko did not want Still's pictures to be visible from his doorway. Miller explained that the entry had to be six feet wide to accommodate crowds, and suggested that they use plants to block the view. Rothko seemed to find this acceptable.[104] But one day, after Miller and Still had arranged Still's gallery, Rothko persuaded him, behind Miller's back, to re-hang it entirely. Rothko was worried about the impact on his work of a very large black painting by the other artist that could be seen from his space. Miller convinced Still to return to the original hanging, and then reinstalled the room. The show did not travel because Rothko and Still refused to participate in the tour.[105]

Kiesler was also very demanding, telephoning Miller several times a day and repeatedly insisting that she visit his studio, where he would attempt to persuade her to allow him to overcrowd his gallery.[106] What a relief it must have been that Pollock did not participate in the installation, leaving it to Miller's discretion! He wrote a note of thanks, which she received on April 14, 1952: "Dear Dorothy, I want you to know what a wonderful job I think you did in hanging my room at the Museum. There was probably extra work for you (or was there?) in my staying away. At any rate, I think it was wise of me."[107]

Documentary photographs indicate that the exhibition had exceptionally

8. Installation view of the Jackson Pollock gallery, with Frederick Kiesler's *Galaxy* (1947–48) visible at far right, "15 Americans," The Museum of Modern Art, New York, 1952

beautiful passages. In a dramatic progression, the galleries gradually darkened as the installation moved from Baziotes to Pollock to Kiesler, and then became light again with Tomlin. The Pollock gallery must have been spectacular, with black-and-white paintings, long, narrow oriental scroll-like works, and the eighteen-foot-wide *Number 30*, of 1950, each occupying their own wall (fig. 8). Ultimately, Miller managed Kiesler very well. His painting in nineteen sections, configured in an "X," was positioned on the wall least visible upon entering the room, and took nothing away from *Galaxy*, of 1947–48, the fine monumental sculpture that dominated the space (fig. 9). The selection of works by Still (fig. 10) appears to have been as strong as that by Pollock, with his thirteen-foot-wide black painting as powerful as Rothko had been afraid it would be. Rothko's gallery seems to have lacked some of the impact one expects from a collection of his best paintings. Tomlin and Baziotes were well represented.[108] However, Ferber's ambitious sculpture, *. . . and the bush was not consumed,* of 1951, looks a bit ungainly. Made for the outside of a synagogue in New Jersey, it was over twelve feet high and almost eight feet wide, and it opened the exhibition.[109] The art of Corbett and Wilfrid could live reasonably comfortably with that of the New York School, but paintings by Glasco, Katzman, Kreisberg, and especially Dickinson (fig. 11) and Rose, were strongly overshadowed by the sheer size of the Abstract Expressionist works.[110]

The records regarding sales indicate that paintings and sculptures by seven artists sold from the 1952 exhibition. The Museum acquired four works, one through purchase and three as gifts. The acquisition of Rothko's *Number 10* was also related to its inclusion in the show.[111] On April 14, 1952, on his way out of town, Barr sent a memorandum to d'Harnoncourt: "Just a thought on the way to the boat. If *Fifteen Americans* is a real success, maybe we should keep it on through the summer."[112] The

9. Frederick J. Kiesler. *Galaxy*. (1947–48; base remade 1951). Wood and rope, 11'11" x 13'10" x 14'3" (363.2 x 421.6 x 434.3 cm). The Museum of Modern Art, New York. Gift of Mrs. Nelson Rockefeller, 1991. Included in "15 Americans"

Left.
10. Installation view of the Clyfford Still gallery, "15 Americans," The Museum of Modern Art, New York, 1952

Right:
11. Installation view of the Edwin Dickinson gallery, "15 Americans"

exhibition seems to have been counted something of a triumph since they did extend it, not to the end of the summer, but for an extra month, to the end of July.

"15 Americans" was an unwelcome shock for much of the Modern's audience, engendering a great deal of anger from the public and the press. The Museum's administration had prepared for the onslaught. In Miller's words, "*Fifteen Americans* was supposed to be a very far-out show. I was ready to stick to my choices but I didn't know how it would be accepted. I had a twenty foot wall filled with one Pollock. I think some of our Trustees were worried about what the critics would say. Some of them came and looked at the show the morning before the preview. The President of the Board was brought through by René d'Harnoncourt, Director of the Museum, to break him in gently."[113] But at the opening, as Miller entered, Barr's wife, Marga, rushed up to congratulate her on a great success.[114]

Walking through the galleries during public hours, Miller often overheard derogatory comments about Rothko and Still, and a painting by Still was vandalized during the show.[115] The files in the Museum Archives, filled with protest letters, confirm the fact that these artists excited great hostility.[116] One $100-a-year member resigned his membership over the exhibition.[117] Worried, Miller sent a copy of his letter to Barr, who was vacationing in Sicily. She wrote along the bottom of the member's letter: "Alfred—I haven't answered—don't know what to do—gave Jim [Soby] a copy at his request as he said he would argue with him. [He] has been a $100 member for three years. Ah me!" On June 4, 1952, Barr wrote to the man, whom he knew personally, expressing his dismay in reading the letter: "For me, '15 Americans' is the most compelling and dramatic demonstration of the vigor of our art that I have ever seen—at least our contemporary art."[118] The concern was such that Soby also wrote to the man.[119]

The press response to the exhibition may have fueled that of the public. In May 1952, the *New Yorker* critic, Robert M. Coates, charged that, "For the most part, the exhibition is a reflection of a rather supercilious attitude the Museum has shown before toward contemporary American art—that it's a field of no great consequence or validity, fun to cull through for oddments and curiosities but hardly worth serious investigation."[120] From Sicily, Barr once again wrote on Miller's behalf, reiterating to Coates the Museum's record on American art.[121] Coates responded, ". . . I appreciate a point of difficulty in your position that you're kind enough not to mention in your letter: that you, after all, are supposed to present all modern art, European and American, and it must be a constant struggle (and seem often an ungrateful one) to try to maintain a balance among them all" (June 15, 1952). He then elaborated on his complaint about the Museum's attitude: ". . . the whole thing revolves around 'showmanship' . . . [W]hile your European shows—Klee, Braque, Matisse, etc.—are put on with great soberness and thoroughness, the Americans, one feels, are put on as if they were something to be played with, a little. One result (again, to me) is that they don't have the honesty of your European shows. . . ."

Barr replied, thanking Coates for the "thoughtfulness and friendly spirit" of his correspondence, but adding, "Golly, when I think of the sweat and soul searching that went into *15 Americans* it does make me pretty mad to have had you damn it as 'a reflection of a supercilious attitude' without even bothering to glance at the catalog" (September 9, 1952). And, voicing the Museum's long-standing position, he added, "As to showmanship—we are conscious of no difference between our presentation of American and European art." Coates had erroneously claimed that the catalogue was not ready for the opening. Miller defended herself on that point, writing him on July 9 that, in fact, the book had been available at the press desk. Coates's tone, when he answered her, was very different from the one employed in his correspondence with Barr. He wrote to Barr on September 27, 1952, after reflecting on a philosophical difference that he perceived between them: "I don't think we're as far apart as that, thank God, and in fact I'm sure of it. But I do think our present split leads in that direction. Can't we get together for a drink, or lunch maybe, some time, and see if we can heal the fissure?" (There is no evidence that Barr responded.) To Miller Coates stated that, although he had liked other shows of hers, ". . . I didn't . . . like this one. Can't we just let it go at that and hope for better agreement next time?" (July 17, 1952).[122]

In *The Nation,* S. Lane Faison, Jr., cited Pollock and Tomlin as the highlights of an exhibition whose variety was a bit bewildering.[123] There was a negative review in *Art digest* that approved of only Wilfrid and Ferber.[124] The critic for the *New York Times,* Howard Devree, disliked what he considered extreme forms of Abstract Expressionism, epitomized by Pollock, Still, Rothko, and Tomlin.[125] Genauer published a short piece in the *Herald Tribune,* calling the exhibition "Avant-chic" and deploring the "enormous panorama of emptiness" in Still and Rothko and the "tangled skein-of-wool panels" of Pollock.[126] (Genauer usually attacked by claiming that the art shown at the Modern was not as radical as it purported to be. In actuality, her taste ran to the more conservative end of a given spectrum, which, in this case, included Dickinson, Katzman, and Rose.)

Miller and Barr most enjoyed a review by Henry McBride, an elder statesman among U.S. critics, who wrote about the exhibition in *Art News,* at the end of a longer piece on art from the United States. McBride told Miller that, viewing the exhibition for the first time, he had been unable to understand those "acres of canvas with so little on them"; on his second visit, however, he had been "overcome" by the show.[127] In his review McBride observed, "A few American artists, at long last, seem to have gone completely native, and for the first time since these wars, it has not been necessary to stumble over references to Matisse, Juan Gris, Picasso, Léger, etc., etc. before arriving at the exhibitor's part of the work."[128] He believed that the negative press had resulted from the need to see the show more than once, as it could be daunting on first contact—for instance, Tomlin, Pollock, and Rothko "use size as a weapon." McBride wrote that "15 Americans" marked the beginning of a "new cycle."

"12 Americans"

"12 Americans," of 1956, was easier to organize than the previous exhibition in the series, since it included fewer artists, and they were less demanding. The show consisted almost entirely of abstract painting and sculpture, although John Myers, co-director of Tibor de Nagy Gallery in New York, claimed that Larry Rivers and Grace Hartigan transcended the "tiresome" art-world dichotomy between the abstract and the representational.[129] The exhibition mixed first-generation New York School artists James Brooks, Philip Guston, and Franz Kline with members of the second generation—Ernest Briggs, Hartigan, and Rivers, and West Coast abstractionist Sam Francis. Fritz Glarner, the only real anomaly among the painters, had been long-associated with Mondrian-derived geometric abstraction. Raoul Hague, Ibram Lassaw, Seymour Lipton, and José de Rivera contributed abstract sculpture (fig. 12).

Miller also asked Joseph Cornell to participate in the 1956 exhibition. When he met with her at the Museum early that year, Cornell proposed integrating his sculptures into a single environmental work that would occupy an entire gallery. Miller thought they had reached an agreement, but by the beginning of March he had telephoned to decline her invitation. He felt that there was not sufficient time to realize a project as ambitious as the one he envisioned.[130]

Guston was the first artist Miller chose: "He had just broke through with . . . the red paintings."[131] She went to his studio on Twelfth Street and liked his new work so much that she immediately invited him to take part: "Sometimes it's a mistake to do that and sometimes it isn't."[132] Hartigan was among the last that she asked to participate:

One of the people in last year's show about whom I was very enthusiastic is Grace Hartigan. . . . Curiously enough, she was one of the last persons that I put in the show, because I didn't like the painting she'd been doing during the last year. . . . However, I decided that I could get enough things that I did like together to represent her, and I was so glad that I put her in, because she responded to the invitation with two or three magnificent new canvases. One of them, which I think is perhaps her best to date, was bought from the show by Nelson Rockefeller, who has very discriminating taste.[133]

Following the 1952 show, the "Americans" exhibitions apparently had taken on added significance within the art world.[134] In January 1956, Miller received a letter from six prominent members of Chicago's art community, who reported that many Chicagoans were disturbed because "various museum directors and curators . . . so rarely visit this city."[135] Knowing that she was at work on the next installment of her series, they invited Miller to come to Chicago, offering to provide a car, driver, and list of galleries and artists to visit. She took them up on their offer, but none of the Chicago artists on the list they provided were included in the show.[136]

She also received a letter from John Myers:

All I do these days in the face of complete ignoring by the New York Times, Herald Tribune, and The Arts Magazine . . . is think about whatever is going to happen to my artists whom I'm so crazy about. . . . Particularly I think about Grace H. and Larry R. and that some time in the future you are going to be deciding on Fifteen Americans. *. . . What worries me is that perhaps you and Alfred have forgotten us since last year[.] . . . [T]he new work is better, the impulse just as forward going. I know it's awful to try to influence you this way. But we are all so forgetful (I am at times)—and since both artists are in the Museum of Modern Art's collection—I would feel so much better if there was a continuity of faith shown.*[137]

A day after Myers's concerns spurred him to write, those of art historian and curator Sam Hunter did the same:

The announcement of your spring show has come, and set off a train of thought. . . . I have spent a good deal of time recently with the abstract artists, and seen much of their most recent work. I have the impression . . . that they are disgruntled about museum policy vis-à-vis their work. No museum has isolated them in a single exhibition and thus acknowledged the unity of their work, or its centrality to contemporary painting. . . . It has struck me that your show might present a unique opportunity for doing some such thing. . . . In thinking about your very excellent shows of the past . . . it struck me that some of the more interesting older [artists] like Kline, Gottlieb, Hofmann, Guston, Tworkov, Brooks in painting, and Lipton, Smith, Lassaw in sculpture, haven't been dealt with yet . . . [and] it would make a really stunning exhibition to show these artists with a few younger painters working in abstract modes. . . .[138]

Hunter also advised Miller to write a real essay, in order to give these artists the critical consideration they deserved:

And why not a catalogue introduction in addition to the artists' statements, tracing their evolution and the main currents within so-called abstract expressionism? Curiously enough, there has been more serious exegetical writing for foreign shows (I think of the excellent introduction Holger Cahill did for the European show recently) than there has been at home.

Hunter was delicate in framing his suggestions, not only citing Miller's husband as a model but also apologizing for his own presumptuousness both at the beginning and end of his letter. Miller, who was gracious in her response to him,[139] would, of course, include in her 1956 exhibition a number of the artists Hunter mentions, but she would not mount the kind of show he was suggesting. Barr and Miller may have felt that a mix of styles offered some protection not only from charges of favoritism, but also from the belligerence of the press in the face of the more radical abstraction contained in the shows—consciously or not, in each exhibition Miller gave reactionary critics such as Genauer some work they could like.[140]

Miller saw it as part of her mission in these exhibitions to present unknowns to the art world. Hague was then fifty-one and had never been the subject of a one-person exhibition; he was the show's "discovery," and she was especially concerned for him. She attempted to help him find a gallery and relocate to New Haven, Connecticut, from upstate New York. In a letter to a mutual friend, she wrote, "Please don't tell [Hague] because I am afraid of possible disappointments, but I have two other pieces of his on reserve now. I do hope these purchases will go through but I won't know for a while yet."[141]

Miller's feeling for the artists she fostered in the "Americans" shows is also evident in a June 29, 1956, memorandum to Barr, in which she mentioned that "Robert Hale of the Met . . . [came] here to see [Hartigan's] *City Life* with [the collector] Roy Neuberger, who wants to buy a Hartigan for the Met. It was my feeling that unless our Museum definitely wants the *City Life,* we probably ought to release it to the Met, as this would mean a great deal to the artist."[142] And after the Modern acquired Brooks's *Qualm* (1954), Miller received a letter from Brooks acknowledging her support: "Your interest in my work and efforts to do something about it are a great lift to me . . . my deepest thanks to you."[143]

Sales from the 1956 exhibition were lively, with interest shown in all the artists.[144] Regarding the press, Miller wrote to Brooks on June 11, 1956:

I never worry about Genauer or Coates—Genauer hates me and has only two techniques of [sic] dealing with any exhibition I organize—to pan it or to ignore it. I prefer the latter. Coates is so stupid that one can only feel sorry for him. However, I am not sorry for the New Yorker *and think it scandalous that they do not have a good art critic. The Sunday* Times *review, as well as the news story following the opening of the show, were both excellent. Have you seen the current* Art News? *[Thomas] Hess is not too bad there. The magazine* Arts *will run a review by Leo Steinberg in the July issue.*[145]

Steinberg's review appeared in two parts, the first of which is concentrated on Glarner and Guston. In part two, he faulted Hartigan for the quality Myers extolled in his letter—that the works were neither abstract nor figurative. Brooks, he thought, had gotten academic. Briggs and Francis were accomplished painters who created "backdrops," but Guston and Kline had "the power to turn a picture into a total experience."[146] In the *Herald Tribune Book Review,* Genauer wrote in a predictable fashion: ". . . the museum, so long in the vanguard of the abstract expressionist movement is now, since younger artists are definitely changing their direction, in the unaccustomed position of bringing up the rear."[147] In the *New York Times,* Stuart Preston actually gave the show a rave: "A spectacular variety of up-to-the-minute personal statements is offered in The Museum of Modern Art's current exhibition, *Twelve Americans.*"[148]

Except for Glarner, the 1956 exhibition was the most cohesive in the "Americans" series. (This may have been an unconscious response on Miller's part to mounting pressure from supporters of the New York School like Sam Hunter.) Though with the aid of hindsight one might quarrel with who Miller chose for her exhibitions, in the 1956 show, her eye for the best of what her artists produced was in evidence. Briggs's work was especially strong around 1956; it appears that Miller showed him at the optimum moment[149] (fig. 13). Francis and Kline (fig. 14) were

both represented by major paintings—*Big Red* (1953) and *White Forms* (1955), respectively—that would eventually find their way into the Modern's collection. Rivers's *Washington Crossing the Delaware* (1953), already in the Museum's holdings, and *Double Portrait of Birdie* (1955), on loan from the Whitney, were exhibited.

"Sixteen Americans"

Originally, "Sixteen Americans" was to open in the autumn of 1958, allowing Miller the shorter interval that she had always desired between shows. However, in a December 1957 meeting to which she was not invited, postponement was discussed because of "scheduling conflicts." Once again, Barr wrote in Miller's behalf, this time to Museum Director René d'Harnoncourt. Barr stated her concern that, with the exhibitions so far apart, the Museum was thought to be slow in its recognition of a number of important artists, and explained that, while Miller was not insisting on having her way, she felt strongly about this point and he, Barr, concurred.[150] But Barr did not hold sway, and "Sixteen Americans" was delayed until December 1959.

Abstraction again predominated in the 1959–60 exhibition, but within that category there was greater variety. There were different forms of painterly abstraction by J. de Feo, James Jarvaise, Alfred Leslie, Richard Lytle, Albert Urban, and Jack Youngerman; hard-edge abstraction by Ellsworth Kelly; geometrically-based monochrome black paintings by Frank Stella; abstraction based on symbols by Wally Hedrick; the figurative abstraction of Landès Lewitin; what was then called neo-Dada by Jasper Johns and Robert Rauschenberg; abstract reliefs by Robert Mallary; welded sculpture by Richard Stankiewicz and Julius Schmidt; and a sculptural environment by Louise Nevelson.

A handwritten list in the files of the Museum Archives headed "1958 possibilities" indicates that Miller at one point had considered Leonard Baskin, Bourgeois, Cornell (again), Richard Diebenkorn, Helen Frankenthaler, Frank Lobdell, Conrad Marca-Relli, Joseph Messina, Joan Mitchell, Reuben Nakian, Ray Parker, Marianna

Left:
12. Installation view of the Ibram Lassaw gallery, with James Brooks's *Altoon* (1956) in the background, "12 Americans," The Museum of Modern Art, New York, 1956

Right:
13. Installation view of the Ernest Briggs gallery, with Larry Rivers's Studies for *Washington Crossing the Delaware* (1953) in the far background, "12 Americans"

14. Installation view of the Franz Kline gallery, "12 Americans," The Museum of Modern Art, New York, 1956

Pineda, Giorgio Speventa, Hedda Sterne, Harold Tovish, and Elbert Weinberg for her show.[151] In June 1958, she visited Kenneth Noland's studio in Washington, D.C.[152] And she received a letter from John Myers, dated the following September, asking her to consider Robert Richenberg for her show: "I hate to try to influence you; on the other hand, my conscience tells me that I should speak up for what I think is right. At least I won't feel guilty for not having tried. lots of love, John."[153]

At twenty-three, Frank Stella was one of the two youngest artists ever included in an "Americans" exhibition.[154] William C. Seitz, who had been Stella's professor at Princeton, first told Miller about him and gave her the artist's name and address, but she was not immediately able to visit him. A few months later, Myers included one of Stella's black paintings in a "New Talent" exhibition at Tibor de Nagy Gallery. Then, over lunch in early September 1958, the dealer Leo Castelli told Miller that he planned to visit Stella, and they decided to go together. Later, Miller recalled a very thin young man who was missing his front teeth, in a small studio with a large stack of paintings leaning face to the wall. In order to show his work, Stella had to grab a painting by the stretcher, carry it out into the hall, turn it so that it was facing forward, and reenter the studio: "It was like a ballet."[155] A couple of days later, Miller took Barr to Stella's studio and he was very enthusiastic: "It was just by sheer chance that Leo and I went down together because we were very friendly and all that. That's why in the catalogue [Stella's works] were credited as lent by [Castelli Gallery]—because Leo took him on immediately."[156] However, it was Miller who gave Stella his first solo showing, within "Sixteen Americans" (fig. 15).

Miller first saw a Johns flag painting in a group show at Castelli's. Then, on a Saturday morning, in pelting rain, Barr called her asking how soon she could get to the gallery. She rushed to East Seventy-seventh Street to see Johns's first one-person exhibition, and she and Barr spent an hour discussing what to buy: "It wasn't a question of one picture, we chose four pictures. They were inexpensive and they were just so remarkable."[157] Johns was twenty-seven at the time.

Barr and Miller responded differently to Rauschenberg, who was represented by the same gallery. According to Castelli, the Modern did not acquire an early Rauschenberg because Barr did not like the work. The dealer was hopeful that the Museum would purchase a piece from "Sixteen Americans," ". . . but Dorothy wasn't that sure about Rauschenberg either, so . . . no acquisition of a Rauschenberg was made at that time."[158] Although Rauschenberg had been showing in New York since 1951, the Museum did not acquire a combine painting until 1972, when *First Landing Jump*, of 1961, entered the collection as a gift of Philip Johnson.[159]

Miller first visited Kelly's studio in June 1955, on the recommendation of Alexander Calder, who had met the younger artist in Paris. Clearly, she was interested in Kelly, since during that summer she kept a few of his smaller works in her office for the curatorial staff to see. On September 26, 1955, she sent to Andrew Carnduff Ritchie, then Director of the Department of Painting and Sculpture, a memorandum "for possible future reference," giving him the name and address of "the painter of the two 'pure' abstract pictures and the 'relief' you saw in my office."[160] Since there was no immediate response to Kelly's work on the part of the Museum, this may be an instance where Barr lacked interest in work about which Miller was enthusiastic. Although she did not include Kelly in an "Americans" exhibition until 1959, it was in a context that was far more hospitable to the artist than the 1956 show would have been[161] (fig. 16).

From the beginning, Miller wanted to include Nevelson in the 1959 show. She asked her to participate with some timidity, because by that time, "she had made it in a big way."[162] But Nevelson immediately responded: "[She said,] 'Dear, we'll make it a white show.' Just like that. Everything up until then had been black. It just came into her mind; she said, 'Don't tell a soul. We'll surprise them.' And that's what happened. She spent the entire summer making this tremendous roomful. I gave her the biggest gallery I had."[163]

If by 1959 the market for contemporary art was not yet what it would be in the 1960s and after, the situation had changed radically from what it had been in 1942. In a memorandum, Miller informed Museum Registrar Dorothy Dudley that, including sales to the Modern, twelve out of a possible fifty-three works were sold in 1952; eighteen out of a possible forty-nine were sold in 1956; and as of January 4, 1960, with a month and a half left of the exhibition's run, forty-five out of a possible fifty-one works were sold.[164] In 1959–60, Miller had lists of two and three people who wanted particular works.[165]

Earlier in 1959, before "Sixteen Americans" opened, the collector Larry Aldrich had made an offer to William S. Lieberman, then Curator in the Department of Prints. Aldrich proposed giving the Museum $10,000 a year for ten years to spend on works by emerging U.S. artists that were priced under $1,000. His only condition was that he be shown each work before it was purchased. An active businessman living in Ridgefield, Connecticut, with no connection to the New York art scene and little time to browse the galleries, Aldrich was looking for a feasible way to become familiar with, and to begin collecting, contemporary U.S.

art.[166] Lieberman introduced him to Miller and Barr. As Aldrich later recalled, "I told them my proposal. I didn't tell them what my reasoning was—they didn't ask me and I didn't tell them—but my reason was I hoped they would do my shopping for me, since I didn't have time to do it. Unfortunately, it didn't work that way."[167] The first purchase the Museum made with the Larry Aldrich Foundation Fund was Stella's *The Marriage of Reason and Squalor* (1959). Although the mood regarding current art had changed somewhat, there was still some difficulty in getting the painting approved by the Acquisitions Committee. Had only Museum funds been available for its purchase, it might have been impossible.[168]

The Museum of Modern Art Archives holds a file full of letters, positive and negative, about "Sixteen Americans." Miller felt the nastiest responses were encouraged by John Canaday of the *New York Times*, who attacked the exhibition no less than four times, the last of which was four years after the show had closed, in a review of works shown in the United States Pavilion at the New York World's Fair.[169] Stuart Preston, who had reviewed the exhibition for the *Times* in December 1959, felt the work was "egocentric" in the mode of Abstract Expressionism, and decried the absence in the catalogue of any attempt to relate the artists to "the intellectual and moral climate of modern times."[170] But he was nonetheless relatively even-handed in his analysis. On January 31, 1960, Canaday used an exhibition at the Museum from the Art Lending Service to launch an attack:

I found that although I would have enjoyed owning any one of at least half the objects in the show, I was restless to get upstairs for a third visit to . . . Sixteen Americans, where there is not a single painting, and very little sculpture, that I could imagine living with, but where a series of intellectual stunts and a couple of fresh ideas, combined with other examples of painting that seemed to me utterly stale and pointless, were displayed as a spectacle. . . .[171]

Two months later, he called "Sixteen Americans" "a show that continues to haunt me because it was such a disastrous exhibition yet such an 'exciting one' to talk about. . . . I'm wondering what *Sixteen Americans* would look like if it hung again next year. Pretty stale, no doubt."[172] And then, the following September, in preparing for the coming season, he wrote that he would like to call a moratorium on the showing of work that is less than ten years old. Then The Museum of Modern Art would not need to expand. It could hang its collection in "the space normally allotted to such breath-takers as last year's *Sixteen Americans*."[173]

In the midst of this barrage, on March 9, 1960, Miller received a note from Canaday. She had selected the paintings featured in "New Talent USA," an article that had appeared in *Art in America* earlier that year. In a letter to the editor of the magazine, John Myers had accused Canaday of launching an attack on the art reproduced in that article without having seen the works themselves, based solely on black-and-white photographs.[174] Canaday must have been worried about the charge, as the tone of his note to Miller is unctuous, as if trying to charm: "Mr. Myers does not like me at all. . . . I hope that you do not share—too much—his irritation with my shortcomings."[175] And then in closing, "I would not like to think that you find me objectionable." In response to this letter, Barr wrote to Elizabeth Shaw, the Museum's Director of Publicity,[176] asking that she gather all available correspondence, along with Canaday's pieces mentioning Miller or "Sixteen Americans": "Think answer to Canaday's letter very important."[177]

In general, the press for this exhibition was not particularly good. On the whole, critics responded negatively to Youngerman, de Feo, and especially Stella. However, Katharine Kuh wrote positively about the exhibition in *The Saturday Review*[178] and Hess did the same in *Art News*.[179] The critic for the *Philadelphia Inquirer* found it "difficult to accept the works of artists such as Frank Stella, Jack Youngerman, or J. de Feo. . . . In contrast the work of Louise Nevelson is full of implication and association,"[180] while the *Hartford Times* found the whole effort "Self-conscious, exhibitionistic, and lacking in depth. . . ."[181] In *The New Yorker,* Coates had to confess, "I felt tepid about the collection as a whole. I could discern no central purpose or 'point' to the show . . . [It was] chaotic but stylish."[182] He disliked Stella and found Johns and Rauschenberg "severely limited in subject matter." In her review in the *Herald Tribune,* Genauer called Stella "unspeakably boring."[183] Two weeks later, she reprinted a letter from the artist that took issue with her description of his works, insisting that the light areas on his paintings were not stripes, but ground. She also reprinted the statement on Stella by Carl Andre from the catalogue. Clearly, she considered both self-damning.[184]

In organizing "Sixteen Americans," Miller was remarkably sensitive to an important transitional moment, when Abstract Expressionism was still a vital force, and Minimalism and Pop were poised to make their presences felt. Identifying incipient currents, particularly through the work of Stella, Johns, and Rauschenberg, and containing excellent art by others, the show clearly generated real energy and excitement, even though it presented much disparate work. It may have helped that nine of the sixteen artists, all under the age of thirty-five (Lytle was only a year older than Stella), worked from the same generational perspective. However, Nevelson, at fifty-nine the second oldest of the artists, obviously provided one of the exhibition's highlights with her dramatic all-white installation. Stella, represented by four of his

15. Installation view of the Frank Stella gallery, with paintings by James Jarvaise in the middle background, "Sixteen Americans," The Museum of Modern Art, New York, 1959

Left:
16. Installation view of the Ellsworth Kelly gallery, with J. de Feo's *Veronica* (1957) in the far background, "Sixteen Americans," The Museum of Modern Art, New York, 1959

Right:
17. Installation view of the J. de Feo gallery, "Sixteen Americans"

famous black paintings, was perhaps the most important "discovery" of the entire "Americans" series. Kelly showed eight fine canvases from that year, among them, *Running White,* which the Museum acquired from the show. Johns's gallery contained works from 1955 through 1959, including the Modern's *Green Target* (1955), purchased by Barr and Miller from the 1958 Castelli exhibition, and the *Large White Flag,* of 1955. Rauschenberg showed seven combine paintings. Alfred Leslie admirably represented an Abstract Expressionist perspective. Youngerman, in top form, showed, among other works, *Coenties Slip* (1959), now in the collection of the Whitney Museum.[185] Miller's inclusion of de Feo and Hedrick, members of the San Francisco Bay Area art scene, was inspired (fig. 17). Stella's paintings did not hang easily with any of the other work in the exhibition, but it was Lewitin's relatively small canvases that truly seemed out of place.

"Americans 1963"
Although it was not intended as such, Miller's last "Americans" show was viewed in many quarters as an endorsement of Pop art, and thus as a rejection of Abstract Expressionism.[186] The exhibition included Robert Indiana, Marisol, Claes Oldenburg, and James Rosenquist. In addition, Chryssa, Edward Higgins, and Jason Seeley contributed Pop-related works. However, also featured were Op art canvases by Richard Anuskiewicz, pointillist abstractions by Sally Hazelet Drummond, geometric abstraction with a softer edge by Bay Area artist David Simpson, Weimaresque figuration by Richard Lindner, and five-foot-square black paintings by Ad Reinhardt, a first-generation member of the New York School. In the introduction to the catalogue, Miller mentioned that this was the only one of her exhibitions to include an equal number of sculptors and painters. (If she was responding to a nascent Minimalist trend, then it was exclusively to its privileging of the three-dimensional object and not to its geometric form.) Non-Pop sculptors were Lee Bontecou, Gabriel Kohn, and Michael Lekakis.[187]

The files on this exhibition yield little regarding Miller's thinking on it. Notes indicate that she considered including Mel Ramos and Ernest Trova, and she received what must have begun to seem like the usual plea from John Myers, this time on behalf of Fairfield Porter.[188] By 1963, everyone in the art world knew when Miller was about to launch one of these shows, and John Gruen, in the *Herald Tribune,* archly described the mounting fever as the (unidentified) "official" of the Museum made the rounds: "Every few years artists and galleries alike become ever so restless in the knowledge that the Museum of Modern Art is once again preparing for a big group exhibition. The questions begin to fly. 'Who's going to be in it?'; 'Who's going to be left out?'; 'What faction will be favored?; Is "Pop" Art in?; Will they even touch Abstract-Expressionism?'"[189]

In fact, as late as December 1962 Miller was uncertain about who would be in her show of the following May, and was inclined to keep to herself whatever she did know, so as not to ease the tension Gruen described. As she wrote to Charles Parkhurst of the Baltimore Museum, who was interested in taking the exhibition:

I know it sounds foolish, but I have as yet no final list of artists for this show. There are a number of reasons for this. . . . One is that I never have time to start work on these exhibitions until very close to the catalogue deadline. . . . Another reason is a feeling that if the show is set up far in advance and everyone knows exactly who will be in it, it loses its edge. . . . This exhibition will emphasize, perhaps more than any previous one except "Sixteen Americans" of 1959–60, a variety of youthful artists who have developed in the last four or five years and who in my opinion have great promise.[190]

At that point, Miller thought the show would contain more sculpture than usual; it would definitely not be devoted to Pop art, although it was possible that someone associated with that style might be included.

She was probably truthful with Parkhurst, although she undoubtedly could have given him some names. She did not invite Reinhardt to be in the exhibition until early March 1963, only two months before the opening. On March 7, she sent the artist a list of those included; under the heading "possible" are Drummond, Simpson, and Morris Louis.[191] But Simpson's letter accepting Miller's invitation to participate is dated February 26, 1963, before Miller asked Reinhardt to show. In addition, among her papers Miller had an advance-schedule press release from the Guggenheim announcing a Louis retrospective for September 1963. In all likelihood, she had discounted Louis earlier so as not to cause a conflict. Since Drummond's works entered the Museum on March 13, she, too, may have been asked to join the project before Reinhardt, as packing and shipping arrangements are usually made more than six days in advance. It hardly matters, however, if Reinhardt was the last to be invited, since he would prove to be a vitally important addition. A late-blooming Abstract Expressionist who had led the protest against the Museum in 1940,[192] he was a first-rate painter whom Miller hit upon just as his star was rising. The most formally radical artist in the exhibition, he would garner the most attention.

Reinhardt accepted the invitation.[193] He was, however, concerned with the conditions under which his extremely subtle works would be seen. In a card postmarked April 2, 1963, he stated to Miller: "I'd like to talk to you again about the "rooms" and "light" (Daylight or etc.) . . . I'd not only want not to get sandwiched in between a Ben-Day-ice-cream-cone and plaster hamburger, but not some other things too." Reinhardt was never satisfied with the way his works looked at the Modern. On May 29, he wrote Miller that he was unhappy with his gallery and did not know what to do about it. On June 16, in a letter from France, he reported that his show at Galerie Iris Clert, in Paris, was going well, and that he liked the installation because the structure of the gallery allowed each of the paintings to be hung in its own alcove. He included a drawing, presumably in order to share with her his discovery of a desirable way to display his art.

By the time she showed Reinhardt, Miller had a well-honed sense of what would offend viewers. A wall text was hung in his gallery explaining that, although the paintings first appeared to be uniform black squares, a few minutes of concentrated looking would reveal their configurations.[194] This did not help with all factions of the public. Stanchions had to be erected to keep people from defacing the work,[195] and Miller received some angry letters.

While the Museum did acquire a number of works from the show,[196] there is little information about sales in the files for this exhibition—the result, perhaps, of changes within the art world for which Miller and her exhibitions bore some responsibility. The audience for contemporary art from the United States was growing, and the art was becoming increasingly commercially viable. A greater number of dealers and collectors may have rendered sales by the Modern almost moot.[197]

Sympathetic and unsympathetic critics alike saw "Americans 1963" as a victory for Pop art over Abstract Expressionism, so focused was the art world of the time on the war between the two styles. In *The New Yorker*, Harold Rosenberg reported that "Abstract Expressionism may not be as dead as we keep being told it is, but there is no denying the will to see it dead. For professionals of the art world—dealers, museum directors, critics, contemporary historians—the largest flaw in the success achieved by American painting during the past dozen years has been the overemphatic presence of the artist and his personality in the work."[198] He devoted much space to Reinhardt, terming him a "Neo-aesthete par excellence" and "The 'black monk' of the Abstract Expressionist crusade," and stating, "Reinhardt's idea is the most powerful, since it seeks not to oppose other ideas or insights but to obliterate them."[199] Rosenberg noted the predominance of the concept as an impetus for art-making—he called the artist the "idea man"[200]—identifying a characteristic that, in the ensuing decade, would prove central to Pop art, Minimalism, and Post-Minimalism.

Like Rosenberg, Irving Sandler devoted the bulk of his review to Reinhardt: "The outstanding artist in the exhibition is Ad Reinhardt. His room of 'black paintings' alone warrants repeated visits."[201] Canaday, ever eager to be critical, wrote: "A thesis could be written on what has happened in New York by comparing "Sixteen Americans" with "Americans 1963," which has forgotten that abstract expressionism ever existed and admits that pop art is here to stay at least until the next survey."[202] He described the show as "a gadgety and gimmicky collection" and an "esthetic circus." In *The Nation*, Hilton Kramer spent almost his entire review denouncing Reinhardt's paintings, which he believed were nihilistic.[203]

The 1963 show appears to have lacked the vitality that characterized the 1959 exhibition, at least partially because the various contributions did not coalesce into a cohesive statement. This was despite strong individual presentations. Oldenburg, Reinhardt, and Rosenquist have remained extremely influential over the years, and

18. Installation view of the James Rosenquist gallery, "Americans 1963," The Museum of Modern Art, New York, 1963

Bontecou, in the midst of her much-tauted early period, was producing significant work (see figs. 18, 19). Edward Higgins, Indiana, and Marisol were also of genuine interest. But, again with the advantage of hindsight, it is clear that Lindner's work was too different in character from everything else in the exhibition not to seem anomalous. Paintings by Simpson and Drummond, though sensitive and accomplished, were less challenging than other work of the time.[204] In 1963, Andy Warhol and Roy Lichtenstein were generating real excitement, and Minimalists such as Donald Judd, Dan Flavin, and Robert Smithson had had their first one-person exhibitions in New York during the preceding three or four years.

"The New American Painting"

As we have seen, the "Americans" series coincided with the development of Abstract Expressionism, and New York School painters and sculptors played an important role in the exhibitions. However, the Modern did not acknowledge the significance of that group as a whole with an exhibition devoted exclusively to them until 1958, almost a decade after most of the artists had found their mature styles, and even then, the show was not originally destined for New York.[205] Directed by Miller and conceived as an international touring exhibition, "The New American Painting," of 1958–59, apparently appeared at the Modern only after pressure was brought to bear by the artists and their supporters.[206] Even the impetus for the project came from outsiders—European curators who were persistent in their requests that the Museum provide such an exhibition.[207] The show contained work by all the first-generation New York School artists who had until then appeared in the "Americans" series—Baziotes, Brooks, Gorky, Guston, Kline, Motherwell, Pollock, Rothko, Still, and Tomlin—along with de Kooning, Gottlieb, Barnett Newman, and Jack Tworkov, and younger painters Francis, Hartigan, and Theodoros Stamos. Newman and Tworkov were added at the last minute.[208]

There had been no exhibition of Newman's work in New York since 1951, so

19. Installation view of the Lee Bontecou gallery, "Americans 1963," The Museum of Modern Art, New York, 1963

collector Ben Heller installed a group of paintings in the artist's studio in an effort to convince Barr and Miller that he should be represented in the exhibition. (Newman was recovering from a heart attack at the time). Barr at first resisted, feeling that Newman was not a true Abstract Expressionist, but had developed out of Kasimir Malevich. Eventually, however, he relented.[209] In Heller's view, Barr came to appreciate Newman's work, but the nature and extent of that appreciation remain in question.[210] What is clear, however, is that Heller's cooperation was important to the realization of the exhibition. "The New American Painting" had to be organized quickly; with Pollock dead, it was difficult to borrow important paintings by him, and Still and Rothko refused to cooperate, so works had to be lent by private collectors and institutions.[211] In the late fifties, Heller had one of the few important Abstract Expressionist collections, and Barr and Miller were depending on him to lend. A disparaging comment made by Miller in 1985 indicates that she, for one, never changed her opinion about Newman.[212] It is possible that she and Barr were somewhat influenced in their decision to include him—albeit in the light of growing recognition of his achievement—by their wish to accommodate Heller.[213]

Frank O'Hara, then on the staff of the Museum's International Program, worked on the exhibition with Miller. Among his papers are notes indicating that before the show was limited to painting, Miller considered including the sculptors Hare, Ferber, Lassaw, Lipton, Roszak, and David Smith, as well as the painters Rivers and Tobey. The exhibition was at various points titled "Americans 1947–1957" (underscoring the link between the series and the New York School), "American Art of the Past Decade," and "Abstract Expressionism in America."[214] Motherwell hit upon the title "The New American Painting" in an effort to avoid the term "Abstract Expressionism."[215] The New York showing bore the subtitle "As Shown in 8 European Countries 1958–1959" (figs. 20, 21, 23).

The Museum may have been somewhat more willing to feature these artists as a group in its internationally circulating exhibitions than at home, perhaps believing that general audiences abroad were more sophisticated and less emotionally invested in the issues raised by the work. During the McCarthy era, the atmosphere in the United States was especially hostile to vanguard art. Away from the fishbowl that is the New York art world, the Modern's Trustees were less likely to be upset by exhibitions, and in foreign countries the Museum did not run the risk of having its patriotism impugned.[216] Abroad, it must have seemed easier to give the Modern's imprimatur to Abstract Expressionism as a movement. In 1957, in addition to a Pollock exhibition,[217] The Museum of Modern Art sent to the São Paulo Bienal a group show, organized by O'Hara (with McCray, Soby, Miller, and Hunter), that included Brooks, Guston, Hare, Hartigan, Kline, Lassaw, Lipton, and Rivers. The 1958 Venice Biennale featured Lipton, Rothko, Smith, and Tobey, while the 1960 Venice exhibition presented a major show-ing of works by Motherwell.[218] Nevertheless, "The New American Painting" remains the first comprehensive Museum exhibition devoted to the group.

Some European press reaction to "The New American Painting," by no means all of it positive, was reprinted in the New York catalogue. A Milanese critic wrote, "It is not new. It is not painting. It is not American. There is no deep necessity, no inner torment, not even a serious formal research. Not one of these painters goes against the current. Not one of them is anti-conformist. There is no spiritual light."[219] Yet a number of European critics were extremely generous and open to this work. In Berlin, a journalist wrote:

Pollock was a genius, but by European standards, one can easily count half of the other sixteen to be exceptional talents. They are painters without regard for the ready-made world. . . . Here, there is no comfort, but a struggle with the elements, with society, with fate. It is like the American novel; something happens, and what happens is disquieting and at the same time pregnant with the future.[220]

20. Installation view of "The New American Painting: As Shown in 8 European Countries 1958–1959," The Museum of Modern Art, New York, 1959, with paintings by William Baziotes and, in the background, Willem de Kooning

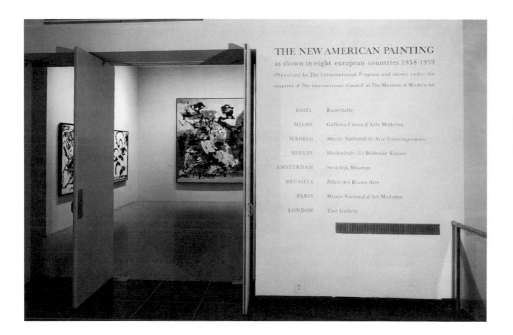

21. Entrance to "The New American Painting: As Shown in 8 European Countries, 1958–1959," The Museum of Modern Art, New York, 1959, with paintings by Jackson Pollock in the background,

The U.S. critics' responses were mixed, but in comparison to earlier in the decade, an increased number understood Abstract Expressionism and supported it.[221] Predictably, Genauer disparaged the show, calling it "tame."[222] Ironically, in light of the context in which the term is used today, Kramer reported that "It is the *otherness* [the italics are his] of this art that excites the European imagination[.] . . . [T]hey responded especially to its raw power, its daring, and its scale. They insisted a little too much perhaps on its physical vigor and on its violence."[223] Kramer believed that "in this country, Abstract Expressionism is now our certified contemporary art style so far as museums, the critics, and the big investors in modern painting are concerned," and described the opening-night festivities at the Museum as having "the air of a college town after the big game."[224]

Curatorially, "The New American Painting" accomplished what was required. It contained significant paintings by a majority of the most prominent artists of the New York School. In selecting the art, Miller was aided by the number of classic works that she, Barr, and others had managed to acquire for the Museum's collection. Despite the difficulties, even Rothko and Still were well represented. Indeed, Rothko appears to have been given a stronger showing than in "15 Americans" (fig. 23). The installation photographs reveal some graceful juxtapositions: Miller hung Gorky and de Kooning together at a time when their work could not often have been seen in depth in that way; Guston and Still also worked well in concert. Only the inclusion of second-generation artists Francis, Hartigan, and Stamos seems arbitrary. Why not Frankenthaler, Mitchell, and Rivers? Miller would have made a more complete and meaningful statement had she confined the show to the first generation. She might have added Hans Hofmann, Lee Krasner, Richard Pousette-Dart, or Reinhardt to those already on her roster.[225]

•

Opinions about the extent of The Museum of Modern Art's commitment to the New York School are widely divergent. Some have claimed that the institution used

Abstract Expressionism as a tool of cultural imperialism during the Cold War;[228] others have asserted that the Modern was never as responsive to New York School artists as their importance warranted.[227] The nature and composition of the "Americans" series, for much of its existence the Museum's primary venue for contemporary U.S. art, suggests that, although she recognized individual achievement in a high percentage of Abstract Expressionists, Miller, along with Barr and others at the Museum, lacked commitment to the group as a whole. William Rubin reports "a widespread feeling among the Abstract Expressionist painters that The Museum of Modern Art, despite the 'Americans' shows and everything else they did, was treating that group of artists as just one aspect of the local provincial product . . . as compared to the pedestal on which they placed leading European artists."[228] By the mid-1950s, the New York School saw itself on a par with the great pre–World War II European movements and wanted to be treated as such. Thomas Hess was speaking for the artists as well as himself when he said that "the most important *public* action the Museum takes is its exhibitions. When represented at all by the Museum, Abstract-Expressionism was included in surveys as just another phase of the current scene, as against, for example, Magic Realism, which the Museum considered important enough a style to devote a major historical exhibition ['American Realists and Magic Realists'] to it alone. . . ."[229]

However, Barr and Miller faced difficulties that were unique to the Museum in supporting more extreme forms of abstraction. In addition to the vitriolic reactions of much of the press and public, the Modern came under especially fierce attack around 1948 from the U.S. Congress and President Harry S. Truman, who considered modern art "Communistic."[230] And there were also difficulties involving Trustees and friends on whom the Museum depended.[231] Barr reported that early in 1948, some of the older members of the Committee on Museum Collections, encouraged by adverse press, vigorously questioned the validity of certain Abstract Expressionist acquisitions: "Purchase was difficult."[232] Miller concurred:

22. Clipping from *The Star* (London), February 23, 1959, with commentary on The Tate Gallery showing of "The New American Painting"

The old committee of course was the old Trustees—Stephen Clark and Sam Lewisohn and Conger Goodyear and Mrs. [Simon] Guggenheim and so on. They were wonderful up to a certain point. And then they couldn't take what was happening around 1949, 1950 on, when the Museum wanted to buy a Rothko. Alfred Barr brought a beautiful Rothko before the committee—in fact he brought three Rothkos before the committee just to try and get them used to it. And then, say, a year later, he brought one he wanted to buy— this was about 1950, 1951—that was when those old Trustees were outraged. . . . Stephen Clark left the committee because he didn't like Giacometti (I suppose this is frightfully indiscreet of me). Conger Goodyear left the committee because of Rothko.[233]

Irving Sandler later maintained that, had Barr not been hampered by powers within the Modern's family, he would have done more for Abstract Expressionism earlier.[234]

To the Museum's credit, they bought Pollock's *She Wolf* in 1944, soon after it was painted, having seen it first in a 1943 exhibition at Peggy Guggenheim's New York gallery, Art of This Century.[235] The only work to sell from that exhibition, it was also the first Pollock to enter a public collection. The Modern also bought a "drip" Pollock in 1950.[236] Dealers Betty Parsons and Samuel Kootz both felt that the Museum was extremely supportive of the Abstract Expressionists.[237] Kootz

23. Installation view of "The New American Painting: As Shown in 8 European Countries 1958–1959," The Museum of Modern Art, New York, 1959, with paintings by Mark Rothko

observed that the Modern encouraged its more adventurous Trustees to collect this work:

I must say that the Modern Museum was one of the first to accept people like Motherwell, Gottlieb, Baziotes, people we were handling at that time. Barr was an enthusiast for those particular three men and conveyed this enthusiasm to people like Burden, or Nelson Rockefeller, and others of the Modern group of Trustees. And we find that in the late forties we had pictures by these men well represented in such collections.[238]

In fact, Barr and Miller not only advised certain Trustees regarding the purchase of U.S. art, they also bought Abstract Expressionism for Blanchette Rockefeller in the late forties and for David Rockefeller in the late fifties.[239]

Nevertheless, by 1958 or 1959, while "The New American Painting" was touring, Barr and Miller were becoming interested in other forms. In 1958, at a meeting of the Club, the organization founded in 1948 to provide a forum for New York School artists, Barr challenged second-generation Abstract Expressionists to be more rebellious toward their elders.[240] That same year, in buying three paintings from Jasper Johns's first exhibition and enlisting Philip Johnson to purchase a fourth, Miller and Barr did something they had never done for an Abstract Expressionist— there had been no urgency about collecting those artists in depth. Rothko and Kline, for example, were represented by only one work in the collection for seven and fifteen years, respectively.[241] One is left with the impression that while Barr and Miller had an intellectual understanding of the achievements of the first-generation New York School, on a gut level they preferred an artist like Johns to one like Rothko. Rubin remarks that Johns's early works "had the sophisticated cuisine of European painting; despite their unexpectedness as images, they were not—as regards facture—the in-your-face pictures that Abstract Expressionist painters made." They also exhibited some reassuring continuity with Dada and Surrealism, favored movements at The Museum of Modern Art.[244]

Miller once stated that "the 1960s and Pop art opened up so much that you'd never hesitate to buy things. But back in 1942, or whatever it was, we didn't."[243] In the sixties, there was a different economy, more money was available, and the collective attitude toward spending had changed. However, in the late fifties, Barr was not disposed toward spending substantial sums for art from the United States. Waldo Rasmussen, former Director of the Modern's International Program of Circulating Exhibitions, is one of many who remember Barr's outraged rejection of Pollock's *Autumn Rhythm* (November 30, 1950) in 1957 because of its $30,000 asking price.[244]

Miller and Barr initiated and oversaw the acquisition of some of the Museum's finest Abstract Expressionist works, but they did not collect these paintings in great numbers. And in the sixties, when it would have been possible to do so, they did not make the acquisition of works by the first generation of the New York School a priority. As Miller would later recall, the artists felt this absence of patronage keenly:

We had the problem of holding the hands and heads of all the ab ex people because they were in such distress over [the emergence of new art forms in the sixties] and felt their thunder had been stolen and they were on the skids . . . and there were even a few personal friends completely lost forever because the Museum naturally was interested in these very big new artists. How could you help but be?[245]

•

In her "Americans" series, Miller was neither remiss nor remarkable in her foresight with regard to the first generation of the New York School. She showed Gorky, Hare, and Motherwell in 1946, which was early, and Baziotes, Brooks, Guston, Kline, Pollock, Rothko, Still, and Tomlin, along with the sculptors Ferber, Lassaw, Lippold, and Lipton, once they had reached their prime. We know that she would have exhibited some members of the second group sooner, had she not been restricted regarding the frequency of the shows, and that she tried to include de Kooning in the 1952 exhibition. As a sculptor with connections to the Abstract Expressionist circle, David Smith would have been an obvious choice for an "Americans" exhibition, but once his one-person show at the Museum was scheduled for 1957, he probably was no longer considered eligible for the series. Newman, arguably among the most influential artists of the second half of the century, is Miller's most significant omission, but she and Barr had an unfortunate blind spot about him.[246] Gottlieb, central to the Abstract Expressionist milieu and the history of the time, was not included; neither was Hofmann. But Barr and Miller did not favor them either.[247]

The series' innovative importance can be measured by the fact that in 1957, fifteen years after "Americans 1942," the Whitney began its "Young America" shows, obviously modeled on Miller's exhibitions. Although the Whitney exhibitions contained more artists, included fewer works by each, and were confined to younger people, they were nonetheless touted in the catalogues as an alternative to the larger annuals.[248] These publications, apparently conceived along the lines of the ones for the "Americans" shows, are approximately the same size as the Modern's and contain short introductions that trace the institution's involvement with new talent. They also include artists' statements, a plate section, and biographies.

The "Americans" series was a major curatorial achievement and a milestone in the history of the art of the period. The three installments in the 1950s in particular were significant for the work they featured and the elegance and insight with which it was presented. With the single exception of the 1942 exhibition, which had a unique purpose, all of the shows contained important statements by some of the most influential painters and sculptors of the postwar period, as well as moving and beautiful works by artists whose achievement is less familiar to us today.[249] I believe that the series was Miller's creation, the product of her strengths and weaknesses. She may have reflected too closely the needs and desires of the institution; she and Barr certainly shared opinions, and if he made suggestions, she was probably influenced by them to some degree. Yet I have found no evidence that he or anyone else interfered with her choices or required that she rethink her decisions.

The ending of the "Americans" series paralleled the ending of an era. Barr retired in 1967 and Miller in 1969. The sixties was a period of great expansion in museum audiences; galleries for contemporary art were proliferating, and throughout the decade, tolerance for new cultural forms increased in American society at large. In the international art arena, the United States held center stage. The Modern as well the Whitney and Guggenheim museums mounted numerous one-person and group shows devoted to or including U.S. artists.[250] Built into the "Americans" exhibitions were self-protective mechanisms that served the institution when it was difficult to show radical abstraction made in the United States. By 1963, however, the New York School had allowed us to see ourselves as the makers of movements of international consequence. After that, for The Museum of Modern Art to mount exhibitions of a limited number of artists working in a variety of styles would have made little sense. The time for the "Americans" shows had passed.

Appendix

This appendix lists the artists included in each exhibition in the "Americans" series, itineraries for the shows that traveled, and exhibited works that entered the Museum collection, both direct purchases and works acquired by Museum Trustees and later given to the Modern. The date of acquisition is provided only for works that entered the collection subsequent to the year in which they were exhibited.

"Americans 1942: 18 Artists from 9 States"

January 21–March 8, 1942

Darrel Austin, Hyman Bloom, Raymond Breinin, Samuel Cashwan, Francis Chapin, Emma Lu Davis, Morris Graves, Joseph Hirsch, Donal Hord, Charles Howard, Rico Lebrun, Jack Levine, Helen Lundeberg, Fletcher Martin, Octavio Medellin, Knud Merrild, Mitchell Siporin, Everett Spruce

Tour Itineraries

Following its close in New York, the show was divided into two exhibitions— "Americans 1942" and "18 Artists from 9 States"—both of which circulated for one year.

"Americans 1942": Institute of Modern Art, Boston, March 23–April 21, 1942; Portland Art Museum, Portland, Oregon, May 6–June 2, 1942; Seattle Art Museum, June 10–30, 1942; San Francisco Museum of Art, July 8–August 5, 1942; Denver Art Museum, October 1–30, 1942; The Art Gallery of Toronto, December 11–21, 1942; City Art Museum of St. Louis, January 4–February 1, 1943; Society of the Four Arts, Palm Beach, Florida, February 13–March 7, 1943

"18 Artists from 9 States": Vassar College, Poughkeepsie, New York, April 27–May 18, 1942; Washington County Museum of Art, Hagarstown, Maryland, September 26–October 17, 1942; University of Minnesota, Minneapolis, November 29–December 20, 1942; Carleton College, Northfield, Minnesota, January 4–25, 1943; Currier Gallery of Art, Manchester, New Hampshire, February 4–25, 1943; Flint Junior College, Flint, Michigan, March 7–28, 1943; Lehigh University, Bethelehem, Pennsylvania, May 3–24, 1943

Acquisitions

Hyman Bloom: *The Bride,* 1941 (Purchase); *The Synagogue,* c. 1940 (Acquired through the Lillie P. Bliss Bequest)

Emma Lu Davis: *Cosmic Presence,* 1934 (Purchase); *Chinese Red Army Soldier,* 1936 (Abby Aldrich Rockefeller Fund)

Morris Graves: *Fledgling,* 1940 (Purchase). Fifteen works were purchased as a group in 1942: *English Nightfall Piece,* 1938; *French Nightfall Piece,* 1938; *German Nightfall Piece,* 1938; *Roman Nightfall Piece,* 1938; *Bird Singing in the Moonlight,* 1938–39; *In the Moonlight,* 1938–39; *Snake and Moon,* 1938–39; *Bird Alone,* 1940; *Blind Bird,* 1940; *Grail (Chalice or Cup),* 1940; *Nestling,* 1940; *Little-Known Bird of the Inner Eye,* 1941; *Unnamed Bird of the Inner Eye,* 1941; *Woodpeckers,* 1941. *Bird Alone* and *Grail (Chalice or Cup)* were traded in 1945 for *Joyus Young Pine* (1944).

Jack Levine: *The Passing Scene,* 1941 (Purchase). Correspondence in the Museum Collection files in the Department of Painting and Sculpture confirms that this work, though not on the checklist published in the exhibition catalogue, was included in the show (Dorothy Miller to Edith Halpert, Downtown Gallery, February 13, 1942).

"Fourteen Americans"
September 9–December 8, 1946
David Aronson, Bel L. Culwell, Arshile Gorky, David Hare, Loren MacIver, Robert Motherwell, Isamu Noguchi, Irene Rice Pereira, Alton Pickens, C. S. Price, Theodore J. Roszak, Honoré Sharrer, Saul Steinberg, Mark Tobey, George Tooker

Tour Itinerary
Vassar College, Poughkeepsie, New York, January 5–26, 1947; Society of the Four Arts, Palm Beach, Florida, February 7–March 7, 1947; Cincinnati Modern Art School, March 20–April 17, 1947; San Francisco Museum of Art, May 1–June 1, 1947; Louisiana State University, Baton Rouge, June 15–30, 1947

Acquisitions
Ben L. Culwell: *Death by Burning,* c. 1942 (Purchase); *Men Fighting and Stars in the Solomons,* 1942 (Purchase)
Arshile Gorky: *Diary of a Seducer,* 1945 (Gift of Mr. and Mrs. William A.M. Burden, 1985). Purchased by Burden from the Julian Levy Gallery, New York, lender to the exhibition; the work became a promised gift in 1967.
Mark Tobey: *Remote Field,* 1944 (Gift of Mr. and Mrs. Jan de Graaff, 1947). The donors also lent the work to the exhibition.

"15 Americans"
April 9–July 27, 1952
William Baziotes, Edward Corbett, Edwin Dickinson, Herbert Ferber, Joseph Glasco, Herbert Katzman, Frederick Kiesler, Irving Kreisberg, Richard Lippold, Jackson Pollock, Herman Rose, Mark Rothko, Clyfford Still, Bradley Walker Tomlin, Thomas Wilfred

Tour Itinerary
The exhibition did not travel.

Acquisitions
Edward Corbett: *Number 11,* 1951 (Katherine Cornell Fund); *Number 15,* 1951 (Purchase)
Edwin Dickinson: *Composition with Still Life,* 1933–37 (Gift of Mr. and Mrs. Ansley W. Sawyer)
Herbert Katzman: *The Seine,* 1949 (Gift of Mr. and Mrs. Hugo Kastor)
Frederick J. Kiesler: *Galaxy,* 1947–48 (Gift of Mrs. Nelson Rockefeller, 1991)
Mark Rothko: *Number 10,* 1950 (Gift of Philip Johnson)
Bradley Walker Tomlin: *Number 20,* 1949 (Gift of Philip Johnson)

"12 Americans"

May 30–September 9, 1956

Ernest Briggs, James Brooks, Sam Francis, Fritz Glarner, Philip Guston, Raoul Hague, Grace Hartigan, Franz Kline, Ibram Lassaw, Seymour Lipton, José de Rivera, Larry Rivers

Tour Itinerary

The exhibition did not travel.

Acquisitions

James Brooks: *Qualm,* 1954 (Gift of Mrs. Bliss Parkinson)

Sam Francis: *Big Red,* 1953 (Gift of Mr. and Mrs. David Rockefeller, 1958). Purchased by David Rockefeller with the understanding that if it was not installed at the Rockefeller Institute in New York it would be given to the Modern.

Fritz Glarner: *Relational Painting, Tondo 37,* 1955 (Gift of Mr. and Mrs. Armand P. Bartos)

Philip Guston: *Painting,* 1954 (Philip Johnson Fund)

Raoul Hague: *Ohayo Wormy Butternut,* 1947–48 (Katherine Cornell Fund); *Plattekill Walnut,* 1952 (Elizabeth Bliss Parkinson Fund)

Franz Kline: *White Forms,* 1955 (Gift of Philip Johnson, 1977). Purchased by Johnson from the Sidney Janis Gallery, New York, in 1956, and lent to the exhibition that same year.

"Sixteen Americans"

December 16, 1959–February 17, 1960

J. de Feo, Wally Hedrick, James Jarvaise, Jasper Johns, Ellsworth Kelly, Alfred Leslie, Landes Lewitin, Richard Lytle, Robert Mallary, Louise Nevelson, Robert Rauschenberg, Julius Schmidt, Robert Stankiewicz, Frank Stella, Albert Urban, Jack Youngerman

Tour Itinerary

The exhibition did not travel.

Acquisitions

Wally Hedrick: *Around Painting,* 1957 (Larry Aldrich Foundation Fund)

James Jarvaise: *Hudson River School Series, 32,* 1957 (Larry Aldrich Foundation Fund, 1960)

Ellsworth Kelly: *Running White,* 1959 (Purchase, 1960)

Alfred Leslie: *The Second Two-Panel Horizontal,* 1958 (Larry Aldrich Foundation Fund)

Landès Lewitin: *Knockout,* 1955–59 (Promised gift and extended loan from Royal S. Marks, 1963)

Louise Nevelson: Two *Hanging Columns* from *Dawn's Wedding Feast,* 1959 (Blanchette Rockefeller Fund, 1960)

Julius Schmidt: *Iron Sculpture,* 1960 (Gift of Mr. and Mrs. Samuel A. Marx, 1960)

Richard Stankiewicz: *Urchin in the Grass,* 1956 (Gift of Philip Johnson, 1969). Purchased by Johnson from the Hansa Gallery, New York, in 1957.

Frank Stella: *The Marriage of Reason and Squalor, II,* 1959 (Larry Aldrich Foundation Fund)

Albert Urban: *Painting,* 1959 (Purchase)

Jack Youngerman: *Aquataine,* 1959 (Larry Aldrich Foundation Fund). Exchanged (in 1964) for Youngerman's *Black, Red, and White,* 1962; apparently chosen by Aldrich for his own collection and relinquished when the Modern expressed interest in the painting.

"Americans 1963"

May 22–August 18, 1963

Richard Anuskiewicz, Lee Bontecou, Chryssa, Sally Hazelet Drummond, Edward Higgins, Robert Indiana, Gabriel Kohn, Michael Lekakis, Richard Lindner, Marisol, Claes Thure Oldenburg, Ad Reinhardt, James Rosenquist, Jason Seley, David Simpson

Tour Itinerary

National Gallery of Canada, Ottawa, November 8–December 1, 1963; Artist's Guild of St. Louis, December 18, 1963–January 15, 1964; The Toledo Museum of Art, February 3–March 2, 1964; Ringling Museum of Art, Sarasota, Florida, March 18–April 15, 1964; Colorado Springs Fine Arts Center, May 1–29, 1964; San Francisco Museum of Art, June 16–July 14, 1964; Seattle Art Museum, September 16–October 15, 1964; Detroit Institute of Arts, November 1–29, 1964

Acquisitions

Lee Bontecou: *Untitled,* 1961 (Kay Sage Tanguy Fund)

Gabriel Kohn: *Acrotere,* 1960 (Given anonymously [by exchange])

Richard Lindner: *Boy,* 1954 (Gift of Mr. and Mrs. Wolfgang Schoenborn, in memory of René d'Harnoncourt, 1971); *Construction,* 1962 (Philip Johnson Fund)

Ad Reinhardt: *Abstract Painting,* 1960–61 (Purchase [by exchange])

David Simpson: *Red, Blue, Purple Circle,* 1962 (Larry Aldrich Foundation Fund)

Notes

In this essay I have depended especially on the reminiscences of those who were part of the period of which I have written. Larry Aldrich, Philip Johnson, William Lieberman, Waldo Rasmussen, and William Rubin gave very generously of their time, imparting historically valuable and otherwise unattainable information in interviews. I have also quoted from taped interviews with Ben Heller, Sidney Janis, and Dorothy Miller that I conducted some years ago for a different purpose. William Rubin, Kirk Varnedoe, Anne Umland, and Jodi Hauptman provided useful critiques of the essay in progress. In addition, Ms. Hauptman did extensive research for the paper. Christel Hollevoet performed the arduous task of fact-checking the archival material in this essay; she and Jill Carrick also helped with research at critical moments. I am extremely grateful to all those who supported this effort.

The following source material will be cited in abbreviated form: Holger Cahill Oral History, Columbia University, New York, transcript of interviews conducted by Joan Pring, April–June 1957, that include remarks by Miller; Dorothy Canning Miller Oral History, Archives of American Art, Smithsonian Institution, Washington, D.C., transcript of interviews conducted by Paul Cummings, May 26, 1970–September 28, 1971; Museum Collection files, Department of Painting and Sculpture, The Museum of Modern Art, which contain information on individual works in the painting and sculpture collection; the Dorothy C. Miller Papers, housed in The Museum of Modern Art Archives; an interview with Miller conducted by Avis Berman, May 4, 1981, as part of "Mark Rothko and His Times," an oral history project sponsored by the Archives of American Art, 1980–85; and the following frequently cited volumes: Alfred H. Barr, Jr., "Chronicle of the Collection of Painting and Sculpture," in *Painting and Sculpture in The Museum of Modern Art, 1929–1967* (New York: The Museum of Modern Art, 1977); *Defining Modern Art: Selected Writings of Alfred H. Barr, Jr.,* ed. Irving Sandler and Amy Newman (New York: Abrams, 1986); and "Dorothy Canning Miller," in Lynn Gilbert and Gaylen Moore, *Particular Passions: Talks with Women Who Have Shaped Our Times* (New York: Clarkson N. Potter, 1981).

1.   See appendix, pp. 94–97, for listings of the artists included in each exhibition, exhibited works that entered the Museum's collection, and tour itineraries.
2.   Miller has described the "Americans" shows as involving "some artists who were already known but little appreciated. They also aimed at discovering new people and selling their work to collections and [to] the Museum" (*Particular Passions,* p. 27). At this time, museums routinely offered for sale the work they exhibited. For example, in 1953, Irene Rice Pereira complained that only one work sold out of her retrospective at the Whitney Museum of American Art; see Karen A. Bearor, *Irene Rice Pereira: Her Paintings and Philosophy* (Austin: The

University of Texas Press, 1993), p. 225.
Everything in the "Americans" exhibitions not already in public or private collections was for sale. (For "Americans 1942," prices were posted in the galleries.) The Museum routinely took a ten-percent commission if the artist did not have a dealer. If the artist had a New York dealer, collectors were asked to contact the dealer directly, and the Museum took no commission (though there were exceptions). Sales to staff were exempt: In a postscript to a January 22, 1942, memorandum to Ione Ulrich [Sutton], the Museum's Assistant Treasurer, regarding "Americans 1942," she wrote, "Several members of the staff wish to buy pictures by Morris Graves, in which cases we will not add a Museum commission."

That such sales could constitute a conflict of interest seems not to have been an issue. Especially in the 1940s and early fifties, many of the artists lacked representation and presumably were grateful for the opportunity to sell their work. Miller often acted as their advocate: In the postscript to the memorandum cited above, Miller added, "As several of the artists . . . are desperately poor and as sales may be few and far between I wish that we could send checks to them right after sales are made, rather than waiting until the close of the exhibition." Miller Papers, I.1.3c.
3.   Cahill Oral History, p. 604. Cahill was Miller's husband; she was present when his oral history was taken, and her remarks are recorded in it. Here, she was comparing "Paintings by Nineteen Living Americans" to typical salons like the "1946 Annual Exhibition of Contemporary American Painting" at the Whitney Museum, which included one work by each of 170 artists.
"Paintings by Nineteen Living Americans" was held December 13, 1929–January 12, 1930, and included works by Charles E. Burchfield, Charles Demuth, Preston Dickinson, Lyonel Feininger, George Overbury ("Pop") Hart, Edward Hopper, Bernard Karfiol, Rockwell Kent, Walt Kuhn, Yasuo Kuniyoshi, Ernest Lawson, John Marin, Kenneth Hayes Miller, Georgia O'Keeffe, Jules Pascin, John Sloan, Eugene Speicher, Maurice Sterne, and Max Weber.
4.   Dorothy C. Miller, *15 Americans* (New York: The Museum of Modern Art, 1952), p. 5. The form of the catalogues was varied only slightly; for example, artists did not always write their own statements. (The 1959 catalogue contains the well-known instance in which Carl Andre wrote the "artist's statement" for Frank Stella; see Dorothy C. Miller, ed., *Sixteen Americans* [New York: The Museum of Modern Art, 1959], p. 79. The statement appears in n. 184 below.) From 1942 onward, acknowledgments appear in the front of the book, either before or after Miller's introduction, followed by a statement by, and in some cases a photograph of, each artist, along with plates of some of their works. The catalogue of the exhibition, which sometimes includes biographical information, appears at the back of the book.
5.   Knud Merrild, who painted biomorphic abstractions, was the one exception.
6.   *Particular Passions,* p. 24.
7.   This attitude was not unique to Graves. At

the time, many artists seem to have been concerned about compromising their integrity by exhibiting.
8.   *Particular Passions,* p. 25.
9.   "When I opened the package [containing Graves's work] with Alfred Barr, and there were all those marvelous pictures, well, everybody in the office just died. Some of our trustees who were on our painting and sculpture committee came rushing in to look at them. . . . The trustees and staff all wanted to buy, but Alfred said[,] 'The Museum gets the first choice, then Dorothy gets the next choice because she succeeded in getting them here'" (ibid). According to Miller, all eighty works sent by Graves to the Museum were sold at that time; it is impossible to corroborate this, but it is clear from the Museum Registrar's files that works were sold that had not been hung in the exhibition. Miller also recalled that the Museum purchased ten paintings by Graves, but a January 31, 1942, memorandum in the Museum Collection files indicates that fifteen works were approved for purchase on January 27 (see appendix, p. 94). *The Fledgling* (1940), which arrived at the Museum, apparently in a "second shipment" of Graves's works on February 20—almost a month after "Americans 1942" opened—was approved for purchase at a later acquisitions meeting. Miller, memorandum to Dorothy Dudley, February 20, 1942. Museum Registrar's files, The Museum of Modern Art.
10.   Miller Oral History, p. 48.
11.   Ibid.
12.   It is difficult to determine exactly how many works were sold from the "Americans" exhibitions. Documents in the Archives and in the Registrar's files are full of notations that reveal an extremely changeable situation; reserves were often cancelled and potential buyers frequently changed their minds. Although in 1960 Miller was able to provide precise information on sales from the 1952, 1956, and 1959 shows (see p. 80 of this essay), I have not found a list of sales for any of the exhibitions that I feel certain is definitive. Nevertheless, it is clear that sales were good in 1942. In addition to Graves and Bloom, works by Cashwan, Chapin, Davis, Hirsch, Hord, Lebrun, Levine, Lundeberg, Martin, and Spruce appear to have sold.
13.   Emily Genauer, *New York World Telegram,* January 24, 1942. The Museum of Modern Art Archives: Public Information Scrapbook no. 59.
14.   Edward Alden Jewell, "18 American Artists Display Work at Museum of Modern Art Opening," *New York Times,* January 21, 1942; and "Melange: Rembrandt's Work—Sundry Americans," *New York Times,* January 25, 1942. The Museum of Modern Art Archives: Miller Papers, I.1.3d.

By right- and left-wing academism Jewell presumably was referring to what he felt were the pitfalls of Regionalism and Social Realism, two categories commonly subsumed under the broad heading of American Scene Painting in the 1930s. The Regionalists were thought to endorse or even glorify national traditions, while Social Realists were considered "message painters" who provided a left-wing critique of American society. This is, of course, an oversimplification. See, for example, Nancy Heller and Julia Williams, *The Regionalists* (New York: Watson-Guptill Publications, 1976), pp. 144–45, 165.

15. "Eighteen Artists from Nine States Reviewed," *Art digest*, February 1, 1942. Miller Papers, I.1.3d.

16. George Baer, "Young American Artists—1942: Modern Museum Show Proves Great Democratic Possibilities of Art," *Daily Worker*, February 4, 1942. Miller Papers, I.1.3d.

17. "To the art lover it is distressing to see this museum, which from its inception [has shown] the finest in modern art, reducing American art to a demonstration of geography. The region in which the work was produced was undoubtedly of greater importance than the quality of the art" (quoted in "Art Show Protested: Modern Painters and Sculptors Assail 'Americans—1942,'" *New York Times*, February 3, 1942). Miller Papers, I.1.3d.

18. Although Wheeler's title was Director of Publications, many administrative and diplomatic matters not conventionally associated with that title fell to him—as is often the case with staff members in small institutions. See Russell Lynes, *Good Old Modern: An Intimate Portrait of the Museum of Modern Art* (New York: Atheneum, 1973), p. 167.

19. Kamrowski to Wheeler, September 26, 1941. Miller Papers, I.1.3b.

20. Miller, letter to Norman Barr (United American Artists), October 22, 1941. Miller Papers, I.3.1d.

21. "Museum of Modern Art Announces New Schedule of Exhibitions," MoMA press release no. 63, [1941]. Department of Public Information, The Museum of Modern Art. Since it is doubtful that such a release could have been distributed without Miller's approval, it is likely that "New American Leaders" was part of her original title.

22. *Particular Passions*, p. 24. Miller also mentioned this in her oral history: "The Trustee committee or whoever was deciding those matters wanted it to be Americans not in New York" (p. 93). And again: ". . . the first show I did in 1942, the exhibitions committee—the Trustees—specified that it should be on non–New Yorkers" (p. 172).

23. In April 1941, at the time they issued their "Report on the Museum Collections," the Advisory Committee was chaired by William A.M. Burden and included Lincoln Kirstein, Mrs. Duncan H. Read, James Thrall Soby, and Wheeler. Barr had worked with them and was in general agreement with the report. They recommended that the "American Section" of the painting and sculpture collection "cover more of the country and be more representative of advanced . . . American painting and sculpture" (quoted in "Chronicle of the Collection," p. 628).

24. Miller Papers, I.1.3b.

25. Through Cahill, Miller had intimate knowledge of the WPA, and she believed in it fully: "Although the Depression was horrible, there was great hope in the WPA. All the Museums were cooperating and there were advisory committees everywhere to help the Project. Before that there was very little support for American art. The Met had the Altman fund to spend on American art only and

bought art of the 1930s, but no one was very excited about it until it was seen as part of an important movement" (Miller Oral History, p. 99). Miller also stated that her association with the WPA ultimately led to the first "Americans" show: "That first one I did . . . these marvelous young artists, you see, had appeared on the [WPA] Project and I was very close to the Project naturally and so I knew about them" (ibid., p. 47).

26. See Jane de Hart Matthews, "Arts and the People: The New Deal Quest for a Cultural Democracy," *The Journal of American History* 62 (September 1975), pp. 325, 327.

27. Barr had worked himself to the point of exhaustion but could not sleep, and he had digestive ailments; his mentor, Museum Trustee Paul J. Sachs, thought he was "on the verge of a nervous breakdown." In the spring of 1932, having consulted a "nerve specialist," Barr was granted a year's leave of absence from the Museum. He spent the year in Europe. See Lynes, *Good Old Modern*, pp. 102–04.

28. Rockefeller Center was newly opened at the time, and the Rockefellers had donated an enormous space to the City of New York. It was to be used as a permanent municipal art gallery, modeled on the idea of a European *kunsthalle*. Cahill was chosen to direct a large exhibition of contemporary U.S. art there. See Miller Oral History, p. 15.

29. According to their biographies in the 1942 exhibition catalogue, Austin, Bloom, Breinin, Cashwan, Graves, Hirsch, Hord, Howard, Levine, Lundeberg, Martin, and Siporin had been involved with the WPA. This is not surprising, since many artists, including many first-generation Abstract Expressionists, participated in these programs. See Dorothy C. Miller, ed., *Americans 1942: 18 Artists from 9 States* (New York: The Museum of Modern Art, 1942).

30. For example, Soby was a Museum Trustee as well as a department head and curator. When asked about his dual role, he replied, "At first I really didn't want to be a Trustee because I thought it would make a conflict. . . . [I] remember Alfred saying to me, 'Don't be foolish. It'll be a help because you'll learn more quickly that way.' And he was absolutely right. He had been a Trustee. Our Museum had that policy very early of putting staff members on the board . . ." (Archives of American Art, Smithsonian Institution, Washington, D.C.: James Thrall Soby Oral History, interview conducted by Paul Cummings, July 7, 1970; transcript, p. 20).

31. By 1940, the Museum had presented nineteen one-person exhibitions by European or Latin American painters and sculptors, as opposed to only seven by artists from the United States. The group shows were more balanced in number.

32. An undated letter to Soby from the Federation of Modern Painters and Sculptors was, in part, a reaction to the 1942 "Americans" show, as well as to the 1943 exhibitions "Magic Realists" and "Romantic Painting in America": "We favor (1) the abandonment of shows which emphasize works rightly considered academic and outmoded even in the Victorian era and (2) a curtailment of such displays as are interesting only on scientific or ethno-

graphic grounds. (3) We criticize the museum for adopting one set of standards for the European art which it displays and a thoroughly different one for its American selections. When exhibiting the art of Europe there have been commendable efforts toward showing the new and progressive movements of this century. On the other hand when American painting is presented it is invariably on such superficial grounds as fantasy, romance, and (most of all) geographical and regional interest." Archives of American Art, Smithsonian Institution, Washington, D.C.: Federation of Modern Painters and Sculptors Papers (N69-75; 564–65).

33. Man Ray's contribution to the exhibition was limited to photography. E. McKnight-Kauffer, a U.S. citizen living in England, was included in the graphics section, represented by a poster. See Alfred H. Barr, Jr., *Cubism and Abstract Art* (New York: The Museum of Modern Art, 1936; rpt. Cambridge, Mass., and London: The Belknap Press of Harvard University Press, 1986), pp. 92, 170, 174.

34. In describing these artists as "relatively conservative" or "more traditional than revolutionary" I am speaking not of the critical reception of their work but of its formal properties in comparison to the Cubist-derived abstraction of Marsden Hartley or Stuart Davis, for example, or to the compositions of Ilya Bolotowski or Carl Holty. This was the context within which artists of the early forties saw the argument (see p. 63 of this essay).

The preference for figurative art may have been connected to the notion of "cultural democracy" mentioned above, and the desire for accessibility in art. It may also have been predicated on Barr's notions about the nature of art from the United States: "Barr's approach drove a theoretical wedge between the Europeans and the Americans. In Barr's view, if one could speak of a tradition of American art at that point, it was a tradition of representational painting" (Michael Auping, *Abstraction, Geometry, Painting: Selected Geometric Painting in America Since 1945* [New York: Abrams in association with the Albright-Knox Gallery, Buffalo, 1989], p. 25). Bolotowski, for instance, felt that the Modern "was against abstraction for American art. Barr felt it was a foreign development" (quoted in ibid.).

35. James Abbott McNeill Whistler was born in 1834 and died in 1903. The Museum, almost from the beginning, had defined its area of concern as up to fifty years before the present. Eventually, 1880 became the established starting date for the collections, except for those of photography and film, which cover the entire history of those mediums. At different times the institution has violated both guidelines; see John Elderfield, "The Precursor," in *Studies in Modern Art 1: American Art of the 1960* (New York: The Museum of Modern Art, 1991), p. 88, n. 5. However, in 1934, Whistler actually fell within the fifty-year limit, having died only thirty-one years before.

36. In a memorandum to Miller of October 10, 1940, Barr called painting and sculpture "two fields in which America is not yet, I am afraid, quite the equal of France. . . ." The Museum of Modern Art Archives:

Alfred H. Barr, Jr., Papers, 9b. The full text of the memorandum appears on pp. 63–64 of this essay.

37.   The Museum was founded in 1929 by Lillie P. Bliss, Mrs. Rockefeller, and Mrs. Cornelius J. (Mary Quinn) Sullivan. The women asked businessman A. Conger Goodyear to act as President of the Board of Trustees and, with the help of a trusted advisor, Paul Sachs, then a professor at Harvard University, hired the twenty-seven-year-old Alfred Barr as Director.

38.   On May 28, 1936, Mrs. Rockefeller donated $4,500 for the establishment of two purchase funds: $2,500 for the acquisition of works by U.S. artists and $2,000 for art from abroad. She contributed $20,000 in unrestricted acquisition funds in both 1938 and 1939. See "Chronicle of the Collection," p. 624.

39.   Lynes, *Good Old Modern*, pp. 300–01.

40.   Ibid., p. 54.

41.   "Chronicle of the Collection" p. 623.

42.   *The Bulletin of The Museum of Modern Art* 8 (November 1940), p. 6.

43.   Quoted in Irving Sandler, Introduction to *Defining Modern Art*, p. 27. See also Lynes, *Good Old Modern*, pp. 229–30. "Modern Masters from European and American Collections" ran from January 26 to March 24, 1940. In addition to the U.S. artists named in the protest leaflet, the exhibition included Brancusi, Braque, Cézanne, Degas, Derain, Despiau, Epstein, Gauguin, van Gogh, Gris, La Fresnaye, Lehmbruck, Maillol, Matisse, Miró, Picasso, Renoir, Rouault, Rousseau, Seurat, and Vuillard.

44.   In 1943, artists protested the exhibition "Realists and Magic Realists," claiming that it was not the Museum's business to define tendencies in modern art but only "to search for true art" (Lynes, *Good Old Modern*, p. 230). This contradicts another complaint lodged by the Federation of Modern Painters and Sculptors (see point [3] of their letter, in n. 32 above), which would also be made by artists and their supporters in the 1950s, when the Museum's failure to fully recognize the New York School with an exhibition devoted to it was, in the minds of some, a paramount concern.

45.   The Museum of Modern Art Archives: Alfred H. Barr, Jr., Papers, 9b. This memorandum, though private, reads as if it were written for publication.

46.   John Hay Whitney, Foreword to *Painting and Sculpture in the Museum of Modern Art* (New York: The Museum of Modern Art, 1942), p. 7; quoted in "Chronicle of the Collection," p. 633.

47.   James Thrall Soby, "Acquisitions Policy of the Museum of Modern Art, Painting and Sculpture," *The Museum News* 22 (June 15, 1944), p. 7.

48.   See Dorothy C. Miller, Acknowledgments and Foreword to Miller and Alfred H. Barr, Jr., eds., *American Realists and Magic Realists* (New York: The Museum of Modern Art, 1943), p. 5; see also Miller Papers, I.4a.

49.   The catalogue mirrors the exhibition, which began with nineteenth-century artists, moved on to Sheeler and Hopper as "pioneers of the new direction," then closed with contemporary paintings, drawings, and prints. See ibid.; the quotation appears on p. 9.

50.   See Dorothy C. Miller, ed., *Americans 1942–1963: Six Group Exhibitions* (New York: Arno Press for The Museum of Modern Art, 1972).

51.   Cahill Oral History, p. 584.

52.   Miller wrote to Gorky on November 28, 1942, asking him to participate in the 1943 show. In a letter of December 6, 1942, she notified the artist that the plan for the second "Americans" show had been completely altered and the abstract component postponed. She said that she hoped to present the abstract section as its own show the following winter. Museum Collection files.

53.   An undated press release in the Museum Registrar's files states that Tooker's work was "added during the three month interval between the time the catalogue went to press and the opening of the exhibition." William Lieberman has speculated that the last-minute addition may have been an instance of Barr's interference (interview with the author, October 22, 1993). Currently Director of the Department of Twentieth-Century Art at The Metropolitan Museum of Art, Lieberman was on the staff of the Modern from 1943 to 1979, entering as Barr's assistant and leaving when he was Director of the Department of Drawings.

54.   Miller Oral History, pp. 115–16. This is an almost verbatim restatement of a comment by Miller in the Cahill Oral History, pp. 605–06.

55.   Documents in the Miller Papers and in the Museum Registrar's files confirm that Barr, Kirstein, Lieberman, Soby, and Wheeler were among the buyers, and Culwell, MacIver, Pickens, Sharrer, Steinberg, and Tooker sold works. It does not appear that abstraction was very saleable at the time; there is no mention of purchases of works by Gorky, Hare, Motherwell, Noguchi, or Pereira. (Gorky's *Diary of a Seducer* [1945], which was lent to the exhibition by the Julian Levy Gallery, entered the Museum collection in 1985, a gift of Mr. and Mrs. William A.M. Burden; the Burdens acquired the work, either during the exhibition or sometime thereafter.)

56.   Emily Genauer, "Curtain Goes Up," *New York World Telegram*, September 14, 1946. Regarding Genauer's criticism of Miller's show, it is difficult to imagine that, at twenty-three, Aronson had become a perennial of any sort. Jon Stroup defended the exhibition against Genauer's accusation; see "Time Out: . . . 14 Americans," *Town and Country* (November 1946), p. 108. The response of other critics was generally positive: See Helen Carlson, "Current Exhibitions: Modern Museum Shows More American Art. . . ," *New York Sun*, September 14, 1946; Carlyle Burrows, "Art of the Week," *New York Herald Tribune*, September 15, 1946; and Edward Alden Jewell, "Museum Displays Work of 15 Artists: Modern Art Opens Exhibition of Painting and Sculpture of Contrasting Aims," *New York Times*, September 15, 1946, and "New Show at the Modern," *New York Times*, September 22, 1946. Miller Papers, I.2.5a.

On May 8, 1946, Miller received a typed note from an unidentified source stating that Genauer was writing a piece on the upcoming season but that she would not include anything about Miller's show unless given a list of the artists. Miller refused to cooperate: "[I] told [Sarah] Newmeyer [head of

Publicity] I w[oul]d not give out names at all until last moment before show." If Genauer's assault on Miller's 1942 show was not enough to justify this treatment, the critic's scathing, opportunistic 1944 article on Barr and the Modern, "The Fur-Lined Museum," hardly would have endeared her to Miller; see *Harper's* 189 (June 1944), pp. 128–38.

57.   Manny Farber, "An American Show," *The New Republic*, October 14, 1946. Miller Papers, I.2.5a.

58.   The process by which a work of art becomes an icon of a period is, of course, a complex one. Any number of works acquired by the Museum from exhibitions organized by Miller became icons because of their visibility within the institution as well as their aesthetic and historical significance.

59.   Lieberman, in an interview with the author, October 22, 1993.

60.   The Museum owns two small works on paper that are related to the ones Culwell showed in the 1946 exhibition. One of these, a small watercolor and gouache, *Death by Burning* (1942), was also done while the artist was in the Navy.

61.   *The Nation*, November 23, 1946, p. 594. Miller Papers, I.2.5a. Because the masculine pronoun today usually denotes an exclusively male subject, Greenberg's review may now read as if he assumed that the curator of Miller's exhibition was male—a flagrant example of sexism. At the time, however, it was acceptable to use "he" to denote either man or woman where gender was in question.

62.   This was clearly Barr's view. On June 2, 1943, he sent a memorandum to John E. Abbott, Executive Director of the Museum, outlining his difficulties with Trustee Stephen C. Clark regarding budget proposals that Barr and Soby had made: "Our gravest error seems to have been proposing a secretary for Dorothy Miller's office." He added, "Dorothy is our expert in American painting and she can't keep up her knowledge without more time to see shows, studios, dealers' stocks, annuals in other cities. And she needs some time for research—months actually, for this fall show of Romantic American painting." Miller Papers, III.3.a.i.

63.   *Particular Passions*, p. 21.

64.   Miller termed John Cotton Dana "a practical visionary and a great librarian" (*Particular Passions*, p. 22). A man devoted to providing service to the community, Dana began open stacks in U.S. libraries and was a great supporter of the arts in the United States.; his 1914 book was titled *American Art: How It Can Be Made to Flourish* (rpt. Woodstock, Vt.: [Elm Tree Press], 1929). After finishing the course, Miller stayed on to work at The Newark Museum. Ibid., pp. 22–23.

65.   Miller Oral History, pp. 39–40. In 1934, Miller was Assistant to the Director of the Museum, (Barr); 1935–41, Assistant Curator of Painting and Sculpture; in 1942, Associate Curator of Painting and Sculpture; 1943–47, Curator of Painting and Sculpture; 1947–67, Curator of Museum Collections; and 1968–69, Senior Curator. Rona Roob, "Biographical Note," in *Guide to the Dorothy C. Miller Papers* (New York: The Museum of Modern Art Archives, 1989), p. ii.

66. The collector Larry Aldrich observed that, as late as 1959 or 1960, when artists came to the Museum it was to see Miller, who made herself available to them. To his recollection, Barr had no involvement with the artists at this time: ". . . that was all Dorothy." Aldrich saw Jack Youngerman's work for the first time in Miller's office, where the artist had left it. Aldrich, in an interview with the author, September 29, 1993.

67. A number of those who were at the Museum during Miller's tenure believe that she had a writer's block. According to Lieberman, "Dorothy had a block about writing . . . and subconsciously Alfred encouraged that block." Although Barr would not have admitted to himself that he wanted Miller to be entirely at his disposal, Lieberman's impression was that that was in fact the case: "Had he said at . . . the beginning, 'Now you just lock yourself in a room and write it out,' Dorothy, I'm sure, would have." Lieberman, in an interview with the author, October 22, 1993.

68. Milton W. Brown, "From an Evangelical Tent Show into a Modern Museum," *Art News* 50 (October 1979), special issue, "The Museum of Modern Art at 50," p. 77.

Regarding responsibility for the "Americans" shows, these comments by Leo Castelli illustrate the confusion: "I suppose Alfred played a political role there, too. [Miller] was not doing it all by herself; she had to have Alfred's approval. . . ." But then, rethinking the issue: "She made the choices. . . ." The Museum of Modern Art Archives: Leo Castelli Oral History, The Museum of Modern Art Oral History Project; transcript, p. 60. Sandler gave Barr the credit: "Barr's recognition of Abstract Expressionism encouraged Dorothy Miller to include Pollock, Rothko, Still, Baziotes, and Tomlin in her '15 Americans' show of 1952. The show marked the Museum's official acceptance of a number of Abstract Expressionists, only four years or so after their 'breakthroughs' to mature styles" (Sandler, Introduction to *Defining Modern Art*, pp. 39–40).

Robert Rosenblum, in the pamphlet for the exhibition *A Curator's Choice 1942-1963: A Tribute to Dorothy Miller* (New York: Rosa Esman Gallery, 1982), provided a welcome alternative to this view of Miller's role: "Most of [Miller's] judgments . . . now appear so bull's-eye accurate that even in the case of those artists she favored whose subsequent reputations have dimmed, we feel we had better check up on them to see that we weren't missing something all along. Dorothy Miller, in short, played a brilliant role in tracing . . . two astonishing decades of American art. She wrote a major history of those incredible years not through the printed word, but through a series of living, visual events that steered spectators, both sophisticated and naive, through the most uncharted and thrilling seas the New York art world has ever known."

69. In a letter of April 25, 1958, sent to Miller in Paris, Barr asked her to ponder the following: ". . . Porter [McCray] has been asked by the Biennale in Italy to send work by three 'young' American artists,

two painters and one sculptor, to be shown in the big tent rather than in the national pavilion. . . . Jim [Soby], I think, has submitted suggestions. I haven't yet. This is urgent." Barr also asked Miller to help him select five worthy paintings, exhibited in the previous two years, for consideration in a "Guggenheim" competition. In a handwritten postscript: "How wonderful it'll be to see you. I realize you won't be at all rested, but I hope the mill here will grind a bit more slowly than during the past nightmare. A great deal of love and expectations —A." Miller Papers, III.3.a.iii.

Barr also gave Miller a copy of a letter he was preparing for the art historian and curator Sam Hunter, along with a list of artists that Barr was suggesting for a large international exhibition. She reviewed the list, making comments in the margin: "Yes" next to Joan Mitchell, Robert Rauschenberg, George Spaventa, Sam Francis, Grace Hartigan; she questioned the inclusion of others. Miller Papers, I.7.15a.

70. In November 1943, Barr was fired as Director of the Museum and made Director of Research. Soby was appointed Director of the Department of Painting and Sculpture and Miller was made Curator. James Johnson Sweeney served as Director of the department from January 1945 until the fall of 1946, when Andrew Carnduff Ritchie was appointed to the post; Ritchie remained until 1957.

71. In *The Feminization of American Culture* (New York: Knopf, 1977), historian Ann Douglas considered the manner in which culture became the province of middle-class women in an industrialized society. At a recent conference on gender issues in museums it was noted, "Once it became allowable for women to work in an intellectual arena, they naturally came to museums because, in American society, cultural work is traditionally women's work. It is an attitude that European society considers ridiculous, but in the United States, culture was often considered frivolous. And as something frivolous, it was consigned largely to women" (Marc Pachter, quoted in Jean Weber, "Changing Roles and Attitudes," in Jane Glaser and Artemis A. Zenetou, eds., *Gender Perspectives: Essays on Women in Museums* [Washington, D.C.: Smithsonian Institution Press, 1994], p. 33). The traditional museum hierarchy has involved "male curators and directors, maintained by countless female assistants" (Heather Paul, "In Preparation for the Future," in ibid., p. 117). In a recent article, a California critic contended that art museums lag behind corporations and other kinds of institutions regarding the numbers of women holding top positions. He put forth the thesis that, in order to be taken seriously, museums place an "out-sized emphasis on masculinity. They overcompensate" (Christopher Knight, "These Are the Only Women Running Major Art Museums in the United States. Can You Believe It?," *Los Angeles Times*, March 27, 1994, p. 90).

72. Rubin was working on the exhibition "Dada, Surrealism and Their Heritage," which ran from March 27 to June 9, 1968, at the Modern and then traveled to the Los Angeles County Museum of Art and The Art Institute of Chicago.

73. Rubin, in an interview with the author, October 15, 1993.

74. Miller was "looked upon by artists either as a benign goddess or as a disdainful one, depending on whether or not she smiled on their work and included them in her shows" (Lynes, *Good Old Modern*, p. 120). Although it was certainly not the case, Pereira actually believed that Miller blackmailed galleries into refusing to carry her work; she also thought that only one work sold out of her 1953 retrospective at the Whitney Museum because her art was being systematically suppressed by the Modern. See Bearor, *Irene Rice Pereira*, pp. 224–25.

75. In a March 3, 1958, memorandum to Porter McCray, Director of the International Program, Helen M. Franc, who was then editing the catalogue for the 1958–59 international tour of "The New American Painting," reported that she was horrified to find that, regardless of any other considerations, Miller was adamant that every lender must be represented in the illustrations for the publication. The Museum of Modern Art Archives: Frank O'Hara Papers, 2.14b. Although McCray recently characterized Miller as being "the absolute slave of Alfred Barr" (quoted in Brad Gooch, *City Poet: The Life and Times of Frank O'Hara* [New York: Knopf, 1993], p. 313), this contradicts virtually everyone else's recollections of their relationship and her persona.

76. Johnson has described Miller as having been Barr's alter ego, but not powerful in and of herself (interview with the author, October 19, 1993). Rubin has also remarked that, once Barr left the Museum, Miller had no real power of her own (interview with the author, October 15, 1993).

77. *Particular Passions*, p. 27.

78. Miller Oral History, p. 106.

79. These exhibitions are included in "The Museum of Modern Art: Painting and Sculpture Loan Exhibitions, 1940–63," compiled by Rona Roob, pp. 200–04 of the present volume.

80. Soby wrote the catalogue essay for "Romantic Painting in America"; presumably for this reason, the show is often treated as his. In fact, though well versed in European Romanticism, Soby did not know a great deal about American Romantic painting when he took on the project, and recalled spending months "working like fury" to educate himself on the topic (Archives of American Art: Soby Oral History; transcript, p. 16).

81. The Museum of Modern Art Archives: James Thrall Soby Papers, III.53(3). Miller's sense that she would not be allowed to organize another exhibition was not hyperbole. It no doubt had to do with an impending reorganization of the Museum, which, beginning in 1947, moved Miller, with Barr, into the Department of Painting and Sculpture Exhibitions. The letter to Soby, written only ten days after the opening of "Fourteen Americans," suggests that interpersonal tensions also may have given Miller cause to worry about her position; she clearly felt no support from Sweeney, then Director of the Department of Painting and Sculpture. The Museum bought little from the exhibition, which could indicate that the

show was not well received within the institution. The mechanics of recordkeeping—registration, maintaining the department's albums of photographs of works—fell to Miller as Curator of Museum Collections; although she did not officially hold this title until 1947, this may be what Miller meant by "a barren period . . . of routine work" in her letter to Soby. Lieberman, in an interview with the author, October 22, 1993.

82.   *The Museum of Modern Art Bulletin* 14 (Summer 1947), special issue, "Ben Shahn," p. 3. In his acknowledgments, Soby thanked "Miss Dorothy C. Miller, who acted as Assistant Director of the exhibition."

83.   The arrival of Ritchie, who apparently had a strong interest in contemporary art from the United States as well as from Europe, as Director of the Department of Painting and Sculpture, may have had some bearing on the decrease in Miller's activity as a curator of temporary exhibitions. Sara Mazo, Miller's assistant in the Department of Museum Collections, recalled in November 1994, "Dorothy Miller felt she had been pushed back by Ritchie. She never said it, and I shouldn't perhaps assume this, but I know her feelings were hurt" (The Museum of Modern Art Archives: Sara Mazo Oral History, The Museum of Modern Art Oral History Project; transcript, p. 27–28). Beginning in 1950, Ritchie organized a series of small shows called New Talent, which took place in the Penthouse gallery, outside the Members' Dining Room, and to some degree prefigured the Museum's ongoing Projects series, which began in the early 1970s. New Talent exhibitions featured artists who had not yet had one-person shows in New York, and were only open to the general public during special hours. The Museum encouraged members to make purchases from these exhibitions and did not take a commission on sales. The series included fourteen exhibitions and ran through 1960.

        Within the Museum, competition in Miller's area of specialization grew steadily stronger. In 1956, Sam Hunter, who was primarily concerned with contemporary American art, joined the department; in 1958, Peter Selz became its director; and, in the 1960s, William C. Seitz organized exhibitions of U.S. art at the Modern. Frank O'Hara, a departmental curator formerly on the staff of the Museum's International Program of Circulating Exhibitions, directed painting and sculpture exhibitions, as did guest curators. With these high-powered men vying for the opportunity to work within Miller's accustomed field, she probably had little chance to prevail. In a 1964 profile of the Modern published in *Art in America,* Miller is given only a brief blurb, following longer profiles of Barr, René d'Harnoncourt, David Rockefeller, William A.M. Burden, Philip L. Goodwin, Sachs, Edward Steichen, Eliza Bliss Parkinson, Wheeler, Soby, Selz, and Seitz (Seitz was then an associate curator; Miller was Curator of Museum Collections). See Geoffrey T. Hellman, "Profile of a Museum," *Art in America* 52 (February 1964), pp. 27–40, 58–64.

        Beginning in the 1950s, one-person exhibitions of U.S. artists at the Modern included Jackson Pollock (directed by Hunter, 1956); Matta (Rubin,

1957); David Smith (Hunter, 1957); Mark Rothko (Selz, 1961); Mark Tobey (Seitz, 1962); Arshile Gorky (Seitz, 1962); Hans Hofmann (Seitz, 1963); Robert Motherwell (O'Hara, 1965); Reuben Nakian (O'Hara, 1966); Pollock (begun by O'Hara; completed by Lieberman, 1967); John Graham (Elia Kokkinen, 1968); and Willem de Kooning (Thomas B. Hess, 1969).

84.   *Particular Passions,* p. 25.

85.   Miller Oral History, p. 94.

86.   Despite the frustrations, Miller on one occasion called the "Americans" series "One of my chief satisfactions at the Museum," adding, "I have a tremendous passion for making a good exhibition. You've got fifteen artists; who's going to be in the first gallery? The order in which you place the artists, that's so important. What you look for and what you try to achieve are climaxes—introduction, surprise, going around the corner and seeing something unexpected, perhaps several climaxes with very dramatic things, then a tapering off with something to let you out alive" (*Particular Passions,* p. 27). ". . . [T]he space was generally about the same for all those shows. It was the third floor of the old Number 11 building. Of course, I felt I was really a skillful crowder; my shows were always very crowded and I tried to make them look uncrowded" (Miller Oral History, p. 47).

87.   Baziotes, Pollock, Rothko, Still, and Tomlin were all first-generation Abstract Expressionists. Ferber and Lippold were among the sculptors associated with them.

88.   Cahill Oral History, p. 607. Miller added, "Howard Devree reviewed the show, but he couldn't really take it. Genauer ignored it. I always prefer being ignored by her to getting the full treatment from her, because she's always been very antagonistic to everything I've done. In fact, I shiver when I see her walking into one of my shows, because I know she's going to pan it. It's just inevitable, so when she ignores it, as she almost did with the 1952 Americans [exhibition], I'm relieved."

89.   Miller first "reserved" a de Kooning in the collection so that it would not be lent elsewhere, but "out" is written next to his name on a list that includes Baziotes, Pollock, Rose, and Rothko. Miller Papers, I.2.6a.

90.   Miller, in an interview with the author, November 12, 1985. In appraising the Museum's role in relation to U.S. art for *Art News* in 1978, Irving Sandler noted that, along with Gottlieb and Barnett Newman, de Kooning did not appear in the "Americans" series; see "When MoMA Met the Avant-Garde," *Art News* 78 (October 1978), 50th Anniversary Issue, p. 79.

91.   *Particular Passions,* p. 25.

92.   Miller Oral History, p. 79. In 1981, Miller recalled that it was during Still's third show at the Betty Parsons Gallery that Cahill called her at the Museum and told her to come over to the exhibition (*Particular Passions,* p. 25). In a letter of August 3, 1994, Wendy Jeffers kindly pointed out to me that, according to the transcript of Miller's oral history, which was recorded in 1971, it was with Still's second Parsons exhibition

that Miller became conscious of his work. This earlier interview is probably the more accurate of the two, since it is closer to the period in question.

93.   Initially, Miller had difficulty finding either Still or his work. She traveled to the West Coast, where she expected to find Stills for the exhibition, only to learn that there were none. When she got back, Still wasn't in New York—he was out West: ". . . I couldn't get hold of him. He was gone and nobody knew when he was coming back. It was really crazy" (Miller Oral History, p. 79). Once he had agreed to be in the exhibition, Still asked Miller to come up to his studio a number of times. His paintings were all rolled. They picked about two or three times the number of canvases they needed in order to have a selection. After the catalogue had gone to press, Still called to say he wanted to include a huge black painting, to which Miller agreed. Ibid., p. 132.

94.   Ibid., p. 79.

95.   When Still asked who else would be in the 1952 show, Miller did not name the realists, although she did tell him that there would be a realist section, since the exhibitions were meant to be varied; see *Particular Passions,* p. 26. See also Rothko Project, p. 8.

96.   Rothko Project, p. 25.

97.   Both Miller and Barr had known Rothko for many years. Miller has implied that, by 1952 Rothko was already beginning to deteriorate emotionally. She used to take people to his studio early on; for example, she took Henry Moore there, and Moore was fascinated, "because Rothko was rather a special sight in America for a year or two. He was so different from other artists in what he was doing" (ibid., p. 18). Rothko liked the attention at that time, which was before he began to become remote and "no one dared visit him" (ibid.). Moore may have visited Rothko in 1950, when the sculptor exhibited in Mexico City and Guadalajara—and would undoubtedly have traveled to Mexico via New York—or in 1951, when he had a one-person show at the Buchholz Gallery in New York.

        Miller did not see much of Rothko after the 1952 show. She has stated that the artist felt museums were trying to use him, and he became fixated on the idea that no one could buy one painting: They had to buy a group of works. With Rothko and Still, Miller has said, there was a sense that their "air" could be contaminated by other people's. Miller had nothing to do with the Museum's 1961 Rothko retrospective, which was directed by Peter Selz: "I went to the opening, said hello [to Rothko] and all; but by then we had drifted very far apart." Ibid., p. 26.

98.   Miller Oral History, p. 134. It was Miller's habit to bring more works to the Museum than could be hung, which gave her flexibility during the installation. She did the same with Still (see n. 93 above).

99.   Ibid., p. 135.

100.   Ibid.

101.   Rothko even suggested that Miller include Still in the exhibition, which she had already intended to do; see Rothko Project, p. 27.

102.   In a letter of April 4, 1955, to Sidney Janis, Still wrote, "When [Rothko's paintings] are hung in

a tight phalanx, as he would have them hung, and flooded with the light he demands they receive, the tyranny of his ambition to suffocate or crush all who stand in his way becomes fully manifest. This is the way he would have his work seen, and act, in the Modern Museum show of the '15.'" Archives of American Art, Smithsonian Institution, Washington, D.C.: Alfred Ossario Papers; quoted in James E.B. Breslin, *Mark Rothko: A Biography* (Chicago: University of Chicago Press, 1993), p. 344]. Rothko would later require as little light as possible on his paintings, a decision that seems more appropriate for the work: With less light, colors that could become bleached out are richer, and the contemplative atmosphere better suits the spirit of the paintings.

103. Rothko Project, p. 8.

104. Ibid., p. 23.

105. Miller Oral History, pp. 135–36.

106. Ibid., p. 133.

107. Miller Papers, I.2.6b.

108. Baziotes showed *Dwarf* (1947), already in the Museum's collection in 1952, along with seven other works; Tomlin's representation included *Number 20* (1949) and *Number 9, In Praise of Gertrude Stein.* (1949).

109. This was one of three works commissioned by Congregation B'nai Israel, Millburn, New Jersey. The others were by Motherwell and Gottlieb. See Miller, ed., *Americans 1942–1963*, p. 46.

110. It was then common practice to mix artists as different as these. In 1958, Sweeney presented Glasco and Katzman in an exhibition in Rome that also featured Richard Diebenkorn, Mitchell, and others; see *American Artists of Younger Reputation* (Rome: New York Art Foundation, 1958). At around the same time, Alfred Frankfurter showed Rose in a group that included Mitchell, Hartigan, Elaine de Kooning, Alfred Leslie, Rauschenberg, and Larry Rivers. See Miller Papers, I.5.9b.

111. See appendix, pp. 95–96, for a complete listing of works acquired from the exhibition.

112. Miller Papers, I.2.6d.

113. *Particular Passions*, p. 27.

114. Ibid.

115. See Rothko Project, p. 10.

116. Miller Papers, I.2.6b.

117. Letter from Museum member to Miller, May 15, 1952. All correspondence concerning this $100-a-year member is found in the Miller Papers, I.2.6d; subsequent references are identified by date only within the text. Miller's note to Barr, written at the bottom of the copy of the member's letter, is undated.

118. This is relatively modest praise from Barr, as it implies that the quality, importance, or energy of earlier U.S. art surpassed that of the New York School. It may have been designed to placate the recipient.

119. ". . . I think it only fair to admit that for a considerable period of time I shared your doubts as to the validity and worth of some of the artists included in the current Americans Show at the Museum. . . . Today I'm convinced that the so-called New York School, many of its members shown in the present exhibition, is more interesting and stronger than the post-war schools in France, Italy, England, and Germany" (Soby to $100-a-year member, June 4, 1952). Soby reiterated a basic point of Museum policy: It is the role of the Museum to show current tendencies in contemporary art, not to tell artists what these tendencies should be. He then cordially invited the man to do battle on these points over some good Irish whiskey.

120. See Robert M. Coates, *The New Yorker,* May 3, 1952, p. 97. Miller Papers, I.2.6d.

121. Barr to Coates, May 31, 1952. All Coates correspondence, Miller Papers, I.2.6d. Subsequent quotations are identified by date only within the text.

122. It appears that Miller had not gained much visibility since Greenberg's review of the 1946 show: Coates was apparently under the impression that Soby had directed "Romantic Painting in America." See Coates, letter to Barr, June 15, 1952.

123. S. Lane Faison, Jr., "Art," *The Nation,* May 10, 1952, pp. 457–59. Miller Papers, I.2.6d. Faison faulted Miller for eliciting statements from the artists that he found largely impenetrable, declaring that she should have written an essay "instead of limiting herself to a purely general and unarguable preface."

124. Ralph M. Pearson, "A Modern View: Merit at the Modern," *Art digest*, May 1, 1952. Miller Papers, I.2.6d.

125. Howard Devree, "Diverse Americans: Fifteen in Museum of Modern Art Show," *New York Times,* April 13, 1952. Miller Papers, I.2.6d.

126. Emily Genauer, "Exhibits of Church Art, da Vinci Inventions, Modern Museum Choices," *Herald Tribune,* April 13, 1952. Miller Papers, I.2.6d.

127. Miller Oral History, p. 79.

128. Henry McBride, "Half-Century or Whole Cycle," *Art News* 51 (Summer 1952), p. 125.

129. Myers, letter to Miller, November 1955. Miller Papers, I.5.9b.

130. In a February 10, 1977, letter to Lynda Roscoe Hartigan, now curator of the Joseph Cornell Study Center, National Museum of American Art, Washington, D.C., Miller explained that in late 1951 she had asked Cornell to be in "15 Americans," to take place in the summer of 1952. However, correspondence from 1956 indicates that Miller was probably wrong about the dates as she reported them in 1977. In a memorandum to Museum Registrar Dorothy Dudley dated February 20 of that year, Miller mentioned that she intended to include Cornell in "12 Americans," and in a letter of February 21, Soby expressed delight at the news that Miller would include Cornell in the upcoming show. But in a March 7 letter to Miller, Soby said he understood why Cornell could not participate in the exhibition; the artist was "too complicated" to work with, given the short lead time. All correspondence, Museum Collection files, Department of Painting and Sculpture, The Museum of Modern Art.

131. Miller Oral History, p. 139.

132. Ibid., p. 140.

133. Cahill Oral History, p. 617.

134. On February 23, 1956, Sam Francis wrote to Miller from Paris, where he had been living since 1950: "Have heard rumors about your show—already here—one was that there would be 100 painters in it, another that you had gone to see Joan Mitchell's work and she declined because of not hav[ing] enough work, etc. etc. Artists are the biggest gossips." Miller Papers, I.5.9a.

Although the Museum did not directly acquire a work by Francis from the exhibition, *Big Red* (1953) came into the collection in 1958, a gift of Mr. and Mrs. David Rockefeller. Rockefeller bought the painting that year with the understanding that he would give it to the Museum if it did not seem right for the Rockefeller Institute. On March 10, 1958, Barr wrote him a letter of thanks: "It is a picture we all admired tremendously when it was in . . . *12 Americans* . . . , but we had just acquired a smaller work by Francis and did not feel we ought to buy another immediately. . . ." Museum Collection files.

135. The letter, dated January 10, 1956, was signed by Sally Fairweather and Shirley G. Hardin of Fairweather-Hardin Gallery, Katharine Kuh, Curator of Modern Painting and Sculpture, The Art Institute of Chicago; Earle Ludgin of Earle Ludgin & Co.; Daniel Catton Rich, Director, The Art Institute of Chicago; and the collector Joseph R. Shapiro. Miller Papers, I.5.9a.

136. The Midwestern artists on the list subsequently sent by Kuh were Don Baum, Fred Berman, Cosmo Campoli, Joseph Friebert, Roland Ginzel, Gerald McLaughlin, Robert Nickel, Kemper Quabius, Shoshanah, Evelyn Statsinger, Natsuko Takehira, Joyce W. Treiman, and James Walker. Kuh noted that she did not include Leon Golub, Joseph Goto, or Richard Koppe because she was certain that Miller was aware of their work. Miller Papers, I.5.9a.

137. Myers to Miller, November 4, 1955. Miller Papers, I.5.9c.

138. Hunter to Miller, November 5, 1955. Miller Papers, I.5.9b.

139. A pencilled note at the top of Hunter's letter indicates that Miller responded by telephone on November 16, 1955, very shortly after she received his letter; she also sent him an exhibition catalogue, for which he thanked her in a note dated June 6, 1956. Miller Papers, I.5.9b. Hunter was referring to Cahill's introduction to the catalogue for "Modern Art in the United States: A Selection from the Collections of the Museum of Modern Art," which Miller had organized in consultation with Barr and which toured Europe in 1955 (see n. 207 below).

140. Philip Johnson has suggested that mixing artists of widely different styles and concerns may have allowed Miller to include more radical art in the shows without being subject to a destructive level of criticism (interview with the author, October 9, 1993).

141. Miller to Jean Wrolsen, June 21, 1956. Miller Papers, I.5.9b.

142. Miller to Barr, June 9, 1956. Miller Papers, I.5.9b. The painting was ultimately purchased by Nelson Rockefeller.

143. Brooks to Miller, June 9, 1956. Miller Papers, I.5.9b.

144. With each successive "Americans" exhibition

the recordkeeping became more professional and more extensive. Nevertheless, it is difficult to know whether records for sales, for example, for any given show are absent from the files because sales were low, or because sales were not properly recorded. With this in mind, it does seem that sales were particularly strong in 1956.

145.   Miller Papers, I.5.9a.

146.   Leo Steinberg, "Month in Review," *Arts Magazine* 30 (July 1956), p. 28. Miller Papers, I.5.9d.

147.   Emily Genauer, "Art: Modern Museum Show," *Herald Tribune Book Review,* June 3, 1956. Miller Papers, I.5.9d.

148.   Stuart Preston, "Twelve Americans: Advance Guard Arrives at Modern Museum," *New York Times,* June 3, 1956. Miller Papers, I.5.9d. Like other critics, Preston noted in his review that Hague was the one unfamiliar figure in the show.

149.   Sandler recently stated that "Briggs injected Still's demands for a visionary art, and his moralist and iconoclastic stance, into the thinking of the second generation" (quoted in the press release for "Abstraction," Anita Shapolsky Gallery, New York, April 9–May 21, 1994).

150.   Barr, memorandum to d'Harnoncourt, December 3, 1957. Miller Papers, I.7.15a. Barr added, "In any case, I hope [Miller] will have a chance to discuss the problem tomorrow. Indeed, she should have been at the previous discussion of the schedule."

151.   Miller Papers, I.7.15a.

152.   A notation in Miller's date book for June 21, 1959, reads: "To Wash." Miller Papers, V.35. It appears, however, that Miller did not travel to the West Coast in 1959 because Cahill was sick. He died the following year.

153.   Myers to Miller, September 18, 1959. Miller Archives, I.7.15a.

154.   The other twenty-three-year-old included in the series was David Aronson, who was born in 1923. His work was shown in "Fourteen Americans" in 1946.

155.   Miller Oral History, p. 138. Stella's name first appears in Miller's 1959 date book, on September 2, but is crossed out. On September 3, there is a notation that reads: "5:30 Castelli; 6:00 Stella." Miller Papers, V.35. This seems to corroborate Castelli's recollection that he saw Stella a few days before Miller and then took her to the artist's studio; see The Museum of Modern Art Archives: Castelli Oral History; transcript, p. 30.

156.   Ibid.

157.   Barr and Miller bought two works by Johns with Museum funds: *Green Target* (1955), Richard S Zeisler Fund; and *White Numbers* (1957), Elizabeth Bliss Parkinson Fund. *Target with Four Faces* (1955) was acquired by Mr. and Mrs. Robert C. Scull and given to the Museum in 1958. *Flag* (1954–55) was a gift of Philip Johnson in 1973—another instance of Johnson buying a painting for the Museum because the Acquisitions Committee would have refused it if Museum funds had been used for its purchase. Johnson says there was the fear that the Johns would be seen as desecrating the American flag (interview with the author, October 9, 1993). Miller bought

Johns's *Grey Numbers* (1957) for herself; see Miller Oral History, p. 255.

158.   Castelli has stated that it was exceptional for the Museum not to buy a work by each artist out of these shows. As is evident from the appendix to this essay (pp. 94–97), this was not actually the case, but many works were acquired from the 1956 and 1959 exhibitions, and this may have led to Castelli's misunderstanding. There is no question that Miller and Barr missed the mark regarding Rauschenberg, yet despite the obvious lack of support, Castelli seems to have felt that on some level Barr understood the artist's importance; see The Museum of Modern Art Archives: Castelli Oral History; transcript, p. 33.

159.   On June 23, 1955, Miller wrote Calder: "Dear Sandy: I went to see Ellsworth Kelly's work yesterday and found it very interesting. He has done some good things recently. Thanks for telling us about him. I am going to keep three or four of the smaller ones in my office this summer." Museum Collection files.

160.   Museum Collection files.

161.   See Yve-Alain Bois, "Ellsworth Kelly in France: Anti-Composition in Its Many Guises," in *Ellsworth Kelly: The Years in France, 1948–1954* (Washington, D.C.: National Gallery of Art, 1992). Bois reported that Barr was too busy to visit Kelly's studio that summer: "The matter would have ended there had it not been for the tenacious Dorothy Miller, who had her eyes and ears open and, not being one to hang back, visited Kelly's studio, emerging much impressed" (p. 11).

162.   Miller Oral History, p. 173.

163.   Ibid.

164.   Miller to Dudley, January 4, 1960. Miller Papers, I.7.15a.

165.   On December 8, 1959, Miller received a telephone message left by a woman inquiring into the purchase of works in the show. The woman was told that most were on reserve, but she was very insistent and asked to have her call returned. This was a sea change from 1942, when price lists were posted in the galleries.

On December 18, Miller wrote Louise Boyer in Nelson Rockefeller's office with a list of items she had reserved for Rockefeller's consideration.; included were Johns's *Black Target* (1959), Youngerman's *Coenties Slip* (1959), and Mallary's *Head of a Bull* (1958). She also sent along a catalogue and mentioned Nevelson's "columns," which were to be sold in pairs. Miller Papers, I.7.15b.

166.   Aldrich's name first appears in Miller's date-book on August 27, 1959. Miller Papers, V.35. According to Aldrich, he and Lieberman met at a party (interview with the author, September 29, 1993).

167.   Aldrich, in an interview with the author, September 29, 1993. Aldrich began collecting after World War II, primarily Impressionist and Post-Impressionist works. He became interested in contemporary art in Paris, to which he traveled several times a year on business. In New York, he met the dealer John Myers, who introduced him to the work of Hartigan. Hartigan became the first U.S. artist whose work Aldrich acquired.

Aldrich liked a number of works in the first group Miller showed him but discovered that the

exhibitions from which they came, some of which had taken place months before, had sold out. He soon began to devote one day a week to shopping for art,. He became friends with Miller and Barr, was known in the galleries, and was usually among the first to become aware of emerging artists. Often, when he went to an exhibition he would choose one work for himself and one for the Museum; Miller and Barr frequently wanted the Museum to have works he had earmarked for himself, which was agreeable to him. After 1963, he instituted a similar arrangement with the Whitney Museum.

168.   In the end, the painting was approved unanimously for acquisition because of its low price and in support of the staff's professional judgment. Museum Collection files, Department of Painting and Sculpture, The Museum of Modern Art.

169.   Miller Papers, I.7.15i.

170.   Stuart Preston, "The Shape of Things to Come," *New York Times,* December 20, 1959. Miller Papers, I.7.15i.

171.   John Canaday, "Evolution of a Public: The Audience Created for Modern Art May in Turn Be on the Point of Redirecting That Art," *New York Times,* January 31, 1960.

172.   John Canaday, "It Talks Good: Story-Telling Is Taboo, But Painting Today Is an Adjunct to Words," *New York Times,* March 6, 1960.

173.   John Canaday, "Perhaps Drastic: A Moratorium on Art Might Be Nice for a while But Could Be Dangerous," *New York Times,* September 4, 1960.

174.   "New Talent U.S.A.," *Art in America* 48 (1960), pp. 23–60. Miller Papers, I.7.15d. Miller selected works by Edward Avedisian, Frederick Franck, Alfred Jensen, James McGarrell, Robert Richenberg, and Myron Stout. Katharine Kuh chose sculpture; Lieberman, prints and drawings; Beaumont Newhall, photography; David Campbell, crafts; and Henry-Russell Hitchcock, architecture. Canaday's commentary, which is actually part of the feature, appearing as an introduction and at the beginning of each section, is surprisingly negative, given its context.

175.   Canaday to Miller, March 9, 1960. Miller Papers, I.7.15d.

176.   The Publicity Department was renamed the Department of Public Information in 1963.

177.   Barr in an undated memorandum to Shaw. Miller Papers, I.7.15d. I have been unable to locate a response from Barr or Miller to Canaday's letter, so it is uncertain what action they took.

178.   Katharine Kuh, "A Contemporary Canvass of the American Canvas," *The Saturday Review,* January 23, 1960, pp. 29, 40. Miller Papers, I.7.15i.

179.   Thomas B. Hess, "U.S. Art: Notes from 1960," *Art News* 58 (January 1960), pp. 24–29. Miller Papers, I.7.15i.

180.   Dennis Leon, "16 Americans on View," *Philadelphia Enquirer,* December 27, 1959. The Museum of Modern Art Archives: Public Information Scrapbook no. 35D.

181.   Florence Berkman, "Abstract Art Losing Its Way, Seen Reverting to Dadaism," *Hartford Times,*

January 30, 1960. The Museum of Modern Art Archives: Public Information Scrapbook no. 35D.

182.   Robert M. Coates, "The 'Beat' Beat in Art," *The New Yorker,* January 2, 1960, p. 61. Miller Papers, I.7.15i.

183.   Emily Genauer, "16-Artist Show Is on Today at Museum of Modern Art," *Herald Tribune,* December 16, 1959. Miller Papers, I.7.15i.

184.   Emily Genauer, "The Fifties Will Go Down As Decade of Abstraction," and "An Artist Writes to Correct and Explain"; in *Herald Tribune,* December 27, 1959. Miller Papers, I.7.15i. *Time* Magazine, clearly amused, reprinted this exchange in its November 11, 1960, issue. Andre's statement reads: "Art excludes the unnecessary. Frank Stella has found it necessary to paint stripes. There is nothing else in his paintings. Frank Stella is not interested in expression or sensitivity. He is interested in the necessities of painting. Symbols are counters passed among people. Frank Stella's painting is not symbolic. His stripes are the paths of brush on canvas. These paths lead only into painting." Reprinted from Miller, ed. *15 Americans,* p. 79.

185.   This work was purchased by Nelson Rockefeller and ultimately given by him to the Whitney.

186.   This despite the press release for the show, which reads, "The exhibition offers little comfort to trend-spotters because, as in past years, the emphasis is on variety rather than on a single style or movement." MoMA press release no. 64, May 22, 1963 (draft). Miller Papers, I.9.20a.

187.   Although Bontecou's and Higgins's works do not contain explicit references to pop culture, a compelling, sometimes amusing, tension between abstract art and recognizable objects is central to their production.

188.   Myers to Miller, February 12, 1963, Miller Papers, I.9.20d.

189.   John Gruen, "Pop Goes the Easel," *Herald Tribune,* May 2, 1963. Miller Papers, I.10.20i.

190.   Miller to Parkhurst, December 13, 1962; written in response to Parkhurst's letter of December 11, 1962. Miller Papers, I.9.20c.

191.   Miller to Reinhardt, March 7, 1963. All Miller–Reinhardt correspondence Miller Papers, I.9.20d. Subsequent quotations are identified by date only within the text.

192.   See p. 63 of this essay. For a discussion of artist led protests against the Museum's exhibition and acquisition policies, see Michael Kimmelman, "Revisiting the Revisionists: The Modern, Its Critics, and the Cold War," pp. 38–55 of the present volume.

193.   Reinhardt's letter to Miller is undated; it was received on March 11, 1963. He wrote: "The only possible reason I could think of why I would not want to show in your Fifteen or Sixteen 'Americans—1963' is some possible relation the Museum might make with that 'New-York-School' or what you called 'New-American-Painting' business of the last fifteen or sixteen years. I don't have to forgive you for that, ('you'='museum')? Yes, I'd like to show in the show." He adds, "That's a nice group of pretty girls (Bontecou, Marisol, Chryssa,

Hazelet [Drummond]) and I'm very pleased to see Richard Lindner's name." Miller Papers, I.9.20d.

194.   See Miller Papers, I.9.20f.

195.   Reinhardt later recalled, "When the Museum of Modern Art had its last fifteen or sixteen Americans show in nineteen sixty-three they had to rope off my room, and the public got angry only with that room. They accepted everything in the rest of the show—the pop art, the plaster hamburgers and everything else" (quoted in Bruce Glaser, "An Interview with Ad Reinhardt," in *Art As Art: The Selected Writings of Ad Reinhardt,* ed. Barbara Rose [New York: Viking Press; Berkeley: University of California Press, 1975], p. 15). Reinhardt clearly regarded this as a testament to the power of his work.

196.   See appendix, p. 97, for a complete listing.

197.   William Burden commissioned Drummond to do a painting. He sent Miller a blind copy of his letter to the artist: "I should like to commission you to do a painting for me in a turquoise blue color, approximately 30 x 32." It is my understanding that the price will be somewhere between $900 and $1200." Miller Papers, I.10.20h. The file also contains Miller's reminder to herself to tell the front desk that a Rosenquist had been sold: "Put a star on the label."

198.   Reprinted in Harold Rosenberg, "Black and Pistachio," in *The Anxious Object* (Chicago: University of Chicago Press, 1966), p. 49. Rosenberg discerned an expressionist flavor in Kohn and Lekakis, and somewhat in Oldenburg, too, and wondered why Jack Tworkov and Esteban Vicente weren't included in the exhibition.

199.   Ibid., pp. 52, 53.

200.   Ibid., 53.

201.   Sandler saw the exhibition as an endorsement of Pop art but felt that the artists included, with the exception of Oldenburg, were on the safe end of the Pop spectrum; see "In the Art Galleries," *New York Post,* June 9, 1963. John Gruen also discerned in the show a full commitment to Pop art; see "The Trend of the Times in Modern Art." *Herald Tribune,* May 22, 1963. Miller Papers, I.10.20i.

202.   John Canaday, "Americans Once More: Museum of Modern Art Makes New Choices," *New York Times,* May 26, 1963. Miller Papers, I.10.20i.

203.   Hilton Kramer, "Art," *The Nation,* June 22, 1960. Miller Papers, I.10.20i.

204.   Drummond's *Hummingbird* (1961) came into the Museum collection in 1962. This small (12-by-12-inch) painting is like a detail of a Georges Seurat. Simpson's *Red, Blue, Purple Circle* (1962), which came into the collection the year of the show, is a painting of thin horizontal stripes within a 48-inch-diameter tondo.

205.   The Modern was not alone in being slow to recognize Abstract Expressionism as a phenomenon. In fact, "The New American Painting" was the first exhibition mounted by a major U.S. institution to offer a more-or-less comprehensive look at the first generation of the New York School.

206.   The decision to bring the exhibition to New York was made a few months before its first European showing. Rubin has confirmed that, as the

show was being assembled, pressure was applied by individuals such as Seitz and Heller, who felt it was scandalous that the Modern would send this exhibition to Europe and not show it at home (interview with the author, October 15, 1993).

207.   In 1955, Miller, in consultation with Barr, selected the painting and sculpture sections for a large survey exhibition for the Musée National d'Art Moderne in Paris. The exhibition opened in Paris under the title "50 Ans d'Art aux Etats-Unis: Collections du Museum of Modern Art de New York." In 1955–56, the painting and sculpture sections and the print section (selected by Lieberman) were circulated throughout Europe as "Modern Art in the United States: A Selection from the Collections of the Museum of Modern Art," together, on occasion, with one or more of the other sections (architecture, photography, film, and design). Thirteen artists in the Contemporary Abstract Painting section were from the New York School: Baziotes, Gorky, Guston, Hartigan, Kline, de Kooning, Motherwell, Pollock, Pousette-Dart, Rothko, Stamos, Still, and Tomlin. The section also included Tobey, who is sometimes counted among the Abstract Expressionists. Other categories of painting and sculpture included First Generation Modernists, Realist Painters, Romantic painters, and Modern Primitives. Miller felt that "Modern Art in the United States," which provided many Europeans with their first exposure to Abstract Expressionism, created a demand abroad for more work by the New York School. According to Miller, Arnold Rüdlinger, then at the Kunsthalle, Basel, was "the first European . . . to be passionately interested in the new American art" (Miller Oral History, pp. 142–43). See also Kimmelman, "Revisiting the Revisionists," pp. 45–19 and p. 54 (n. 60) of the present volume.

208.   See O'Hara, memorandum to McCray, February 19, 1958. The Museum of Modern Art Archives: O'Hara Papers, 2.14b. Once Gottlieb, Newman, Stamos, and Tworkov were included in "The New American Painting," they were probably considered ineligible for the 1963 "Americans" exhibition.

209.   Heller, in an interview with the author, October 24, 1985.

210.   The sale of Newman's *Abraham* (1949) to the Museum in 1959 resulted from that meeting (ibid.).

211.   According to Miller, in 1958 it was difficult to borrow Pollocks; see Miller Oral History, p. 144. Two of the Pollocks in the exhibition were lent by the Sidney Janis Gallery, which represented the Pollock estate; a third was lent by Mr. and Mrs. Roy R. Neuberger; and a fourth by Nelson Rockefeller. Many others were no doubt already reserved for the 1958–59 touring Pollock retrospective organized by the Museum's International Program, which traveled during the same period, and in three cities coincided with "The New American Painting."

212.   "[Newman's] work didn't seem as interesting to us as some of the others. Never did seem up to Rothko and Pollock, . . . and de Kooning" (Miller, in an interview with the author, November 12, 1985).

213.   "The New American Painting" included five works from Heller's collection; see The Museum of

Modern Art Archives: O'Hara Papers, 2.14a. Miller later recalled, ". . . there were artists who wouldn't cooperate, like Rothko and Clyfford Still. And so I had to go to Ben Heller and enter his living room on my knees [and ask], Will you lend some of your paintings, and he said, Well, is this a big major effort of the Museum? And I said Yes, indeed it is, and he said, Alright I will" (Miller Oral History, p. 245).

By the spring of 1958, when Miller and Barr were considering Newman for inclusion in the exhibition, things had begun to improve for the artist. Clement Greenberg had featured him prominently in his essay "American Type Painting," which was published in the *Partisan Review* in the spring of 1955. Heller had purchased two paintings from Newman in 1956. At the instigation of Tony Smith and Paul Feeley, who were teaching at Bennington College, Newman had been invited to have a retrospective at the college as part of an annual series that had already featured Pollock and Hofmann. In March 1959, during the tour of "The New American Painting," Newman would show many of the works from the Bennington exhibition at French & Co. in New York. See Thomas B. Hess, *Barnett Newman* (New York: The Museum of Modern Art, 1981), pp. 93–96.

214.   The Museum of Modern Art Archives: O'Hara Papers, 2.14a.

215.   Miller Oral History, p. 142.

216.   It is difficult to know how important a role these political factors actually played. Rubin has observed that Rivers could have been as offensive to U.S. audiences as Pollock, and that Barr did not "pull his punches" (telephone interview with the author, November 9, 1994). According to Waldo Rasmussen, who succeeded McCray as Director of the International Program in 1962, the Program had a kind of autonomy, partially because its shows took place outside the New York art world, and also because many of its exhibitions resulted from requests from foreign institutions and governments (interview with the author, October 8, 1993). But until "The New American Painting," the Museum did not feature the New York School as a group even in international exhibitions, and continued to include those artists whom it had supported earlier and to omit those, like Newman, for whom there was less institutional regard. (The U.S. contribution to the 1957 São Paulo Bienal focused on the New York School, but excluded many of the most pivotal first-generation Abstract Expressionists.)

217.   The Pollock exhibition in São Paulo was actually larger than the one that had been mounted at the Modern in 1956. It included thirty-four oils and twenty-nine drawings and watercolors, as opposed to the thirty-five oils and nine works on paper in the New York show. The exhibitions contained twenty-four of the same works.

218.   In 1950, when asked to collaborate on the U.S. exhibition at the Venice Biennale by choosing three artists and assembling their work, the Museum picked Gorky, de Kooning, and Pollock. In the 1955–56 touring exhibition "Modern Art in the United States," thirteen of the seventeen artists

included in the Contemporary Abstract Art section were members of the New York School.

It should be noted that in 1951, at the Modern, Ritchie organized the exhibition "Abstract Painting and Sculpture in America," which featured Abstract Expressionists in the categories "Expressionist Geometric" (Ferber, Hofmann, Lassaw, Motherwell, Reinhardt, Smith, Tomlin) and "Expressionist Biomorphic" (Baziotes, Brooks, Gorky, de Kooning, Lassaw, Pollock, Pousette-Dart, Rothko, Smith, Stamos). However, both sections also included a sizeable proportion of artists not associated with that group. In this way, Ritchie's show resembled the "Americans" exhibitions and "Modern Art in the United States."

The other São Paulo and Venice biennials organized by the Modern were more in keeping with the mixture of styles that was the rule at home. In 1953, in São Paulo, the United States presented a major showing of Calder's work, as well as paintings by Baziotes, Bloom, Corbett, Glasco, de Kooning, Motherwell, Shahn, and Tomlin. In 1954, in Venice, de Kooning was coupled with Shahn, and Lassaw and Smith were shown with Lachaise. An exhibition of eleven artists—Bontecou, John Chamberlain, Diebenkorn, Burgoine Diller, Robert Engman, Gechtoff, Golub, Stephen Greene, Kelly, Pousette-Dart, and Richard Stankiewicz—accompanied the Motherwell show to São Paulo in 1961. And in 1962, Dimitri Hadzi, MacIver, and Jan Müller represented the United States at the Venice Biennale.

219.   Leonardo Borgese, "Candore e conformismo della 'nuova pittura americana,'" *Corriere della Sera,* June 8, 1958.

220.   Will Grohmann, "Die neue amerikanische Malerei," *Der Tagesspiegel,* September 7, 1958.

221.   See, for example, Aline Saarinen, "New Humanism in Art," *New York Times,* June 28, 1959; and Betty Kaufman, "An Impressive Display of U.S. Paintings," *The Commonwealth of New York,* July 17, 1959. The Museum of Modern Art Archives: Public Information Scrapbook no. 35D. Kaufman noted that this was the first time the United States had produced a school of artists that later achieved prominence abroad.

222.   Emily Genauer, "Abstract Art That Toured Europe Is Displayed Here," *Herald Tribune,* May 28, 1959.

223.   Hilton Kramer, "The End of Modern Painting," *The Reporter,* July 23, 1959. Reprinted in Clifford Ross, ed., *Abstract Expressionism: Creators and Critics* (New York: Abrams, 1990), pp. 293–94.

224.   Ibid. In fact, at this time there were few "big investors" in Abstract Expressionism. Kramer, like Genauer, typically disparaged vanguard art by claiming that it was actually "tame" or, as in this case, in the pocket of the rich and powerful, which amounts to the same thing, only worse, since it implies that the art, like its patrons, is elitist.

225.   In 1965, Maurice Tuchman, in his exhibition "New York School, The First Generation: Paintings of the 1940s and 1950s," held at the Los Angeles County Museum of Art July 16–August 1, 1965,

showed Reinhardt and Hofmann as well as Pousette-Dart, but he omitted Brooks and Tworkov. Tuchman provided a fuller representation of the artists, showing often double the number of works by each that Miller did. (Miller was restricted to an average of five.) There was overlapping among the works included in each show, but Miller had the edge in terms of quality, in part because the Museum was able to draw upon its own classic stock, including Baziotes's *Dwarf,* Gorky's *Agony* (1947), and de Kooning's *Woman, I* (1950–52).

Henry Geldzahler's "New York Painting and Sculpture 1940–1970," held at The Metropolitan Museum of Art in 1969, contained a far greater variety of painting and sculpture than did Miller's show and was not really comparable.

226.   See, for example, Eva Cockroft, "Abstract Expressionism, Weapon of the Cold War," *Artforum* 12 (June 1974), pp. 39–41. Reprinted in Francis Frascina, ed., *Pollock and After: The Critical Debate* (New York: Harper & Row, 1985), pp. 125–33. See also Serge Guilbaut, *How New York Stole the Idea of Modern Art: Abstract Expressionism, Freedom, and the Cold War* (Chicago and London: University of Chicago Press, 1983). This literature is discussed at length in Kimmelman, "Revisiting the Revisionists," pp. 38–55 of the present volume.

227.   Thomas Hess, editor of *Art News,* complained of this as early as 1954; see "Eros and Agape Midtown," *Art News* 53 (November 1954), p. 17.

228.   Rubin, in an interview with the author, October 15, 1993.

229.   Thomas B. Hess, response to letter to the editor from Alfred H. Barr, Jr., *Art News* 56 (September 1957), pp. 57–58. Barr's letter appears on pp. 6 and 57.

230.   Truman had called modern art "the ham and eggs school" and "the vaporings of half-baked, lazy people" (quoted in Sandler, Introduction to *Defining Modern Art,* p. 31).

231.   The Museum had sustained an earlier attack from insider Lincoln Kirstein, whose "State of Modern Painting" was published in *Harper's* in October 1948. A piece by Barr titled "Is Modern Art Communist?" appeared in *The New York Times Magazine,* December 14, 1952; it is reprinted in *Defining Modern Art,* pp. 214–19.

232.   "Chronicle of the Collection," p. 636.

233.   Miller Oral History, pp. 43–44. The Museum lost the Clark, Goodyear, and Lewisohn collections because of these controversies. Over the years, acquisitions frequently caused dissension. As has been noted, Philip Johnson repeatedly bought works for the Museum that would not have been approved for acquisition had Museum funds been used, among them, Rothko's *Number 10* (1950), which caused dissent in 1952; Johns's *Flag;* and Newman's *Abraham.* In addition, according to Miller, ". . . several times we took a work of Nevelson's to our acquisitions committee and couldn't put it over" (ibid., p. 172).

234.   "Had Barr not been held in rein by conservative members of the Acquisitions Committee and had the art-critical climate been more favorable to avant-garde art in the late forties, he would have

acquired Abstract Expressionist paintings earlier and in greater numbers than he actually did, although what he did manage to introduce into the permanent collection was impressive indeed" (Sandler, Introduction to *Defining Modern Art*, p. 38).

235.   According to his memorandum to Agnes Rindge of November 9, 1943, Soby, then Chairman of the Acquisitions Committee, initially put a reserve on *She-Wolf* during Pollock's 1943 Art of This Century exhibition. A memorandum from Rindge to Sidney Janis and Meyer Schapiro, dated November 22, 1943, indicates that these two men instigated the purchase. Janis later recalled: "Two members of the Acquisition Committee of the Advisory Committee, Meyer Schapiro and myself, strongly recommended the purchase of [*She-Wolf*] by the Museum" (quoted in William Rubin, Introduction to *Three Generations of Twentieth-Century Art: The Sidney and Harriet Janis Collection of The Museum of Modern Art* [New York: The Museum of Modern Art, 1972], p. xiv). In a memorandum to Barr of December 7, 1941, Helen Franc, of the Department of Publications, suggested rewriting Janis's quotation, to give credit for the purchase to Soby and James Johnson Sweeney, then Vice-Chairman of the Acquisitions Committee, as well as to Schapiro and Janis himself. Apparently, this idea was rejected. All memoranda, Museum Collection files.

236.   *Number 1, 1948* was not the first of Pollock's drip paintings to enter a museum collection. Peggy Guggenheim gave *Galaxy*, of 1947, to the Joslyn Art Museum in Omaha in 1949, and Mr. and Mrs. Bernard J. Reis gave *Cathedral*, also of 1947, to the Dallas Museum of Fine Arts in 1950, the same year the Modern bought *Number 1, 1948*. The Modern's painting does appear to be the first classic Pollock to have been acquired by a public institution by direct purchase; see Francis Valentine O'Connor and Eugene Victor Thau, eds., *Jackson Pollock: A Catalogue Raisonné of Paintings, Drawings, and Other Works* (New Haven, Conn., and London: Yale University Press, 1978).

237.   When Parsons opened her gallery in 1946, ". . . Alfred Barr and Dorothy Miller came to nearly every show. And of course they were crazy about the Rothko's. . . ." And: ". . . the museums had a tremendous influence . . . [and] the Modern Museum was the leader for years [in helping the public to realize] . . . that the painters of today can be just as important as the painters of yesterday" (Archives of American Art, Smithsonian Institution, Washington, D.C.: Betty Parsons Oral History, interviews conducted by Paul Cummings, June 4 and June 9, 1969; transcript, pp. 13, 34).

238.   Archives of American Art, Smithsonian Institution, Washington, D.C.: Samuel Kootz Oral History, interview conducted by Dorothy Seckler, April 13, 1964; transcript, p. 12.

239.   In 1951, the Museum's exhibition of the "'experimental' and newly formed collection of Blanchette Rockefeller" included a Baziotes, a Motherwell, a Pollock, a Rothko, and a Tomlin; see

Diedre Robson, "The Avant-Garde and the On-Guard: Some Influences on the Potential market for the First Generation Abstraction Expressionists in the 1940s and Early 1950s," *Art Journal* (Fall 1988), p. 219. Regarding David Rockefeller's collection, see Miller Oral History, p. 163.

240.   See Sandler, Introduction to *Defining Modern Art*, p. 41. Miller and Barr were regulars at the weekly meetings of the Eighth Street "Club": "That was right at the beginning . . . of the Abstract Expressionist, New York School thing, when the Club was going on. We all went like going to a prayer meeting" (Miller Oral History, p. 116). And, whatever the New York School artists' feelings about Barr, they invited him to a three-day Artists' Session at Studio 35 in April 1950. He was the only non-artist present, and served, along with Lippold and Motherwell, as moderator. See Sandler, p. 39.

In Robert Motherwell's diagram of the development of the New York School, Barr appears in the bottom quarter, at the center, after Marion Willard, Kootz, and Parsons, but before Hess and Charles Egan. According to Motherwell, the diagram is "an impression of the true chronology and of the separate clusters that taken together are sometimes called Abstract Expressionism, sometimes called the New York School" (quoted in William C. Seitz, *Abstract Expressionist Painting in America* [Cambridge, Mass.: Harvard University Press, 1983], n.p.). Motherwell's chart seems to have been inspired, at least in part, by Barr's famous diagram of the development of modern art, which was on the dust jacket of the 1936 exhibition catalogue *Cubism and Abstract Art* and is now the frontispiece for the 1986 reprint edition.

241.   *Number 10* (1950) was the only Rothko in the Museum collection between 1952 and 1959. *Chief* (1950) was the only Kline in the collection between 1952 and 1967. Philip Johnson owned Kline's *White Forms* (1955), which he lent to the 1956 "Americans" show and eventually gave to the Modern, in 1977. He had purchased the work from the Sidney Janis Gallery, New York, in 1956. Johnson gave Rothko's *Yellow and Gold* (1956) to the Museum in 1970. It is unclear whether he was encouraged by Miller or Barr to buy these works.

242.   Rubin, in an interview with the author, October 15, 1993.

243.   Miller Oral History, p. 172.

244.   Rasmussen, in an interview with the author, October 8, 1993. In a 1985 interview with the author, Sidney Janis once recalled that "The Museum of Modern Art had an option to buy [Pollock's *Autumn Rhythm*] at $8,000 and the committee wouldn't go for it. . . . Alfred came back after Jackson died and I said, 'You know, Lee [Krasner] has moved up the price—it's now $30,000,' and he almost dropped dead! Nothing happened. We sold it to [Robert] Hale, who was curator of American art at [the Metropolitan Museum]. . . . [He was] very much in tune with the painters because he lived in Easthampton, or in the Springs, and Pollock lived there and de Kooning, and so he was buying those artists and paying a good price, and we got our

$30,000. . . ." Hale's purchase of *Autumn Rhythm* involved a partial exchange in which Krasner took back a Pollock valued at $12,000.

245.   Miller Oral History, p. 224.

246.   See n. 213 above. In the 1950s, the majority of Miller's and Barr's colleagues probably shared their view of Newman. However, others—Greenberg and Heller, for example—recognized the value of his work at that time.

247.   "I didn't care for Gottlieb's work particularly and that's why I didn't have it" (Rothko Project, p. 27). This contradicts the perception of Samuel Kootz, cited on pp. 90-91 of this essay.

248.   The 1957 Whitney Museum show was subtitled "Thirty American Painters and Sculptors Under Thirty-five." This was in contrast to the 1942 Whitney annual, for example, which contained over 200 paintings, sculptures, drawings, and prints, with most artists represented by a single work.

249.   Excluding the 1942 exhibition, thirty-three of the seventy-five artists who participated in the "Americans" series remain widely recognized: Gorky, Hare, Motherwell, Noguchi, Steinberg, and Tobey ("Fourteen Americans"); Baziotes, Ferber, Kiesler, Lippold, Pollock, Rothko, Still, and Tomlin ("15 Americans"); Brooks, Francis, Guston, Kline, Lipton, and Rivers ("12 Americans"); Johns, Kelly, Leslie, Nevelson, Rauschenberg, Stankiewicz, Stella, and Youngerman ("Sixteen Americans"); and Bontecou, Marisol, Oldenburg, Reinhardt, and Rosenquist ("Americans 1963"). This list is, of course, subjectively drawn. Some might reasonably add Glarner, Hartigan, Indiana, and others; they might subtract Leslie, Lippold, Lipton, or Stankiewicz.

Of the artists who are now less well-known but who also contributed fine works to the program, I count Briggs, de Feo, Hedrick, and Higgins. Again, others would, no doubt, construct a different list.

250.   In addition to the one-person shows listed in n. 83 above, The Museum of Modern Art mounted the following exhibitions between 1961 and Miller's retirement in 1969: "Art of Assemblage" (1961; a survey including art from Marcel Duchamp to de Kooning, Rauschenberg, and Johns), "Recent Painting U.S.A.: The Figure" (1962), "The Intimate World of Lionel Feininger" (1963), "The Responsive Eye" (1965), "American Collages" (1965), "Rauschenberg: Thirty-four Drawings for Dante's Inferno" (1965), "Calder: Nineteen Gifts from the Artist" (1967), "The 1960s: Painting and Sculpture from the MoMA Collection" (1967), "Lionel Feininger: 'Ruin by the Sea'" (1967), "The Sidney and Harriet Janis Collection" (1968), "Art of the Real" (1968), "Rauschenberg: Soundings" (1968), "Ben Shahn, 1898–1969 (Memorial)" (1969), "The New American Painting and Sculpture: The First Generation" (1969), "Lucas Samaras: 'Book'" (1969), "Robert Motherwell: 'Lyric Suite'" (1969), "Claes Oldenburg" (1969), "A Salute to Alexander Calder" (1969), and "Spaces" (1969). The Whitney and Guggenheim museums also presented numerous one-person and group shows of U.S. during this period.

1. Loading cases in New York for the shipment of the U.S. representation to the IV Bienal de São Paulo, 1957

The Early Years of the International Program and Council

Helen M. Franc

At a meeting of the Board of Trustees of The Museum of Modern Art on April 10, 1952, its President, Nelson A. Rockefeller, announced that a foundation was giving favorable consideration to a tentative application from the Museum for a five-year grant of $125,000 per annum to establish a program of circulating exhibitions abroad, to be directed by Porter A. McCray, since 1947 Director of the Department of Circulating Exhibitions. A committee, with Wallace K. Harrison as Chairman, in consultation with McCray, formulated a program that was presented to the Board on June 12. It stipulated that if funds were made available, the Museum would initiate a five-year program of exhibitions presenting in foreign countries and the United States the most significant achievements of the art of our time, with the aim of promoting greater international understanding and mutual respect. The United States government, unlike those of other countries, had not recognized the need for this form of cultural exchange, but it was hoped that the Museum's initiative might ultimately lead to governmental support of a comparable program. Upon receipt of funds, the Museum, making use of the existing mechanism of the Department of Circulating Exhibitions, would begin at once the preparation of major exhibitions of contemporary American painting and sculpture, with special emphasis on the younger generation. These would be followed by exhibitions not only on the broader aspects of American culture but would also present the artists, accomplishments, and contributions of other nations.[1] Foreign agencies would be expected to cover the expenses of transportation, the printing of catalogues, and other costs incurred locally.

In setting forth the proposal, Rockefeller was in fact wearing two hats. He was not only President of the Museum's Board of Trustees but also the Treasurer and most active member of the foundation in question—the Rockefeller Brothers Fund (RBF). (It is not unusual for offers of funding from Museum Trustees to be made anonymously so that they can be objectively considered by the Board.) The Fund had been incorporated in 1940 by the brothers John D. Rockefeller 3rd, Nelson A., Laurance S.R., Winthrop, and David for the application of funds for charitable purposes.[2] Not surprisingly, the Museum's application for a grant quickly received a favorable response from the Foundation. A contract was signed between the RBF and the Museum establishing the International Program of Exhibitions, with an initial transfer of funds on July 29, 1952.

The Progenitors

The concept of this program had in fact been formulated through prior discussions among Nelson Rockefeller, the Museum's Director René d'Harnoncourt, and McCray, all of whom had previously worked together in areas relating to international cultural exchange and in various capacities at the Museum.

Of the five sons of Abby Aldrich Rockefeller (Mrs. John D. Rockefeller, Jr.), one of the three original founders, in 1929, of The Museum of Modern Art, it was Nelson who from his college days on had shared her enthusiasm for modern art. The year after the Museum opened, he became a member of the newly created Junior Advisory Committee, a group of bright young people eager to involve themselves actively in the affairs of the institution; in 1931, he became its Chairman.[3] The next year, at the age of twenty-three, he was elected to the Board of Trustees. He became, successively, the Museum's First Vice-President (1936–37), its Treasurer (1937–39), and its President (1939–41, 1946–50).

In 1937, in connection with the large oil holdings in Venezuela of the Creole Petroleum Company, of which he was a director, Rockefeller and a group of business associates made a twenty-nation tour of Latin America, which they found to be in a state of social unrest that made the region highly vulnerable to totalitarian influence. These concerns, shared with a number of businessmen and economists, led to the preparation in 1940 of a memorandum, "Hemisphere Economic Policy," outlining ways by which the United States, by competitively effective measures, should protect its interests in Latin America against totalitarian techniques.[4] Rockefeller personally delivered this memorandum to the White House on June 14, 1940, and in August, President Franklin Delano Roosevelt created the Office of the Coordinator of Inter-American Affairs (CIAA), with Rockefeller as its head.

The cultural program that the CIAA conducted from 1940 to 1944 included the dissemination of material to the Latin American press and radio, exchange scholarships, motion pictures, good-will tours, concerts, and art exhibitions. The funding of the agency, which was not appropriated by Congress but rather came from the President's own discretionary fund, was the first official monetary support for an American propaganda program.[5]

From December 1944 until August 1945, Rockefeller served as Assistant Secretary of State in charge of relations with the Latin American republics. In November 1950, President Harry S. Truman appointed him chairman of the International Development Advisory Board for the Point Four Program (Technical Cooperation Administration) under the State Department, charged with recommending policy and providing technical aid to underdeveloped areas in the world. He resigned a year later, stating that he believed he could "best serve the program of international economic development by again concentrating on the role of private initiative in this field of international cooperation."[6] In 1952, however, he accepted an appointment as Special Assistant to President Dwight D. Eisenhower for Cold War Strategy.

René d'Harnoncourt, a native of Austria, as a young man emigrated to Mexico in 1924. He soon became an expert in the arts and crafts of that country, and organized a large exhibition of its fine and applied arts from the fifteenth century to the present, which toured the United States from October 1930 to September 1931. He became a naturalized U.S. citizen in 1939. As general manager of the newly created

Indian Arts Board of the Department of the Interior, he codirected "Indian Art of the United States," shown at The Museum of Modern Art in 1941. Rockefeller so admired this show that he invited d'Harnoncourt to join the CIAA as Acting Director of its art activities. In several trips to Latin America, d'Harnoncourt helped in placing cultural attachés in embassies and in organizing exchange exhibitions, a number of which were contracted to The Museum of Modern Art.

In 1944, d'Harnoncourt joined the staff of the Museum as Director of the Department of Manual Industries and Vice-President in Charge of Foreign Activities, responsible for conducting relations with cultural organizations in the Latin American republics. In 1946, he became Chairman of the Coordination Committee, which had been established to run the institution—still without a director since the dismissal of Alfred H. Barr, Jr., in October 1943—and was also made Director of Curatorial Departments. In October 1949, he became Director of the Museum, a position for which Rockefeller presumably had been grooming him for years.

The third member of this coterie was Porter A. McCray, who had studied art history, museum administration, and architecture at Yale University, from which he received the degree of Bachelor of Arts in Architecture in 1941. After graduating, he went to work for Harrison, with whom he had taken courses in modern art at Yale. When Harrison was recruited by Rockefeller for the Office of the Coordinator of Inter-American Affairs, McCray moved with him to Washington and became an Exhibition Specialist in the agency. From late 1941 until October 1943, he served as Assistant to the Chief of the Art Section of the Cultural Relations Division. When in November 1943 the cultural exchange program was transferred to the National Gallery of Art under the direction of the Smithsonian Institution, McCray became Chief of its Inter-American Program.

In October 1944, McCray joined the American Field Service as a volunteer ambulance driver, and saw duty first in Europe and then in Asia. On returning to America, he resumed his professional career as an architectural designer with the firm of Harrison & Ambramowitz. In June 1947, he became Director of The Museum of Modern Art's Department of Circulating Exhibitions. He took a year's leave of absence from that position beginning in December 1950 to become an attaché in the U.S. Foreign Service, acting as Deputy Chief of Presentations and Publications in the European Headquarters of the Economic Cooperation Administration. As Rockefeller pointed out, McCray's wide experience in national and international cultural activities, and his diplomatic skills, made him uniquely qualified to become head of the proposed International Program.

Harrison, too, had numerous personal and professional connections with Rockefeller, d'Harnoncourt, and The Museum of Modern Art. He had a personal relationship with Rockefeller through his wife, the former Ellen Milton, who was a sister-in-law of John D. Rockefeller, Jr.'s daughter, Abby. In the 1930s he had executed several architectural projects for Rockefeller and had also frequently been involved in other of the family's projects. Through Nelson Rockefeller, Harrison also had a long-standing relationship with The Museum of Modern Art. In 1939, he was elected a Trustee of the Museum, serving through 1940; reelected in 1945, he remained on the Board until his death in 1981.

In 1940, Rockefeller made Harrison head of the Cultural Relations Division of the CIAA. When Rockefeller moved to the State Department as Assistant

Secretary of State for Inter-American Affairs, Harrison succeeded him as Director of what was renamed the Office of Inter-American Affairs—now placed under the State Department. These positions brought him into contact with d'Harnoncourt, who remained at the CIAA until 1943. As a Trustee of the Museum, Harrison would later deal frequently with d'Harnoncourt in the latter's successive positions at that institution, and, as already noted, he had a longstanding relationship with McCray. It is not surprising that this group of kindred spirits was able to formulate a program of international circulating exhibitions that would be accepted by the Museum's Board of Trustees almost immediately.

The Pre-History of the International Program

The Museum of Modern Art was a logical instrument for carrying out a program of international cultural exchange. Its collections, exhibitions, and publications had always been international in scope. Its Department of Circulating Exhibitions, established in 1933, had by 1952 sent out over 400 exhibitions with more than 7,000 showings at public and private organizations in the United States and Canada, and it had also sent a number of exhibitions to other countries. The earliest and by far the most ambitious of these was "Trois Siècles d'Art aux Etats-Unis," organized at the invitation of the French government and shown at the Musée du Jeu de Paume in Paris, May 24–July 31, 1938. The works were chosen by the Museum's President, A. Conger Goodyear, together with its Director, Barr, and members of the curatorial staff. The exhibition included painting and sculpture; drawings, watercolors, and prints; architecture; photography; film; and a special section of folk painting and sculpture. The works ranged in date from the Colonial period to the present, with the most recent examples presenting a cross-section of twentieth-century American art.[7]

The critical reaction to the show was mixed, the architecture, photography, and film screenings being by far the most favorably received. The consensus was that, except for the American primitives and folk artists, painting and sculpture from the United States was both derivative of European sources and for the most part of lower quality. The nineteenth-century works were regarded as dull, mediocre, and academic, and those of the twentieth century as confused, eclectic, and in no way distinctively "American." Many critics in the United States disapproved of the fact that a show meant to represent American art abroad should have been selected by a single institution, especially one committed to modernism, and like their European counterparts remarked that many of the artists were either foreign-born or the children of immigrants. Both here and abroad, the question was raised whether there was such a thing as American art and, if so, what characterized it.[8]

World War II brought striking changes to the Museum. Rockefeller recruited for various positions at the CIAA John Hay Whitney, Vice-Chairman of the Museum's Board of Trustees; John E. Abbott, Executive Vice-President; and Monroe Wheeler, Director of Exhibitions and Publications, all of whom carried on these offices as volunteers while continuing to fulfill their functions at the Museum. Whitney succeeded Rockefeller as President until commissioned a colonel in the Air Force in May 1942, at which time Stephen C. Clark took over as both President of the Museum and Chairman of the Board of Trustees.[9]

Preceding the United States' entry into the war, "Britain at War," a large exhibition of British paintings selected by Sir Kenneth Clark, Director of the National

2. Entrance to "Road to Victory," The Museum of Modern Art, New York, 1942

Gallery in London, was shown at The Museum of Modern Art from May until early September 1941, then was circulated nationally until 1944. On February 28, 1941, Whitney announced that "In the interest of national defense, The Museum of Modern Art will inaugurate a new program to speed the interchange of the art and culture of this hemisphere among all the twenty-one American Republics." Utilizing film, exhibitions of painting, sculpture, architecture, industrial and graphic design, as well as music, the program would seek to controvert "elements in Central and South America who are doing their best to minimize the achievements and the potentialities of the United States . . . trying to prove that there can be no common ground on which all the peoples of the Western Hemisphere can meet."[10]

In accordance with this initiative, in 1941 the Museum, in collaboration with the CIAA, the American Museum of Natural History, The Brooklyn Museum, and The Metropolitan Museum of Art, organized and circulated the most comprehensive exhibition of contemporary art from the United States ever seen in Latin America. Its 159 paintings and 110 watercolors were apportioned into three sections for showings in Mexico City, Santiago, Lima, and Quito; Buenos Aires, Montevideo, and Rio de Janeiro; and Bogotá, Caracas, and Havana. In 1942, at the instigation of the CIAA, the Museum announced a poster competition on the theme of the united front in the Western Hemisphere. The thirty winning designs chosen from more than 600 submissions from the twenty Latin American republics, the United States and its dependencies, and Canada, were exhibited at the Museum, put on view at the Ministry of Education in Havana, and then circulated in the United States through 1944.[11] "Brazil Builds," a large photographic exhibition organized in 1943 under the joint auspices of the Museum, the American Institute of Architects, and the CIAA, was sent by the CIAA to the Museo del Palacio de Bellas Artes in Mexico City following its showing at the Museum, then returned to the United States to tour domestically for three years.

Other wartime exhibitions included "Road to Victory" (fig. 2), seventy photo-panels showing the United States at war, with photographs selected by Lieutenant Commander Edward Steichen of the U.S. Naval Reserve, accompanied by a text by his brother-in-law, the poet Carl Sandburg.[12] "U.S Housing in War and Peace," prepared at the request of the Council of the Royal Institute of British Architects, surveyed the accomplishments and shortcomings of America's housing program before and during the war.[13] At the request of the Office of War Information (OWI), "America Builds" (fig. 3), a comprehensive survey of American architecture, housing, and city planning, was sent to Sweden to celebrate the twenty-fifth anniversary of the Swedish American Society in Stockholm and the American Scandinavian Foundation in New York.[14]

Altogether, the Museum executed thirty-eight contracts for various governmental agencies during the war years. Nineteen exhibitions of contemporary American painting were circulated throughout Latin America by the CIAA, and documentary films were also shown in that region. A total of fifty-six exhibitions and seventeen slide talks were sold for circulation in Haiti, Brazil, the British Isles, Ireland, India, Egypt, Australia, New Zealand, Spain, Czechoslovakia, Yugoslavia, Italy, Greece, Belgium, and South Africa.[15]

In November 1950, The Museum of Modern Art signed an agreement with the Museu de Arte Moderna, São Paulo, providing for mutual cooperation in loans, exhibitions, and educational activities. The Museum, with its Director as Commissioner, agreed to assume responsibility for organizing the U.S. representation at the I Bienal de São Paulo, in the fall of 1951. Andrew Carnduff Ritchie, Director of the Museum's Department of Painting and Sculpture, was chairman of the group of colleagues from the Modern, the Metropolitan Museum, the Whitney Museum of American Art, The Brooklyn Museum, and the Philadelphia Museum of Art that made the selection of paintings, sculptures, and prints ranging from realism to Abstract Expressionism.[16] Theodore Roszak's *Young Fury* (1948) received the Second Prize in Sculpture.

Through the practical experience gained from these activities, the Department of Circulating Exhibitions was well prepared to take on the new responsibilities of the International Program when it was inaugurated in 1952.

3. Crown Princess Louise, Prince Eugen, Anders Beckman, and Crown Prince Gustav Adolf of Sweden, and U.S. press attaché Karl Jensen, at the opening of "America Builds," Nationalmuseum, Stockholm, 1944

The Climate of the Times: Politics and Censorship

In 1952, the time was ripe for a private institution, concerned with quality and independent of government control or political pressure groups with their own agendas, to undertake the task of cultural interchange with other countries. The government had either foregone any responsibility for cultural exchange or had shown itself completely subservient to the Red-hunting forces in Congress—not only Senator Joseph McCarthy's relatively short-lived hearings of 1950–53 but also the much longer-lasting operations of the House Un-American Activities Committee (HUAC), established in 1946, which published lists of organizations it considered politically suspect; in David Halberstam's words, "The nation was ready for witch-hunts. . . . A peace that permitted Soviet hegemony over Eastern Europe was unacceptable to many Americans. There had to be an answer; there had to be a scapegoat."[17]

For the art world, the first alarm had been sounded in 1947, when Secretary of State George C. Marshall recalled from Prague and Port-au-Prince the two sections of the exhibition "Advancing American Art." Selected by the State Department's Visual Arts Specialist, J. Leroy Davidson, and prepared for circulation in Europe and Latin America, the exhibition was designed to present "a conceptual image of the United States as a nation of humanistic, unprejudiced, and strongly individual people."[18] When shown in the fall of 1946 at the Metropolitan Museum before being sent overseas, the exhibition precipitated a double-pronged attack of a kind that was to continue for many years: on the alleged left-wing affiliation of many of the artists, and on modern art itself. Representative Frank Busbey, Republican of Illinois, asserted that "more than twenty of the forty-five artists were New Deal in various shades of Communism."[19] Simultaneously, the style of the works was attacked. The Hearst newspapers were especially vociferous, abetted by conservative artists' organizations such as the American Artists Professional League, the National Academy of Design, the Salmagundi Club, and the Society of Illustrators, which labeled modern art "Communistic."[20] Matters were not improved when no less an authority than President Truman said of Yasuo Kuniyoshi's *Circus Girl Resting* (1925), "If that's art, I'm a Hottentot."[21] *Look* magazine published a spread of some of the more avant garde works in the exhibition, under the title "Your Money Bought These Paintings," and questioned whether taxpayers' money should support that kind of art; in fact, after the cancellation of the show, Marshall announced that there would be "no more taxpayers' money for modern art."[22]

In the midst of these attacks on modernism, the Boston Institute of Modern Art, on February 17, 1948, issued a "Statement of Principles," announcing that it was substituting the word "contemporary" for "modern" in its name, because modernism, it declared, had become "a cult of bewilderment."[23] At the annual meeting of the American Federation of Arts (AFA) in May 1948, d'Harnoncourt spoke in defense of modern art.[24]

Attacks on modern art and artists intensified throughout 1949. The most vociferous spokesman was George A. Dondero, Republican Representative from Michigan, who, in a series of harangues before the House Committee on Foreign Affairs, singled out specific artists, galleries, institutions, and organizations, "exposing" their "Communist" affiliations. In a speech of August 16, "Modern Art Shackled to Communism," he alleged that modern art sought "to destroy the high standards and priceless traditions of academic art." He listed six of the "isms" used by the Communists as "instruments and weapons of destruction: Cubism aims to destroy by designed disorder. Futurism aims to destroy by the machine myth. Dadaism aims to destroy by ridicule. Expressionism aims to destroy by aping the primitive and insane . . . Abstractionism aims to destroy by the creation of brainstorms. Surrealism aims to destroy by the creation of denial of reason." As the chief citadel of these nefarious movements, The Museum of Modern Art was a particular focus of his invective. Among its "crimes" was its espousal of practitioners of "abstractivism or non-objectivity . . . spawned as a simon-pure, Russian Communist product."[25]

The Cold War became increasingly heated on the rhetorical front as anti-Red hysteria mounted with the victories of Mao Tse-Tung's forces in China and the Soviet Union's explosion of an atom bomb in September 1949. In March 1950, reacting to attacks on modernism, The Museum of Modern Art, the Whitney Museum, and the now-penitent Institute of Contemporary Art in Boston jointly issued "A Statement on Modern Art," affirming their "belief in the continuing validity of what is generally known as modern art" and asserting "that the so-called 'unintelligibility' of some modern art is an inevitable result of its exploration of new frontiers."[26] The government itself began to react to the attacks of the extremists, which were inducing a growing animosity to the United States abroad and leading to disaffection even among its allies. In January 1945, the Senate had passed the Smith-Mundt Act, reorganizing and expanding the Information and Cultural Program, and in March 1950, twelve Senators proposed a resolution that called for a "world-wide Marshall plan in the field of ideas."[27] In September, staff members of the Bureau of the Budget issued a report, stating, "The value of international cultural interchange is to win respect for the cultural achievements of our free society. . . . Cultural affairs are an indispensable tool of propaganda."[28] Notwithstanding official endorsements of the value of freedom of expression, in 1952 the Attorney General began to issue listings of alleged subversives, which for years thereafter continued to be the criterion determining the artists whose works were deemed unacceptable.

•

This was the atmosphere that prevailed when the International Program was founded. Encouragement might have been found, however, when in August 1953 President Eisenhower established the United States Information Agency (USIA) as an independent organization responsible for all the country's information activities abroad. Its purpose was defined as being "to submit evidence to people of other nations . . . that the objectives and policies of the United States are in harmony with and will continue to advance their legitimate aspirations for freedom, progress, and peace" and to avoid "strident and propagandistic material."[29] Furthermore, in a statement titled "Freedom of the Arts," transmitted to The Museum of Modern Art on October 19, 1954, at the ceremonies inaugurating its Twenty-fifth Anniversary Year, the President declared, "Freedom of the arts is a basic freedom, one of the pillars of liberty in our land."[30]

Nonetheless, it was apparent that the State Department and the USIA had no intention either of committing themselves wholeheartedly to freedom of expression or of abandoning the blacklisting of artists. In a speech to the AFA in October 1953, A. H. Berding of the USIA proclaimed that "our government should not sponsor examples of our creative energy which are non-representational. . . . We are not interested in purely experimental art."[31] The agency also announced its intention of continuing to make the political associations of artists the basis for excluding their works from the exhibitions it sponsored.[32]

On October 22, 1954, the AFA, disturbed by several incidents affecting its selection of artists to be included in international circulating exhibitions that it was preparing in cooperation with the U.S. government, issued a "Statement on Artistic Freedom." It declared: "Freedom of artistic expression in a visual work of art, like freedom of speech and press, is fundamental to our democracy. This fundamental right exists irrespective of the artist's political or social opinions, affiliations or activities. . . . We believe that in this period of international tension . . . it is essential that our nation should . . . demonstrate that such artistic freedom and diversity are the most effective answers to totalitarian thought control and uniformity."[33]

One incident in particular had prompted the issuance of this statement. In 1952, the Director of the National Gallery of Art and President of the National Commission of Fine Arts, David E. Finley, had been appointed Commissioner for the U.S. representation at the XXVI Venice Biennale. Under his supervision, the AFA organized an exhibition of four artists, one of whom was Ben Shahn. Under pressure from the USIA, which was partially underwriting the show's expenses, Finley was forced to withdraw Shahn's works and substitute those of another artist.[34]

A particularly raucous controversy arose concerning "Sport in Art," a circulating exhibition of paintings, drawings, and prints from the nineteenth and twentieth centuries illustrating that theme, sponsored by the publishers of *Sports Illustrated* and scheduled for showing in December 1955 at the Dallas Museum of Fine Arts. Patriotic organizations in that city demanded that works by Leon Kroll, Kuniyoshi, Shahn, and William Zorach be withdrawn from "Sport in Art" and neither be shown nor acquired by the museum. Although that institution stood its ground and showed the exhibition in its entirety, the reactionary forces had nevertheless won a victory: Responding to the controversy, the USIA canceled the exhibition's projected tour of Australia, where it was to have been shown in the fall of 1956 during the Olympic Games.[35]

Soon thereafter, the USIA took an action that was to become a cause célèbre. Under a contract with the agency, the AFA had organized an exhibition of one hundred paintings by seventy-five artists, "surveying the major trends in American art from the turn of the twentieth century to the present, including representative examples from realism to abstraction."[36] The USIA declared that ten of the artists were "social hazards," but the AFA refused to alter its selection. When the agency's director sought guidance from the White House, it was decided to cancel the show because "overall program decisions dictate this action," and it was further indicated that from then on there would be no government sponsorship of overseas exhibitions that included paintings made after 1917 (a significant date because it was that of the Russian Revolution).[37]

By now, however, the conflict attracted national attention, even from within the government itself. Reacting to a *New York Times* article on the USIA's withdrawal of support for the AFA's exhibition, Senator Hubert H. Humphrey made a speech on June 23, 1956, in which he referred to President Eisenhower's espousal of freedom of the arts in his message to The Museum of Modern Art two years before. On July 3, Lloyd Goodrich, as Director of the AFA and Chairman of its Committee on Government and Art, drew the attention of Senator J. W. Fulbright of Arkansas, Chairman of the Senate's Foreign Relations Subcommittee, to another *New York Times* report of hearings held the preceding month, when the USIA had stated that its policy was not to include "paintings by politically suspect artists in any of its shows" and admitted that this policy had been adopted because of fear that opposition from "a substantial minority in Congress . . . might endanger the entire USIA program and its appropriations."[38]

President Eisenhower's 1954 statement on the freedom of the arts was also referred to in "An Open Letter to the President of the United States" signed by the publisher and the Chairman of the Board of *Arts* magazine, calling "attention to the recent actions by an agency of the executive branch of the government . . . that you will find to be the very antithesis of the principles announced by you."[39] Though there is no record of a reply to this letter, a slight easing of the Cold War began in 1956, when Eisenhower signed the International Cultural Exchange and Trade Fair Participation Act; and two years later came an agreement between the United States and the Soviet Union for an exchange of national exhibitions. Objections to blacklisted artists nevertheless continued sporadically.[40]

The International Program Is Launched

Thanks to the preliminary discussions, the International Program of Circulating Exhibitions was quick off the mark as soon as the initial installment of funds from the RBF became available in July 1952. The public was made aware of the grant and the Program on April 24, 1953, when John Hay Whitney, Chairman of the Museum's Board of Trustees, announced the opening that day at the Musée d'Art Moderne in Paris of the exhibition "12 Modern American Painters and Sculptors" and described about a dozen other shows underway or in preparation by the Program. He declared: "We at the Museum believe that modern American art has a special contribution to make in the exchange of creative ideas, and that a presentation of our best achievement can enhance the vigor of cultural life throughout the world."[41] On December 16, 1953, the International Program proudly presented at the Manhattan Storage and Warehouse building a "visual report" of its first nine months of operation, in a special showing for invited representatives of the art world, educational foundations, and the press. On view were four complete exhibitions—"Japanese Architecture," "The Skyscraper: U.S.A.," "The American Woodcut Today," and "Twenty-five American Prints—as well as samplings from "Japanese Calligraphy," "Built in U.S.A.: Postwar Architecture," and three additional exhibitions of original graphic work. Supplementing these displays were photographs of installations and events, press clippings from foreign countries, and the itineraries for "12 Modern American Painters and Sculptors," then on tour in Europe; "Seven American Watercolorists," assembled as the U.S. representation at the Second International Art Exhibition in Japan (1953); and the U.S. representation at the recently opened II Bienal de São Paulo. Material also was presented on "The Modern Movement in Italy: Architecture and Design," then traveling in the United States.

Since its inaugural exhibition the year before, the International Program by May 1954 had organized twenty-seven shows—twenty-two for circulation abroad and five for travel in the United States and Canada.[42] Among the most widely viewed was "12 Modern American Painters and Sculptors." Selected by Ritchie in consultation with his colleagues, the exhibition included fifty-six paintings in oil, watercolor, or gouache by nine artists— Ivan Le Lorraine Albright, Stuart Davis, Arshile Gorky, Morris Graves, Edward Hopper, John Kane, John Marin, Jackson Pollock, and Shahn—in addition to sculptures by Alexander Calder, Roszak, and David Smith. In his foreword to the catalogue, Ritchie wrote that his intent was to emphasize both the diversity of modern art in the United States and its individualistic quality. He expressed the hope that the European public would look on the exhibition as a group of works of art, and only secondarily as a collection of American works, for Western painting and sculpture belonged to one world.[43]

The exhibition was presented at the Musée National d'Art Moderne in Paris, April 24–June 8, 1953 (figs. 4, 5; see also p. 38, fig. 1), under the auspices of the French Ministry of Foreign Affairs and the Direction des Musées de France, with the collaboration of the Association Française d'Action Artistique and the U.S. Embassy. The gala opening was attended by d'Harnoncourt, who had installed the exhibition, and by McCray, as Director of the International Program. During its six-week showing, the exhibition attracted 8,500 visitors—"a higher attendance than any other

non-French show held at the Musée National d'Art Moderne in recent years," according to a United States Intelligence Service (USIS) dispatch.[44] It then went on to the Kunsthaus, Zürich; the Kunstsammlungen der Stadt Düsseldorf in West Germany (still under Allied occupation); the Liljevalchs Konsthall, Stockholm; and the Taidehalle, Helsinki, concluding its tour with a showing, February 13–March 7, 1954, at the Kunstnernes Hus, Oslo, an artist-owned cooperative gallery.

The press coverage everywhere was extensive, with a notable diversity of response in the respective countries. Disregarding Ritchie's plea in the catalogue foreword, many viewers sought in the work qualities they regarded as typically American—diversity, vitality, and the inclination for experimentation—while others found no distinctively American traits at all. In France, much of the comment was politically oriented; anti-Americanism was evident both in leftist organs and those of the extreme Right. The Swiss response to the show in Zurich was more temperate and free of political bias. The same was true in Sweden, where the show was welcomed not only as the first introduction to modern American art but also as a strong affirmation of American culture, correcting prejudices and misconceptions derived largely from the movies, the mass media, and advertising. The Public Affairs Office in Stockholm reported to the USIA in Washington, D.C., "It is safe to say that American culture has never before been given such an *éloge* by the Swedish press as on this occasion."[45] In Finland, the exhibition was welcomed for showing contemporary American art—completely unknown in that country previously—and again, independence, free experimentation, and vitality were found to be particularly "American" characteristics, though the art was judged to be in an immature stage of development and not as impressive as American literature.

The reception given to this inaugural show of the International Program made it clear that there was a keen interest in American art, whether it was regarded favorably or unfavorably, and an eagerness to see more of it; and that this manifestation had broadened the perception of this country's culture and enhanced its prestige.[46]

For the II Bienal de São Paulo in 1953, The Museum of Modern Art again

Left:
4. Jean Cassou, director, Musée National d'Art Moderne, and Darthea Speyer, Assistant Cultural Affairs Officer, U.S. Embassy, Paris, at the press opening of "12 Modern American Painters and Sculptors," Musée National d'Art Moderne, Paris, 1953

Right:
5. René d'Harnoncourt (right) at the press opening of "12 Modern American Painters and Sculptors"

assumed responsibility for the U.S. representation, with d'Harnoncourt once more Commissioner. It consisted of three shows: forty-five works by Calder; paintings by sixteen artists ranging from William Baziotes and Willem de Kooning to Alton Pickens and Shahn; and the Latin American version of "Built in U.S.A.: Postwar Architecture."[47] That these exhibitions were organized by a private institution and not a governmental agency did not go unnoticed. An article by Aline B. Louchheim in the *New York Times Magazine* of January 3, 1954—titled "Cultural Diplomacy: An Art We Neglect—How United States Artists Might Win Friends and Influence Allies is Shown in a South American Exhibit"—was read into the record of the Congressional hearings on Federal Grants for Fine Arts Projects on January 18:

Artistically, we could hold up our heads. Our main drawing card was the exhibition of mobiles by Alexander Calder. But what kind of impression did we make? In the first place, everyone was aware that our exhibition was not sponsored by our government. They knew not only that it had been selected by The Museum of Modern Art and installed by its director, René d'Harnoncourt, who served as the American commissioner, but also that it had been paid for out of that institution's Rockefeller Brothers Fund. Although certain members of the State Department came to the official opening as individuals, the American Ambassador neither appeared nor sent a duly authorized delegate to stand with a receiving line in the American exhibition as his colleagues did . . . for the other leading countries. Unfortunately, the lack of official sponsorship surprised neither Europeans nor South Americans; they all speak quite openly of our woeful indifference to culture and specifically of the attitude of our Congress and State Department toward modern art. Those foreigners who are friendly . . . watch the Communists capitalize on it and are powerless to defend us. . . .[48]

Founding of the "Original" International Council

In the late spring and early summer of 1953, discussions took place at the Museum about the founding of an auxiliary organization of community leaders throughout the United States and abroad, interested in furthering the role of modern art in contemporary society, whose annual dues would support a program of cultural exchange. Three men—Rockefeller, d'Harnoncourt, and McCray—had been the progenitors of the International Program. In establishing this new organization, two women—Mrs. John D. Rockefeller 3rd, and Elizabeth (Eliza) Bliss Parkinson—took the lead.

Blanchette Ferry Hooker had married John D. Rockefeller 3rd in 1932. As the daughter-in-law of Abby Aldrich Rockefeller and the sister-in-law of Nelson, she was inevitably exposed to modern art and the activities of the Museum. Her first official connection with it, however, did not come until 1949, when Nelson Rockefeller, then its President, wishing to involve younger people in its operations, urged her to chair a new group, the Junior Council, composed of volunteers eager to explore ways in which the Museum could be of greater service to the community. In the late 1940s, she had begun collecting art in her own right, her first enthusiasm being for the Abstract Expressionists,[49] and installed her artworks in a carriage house on East 52nd Street that had been converted to a Guest House for this purpose by Philip Johnson. (She donated the Guest House to the Museum in 1958.) She was therefore ideally suited to become a supporter of the Museum's contemporary pro-

6. "12 Modern American Painters and Sculptors" being unpacked in New York following its six-city European tour, 1954

grams. In 1952, she was elected to the Board of Trustees.

Eliza Bliss, as a niece of Lillie P. Bliss, one of the three founders of the Museum, had been exposed to modern art from an early age and immersed in the Museum's affairs from the time of its founding in 1929, when she was twenty-two. Her father, Cornelius N. Bliss, was a member of the Museum's first Board of Trustees. After his death, Eliza's mother married Conger Goodyear, President of The Museum of Modern Art from its founding until 1939.

Eliza Bliss had been a friend of Nelson Rockefeller since childhood. In 1930, he had invited her to join the Museum's Junior Advisory Committee. She became one of its most enthusiastic members, with a special interest in developing educational programs, though after her marriage to John Parkinson in 1932, removal to Long Island, and birth of her children, she became less active in its affairs. She was elected to succeed her stepfather, Goodyear, as a Trustee of the Museum upon his death in 1939.

Long interested in music, Mrs. Parkinson had become a member of the Metropolitan Opera Guild, organized in 1935 to publicize, supplement, and contribute funds and equipment for the Metropolitan's events and programs. Believing that the Museum should have something similar, she broached the idea to d'Harnoncourt. With his and Rockefeller's encouragement, she was enlisted to join Blanchette Rockefeller in launching what was to become the International Council.

A Committee for the Formation of the National Council of the Museum of Modern Art was established, with Mrs. Rockefeller as Chairman. At a meeting on June 23, 1953, the proposed organization was described and its name changed from "National" to "International" Council.[50] The regular members were not to exceed one hundred in number, and their annual dues would be $1,000. There would also

7. The United States Pavilion at the XXVII Venice Biennale, 1954, with David Smith's *Hudson River Landscape* (1951) in the foreground

be non–dues-paying Honorary Members, elected for their demonstrated interest in cultural exchange. By-laws adopted on July 29 defined the Council's purpose: ". . . to develop international understanding in the field of the arts, and especially in the field of contemporary art, through the international exchange of exhibitions and the holding of national and international conferences."[51]

Establishment of the International Council was formally approved by the Museum's Board of Trustees October 8, 1953, and on May 4, 1954, the Council's first official meeting took place. Its Charter members, all but three of whom were from New York City, included four of the Museum's Trustees as officers—Mrs. Rockefeller, Chairman; Mrs. Parkinson, Vice-Chairman; Ralph F. Colin, Treasurer; and Wallace Harrison, Secretary—and seven additional members.

The Museum's Twenty-fifth Anniversary Year: Participation of the Program and the Council

On October 19, 1954, The Museum of Modern Art initiated the celebration of its Twenty-fifth Anniversary Year. With the theme "The World of Modern Art," it involved an accelerated program of exhibitions, publications, and events, as well as a fund-raising drive.[52]

The previous March, the Museum's President, William A.M. Burden, had announced the purchase from the Grand Central Galleries, New York, of the United States Pavilion at the Venice Biennale, to insure the continued representation of art from the United States at this important international festival. This was the only pavilion privately owned among twenty others owned by national governments, and because of its poor condition, it required considerable refurbishing. Responsibility for organizing the U.S. representation at the forthcoming XXVII Biennale was entrusted to the International Program, with d'Harnoncourt serving as U.S. Commissioner, but it was stated that other leading institutions would be invited to cooperate in the organization of future exhibitions.[53]

A staff committee consisting of Barr, Ritchie, and Museum Trustee James Thrall Soby, a member of the International Council and a former Director of the Department of Painting and Sculpture, decided to send to the Biennale twenty-seven works by de Kooning; fifty paintings, drawings, prints, and posters by Shahn; and three sculptural works—a welded bronze by Ibram Lassaw, a bronze by Gaston Lachaise, and a steel construction by Smith (fig. 7). The President of the Italian Republic officially opened the exhibition on June 15, 1954, in the presence of the ambassadors and ministers of the thirty-two participating countries, among them, U.S. Ambassador Claire Boothe Luce, who had angrily denounced the selection of "a Communist and [a] foreigner"—referring to Shahn and de Kooning, respectively— and forbidden the staff of the USIA to render any assistance whatsoever.[54] (Shahn had long since been absolved of the charges of being a Communist, and de Kooning, though not yet a naturalized citizen, had emigrated from the Netherlands in 1926 at the age of twenty-two and had lived, painted, and taught in the United States since then.) The International Council made a travel grant to Shahn so that he might attend the opening, and allocated funds providing for a representative to be present at the Pavilion to distribute catalogues and to answer inquiries from the press and the public.

The role of the International Program in presenting the art of the United States overseas was complemented by its exhibition domestically of art from other countries to familiarize the American public with foreign cultural achievements. The first such exhibition was "The Modern Movement in Italy: Architecture and Design," organized by the architectural historian Ada Louise Huxtable and presented through photographic enlargements, plans, and photographs. The exhibition appeared in two cities in Canada and three in the United States before being shown at the Museum, August 18–September 6, 1954; it then went again on tour throughout the United States until 1958.

Two other incoming exhibitions were devoted to architecture. "The Architecture of Japan," assembled by Arthur Drexler, Curator of the Department of Architecture and Design, featured photographs of buildings and gardens from ancient times to the present made available through the Japanese Consulate in New York in cooperation with the Japanese Ministry of Foreign Affairs and the Society for Cultural Relations. Concurrently, a completely furnished Japanese house, re-creating sixteenth- to seventeenth-century prototypes, was made in Nagoya and shipped to the United States as a gift from the America-Japan Society of Tokyo. Reassembled and erected in the Museum's Abby Aldrich Rockefeller Sculpture Garden (fig. 8), it remained for two summers as a feature of the Anniversary Year.

The opening of the second exhibition, "Latin American Architecture Since 1945," planned as a key event in the Anniversary Year, had to be postponed until November 1955. Organized by the International Program in cooperation with the Department of Architecture and Design, it embodied the results of a six-week trip by the architectural historian Henry-Russell Hitchcock and the photographer Rosalie Thorne McKenna, who had been commissioned by the International

Program to make this survey. Assembled and installed by Drexler, the exhibition presented forty-seven buildings by fifty-six architects in ten countries and Puerto Rico, through plans, large-scale photo-panels, and three-dimensional color slides in individual viewers. After three showings in the United States and Canada in 1956–57, the exhibition, with its explanatory texts translated into Spanish, began a tour of Latin America.

Probably no more colorful exhibition has ever been seen at The Museum of Modern Art than "Textiles and Ornamental Arts of India" (fig. 9), the most comprehensive showing of that country's traditional and contemporary folk arts ever presented in the United States. It was directed by Monroe Wheeler, who utilized material selected by Edgar J. Kaufmann, Jr., director of the Museum's Good Design program, and the noted architect and designer Alexander Girard, during a six-week trip to India, England, and Europe, and from museums and private collections in the United States. Rare historic fabrics and ornaments, jewels, enamels, and jade from the sixteenth and seventeenth centuries, as well as contemporary textiles and jewelry from Indian bazaars, were gathered with the assistance of the All India Handicrafts Board and installed in the form of an imaginary bazaar or marketplace designed by Girard. During its five-month showing from April to September 1955 it attracted over 300,000 visitors.

While carrying out its planned activities for the Anniversary Year, the International Program was faced with an unforeseen challenge when given the responsibility of organizing two major exhibitions for the "Salute to France," a program of cultural events arranged in response to a request from the French Ministry of Foreign Affairs and presented in Paris under the auspices of the U.S. Embassy. At the request of Ambassador Douglas Dillon, the Museum's President, Burden, was charged with arranging the Salute's visual arts events, and Robert W. Dowling,

Left:
8. René d'Harnoncourt, Japanese Prime Minister Shigeru Yoshida, and John D. Rockefeller 3rd, in front of the Japanese Exhibition House in the Abby Aldrich Rockefeller Sculpture Garden, The Museum of Modern Art, New York, 1954

Right:
9. Canopy enclosing jewelry, installed by Alexander Girard, in the exhibition "Textiles and Ornamental Arts of India," The Museum of Modern Art, New York, 1954

Chairman of the Board of the American National Theatre and Academy (ANTA), was placed in charge of the performance arts programs.

"De David à Toulouse-Lautrec," a selection of masterpieces of French paintings and drawings of the nineteenth and early twentieth centuries from public and private American collections, was organized at the invitation of the French Ministry of Foreign Affairs. In a press conference following a meeting at the White House on January 19, 1955, Ambassador Dillon revealed plans for this exhibition and stressed President Eisenhower's personal interest in it.

The General Committee for "De David à Toulouse-Lautrec" included sixty-seven museum officials and collectors from throughout the country; the nine-person Selection Committee was headed by Soby. Under McCray as Secretary to the Committee, the International Program assumed responsibility for all organizational arrangements. The loans included such striking paintings as Jacques-Louis David's portrait of Napoleon of 1810–12, from the National Gallery of Art in Washington, D.C.; Pierre-Auguste Renoir's *Luncheon of the Boating Party* (1881), from the Phillips Collection, Washington, D.C.; Edouard Manet's *Woman with a Parrot* (1886), from The Metropolitan Museum of Art; Vincent van Gogh's *Starry Night* (1889) and Henri Rousseau's *Sleeping Gypsy* (1897), from the Museum's own collection; and Paul Cézanne's *Bathers* (1892–1902), from the Philadelphia Museum of Art. The drawings were of no less outstanding quality. During the ten-and-a-half-week period that the exhibition was on view, it attracted more than 188,000 visitors, breaking all records for attendance at the Musée de l'Orangerie (fig. 10). The press coverage was universally enthusiastic, and the exhibition was hailed as the overwhelming success of the entire "Salute to France." The high level of connoisseurship was praised, and it was noted that American collectors had acquired works of the Impressionists before officials and most collectors in France had perceived their importance. Significantly, however, the Communist daily *Humanité* gave the exhibition no coverage whatsoever, and the Communist weekly *Lettres Françaises* published a highly laudatory review without mentioning the auspices under which it was held or the fact that the works of art were lent from American collections.[55]

"50 Ans d'Art aux Etats-Unis," the second exhibition prepared for the "Salute to France," was organized in response to a request from Jacques Jaujard of the Ministere de l'Education Nationale, Paris, for a show of modern American art, was the largest exhibition of modern art from the United States ever to have been sent abroad. Installed at the Musée National d'Art Moderne, it consisted of a cross-section of American works from each of the departmental collections in The Museum of Modern Art, selected by its curators under the general supervision of d'Harnoncourt[56] (fig. 11). Dorothy C. Miller, Curator of Museum Collections, chose 108 paintings and 22 sculptures by seventy artists representing several categories of modern American art: 1) an older generation of founders of the modern movement in the United States; 2) realist artists; 3) romantic painters of the American scene; 4) contemporary abstract painters; and 5) self-taught "primitives." The eighty-two prints by forty-eight artists were divided between "Six Painter-Printmakers, 1900–1925" and "Contemporary Printmaking in the United States." Architecture was represented by seventeen buildings designed since 1946, selected by Arthur Drexler, and shown through photographs, plans, models, and stereoscopic color slides (see p. 47, fig. 9). More than seventy examples of graphic design emphasized

10. Poster for "De David à Toulouse-Lautrec," outside the Musée de l'Orangerie, Paris, 1955

new ideas in typography, while some 150 objects of mass-produced industrial design were chosen to demonstrate that good design and aesthetic merit are independent of price. Approximately one hundred photographs ranged from observed reality to abstract images (see p. 47, fig. 10). Panels of film stills were supplemented by five weekly programs of narrative, experimental, and documentary films, which were screened at the USIS and the Cinéma Lux des Amis de l'Art. The exhibition was installed by d'Harnoncourt and McCray, assisted by Miller and Drexler. A grant from the International Council enabled Richard Lippold to travel to Paris to install his construction, *Variation No. 7: Full Moon* (1949–50).[57]

Though understandably the exhibition did not receive the universal accolades given to "De David à Toulouse-Lautrec," the press coverage was extensive and, with the exception of a few blatantly chauvinist or markedly reactionary critics, showed a real desire to understand American art. Only the "primitive" painters such as Kane were regarded as "pure" and indigenous artists; otherwise, the bewildering diversity of styles and the striking contrast among them did not appear to the writers to result in a truly American expression. "America is, of course, a hash of different people. . . . Accordingly, there is a turmoil of European or even Asiatic influences," wrote René Brécy in the Royalist weekly *Aspect: de la France.*[58] A predilection for what was seen as violent and tormented expressionism, an overstriving for originality, or technical carelessness, was contrasted with the balanced, rational, and finished qualities of French painting. The Abstract Expressionist works in particular were characterized by Maurice Armand in the extreme rightist weekly *Rivarol* (May 5, 1955) as "a mélange of daubs, over-exaggeration and insanity."[59]

11. Eliza Bliss Parkinson, René d'Harnoncourt, Darthea Speyer, and Dorothy Miller (far right) at the opening of "50 Ans d'Art aux Etats-Unis," Musée National d'Art Moderne, Paris, 1955

In general, the sculpture was more highly regarded than the painting, the familiar Calder being especially popular. Prints were praised for their technical proficiency and skillful experimentation, and photography, too, won esteem for its technical mastery, eye for the novel, and interesting subjects. The most highly acclaimed section, however, was that devoted to architecture, for its installation and presentation as well as for the buildings themselves. Frank Lloyd Wright's tower for the Johnson Wax Company was the most admired. The inclusion of architecture, typographic design, and photography, generally not displayed in European art museums, drew comment. The harshest strictures for the inclusion of utilitarian design objects came from the Left. Pierre Descargues wrote in the pro-Communist weekly *Lettres Françaises* (April 4, 1955), "An extensive section has been given over to saucepans, lemon-squeezers, can openers, and plastic chairs. . . . Only a Cadillac, a jet plane, and an H-bomb are lacking but will undoubtedly be included another time."[60]

Following the showing in Paris, the painting, sculpture, and print sections of the exhibition, together on most occasions with one or more of the other sections, traveled to Zurich, Barcelona, Frankfurt, London, The Hague, Vienna, and Belgrade under the title "Modern Art in the United States: A Selection from the Collections of the Museum of Modern Art."[61] D'Harnoncourt provided a new and appropriate introduction for each of the accompanying catalogues.

The showing in Barcelona was requested by the U.S. Embassy in Madrid, which asked The Museum of Modern Art to submit the exhibition as the U.S. representation at the III Bienal Hispánoamericana de Arte. It was presented at two venues, the Palacio de la Virreina and the Museo de Arte Moderna, under the joint auspices of the Instituto de Cultura Hispánica in Madrid, with the assistance of the

U.S. Embassy and the Consulate in Barcelona.[62] A concurrent display of about seventy Museum publications on American art aroused so much interest that it was repeated for each showing, and sets of the books were deposited in an appropriate library in each city. In Barcelona, which early in the century had been an active center of modernism, critics welcomed the exhibition with cordiality and without the chauvinism manifested in France.[63] Enthusiasm for it was instrumental in causing the mayor of the city to pass a budget that included funds with which to convert the Palacio de la Virreina into a new museum of modern art.

"Modern Art in the United States" was shown at the Haus des deutschen Kunsthandwerk in Frankfurt-am-Main under the joint auspices of the Staedelschen Kunstinstitut, the City of Frankfurt, and the USIS (fig. 12). All local arrangements were made by the agency, which published the catalogue, handled publicity, distributed 15,000 handbills to local hotels, schools, travel bureaus, and art-book dealers, and provided an eight-minute television film and newsreels that were shown in 1,750 theaters throughout West Germany. This intensive effort resulted in attracting an attendance of 16,000 during the month the show was on view. American art was found in general to manifest optimism and a belief in progress specific to the New World, in contrast to European art, which expressed despair and *Weltschmerz*. A thorough lambasting of the show was delivered, however, in an unsigned article in the Communist *Sozialistische Volkszeitung* titled "The Art of the Millionaire," which, noting the presence of Ambassador James B. Conant and Rockefeller (as Special Assistant to President Eisenhower), said that the exhibition was a pretext for demonstrating "the freedom-loving United States—an oxymoron, in view of Lenin's thesis that 'no artist can be free in a society which is governed by the power of money'"; the show represented only the viewpoint of the "upper class."[64]

The paintings, sculptures, and prints in "Modern Art in the United States" were shown at The Tate Gallery in London, January 5–February 12, 1956, under the joint auspices of the Gallery and the Arts Council of Great Britain, and in cooperation with the U.S. Embassy (see pp. 46–47, figs. 3–8). Two American authorities, Shahn and the art historian Meyer Schapiro, were invited by the Institute of Contemporary Arts to deliver lectures; their travel expenses were paid by the International Council and the U.S. State Department, respectively. This was the first major exhibition of contemporary American art to be presented in Britain; it attracted an average daily attendance of 1,300 and drew widespread attention in the press, both in England and Scotland and in Bermuda, Canada, and Australia. The first articles to appear evinced admiration for the earlier masters of modernism or more familiar abstractionists such as Marin and Davis, whereas the recent work, especially that of the Abstract Expressionists, was the subject of heated discussion and generally negative or antagonistic comments. Many later reviews by professional critics, however, stressed the diversity, novelty, and vitality of the work, as well as its provocative nature, the "almost reckless spirit of investigation, of inquiry."[65]

The invitation to show "Modern Art in the United States" at the Secession Galerie in Vienna was extended jointly by the Wiener Secession and the USIS; the architectural section was also under the auspices of the Zentralvereinigung der Architekten. The photography section was installed concurrently in the Neue Galerie at Linz, in cooperation with the Amerika Haus. The total attendance in Vienna was 8,749, and in Linz, 3,700. D'Harnoncourt, a native of Austria, was a speaker at the

12. Posters for "Modern Art in the United States: A Selection from the Collections of the Museum of Modern Art," outside the USIS information center, Frankfurt, 1955

opening and later delivered a lecture on The Museum of Modern Art and its activities.

Belgrade had not been on the original itinerary of the exhibition but was added when representatives of the Yugoslav Committee for Foreign Cultural Relations and personnel from the U.S. Embassy visited the show while it was in Vienna and expressed an urgent desire to present it in Yugoslavia. The exhibition was on view July 6–August 6, 1956, under the auspices of the Committee in cooperation with the U.S. Embassy. As this was the first exhibition of modern American art to be seen in a Communist (though not Iron Curtain) country, it aroused great interest. At the request of the USIS in Belgrade, the International Program prepared a special exhibition on the Museum's activities, which was later circulated to other cities in the country; the USIS also displayed photographic panels of the exhibition in the vitrines outside its center in Zagreb.

In marked contrast to their attitude of previous years, the U.S. foreign service officers cordially welcomed "Modern Art in the United States" throughout its entire tour and rendered many services, being particularly helpful in assisting the International Program in its negotiations with local authorities. The USIS was especially cooperative, frequently contributing to the costs of transportation and the printing of catalogues, and energetically publicizing the exhibition through leaflets, wall newspapers, radio interviews, newsreels, and television programs.

Particularly important was the USIA's purchase from the International Program of four near-replicas of the extraordinarily popular exhibition "The Family of Man" for worldwide circulation.[66] (In 1958, it would acquire the original exhibition, which had been circulating domestically, for additional showings in foreign countries.) On January 31, 1954, the Museum had announced that this international photographic exhibition would be a major feature of the Twenty-Fifth Anniversary program, inviting photographers from all over the world to submit for consideration prints consistent with the theme of the project. Stressing that The Museum of Modern Art was the first museum to make photography an important part of its program, Edward Steichen, Director of the Department of Photography since 1947, stated that "The Family of Man" was to portray "the universal elements and emotions and the oneness of human beings throughout the world" and would "be created in a passionate spirit of love and faith in man."[67] Shown at the Museum for three and a half months, it attracted 270,000 visitors before embarking on its worldwide tour.

The USIA assumed full responsibility for the itineraries of the copies it had purchased and for arranging the auspices under which they would be presented. Local USIS bureaus went to great pains to publicize the exhibition and ensure its success wherever it was shown. In 1959, at the request of the USIA, one copy of the exhibition was temporarily withdrawn from domestic circulation so that it might be refurbished with the aid of a grant from the RBF and sent to Moscow as part of the summer-long American National Exhibition in Sokolniki Park.[68] The catalogue accompanying "The Family of Man" included a greeting from President Eisenhower, who stated that it was his "fervent wish" that by means of the American National Exhibition "the people of our two great nations may gain a better understanding of one another. Thus can the foundations be strengthened for our cooperation in the achievement of mankind's greatest goal—a fruitful and flourishing world at peace."[69]

Some contributions that the fledgling International Council made to the celebration of the Twenty-fifth Anniversary Year have already been mentioned. Its most important contribution was the First Annual Conference of the International Council, in May 1955, which was scheduled to coincide with the simultaneous openings at The Museum of Modern Art and the Whitney Museum (then housed in an adjacent building) of the twin "New Decade" exhibitions, devoted to postwar painting and sculpture in Europe and the United States, respectively. The central feature of the Conference was a symposium on "International Exchange in the Arts," during which George F. Kennan, recently returned from the Soviet Union, where he had served as U.S. Ambassador from 1952 to 1954, delivered an address. Kennan stressed the importance to the United States of international cultural exchange in the arts by helping to eradicate impressions of this country as "a nation of vulgar, materialistic *nouveaux riches* . . . contemptuous of every refinement of aesthetic feeling. . . . What we have to do . . . is to show the outside world both that we have a cultural life and that we care enough about it, in fact, to give it encouragement and support here at home, and to see that it is enriched by acquaintance with similar activity elsewhere."[70]

1956—A Critical Year

Nineteen fifty-six was a critical year for both the International Program and the International Council. The fact that the five-year grant from the Rockefeller Brothers Fund was due to expire in June of the following year gave rise to three questions: 1) If the Program were to continue, how would it be financed? 2) What, if anything, should be the responsibility of the Council in this regard? and 3) How should the future relations between the Program and the Council be defined and integrated?

As Chairman of the Council's Ad-Hoc Committee on Foreign Activities appointed to deal with these questions, Nelson Rockefeller, at the Second Annual Meeting of the Council on May 25, stressed the importance of retaining programs of international cultural exchange in private hands, free from government interference. Stating that he believed the RBF should not carry the load to the extent that it had heretofore, he suggested that the Council should no longer be merely an auxiliary body but should rather become the guiding national group, enlisting the cooperation of other museums in international cultural exchange. It was suggested that changing the name from "The International Council *of* The Museum of Modern Art" to "The International Council *at* The Museum of Modern Art" might better convey the national composition of its membership.

Rockefeller emphasized that it would be extremely costly to attempt to replicate the space, staff, and services now being contributed to the Program by the Museum, and that it would also be a mistake for the Council to lose the valuable asset of the Museum's prestige, experienced personnel, and high standards. It was particularly essential that there be one central authority to negotiate with government agencies and institutions abroad. He therefore recommended that the Museum continue to act as central coordinating agency, with its administrative responsibilities handled on a contractual basis, as had been done with the CIAA during the war.[71]

In accordance with the suggestions made at this meeting, it was jointly agreed by the Museum and the Council that the organization's name be changed to "The International Council at The Museum of Modern Art." A Certificate of Incorporation, supplanting the existing charter, was filed with the Office of the Secretary of

State of New York on December 13, 1956.[72] At the first meeting of the newly incorporated Council the following day, announcement was made of the agreement concluded among the Museum, the RBF, and the Council. This stipulated that during each of the twelve-month periods beginning July 1, 1957, and ending June 30, 1962, the Fund would contribute decreasing amounts for support of the Program, and the Council would use its best efforts to increase its contribution gradually, so that by the end of the 1962 fiscal year the RBF would provide $30,000 and the Council would endeavor to raise $125,000.

1957—A Year of Continuity and Change

In 1957, three exhibitions were arranged as the U.S. representations at recurring international festivals. With the aid of a special grant from the Ford Foundation, Sam Hunter, Associate Curator of the Museum's Department of Painting and Sculpture, selected the representation for the III International Contemporary Art Exhibition, organized by the All-India Fine Arts and Crafts Society under the auspices of the government of India. Chosen were thirteen paintings by nine American artists—Davis, Gorky, Adolph Gottlieb, Hartigan, de Kooning, Pollock, Mark Rothko, Niles Spencer, and Mark Tobey—all executed within the preceding fifteen years and preponderantly in various abstract styles not previously exhibited in India. The festival, in which twenty-nine countries participated, opened in New Delhi in February and then traveled to Ahmedabad, Hyderabad, Calcutta, Bombay, and Amritsar. The U.S. representation was well received and, according to the critics of the *Times of India* (February 24, 1957), "topped all others in merit."[73]

The Fourth International Art Exhibition, Japan, at the National Museum of Modern Art in Tokyo was sponsored by the Mainichi Newspapers of Japan with the cooperation of the Japanese Ministry of Foreign Affairs. In accordance with their request that the U.S. representation consist of work by younger artists, the poet Frank O'Hara, then on the staff of the International Program, selected one painting apiece by fifteen artists, among them, Richard Diebenkorn, Sam Francis, Helen Frankenthaler, and Cy Twombly. These works, all executed within the preceding four years, represented a broad diversity of styles and genres. Francis's *Black in Red* (1953) received one of the five prizes awarded by the international jury to non-Japanese artists. Following a three-week showing in Tokyo beginning May 23, where it attracted about 70,000 visitors, the exhibition traveled to eight cities in Japan.

With the termination of the original five-year grant from the RBF on June 30, 1957, the International Council assumed sponsorship of the International Program. The first major exhibition to be sponsored abroad under its auspices was the U.S. representation at the IV Bienal de São Paulo, September–December 1957. Barr served as U.S. Commissioner and as a member of the international jury. The two-part exhibition included a retrospective of thirty-four paintings and twenty-nine drawings by Pollock, who had died the previous year; and twenty-three paintings by James Brooks, Philip Guston, Hartigan, Franz Kline, and Larry Rivers, and fifteen sculptures by David Hare, Lassaw, and Seymour Lipton—all selected by O'Hara in consultation with McCray, Soby, Miller, and Hunter. McCray, aided by Waldo Rasmussen, Assistant Circulation Manager of the International Program, installed both exhibitions. The USIS cooperated by translating, mimeographing, and distributing publicity material and arranging screenings of a color film on Pollock. The top acquisition prize went to Lipton, and the retrospective of Pollock's works (which was not eligible for a prize, since only living artists could compete) received a special *hors de concours* award.

The U.S. representation won high acclaim.[74] An anonymous writer in *O Estado do São Paulo* (October 20, 1957) declared: "The American contribution has been a great stimulus as well as a conscious gesture of gratitude to the Bienal[;] . . . strikingly carried out, it is worthy of the highest praise." In *Correio de Manha* (September 7, 1957), Jayme Mauricio pronounced Pollock's work "one of the high points of the Bienal . . . ," which offered "the opportunity to see his gigantic canvases in rare juxtaposition, didactically illustrating one of the significant aspects of art in the last decades." In *O Estado de São Paulo,* in an article titled "The Two Faces of Tachism" (September 18, 1957), Farreiro Gullar compared Pollock favorably with the European exponents of that movement.[75] Whereas Pollock's work "had a significant vitality and . . . was oriented toward form and structure[,] . . . leading inevitably toward construction and order," his European counterparts were "umbilically linked to the traditional ways of painting, with brushes, on a canvas in its normal position. . . . [The American artists] seem to believe in the metaphysical essence of figurative language . . . [and] that these fragments have a meaning of their own independent of any relation to the whole."

Among the sculptors, Lipton, the prizewinner, found widespread acceptance. The anonymous critic in *O Estado de São Paulo* found that the "infinity of Lipton's spatial scuptures, mysteriously fashioned of interlocking forms, reveals a mystical spirit concerned with introspective research." A dissenting voice was that of Lauricio Gomes Machado, who in an article titled "The Aspect of the New," also in *O Estado de São Paulo* (October 5, 1957), referred to "the unsupportable Lipton," declaring, ". . . although [Lipton] may make a maquette of metal foil, the result will never be sculpture, if the fragility of the material is passed on to the work itself." He had similarly harsh words for Lassaw, who he determined would "never be a sculptor."

•

At the meeting of the Council's Executive Committee in New York on October 7, 1957, Mrs. Rockefeller announced that, while remaining on the Board of Directors, she would not be available for reelection as President. August Heckscher, Director of the Twentieth Century Fund and a Director of the Council, succeeded her as Chairman of the Board;[76] the Council's Vice-President, Mrs. Parkinson, named Acting President, was elected President the following month.

The First Annual Meeting of the newly incorporated International Council at The Museum of Modern Art was held in San Francisco November 6–9,[77] to coincide with the Sixth National Conference of the U.S. National Commission for the United Nations Educational, Scientific, and Cultural Organization (UNESCO), which the Council members were invited to attend as special delegates. This invitation came as thanks to the Council for accepting the proposal of Mrs. Henry Potter Russell of San Francisco, a Director of the Council and a member of the United States National Commission for UNESCO, to take responsibility on behalf of the United States for planning and decorating the Executive Board Room at the UNESCO Conference Building in Paris (fig. 13). Philip Johnson, a Council member, had been commissioned to carry out this project, for which the Council raised from its members and outside sources special contributions amounting to about

$65,000. Besides the election of Mrs. Parkinson as President, other officers elected at this meeting were Colin and John de Menil, Vice-Presidents; Mrs. Gilbert W. Chapman, Secretary; Mrs. Burton Tremaine, Treasurer, with Charles T. Keppel, Assistant Treasurer of the Museum's Board, to hold the same office in the Council.

1958—Theoretical Discussions, Accelerated Activities

During the International Council's Spring Meeting in New York, May 19–20, McCray reviewed the underlying philosophy of the International Program's past activities—the broad framework for which had been outlined when the original grant was requested in 1952—and asked for an expression of ideas concerning future plans. The success of the Program had resulted in a multiplication of demands for its services, including urgent and unforeseen requests. Its activities had also been most useful to the USIA;[78] dispatches sent to Washington by our embassies and consulates regarding favorable reactions to exhibitions circulated abroad by the Program had helped the government overcome Congressional apathy or resistance to making appropriations for cultural exchange. Following McCray's report, it was agreed that it would be a mistake to plan so full a program in advance that it would be impossible to respond to unanticipated requests. It was announced that the Avalon Foundation had made a $25,000 grant for a "sinking fund" to enable the Council to accede to urgent requests unforeseen when the annual budget was prepared.[79]

One of the most intricate projects ever undertaken by the Program was its organization of "Clouet to Matisse: French Drawings from American Collections" (fig. 14). This exhibition came about in response to invitations from J. C. Ebbinge-Wubben, director of the Museum Boymans van Beuningen in Rotterdam, and the Association Française d'Action Artistique and authorities at the Musée du Louvre for a showing at the Orangerie in Paris. The Council voted $5,000 for this project and appointed a General Committee for the Exhibition, composed of more than fifty American museum officials and collectors. With the Museum's President, Burden, as Chairman, it sought the additional funds needed to finance the exhibi-

Left:
13. Executive Board Room, designed by Philip Johnson, UNESCO Conference Building, Paris, inaugurated November 1958

Right:
14. Porter McCray, with Mlle Dubreuil of the Musée du Louvre, at the opening of "Clouet to Matisse: French Drawings from American Collections," Musée de l'Orangerie, Paris, 1958

tion. A Selection Committee of experts from ten museums, headed by Agnes Mongan, Curator of Drawings at the Fogg Art Museum, Harvard University, chose 224 drawings covering a period of five centuries, which were lent by twenty-seven public and forty-one private collections in the United States. The International Program, under McCray as Secretary to the Committee, assumed responsibility for organizing the exhibition and providing text and illustrations for its catalogue. Because of the disruption of the Museum's facilities caused by the fire on April 19, the Metropolitan Museum acted as the central collecting point for the artworks in return for the opportunity to present the exhibition on its return to New York.[80] The exhibition received accolades from the French press, which hailed it as the major artistic event of the season.[81]

Three major exhibitions of American art were sent to Europe during 1958: the United States representation at the XXIX Biennale in Venice, "The New American Painting," and "Jackson Pollock: 1912–1956." For the Biennale, the painters Rothko and Tobey and the sculptors Lippold and Smith were each given a separate gallery in the United States Pavilion. At the request of the Secretary General of the Biennale, the International Program also sent works by three young American artists—the painters Joan Mitchell and Jasper Johns and the sculptor Richard Stankiewicz—for inclusion in a special exhibition of young artists from England, France, Italy, Spain, the United States, and West Germany held in the International Pavilion. McCray served as the U.S. Commissioner, installed the show in the American Pavilion, and was a member of the prize-awarding jury; he and Mrs. Parkinson, representing the Council, were hosts at the official reception on the opening day. The top prize for a non-Italian artist was awarded to Tobey—the first American to receive this honor since James McNeill Whistler in 1895.

"The New American Painting" and "Jackson Pollock: 1912–1956" were sent abroad in response to many urgent requests from European museum directors eager to present in their institutions exhibitions of the recent developments in painting in the United States. These two shows offered the general public in Europe by far the most extensive opportunity to date to see avant-garde American art.

"The New American Painting," eighty-one paintings by seventeen artists representing the advanced tendencies that had developed in America since World War II, was selected by Miller with the assistance of O'Hara.[82] "Jackson Pollock: 1912–1956," an exhibition of thirty-one paintings and twenty-nine drawings and watercolors, was substantially the same as the retrospective selected by O'Hara and presented at the IV Bienal de São Paulo the preceding summer. Its itinerary sometimes included joint showings with "The New American Painting," as in Basel, Berlin, and Paris, and sometimes separate showings, as in Rome, Amsterdam, Hamburg, and London.

Press response in some countries where the exhibitions were shown revealed strong political bias. In Italy, the Pollock exhibition arrived in Rome for its inaugural showing at the Galleria d'Arte Moderna at the time of a heated debate between two camps of avant-garde artists, abstractionists and neo-realists, the latter being passionately supported by the Communists. To the consternation of the left, a young critic who had been strongly critical of the Galleria's director for favoring abstract art recanted his previous stance and acknowledged Pollock as a true artist.[83]

The joint presentation of "Jackson Pollock: 1912–1956" and "The New

American Painting" in Basel came in response to a request by the Kunsthalle's director, Arnold Rüdlinger, who wrote an introduction to the catalogue.[84] Of the artists in "The New American Painting," Pollock generated both the most acclaim and the most criticism. In general, the large format of many of the works in the exhibition drew opposite reactions. Thus, the critic for the *Mannheimer Morgen* (May 13, 1958) wrote of "the pioneering spirit in these paintings . . . an adventure of freedom, a protest against European tradition," whereas the critic Edouard Roditi, writing for *Présence* (July–August 1958), considered the "gigantic format of all these canvases . . . a curious imperialism over the vital space of the wall and an overbearing attitude which from a humane standpoint are in the worst of taste."[85] Roditi also criticized the Museum for having "plumbed the depths of demographic diversity" in selecting the artists. "But this painting, so little American, so little novel or humane, so void of all thought, of all emotion, also gives evidence of a spiritual crisis in America." An even more hostile attitude was that of Emile Biollay, the critic for *Nouvelliste Valaisan,* who decried "American conceptions backed by American money . . . 'daubings' that the Americans with the great force of their dollars come to propose for our admiration." The critic of the *St.Galler Tageblatt* (May 16, 1958), however, admired the American outlook—the paintings' "Large format, dynamic and intense expression, painterly quality . . . quite unlike the refinement of European *peinture*. . . ." New York, he declared, "is now, with Paris, a second center of modern painting." A welcome outcome of this showing was that Hans Theler, President of the Basler Kunstverein, made an initial gift to the Kunstmuseum for the creation of the first gallery in Europe to be devoted to American art.

The showing of "The New American Painting" at the Galleria Civica d'Arte Moderna in Milan (fig. 15) in June was sponsored by the Ente Manifestazioni Milanesi (the organization for cultural activities in Milan). The preponderance of the funds was provided by Romeo Toninelli, a textile manufacturer and art collector, who produced the most elegant of all the catalogues published for the show. Critical reaction ranged from the very negative to the admiring. Leonardo Borghese in *Corriere della Sera* (June 8, 1958) was wholly dismissive: "The New American Painting is not new. It is not painting. It is not American. . . . When will they send us a *real* American show?"[86] Even more virulent was Giorgio Mascherpe, who wrote

Left:
15. Installation view of "The New American Painting," Galleria Civica d'Arte Moderna, Milan, 1958, with paintings by Sam Francis (left), Philip Guston (bottom center), Bradley Walker Tomlin (top center), and Mark Rothko (right)

Right:
16. Installation view of "The New American Painting," Hochschule für Bildende Künste, Berlin, 1958, with paintings by Grace Hartigan (left) and Franz Kline (right)

in *L'Italia* (June 13, 1958), "A sad series of jokes . . . painted as if by a monkey, by cats . . . [and] by babies." A contrary view was that of Marco Valsecchi, who declared in *Il Giorno* (June 10, 1958), "Though American art derives from European art . . . nevertheless its character is so well defined. . . . Because these American artists are not tied down by tradition and deep-rooted cultures like our artists . . . they succeed in reaching greater freedom; more extroverted and pleasing, also gayer and more vibrant."

An enthusiastic reception was accorded the ensuing showing at the Museo Nacional de Arte Contemporáneo in Madrid, July 16–August 11. Installed by d'Harnoncourt and McCray, it was the first extensive collection of avant-garde American art to visit that city. The critic Luis Trabazo asserted unequivocally: "I consider it the most important event since I arrived in Madrid in 1941."[87]

Meanwhile, "Jackson Pollock: 1912–1956" had gone on alone to the Stedelijk Museum in Amsterdam, June 6–July 7, and the Kunsthalle in Hamburg, July 19–August 21, where it was shown under the auspices of the Hamburg Kunstverein. In September 1958, it was reunited with "The New American Painting" at the Hochschule für Bildende Künste in Berlin (figs. 16, 17). The exhibitions had traveled to that city at the request of Joachim Tiburtius, Senator für Volksbildung Berlin, to constitute the U.S. representation at the annual Berliner Festwochen, and their showing was made possible through the cooperation of the U.S. Embassy in Bonn and Michael Weyl of the U.S. Mission in Berlin. These were the first extensive exhibitions to visit Berlin, which for many years had been isolated from the main currents of international art. During the month that they were on view, they attracted 5,461 visitors, including 573 from East Berlin. Once again, the large format of the paintings occasioned comment. Some found that the canvases bore only a slight content, others that the huge dimensions accorded with the wide expanse of the American continent. In a review of "The New American Painting" in *Der Abend* (September 3, 1958), an anonymous critic asked, "What kind of pictures are these?

17. Installation view of "Jackson Pollock: 1912–1956," Hochschule für Bildende Künste, Berlin, 1958

Scratched, punched, smeared, scraped, slit, daubed, sprayed . . . it is as if five pounds of an Italian salad had been poured out. Only Pollock is impressive in several works through the refinement of his tachist effects."[88] The most laudatory comments and detailed analyses of individual artists and their works came, not surprisingly, from Will Grohmann, an Honorary Member of the International Council, who declared in *Der Tagesspiegel* (September 7, 1958), "Pollock was a genius, but one can easily count half of the other sixteen to be exceptional talents."

From Berlin, "The New American Painting," retitled "Young America Paints," went on to the Stedelijk Museum in Amsterdam; for lack of space, only thirty of the works could be shown. The U.S. Embassy in The Hague and the Consulate General in Amsterdam rendered assistance. The show in its complete form then proceeded to the Palais des Beaux-Arts in Brussels. Robert Giron, Directeur Général of that institution's auxiliary Société des Expositions, wrote to McCray: "I do not know whether the public will react immediately to the shock of so explicit an exhibition. Its very power gives it perhaps little chance for the artists' success."[89] His misgivings were prophetic, in view of the more hostile reviews. An unsigned article in *Le Phare* (December 14, 1958) declared: "As to the paintings, they far exceed the worst excesses imaginable in poor quality, for mediocre inventiveness and intellectual poverty."[90] The critic writing in *La Libre Belgique* (December 12, 1958) was more sorrowful and alarmed than indignant: "The show must be seen, even if you leave this encounter in a state of terrible dejection and real anxiety as to the solidity of human reason on this planet in 1958."

In the interim, "Jackson Pollock: 1912–1956" was shown at the Whitechapel Art Gallery in London under the auspices of its trustees and the USIS. The Arts Council of Great Britain aided with a grant, and the USIS assisted with shipping arrangements and provided funds for installation costs. "The exhibition is something of an eye-opener," wrote the critic of the London *Times* (November 7, 1958). "It is the grace and sensibility of these extraordinary paintings that makes the deepest impression and a quality . . . of intense nervous vitality. . . ."[91] John Russell, in the *Sunday Times* of London (November 9, 1958), declared, "Pollock [has] left his mark upon painting in every country in the world where painting is practiced," and David Sylvester, writing from London to the *New York Times* (November 30, 1958), stated unequivocally: "I cannot think of any one-man show seen here since the war which has aroused so much excitement among painters and critics."

In January and February 1959, the Musée National d'Art Moderne in Paris was host to both "The New American Painting" and "Jackson Pollock: 1912–1956." Predictably, the press reaction was polarized between angry rejection and temperate enthusiasm. The artist's avowed intention of breaking with tradition to "make it new" was taken as deliberate provocation. Claude-Roger Marx in the conservative *Figaro Littéraire* (January 17, 1959) said of the seventeen painters: "Their only greatness is in the size of the canvases. . . . We would end up by being disarmed if we did not deplore . . . the impudence of the Réunion des Musées Nationaux in lending official support all too generously to such contagious heresies."[92] In an opposite vein, Bernard Dorival, in *Les Arts* (January 28–February 3, 1959), found analogies in the paintings to American literature: "Far more than the United States of standardization, system, and productivity, there are the qualities of Walt Whitman in these abstract paintings, bursting with vigor, lyrical, and full of vitality." In *Le Monde*

(January 17, 1959), André Chastel wrote: "The exhibitions' great merit is to give
. . . the entire measure of the double relationship of assimilation and rejection that
characterizes American painting."

The final overseas showing of "The New American Painting" was at The Tate
Gallery in London, February 24–March 23, under the auspices of the Arts Council
of Great Britain. The Abstract Expressionists found a more consistently receptive
audience than they had encountered when "Modern Art in the United States" was
presented in the same gallery three years before. There were, of course, dissenting
voices, but in the main, the exhibition proved to be both a critical and a popular
success. Stefan Munsing of the U.S. Embassy in London reported that the paid
attendance of 14,700 was the highest for any comparable one-month period in the
history of the Arts Council's exhibitions at the Tate. The anonymous critic in the
London *Times* (February 24, 1959) stated categorically: "The exhibition . . . is the
finest of the kind we have yet had. It provides concrete evidence . . . why the United
States should so frequently be regarded nowadays as the challenge to, if not actually
the inheritor of, the hegemony of Paris."[93]

While "blockbuster" shows such as these continued to appear in major cities,
the International Program remained mindful of its commitment to provide exhibitions for provincial centers in widely dispersed regions and to reach new audiences
in areas in which it had not previously operated.[94] Negotiating the appropriate auspices for these exhibitions and establishing their itineraries, often with organizations
or individuals with whom these were the initial contacts, was an ongoing and very
time-consuming activity of the Program. Among such shows were smaller versions
of "Built in U.S.A.: Postwar Architecture"; "The Skyscraper: U.S.A."; and six print
shows, selected by William S. Lieberman, the Museum's Curator of Prints and
Drawings, for which the works were purchased outright and planned for indefinitely
extended circulation. Some of these exhibitions were donated in the name of the
International Council to an appropriate institution in the locality of their last showing.

Lieberman also selected three major shows for international circulation.
"Young American Printmakers," comprising seventy prints by seventy artists, was
based on an exhibition sponsored by the Junior Council and shown at The Museum
of Modern Art in 1953. Its year-long tour began in Norway in mid-1957 under the
auspices of Riksgalleriet, Oslo, and included visits to eleven provincial centers before
its final presentation in the capital. A smaller edition of thirty-five prints by thirty-
five artists was shown in Mexico City in the fall of 1958 to coincide with the inauguration of that city's Museo d'Arte Moderno, and the following spring began a
proposed tour of Central America in Guatemala City. The survey exhibition
"Contemporary Printmaking in the United States," comprising forty prints by thirty-
two artists, was circulated from February 1958 through April 1959 to Australia,
Tasmania, and New Zealand by the Contemporary Art Society of Australia. The
exhibition was especially welcomed because it was the first exhibition of American
art to be sent "down under" by the International Program. Finally, "Recent
American Prints in Color," a selection of twenty-five prints by as many artists, began
its tour in Honolulu in 1957 and was then shown in the Philippines, Vietnam,
Singapore, and Ceylon before being circulated among nine cities in India under the
auspices of the New Delhi International Cultural Center.

1959—A Year of Expansion and Crisis

A major event of 1959 was the inauguration in New Delhi of "Design Today in America and Europe." Under a grant from the Ford Foundation, it had been organized by the International Program for a two-year tour of India, at the request of the National Small Industries Corporation (part of India's Ministry of Commerce).[95] It was intended to focus attention on the vital problem of product design in a country whose rapidly developing small-scale industry was in crisis because of a breakdown in traditional patterns of production and distribution. Greta Daniel, Associate Curator of Design, selected in the United States and Europe approximately 350 objects, from furniture and kitchen utensils to laboratory equipment, textiles, and toys. The majority were machine-made, and all were currently in production. Purchased outright so that they might remain in India after completion of the tour to form the nucleus of a permanent design collection, the objects were presented in an installation designed by George Nelson & Company within an R. Buckminster Fuller geodesic dome, donated by the USIA, which had previously been used to house "The Family of Man" during its showings in India.[96] The exhibition was visited by more than 100,000 people during the month it was on view in New Delhi, and by approximately 90,000 people during its seventeen-day stay at its next stop, in Amritsar. Its tour included eight other major cities; it returned to New Delhi in April 1961, to remain permanently.

In 1959, the International Program organized the U.S. representation at two recurring festivals: Documenta II, held in Kassel, Germany, July 11–October 11,[97] and the I Biennale de Paris, October 2–25. It also provided a subsidy to The Art Institute of Chicago, which the International Council had invited to organize the U.S. representation at the V Bienal de São Paulo.

Documenta II, the theme of which was "Art Since 1945," was displayed in three separate buildings: paintings in the Museum Fridericianum, restored after having been severely bombed during the war (fig. 18); sculpture in the nearby Orangerie, a picturesque eighteenth-century ruin, and its surrounding park; and graphics in the small Bellevueschloss. McCray and O'Hara jointly selected works to represent the United States, choosing 144 works by more than forty painters, sculptors, and printmakers. The painters selected included all seventeen artists shown in "The New American Painting" and other Abstract Expressionists, as well as Tobey. The youngest of the group was Robert Rauschenberg.[98] Among the sculptors were Calder, Isamu Noguchi, Roszak, and Smith. There was also a retrospective show of sixteen paintings by Pollock, selected by O'Hara. The USIS arranged a simultaneous exhibition at the Amerika Haus of works by the American printmakers included in the U.S. representation at Documenta. The enormous amount of publicity for the festival in the European press resulted in an attendance of about 130,000 during the three months that Documenta II was on view. The significance of Pollock's work and the extent of its influence were almost unanimously recognized by writers from different countries.[99]

At the invitation of the French government and on relatively short notice, the International Program undertook the organization of the U.S. representation at the newest recurring international art exhibition, the I Biennale de Paris. Devoted to artists between the ages of twenty and thirty-five, and sponsored by the French Ministry of Foreign Affairs and the City of Paris, it was shown at the Musée National

19. Banners announcing the painting section of Documenta II, outside the Museum Fridericianum, Kassel, 1959

d'Art Moderne October 2–25, 1959. The forty-five participating countries came from Africa, Asia, Europe, Latin America, and North America, and included five countries from behind the Iron Curtain (though not the Soviet Union). The U.S. selection of approximately forty paintings, sculptures, prints, and drawings by twelve artists was made by Peter Selz, the Museum's Curator of Painting and Sculpture Exhibitions, who was also named U.S. Commissioner. McCray went to Paris to assist with the installation and serve on the International Jury of Awards.

The press coverage was copious, but the reaction to the exhibition as a whole was not very favorable. The rather low level of quality was deplored, with particularly harsh criticism for the over-large French section. The British and American sections were generally judged the best. Two American artists received awards: Frankenthaler received a stipend providing for a six-month sojourn in Paris, and the Musée Rodin prize of 100,000 francs was given to the sculptor Peter Voulkos. In addition, the printmaker Carol Summers received a prize of 50,000 francs from the Critiques d'Art Français.

While abroad the International Program's exhibitions were winning acclaim for modern, and particularly American, art and were enhancing the Museum's prestige, at home McCray found himself, the Program, and the Council on the receiving end of brickbats rather than kudos. The situation was one manifestation of a general unrest among the younger department heads, who resented the control of their activities by the Coordination Committee—d'Harnoncourt, Wheeler, Barr, and McCray—and believed that they should have more say in setting policy. This was a generational rift between the elder statesmen and the "Young Turks," aggravated in a few instances by personal animosities.

In order to allow the disaffected staff members to discuss their grievances, Burden invited them, as well as Mrs. Rockefeller, as Chairman of the Board, and others of the staff, to spend a long August weekend at his summer home in Northeast Harbor, Maine.[100] In a day-long session entirely devoted to the International Program and the Council, one complaint was that, despite the addition of persons engaged specifically for the Program, its activities took up a tremendous amount of the time and energy of other staff members. The pace of the Program was such that in the course of a year it had been producing five times as many exhibitions as all the curatorial departments together. Because it was independently funded by the RBF, the Council, and contributions for special projects, it did not have to compete for allocations from the Museum's budget. Whereas the curatorial departments had to take turns waiting for gallery space to become available for their exhibitions within the Museum's schedule, the Program had the advantage of a wide range of venues for its overseas exhibitions. Some exhibitions had been directed by members of the Program's staff or outside experts hired for the occasion; while the quality of the selections was not disputed, the Museum's curators felt that they should have been consulted in all cases, if not themselves entrusted with this responsibility. The fact that the Program issued its own press releases was also resented. Another charge was that the Council's annual dues of $1,000 took money away from other Museum membership—an unwarranted accusation, as the growth of the Museum's out-of-town membership undoubtedly had been stimulated both by interest in the Program and by the personal contacts assiduously cultivated by Council members.[101] McCray was deeply hurt and so shaken by the attacks that it was only with some difficulty that he was dissuaded from resigning immediately.[102]

In 1959, the International Council allocated funds for two exhibitions to be presented the following year that honored its commitment to demonstrate American appreciation of the cultural achievements of other countries. "Twentieth-Century Italian Art from American Collections" was initiated at the request of Romeo Toninelli of Milan[103] and selected by Soby, who also wrote the introduction to the catalogue. He chose 191 works by forty-four artists dating from 1902 to 1958, many of which had not previously been on public view in Italy. Cosponsors with the Council were the Italian Ministry of Foreign Affairs, the Ente Manifestazioni Milanesi, and the two exhibiting institutions, the Palazzo Reale in Milan and the Galleria Nazionale d'Arte Moderna in Rome. On its return to New York in October 1960, a special viewing of the show at the Santini Brothers Warehouse was arranged for Council members and invited guests.

A projected exhibition of works by Polish artists, selected by Selz on a visit to Poland in early November, was canceled officially the following month by the Polish government, owing to its desire to tighten control over all manifestations of cultural freedom.[104]

Also in 1959, the Council granted a partial subsidy of $5,000 to the Baltimore Museum of Art, which it had invited to assume responsibility for organizing the U.S. representation at the XXX Venice Biennale in 1960.[105] The exhibition, shown from June to September 1960, consisted of four solo exhibitions by the painters Guston, Hans Hofmann, and Kline, and the sculptor Roszak. The Council also agreed to undertake responsibility for the U.S. representation at the International Exhibition of Modern Art, which, under the sponsorship of the Argentine Office of Cultural Affairs and the Municipality of Buenos Aires, was to inaugurate the new galleries of the Museo de Arte Moderno in that city. The exhibition, held November–December 1960, was a feature of the celebration of the 150th Anniversary of the May Revolution, which had initiated the war of liberation from Spain. O'Hara selected four major paintings by Kline, de Kooning, Pollock, and Tobey.

The Program and the Council Look to the Future

As several members had expressed a desire to have the opportunity to discuss the policy of the Council vis-à-vis the Museum's program, the Executive Committee on December 9, 1959, decided to devote the upcoming Spring Meeting to this topic. In preliminary discussions on January 13, 1960, d'Harnoncourt pointed out that the tripartite agreement among the Council, the Museum, and the RBF would terminate on June 30, 1962, and inasmuch as exhibitions must be planned two or three years in advance, it was essential to consider very soon the question of financing—not only for the next two years but thereafter. First, however, an essential decision had to be made: 1) Should the Council, as under the current agreement, continue to support the Museum's International Program with its character and standards; or 2) Should it become an agency expressing all valid points of view as represented by a wide variety of institutions throughout the United States.

Though other agencies such as the USIA, the Smithsonian Institution, and the AFA had become active in the field of cultural exchange, The Museum of Modern Art, as the only institution with a continuous exhibitions program, did not need to rely on other organizations to carry out its projects and so could retain strict control of standards at every stage of execution. D'Harnoncourt said he believed any attempt to represent all points of view would inevitably result in the compromising of standards. Moreover, since the USIA had to work within a framework determined by political, rather than solely artistic, considerations, its presentations inevitably were tinged with an atmosphere of propaganda. Wide fluctuations in its budget had also resulted either in the cancellation of several major shows or drastic last-minute changes in their content.

Noting that a large proportion of the International Program had been devoted to recurrent international exhibitions, he recommended that the Council should continue its policy of inviting other qualified institutions to assume this responsibility from time to time, and that it should concentrate primarily on exhibitions in the modern field and only under special circumstances undertake projects outside that area.

D'Harnoncourt outlined the following ways that might enable the Council and the Museum to work more closely together: 1) As under the terms of the Agreement currently in force, the Council should sponsor the Museum's International Program and attempt to ensure its continuation and expansion; 2) Major policy and program commitments should be adopted only with the approval of both the Council's Board of Directors and the Museum's Board of Trustees; 3) Routines for the carrying out of projects should be devised and approved by the delegated bodies of both the Council and the Museum; 4) The Council would be represented within the Museum's structure; 5) In accordance with its original concept, membership should be limited to approximately 125 persons throughout the country; and 6) All Council members would maintain their status as Contributing Members of The Museum of Modern Art.

In defining the distinct functions of the Council and the International Program, d'Harnoncourt said that the former was a policymaking, advisory, and supporting group; the latter was the department within the Museum that executed the projects and programs sponsored by the Council. He compared this to the relation between the Board of Trustees and the professional staff in any museum.

At the Spring Meeting of the International Council on May 10, 1960, Heckscher as Chairman presented recommendations regarding the relation of the Council and The Museum of Modern Art. These included representation of the International Council within the Corporation of The Museum of Modern Art; joint meetings of the Exhibitions Committee of the International Council and the Museum's Program Committee to consider proposals affecting the International Program, with all major commitments to be made only with joint approval; representation by a non-Trustee member of the Council's Executive Committee on the Museum's Program Committee to participate in the formulation of such proposals; and similar representation of the Council on the staff sub-committee of the Museum's Program Committee, to enable participation at the earliest stage in the formulation of such proposals. An additional recommendation was that the name of the Council revert from "The International Council *at* The Museum of Modern Art" to the original "The International Council *of* The Museum of Modern Art." All these recommendations were unanimously adopted.

The participation of the International Council in recurring international art festivals was then discussed, in view of their increasing number and the heavy burden they placed on the budget, services, and personnel of the International Program.

19. Wall map illustrating the scope of the International Program, shown concurrently with "The New American Painting: As Shown in 8 European Countries 1958–1959," The Museum of Modern Art, New York, 1959

As yet no government agency had been authorized to undertake the responsibility for organizing the U.S. representations, and the immense costs involved made it difficult for other institutions to accept the Museum's invitations to do so. The greatest problem was the Venice Biennale, because of the state of disrepair of the United States Pavilion. It was voted that a committee be appointed to study the question of asking the government for an appropriation to construct a new pavilion and to review the problems involved in preparing the U.S. representations.

In September 1960, at a meeting of an ad-hoc committee appointed to study these questions, McCray presented a five-year schedule of U.S. representations at international exhibitions and indicated the chief festivals for which the Council had previously taken responsibility, and for which there were already renewed requests. He said that, despite the collaboration of curators in the Museum's other departments and occasionally of outside specialists, not only were the Program's financial and human resources severely taxed by the accelerated pace of activities, but also the Museum's potential borrowing capacity was affected. The question was whether to continue dispersing resources over international shows, whose format was almost always dictated within some predetermined framework, or rather to apply the Council's resources to the presentation of modern American art, with more effective concentration on specific targets. The consensus was that the Council not take responsibility for the Paris Biennale or the Contemporary Art Exhibition in India, unless special circumstances made it advisable to do so, and that the USIA be urged to accept responsibility for financing these shows and delegating their selection to other museums; that the Council accept responsibility for the Venice Biennale until an alternative could be provided through the government's support, and should continue to investigate obtaining a government appropriation for constructing a new pavilion; and that the 1961 São Paulo Bienal be placed on the Council's agenda, but government support for its preparation should be sought and, if possible, its selection be delegated to another institution.

These recommendations were presented to the Council at its Fourth Annual Meeting on October 23, 1960, but definitive action was postponed, pending an outcome of the ongoing discussions with the government, especially with reference to the Venice Biennale and the United States Pavilion. In the meantime, it was decided that the Council should retain control of that exhibition[106] but should be more selective about participating in other recurring international festivals, and should also seek out government support.

A Backward Glance

The magnitude of the International Program as it had developed up to 1960 certainly had not been foreseen when the original proposal was presented in 1952. To exhibitions carefully planned in advance there had been added many organized in response to urgent unanticipated requests. The membership of the International Council—originally a small auxiliary body intended to stimulate countrywide appreciation of the Program's activities, supplement those activities in modest ways, and hold one major annual event, such as a conference—by December 1960 had grown from the thirty-nine directors who signed the Certificate of Incorporation in 1956, plus eight Honorary Members from five countries, to sixty-seven members from twenty-three communities in fifteen states and eight Honorary Members from seven countries.[107] Instead of an ancillary role, it had assumed full sponsorship of the Program and had committed itself to its future continuation and expansion.

The enthusiasm, zeal, and energy of the Program's staff and Council members made possible the greatly increased number of exhibitions and other activities, and

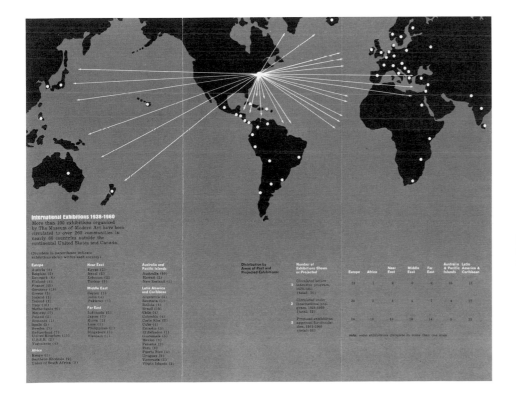

20. Diagram prepared by The International Council of The Museum of Modern Art to document the international circulation of exhibitions, 1938–60

the high quality of these operations enabled fulfillment of their aims of increasing understanding and mutual respect among nations through cultural exchange.[108] Beginning with its inaugural exhibition, "12 Modern American Painters and Sculptors," in 1953, the image of the United States as a cultural wasteland devoted solely to materialism had gradually been altered. "Mutual understanding and respect" had been enhanced by exhibitions honoring the achievements of other countries. Not only major centers but smaller communities in far-flung areas of the world had had the opportunity to see—sometimes for the first time—a wide diversity of modern American art in a variety of mediums.

The Program's activities in the 1950s coincided with the ascendancy of the first indigenous American style of modern painting to attract international attention, Abstract Expressionism. Major exhibitions such as "Jackson Pollock: 1912–1956" and "The New American Painting" led to recognition of its validity and worldwide influence. A further accomplishment was the Program's substantial contribution to the gradual transition on the part of the U.S. government and its agencies from indifference or outright hostility to cultural exchange, to their increasing cooperation and assumption of responsibility for the presentation of American art overseas.

If originally the prestige of The Museum of Modern Art had paved the way for the Program's activities abroad, that prestige had in turn been greatly enhanced by these operations. Particularly important were the close relations that had been established with individuals and institutions in the United States overseas, thanks both to the diplomatic tact of the Program's Director, Porter McCray, and the personal contacts fostered by Council members, who were engaged in "networking" long before that word entered our vocabulary, and whose presence frequently leavened the rigid protocol of official ceremonial occasions.

Much had been achieved; much still lay ahead. But it was the early years of the International Program and the International Council during which standards were established and the groundwork laid for further accomplishments.

Notes

This article has been adapted from a more complete history of the International Program and The International Council of The Museum of Modern Art in the 1950s, which together with documentation has been deposited in The Museum of Modern Art Archives.

Principal sources for this history are: 1) The extensive textual and photographic documentation in the International Council/International Program Exhibition Records (IC/IP Exh. Records) in the Museum Archives, carefully compiled by the late Rose Kolmetz, who was responsible for many of the translations of foreign press reports quoted herein; 2) "Exhibitions Circulated by the International Program," quarterly listings, initiated in January 1957; 3) the departmental records of the International Council, which were kindly placed at my disposal by Carol Coffin and her administrative assistant, Karen L. Madden; 4) and the bound volumes of press releases issued by the Museum, kept in the Department of Public Information.

I am especially indebted to Clive Phillpot, former Director of the Museum Library, and to the patient assistance rendered by the entire Library staff, especially Janis Ekdahl, Daniel Fermon, Eumie Imm, Daniel Starr, John Trause, and Chantal Veraart. Harriet S. Bee, in the Department of Publications, provided constant encouragement and support.

Finally, conversations with former International Program Directors Porter A. McCray and Waldo Rasmussen provided otherwise unattainable information.

1. The Program envisaged large exhibitions of original works of art for showing in three or four major centers, smaller exhibitions of original works available for longer periods, and exhibitions in the fields of architecture, design, and photography treated in photographic enlargements and available for showing in major and secondary centers; and smaller exhibitions of works shown in photographic reproduction or, in some cases, of original works of art purchased outright that could be scheduled for showing throughout the duration of the Program.

2. Certificate of Incorporation of Rockefeller Brothers Fund, Inc., December 23, 1950. Rockefeller Family Archive, Rockefeller Archive Center, Pocantico Hills, North Tarrytown, New York, 1591–1598.

3. This lively group included many who, as Trustees or staff members, would play leading roles in the growth of the Museum. Among them were Lincoln Kirstein and Edward M.M. Warburg, who as undergraduates (together with John Walker, later Director of the National Gallery of Art, Washington, D.C.) had founded the Harvard Society of Contemporary Art; Philip Johnson; James Johnson Sweeney; and Elizabeth Bliss (later Mrs. John Parkinson and Mrs. Henry Ives Cobb).

4. See Peter Collier and David Horowitz, *The Rockefellers: An American Dynasty* (New York: Holt, Rinehart, 1976), p. 209.

5. Organized propaganda was spawned in the 1930s with the rise of the mass media—radio, and later television—and was brilliantly developed by Adolph Hitler's Minister for Propaganda, Joseph Paul Goebbels. There was no central U.S. agency for propaganda during World War I; posters urging enlistment—"Uncle Sam Needs You!"—were done for the U.S. Army, and those promoting the buying of war bonds, for the Treasury.

6. Quoted in *Current Biography* (1951), p. 532.

7. Besides the catalogue of the exhibition, *3 Siècles d'Art aux Etats-Unis* (Paris: Editions des Musées Nationaux, 1938), see *The Bulletin of The Museum of Modern Art* 5 (April–May 1938), pp 12 ff., and 6 (February 1939), pp. 2–12; A. Conger Goodyear, *The Museum of Modern Art: The First Ten Years* (New York: The Museum of Modern Art, 1943), pp. 73–82; and Russell Lynes, *Good Old Modern: An Intimate Portrait of the Museum of Modern Art* (New York: Atheneum, 1973), pp. 183–88. On its return from Paris, the architectural section of the exhibition was shown at the Museum under the title "Three Centuries of American Architecture" and then sent on tour by the Department of Circulating Exhibitions from 1939 to 1941.

8. In 1938, the *New York Times* devoted three of a series of six articles by its leading critic, Edward Alden Jewell, to the question "Have We an American Art?"; the articles were published in expanded form in a book of the same title (New York and Toronto: Longmans, Green, & Company, 1939). Jewell concluded that "much of the art produced in this country bears still a telltale imprint of alien idioms . . . tapped and not assimilated" (p. 198).

This question continued to preoccupy American artists and critics, as evidenced by the symposium, "The State of American Art," *Magazine of Art* 42 (March 1949), pp. 82–102. It was posed again in the 1950s, when the International Program began to send its exhibitions abroad. Even as late as the following decade, Lloyd Goodrich, Director of the Whitney Museum of American Art, wrote an article, "What is American in American Art?," *Art in America* 51 (August 1963), pp. 24–39, which in a revised and condensed version was published as the introduction to the catalogue of an exhibition of the same name shown at M. Knoedler & Co., New York, February 9–March 6, 1971.

9. By the spring of 1943, twenty of the Museum's Board of Trustees and staff members were serving in the Armed Forces, including besides Whitney two other Trustees, David McAlpin and Edward M.M. Warburg; key members of the staff from the Film Library and the departments of Photography, Publications, Exhibitions, and Industrial Design; and guards, electricians, and elevator operators. "Twenty of Museum of Modern Art Staff Now in Armed Services," MoMA press release no. 19, [March] 1943.

In June 1946, Whitney returned to the Museum as Chairman of the Board and Rockefeller resumed the Presidency; Clark, who had served in both capacities during the war years, was named Chairman of the Committee on Acquisitions. "John Hay Whitney Succeeds Stephen C. Clark As Chairman of Board of Trustees of Museum of Modern Art," MoMA press release no. 28, June 6, 1946.

10. "John Hay Whitney Announces Museum of Modern Art Will Serve As Weapon of National Defense," MoMA press release no. 14, February 28, 1941.

11. *The Bulletin of The Museum of Modern Art* 10 (October–November 1942), p. 12.

12. After being shown at the Museum in the fall of 1942, the exhibition was circulated domestically in both a larger and a smaller version; three copies were also sent to Great Britain under the auspices of the Office of War Information (OWI) and to Colombia and Uruguay under the auspices of the CIAA.

13. Under the sponsorship of the OWI, the exhibition was shown in London and then circulated throughout England; duplicates were prepared for Australia and South Africa, and the section on prefabricated housing and building techniques was sent to the Soviet Union.

14. After being shown at the Nationalmuseum in Stockholm—the first American exhibition to be seen there—and circulated throughout Sweden, "America Builds" toured Finland, Turkey, Denmark, South Africa, and Switzerland under the auspices of the OWI; see "The Museum Goes Abroad," *The Museum of Modern Art Bulletin* 12 (November 1944), pp. 3–4.

15. See "Circulating Exhibitions 1931–1954," *The Museum of Modern Art Bulletin* 21 (Summer 1954), pp. 12–13. After the war, additional exhibitions were prepared for circulation by the Civil Affairs Division in Germany and Austria, and by the Reorientation Branch of the Department of the Army in Japan.

16. Ritchie was chairman of both the Bienal's painting and sculpture selection committee (which included Robert Beverly Hale of the Metropolitan Museum, Lloyd Goodrich of the Whitney Museum, John I.H. Baur of The Brooklyn Museum, and Dorothy C. Miller from the Modern) and its print selection committee (which included Carl Zigrosser of the Philadelphia Museum, A. Hyatt Mayor of the Metropolitan, Una Johnson of The Brooklyn Museum, and Dorothy Lytle of the Modern); see *I Bienal do Museu de Arte Moderna de São Paulo: Catálogo* (São Paulo: Museu de Arte Moderna, 1951), pp. 111–12. See also Michael Kimmelman, "Revisiting the Revisionists: The Modern, Its Critics, and the Cold War," p. 49 of the present volume.

17. David Halberstam, *The Fifties* (New York: Villard Books, 1993), p. 9. Renamed the Committee on National Security, HUAC remained active until 1975.)

18. Virginia M. Mecklenburg, *Advancing American Art: Politics and Aesthetics in the State Department (1946–1948),* exhibition catalogue (Montgomery, Ala.: Montgomery Museum of Fine Arts, 1948), p. 40. A full account of this exhibition and the fate that befell it is given in Taylor D. Littleton and Maltby Sykes, *Advancing American Art: Painting, Politics, and Cultural Confrontation at Mid-Century* (Tuscaloosa and London: The University of Alabama Press, 1989).

19. Quoted in Frances K. Pohl, *Ben Shahn: New Deal Artist in a Cold War Climate, 1947–1954* (Austin: University of Texas Press, 1980), p. 35.

20. Ibid., p. 37.

21. Quoted by Leroy Davidson in a speech to

the Chicago Society for Contemporary Art, Fall 1947; excerpted in Marilyn Robb, "Art News from Chicago," *Art News* 46 (January 1948), p. 39. In Robb, the work is erroneously titled *Circus Rider*.

Davidson also reported that while it had been anticipated that the abstract paintings in the show would be the most criticized, in fact it was the representational ones that caused the most fury, particularly those with social content such as Shahn's *Hunger* (1946) and Gwathmey's *Work Song* (1945).

22. Pohl, *Ben Shahn*, p. 37.

23. Quoted in "Modern Art Sham to Boston Institute," *Herald Tribune,* February 7, 1948. The date of the announcement had been chosen because it was the thirty-fifth anniversary of the opening of the Armory Show in New York in 1913, but the modernism it had ushered in was declared by the Institute to have died by 1939. The Museum of Modern Art responded to this defection by a former ally with a forum on May 6, 1948, "The Modern Artist Speaks," at which the participants defended modern art.

24. Published as "Challenge and Promise: Modern Art and Modern Society," *Magazine of Art* 41 (November 1948), pp. 250–52.

25. George A. Dondero, in a speech before the 81st Congress, Second Session, House Committee on Foreign Affairs, *Congressional Record,* August 16, 1949, pp. 11581, 11585.

26. Extensive excerpts of the statement appeared in "Manifesto to End All Manifestoes," *Art News* 49 (April 1950), p. 15.

27. Quoted in Pohl, *Ben Shahn*, pp. 137–38.

28. Quoted in Serge Guilbaut, *How New York Stole the Idea of Modern Art: Abstract Expressionism and the Cold War* (Chicago and London: The University of Chicago Press, 1983), p. 192.

29. Frances K. Pohl, "An American in Venice: Ben Shahn and United States Foreign Policy at the 1954 Venice Biennale," *Art History* 4 (March 1981), pp. 82–83, 108 (n. 14, 15).

30. Published with other addresses delivered on this occasion in *The Museum of Modern Art Bulletin* 22 (Fall–Winter 1954), p. 3.

31. Alfred H. Barr, Jr., letter to the editor, *College Art Journal* 15 (Spring 1956), p. 184.

32. Ibid., p. 185.

33. Published in *College Art Journal* 15 (Winter 1955), inside rear cover, and appended to the AFA *Newsletter,* May 1956. In this and other statements, one may note that the stereotypes adopted by those attacking modern art induced a corresponding rhetoric of its own from its defenders, in which the words "freedom of expression" and "diversity" were reiterated like mantras.

34. In the same year, the USIA had canceled a show of American painting of the decade scheduled for exhibition at the Kunstakademie of Berlin. See Bartlett Hayes, letter to Lloyd Goodrich, June 20, 1954. The Museum of Modern Art Archives: Alfred H. Barr, Jr., Papers [AAA: 3157; 1014].

35. The fracas in Dallas and its aftermath were reported in detail by Charlotte Devree, "The U.S. Government Vetoes Living Art," *Art News* 55

(September 1956), pp. 34–35, 54–56.

36. "An Exhibition Program for U.S.I.A.: A tentative proposal for 1956–7 submitted by the American Federation of Arts, February 1, 1956." The Museum of Modern Art Library Subject File: American Federation of Arts.

37. Devree, "The U.S. Government Vetoes Living Art," p. 34.

38. Goodrich to Fulbright, July 3, 1956. The Museum of Modern Art Archives: Barr Papers [AAA: 3157; 1025–37].

39. *Arts* (incorporating *Arts digest*) 30 (September 1956), p. 11. Besides the three exhibitions mentioned whose foreign tours had been canceled by the USIA, the letter also noted the agency's withdrawal of support for an overseas tour by the Symphony of the Air because some of its performers belonged, or had belonged, to left-wing organizations.

40. See McCray, memorandum to d'Harnoncourt, April 22, 1957; the attachment, a letter to McCray from Edward Stansbury, Chief, Exhibits Division, Information Center Service, State Department, March 27, 1957, reads in part: "The *30 American Printmakers* show which you offered to our London office is one the Agency can not touch . . . it contains the work of William Gropper whom we are unable to use because he comes under . . . the basic instruction under which we must operate." The Museum of Modern Art Archives: Barr Papers [AAA: 3157; 1025–37].

41. MoMA press release no. 33, April 24, 1953

42. "Report of Director of the International Program," May 1954. International Council departmental records, The Museum of Modern Art.

43. There is no printed text of Ritchie's Foreword in English; catalogues for "12 Modern American Painters and Sculptors" were printed in the respective languages—French, German, Swedish, Finnish, Norwegian—translated from texts provided by the Program. The passages paraphrased in the press release cited above were excerpted from a typescript of the complete foreword in The Museum of Modern Art Archives: IC/IP Exh. Records (ICE-F-3-53): Box 1.8.

44. USIS dispatch, June 11, 1953; quoted by McCray in "Report on the International Exhibitions Program," May 1954. International Council departmental records, The Museum of Modern Art.

45. "Summary of Swedish Press Reaction to '12 Modern American Painters and Sculptors,'" March 1, 1956, p. 1. The Museum of Modern Art Archives: IC/IP Exh. Records (ICE-F-3-53; Stockholm): Box 1.3. For the reaction of critics to the showings in Paris, Zurich, and Düsseldorf, see the individual summaries prepared for those showings, also filed in Box 1.

46. An attempt to familiarize the French public with avant-garde American art had been made several years before by the New York dealer Samuel Kootz, who in the spring of 1947 presented at the Maeght Gallery in Paris an exhibition of six artists: Baziotes, Romare Bearden, Byron Browne, Adolph Gottlieb, Carl Holty, and Robert Motherwell, with a catalogue essay by Harold Rosenberg. In general,

criticism of the show was devastating, but a boost was given to the American artists when Christian Zervos devoted three pages to them in the 1947 issue of the highly respected *Cahiers d'Art.*

47. The retrospective exhibition in the Sala Especial Pablo Picasso at the II Bienal de São Paulo was a separate exhibition and was not connected with the U.S. representation organized by the International Program, but the Program did arrange for the shipment to São Paulo of Picasso's *Guernica* (1937), then on extended loan from the artist to the Museum, and provided photographs of works for that exhibition's catalogue.

48. Quoted by Representative Lee Metcalf of Montana in a speech before the House of Representatives, Special Subcommittee on Arts Foundations and Commissions, Committee on Education and Labor, 83rd Congress, Second Session on Bills Relating to the Establishment of a Program of Federal Grants for the Development of Fine Arts Program and Projects, January 18, 1954.

49. In 1987, the Museum named its Abstract Expressionist gallery in her honor.

50. The original name "National Council" had been conceived by analogy with the National Council of the Metropolitan Art Association. "Modern Art Council" was also considered but rejected.

51. "By-Laws of the International Council of the Annual Conference Dedicated to Modern Art and Its Function in Contemporary Society," adopted at the meeting of the Committee on the Formation of the International Council, July 29, 1953, Article II, "Purposes," p. 1. International Council departmental records, The Museum of Modern Art.

52. The activities are summarized in the pamphlet *The Museum of Modern Art Twenty-Fifth Anniversary Year: Final Report* (New York: The Museum of Modern Art, 1956).

53. "Museum of Modern Art Buys Exhibition Pavilion in Venice," MoMA press release no. 32, March 29, 1954. The Museum of Modern Art had cooperated in the organization of several previous U.S. representations. For the XXIV Venice Biennale in 1948—the first after an eight-year interruption—Alfred Frankfurter, President of the Art Foundation of New York, served as Commissioner and enlisted the participation of representatives from Artists Equity and four New York museums in obtaining paintings and watercolors from their holdings and those of private collectors. Dorothy Miller was among those who made the selections; twenty-one of the seventy-nine works were lent by The Museum of Modern Art.

Frankfurter again served as U.S. Commissioner for the XXV Biennale in 1950. The U.S. representation was organized collaboratively by The Cleveland Museum of Art and The Museum of Modern Art, in association with the Art Foundation of New York. Half of the Pavilion was given over to a retrospective of works by John Marin, selected by Duncan Phillips, of the Phillips Collection, Washington, D.C. The other half was divided among six artists: figurative, expressionistic works by Hyman Bloom, Lee Gatch, and Rico Le Brun, chosen by Frankfurter; and Abstract Expressionist works by Gorky, de Kooning, and Pollock, chosen by Barr.

The U.S. Commissioner for the XXVI Biennale in 1952 was David E. Finley, Director of the National Gallery of Art, Washington, D.C., and Chairman of the National Commission of Fine Arts. The exhibition was organized by the AFA, whose Second Vice-President, Eloise Spaeth, headed a selection committee of representatives from six museums, including Ritchie of The Museum of Modern Art, who chose thirteen paintings by Stuart Davis. See Lawrence C. Alloway, *The Venice Biennale: 1895–1968: From Salon to Goldfish Bowl* (Greenwich, Conn.: New York Graphic Society, 1968), and official catalogues for the respective years published by the Biennale.

The Museum of Modern Art continued to administer the Pavilion through 1962, when, owing to funding problems (including the cost of extensive repairs required each time for the dilapidated structure), it relinquished responsibility for organizing the U.S. representation. The Pavilion was placed at the disposal of the USIA, which in 1964 designated Alan R. Solomon, Director of The Jewish Museum, New York, to make the selection; in 1966, it passed the job on to the Smithsonian Institution's National Collection of Fine Arts, but without transferring the requisite funds. In 1986, the Solomon R. Guggenheim Museum acquired the Pavilion, and merely replaced the roof, patched up the structure, made some cosmetic changes, and installed air conditioning.

54. The remark by Luce was recalled by McCray in conversation with the author, 1994. According to William S. Lieberman, who was in Venice for the inauguration of the Biennale, Luce, who had threatened to boycott the opening, ultimately relented.

55. A detailed account of the exhibition and a summary of the press reaction is contained in "A Report on the Exhibition 'De David à Toulouse-Lautrec' Held at the Musée de l'Orangerie, Paris, April 20–July 3, 1955," published and distributed by the International Program following the conclusion of the show.

56. The exhibition catalogue includes a foreword by Jean Cassou, director of the Musée National d'Art Moderne; an introduction by d'Harnoncourt; "American Painting and Sculpture in the Twentieth Century," by Holger Cahill noted authority on American art, a former Acting Director of the Museum, and the husband of Dorothy Miller—and an introduction to each departmental section.

57. A "case history" of the organization of "50 Ans d'Art aux Etats-Unis—"The Preparation and Presentation of an International Program Exhibition"—was appended to the grant proposal made by the Museum to the Ford Foundation, March 7, 1957. International Council departmental records, The Museum of Modern Art.

In conjunction with the opening of the exhibition, Eliza Bliss Parkinson, the Council's Vice President, hosted a reception for about one hundred artists. This and similar subsequent events were arranged by the Council with the intent of establishing cordial relations with foreign officials, artists, and critics on a more personal and informal basis

than was possible at the ceremonial occasions. A secondary purpose was to demonstrate the interest in, and support of, cultural exchange by private citizens in the United States—something almost entirely unknown abroad. The same concern with personal contacts led to the Council's formation of a Hospitality Committee to welcome and assist artists and art specialists visiting the United States. Such contacts were valuable not only to the International Program but to the Museum's own exhibitions program, which depended on good will to obtain loans from abroad.

58. "Summary of French Press Reactions to '50 Ans d'Art aux Etats-Unis,'" May 1, 1956, p. 8. The Museum of Modern Art Archives: IC/IP Exh. Records (ICE-F-24-54; Paris): Box 11.1.

59. Ibid., p. 14.

60. Ibid., p. 9.

61. The painting and sculpture and print sections of "50 Ans d'Art aux Etats-Unis" included a total of 113 painters, sculptors, and printmakers. The subsequent touring exhibition, "Modern Art in the United States" (see pp. 128–29 of this essay), included 112 of these artists, as the sculpture by Lippold did not travel beyond Paris. For further discussion of this exhibition, see Kimmelman, "Revisiting the Revisionists," pp. 41 and 45–48 of the present volume.

62. On Columbus Day, October 12, 1955, Generalissimo Francisco Franco visited the exhibition, accompanied by a number of ambassadors. The Catalans took sardonic pleasure in the reason for Franco's presence in their midst for several weeks: He had required an operation, and the specialist whom he consulted had refused to go to Madrid to perform it, insisting that the Generalissimo come instead to his clinic in Barcelona. This occasion also precipitated a relaxation of the economic and cultural sanctions that had been imposed on Catalonia since 1939 as the center of Republican resistance during the Spanish Civil War.

63. For the responses of critics to "Modern Art in the United States," Palacio de la Virreina, Barcelona, see The Museum of Modern Art Archives: IC/IP Exh. Records (ICE-F-24-54; Barcelona): Box 11.1.

64. "Summary of German Press Reaction to 'Moderne Kunst aus U.S.A.' (Modern Art in the United States)," May 6, 1957, pp. 3–4. The Museum of Modern Art Archives: IC/IP Exh. Records (ICE-F-24-54; Frankfurt): Box 11.1.

65. Colin McGuinness, in the British Broadcasting Company (BBC) overseas radio broadcast "London Calling," March 22, 1956; quoted in "Summary of British Press Reaction to the Exhibition 'Modern Art in the United States,' Held at The Tate Gallery, London, January 5–February 12, 1956," May 1, 1956, p. 7. The Museum of Modern Art Archives: IC/IP Exh. Records (ICE-F-24-54; London): Box 11.1.

The reaction of some critics to the London showing of "Modern Art in the United States" anticipated the more universal acceptance of Abstract Expressionism in "The New American Painting" and Documenta II. For example, Patrick Heron, in his review of the exhibition in *Arts* magazine, stated,

"We shall [now] watch New York as eagerly as Paris for new developments" (ibid., p. 11).

66. In addition to the four copies designed and prepared by the International Program for sale to the USIA, the agency provided designs and negatives for another replica that was produced in Japan and circulated in that country under the joint auspices of the USIA and the newspaper *Nihon Keizai Shimbun*.

67. "Museum of Modern Art Plans International Photography Exhibition," MoMA press release no. 11, January 31, 1954.

68. Besides "The Family of Man," the American National Exhibition, held July 25–September 5, included a large show of mass-produced objects for household use. This was the setting for the much-publicized "kitchen debate" between then–Vice President Richard M. Nixon and Premier Nikita Kruschev.

69. *The Family of Man* (Cleveland: Republic Steel Corporation for The Museum of Modern Art, 1959), n.p. This Russian-language edition of the catalogue was prepared for free distribution; the English translation of Eisenhower's statement is printed on a one-page insert. The Museum of Modern Art Archives: IC/IP Exh. Records (SP-ICE-24-59; Moscow): Box 103.13. The roseate vision presented in this statement was abruptly shattered the following year, when the Russians shot down a U-2 spy plane and imprisoned its pilot, despite the President's initial attempts at a cover-up.

The several copies of "The Family of Man" were shown on every continent but Antarctica in various kinds of venues and under diverse auspices and sponsors. Besides U.S. embassies, museums, art centers, universities, professional organizations, and so on, one encounters some surprises. The sponsorship of the exhibition's Australian tour indicates a particularly sensitive response to the images and to the words in Steichen's introduction and Sandburg's foreword to the catalogue, for example: "Hope is a sustaining human gift. . . . Everywhere love and love-making, weddings and babies from generation to generation keeping the Family of Man alive and continuing. . . . [W]e are on all continents in the need of love, food, clothing, work, speech, worship, sleep, games, dancing, fun. From tropics to arctics humanity lives with the needs so alike, so inexorably alike" (Carl Sandburg, Prologue to *The Family of Man* [New York: Maco Magazine Corporation for The Museum of Modern Art, 1955], p. 2). Regarded as a kind of psychic therapy, the exhibition appeared under the auspices of agencies such as the Family Welfare Bureau, the Oral Deaf Association, the Queen Victoria Maternity Hospital, Guide Dogs for the Blind, and the St. John Ambulance Service. In South Africa, it was shown under the joint sponsorship of the Coca-Cola Corporation and the Witwaterstrand Agricultural Society. At the Government Palace in Johannesburg, Coca-Cola installed in the middle of the exhibition space a refreshment center—a kiosk equipped with dispensers of its soft drinks, surrounded by tables and chairs under sheltering umbrellas in a rock garden.

John Szarkowski, in "The Family of Man,"

pp. 12–37 of the present volume, discusses the genesis of this exhibition and the reaction to it among photographers. As he notes, the USIA did not always furnish the International Program with details on the various showings or on the attendance. On one occasion, however, as McCray reported to the International Council in May 1957, the USIA informed him that a world record for attendance to date had been set in Belgrade, a city with a population of about 1,300,000, where in twenty-nine days the exhibition attracted 276,311 visitors—as compared with 270,000 during the three and a half months that it was on view in New York. Inter-national Council departmental records, The Museum of Modern Art.

70.   This address seemed to the Council so noteworthy that it published it as a pamphlet for circulation to the Museum's membership and other interested persons and organizations; see George F. Kennan, *International Exchange in the Arts* (New York: The International Council of The Museum of Modern Art, 1956).

71.   Scheduled events during this Second Annual Meeting of the Council included visits to the Manhattan Storage and Warehouse Company to see a "visual report" summarizing the Program's accomplishments since its inception in 1952, and a dinner at the Guest House at which Shahn reported on his trip to London for The Tate Gallery's showing of "Modern Art in the U.S.A." The next day, a trip by chartered bus to Jacques Lipchitz's studio at Hastings-on-Hudson was followed in the evening by an address on international cultural relations by Grayson L. Kirk, President of Columbia University, and a private viewing for Council members of the Museum of Modern Art exhibition "Toulouse-Lautrec."

72.   Besides the nine persons named as Incorporators, thirty others were designated as directors and members of the Corporation. The Museum's President, Burden, its Director, d'Harnoncourt, and the Director of the International Program, McCray, were made ex-officio members of the Council's Board of Directors.

73.   Quoted by McCray in "Report to the International Council at The Museum of Modern Art on the Current Status of the International Program," May 1957. International Council departmental records, The Museum of Modern Art.

74.   All excerpts in this and the following paragraph, "Publicity: Press Clippings," U.S. Representation: IV Bienal de Museu de Arte Moderna, São Paulo. The Museum of Modern Art Archives: IC/IP Exh. Records (ICE-F-35-57): Box 16.3.

75.   "Tachism" was the term commonly used in Europe and Latin America for Abstract Expressionism.

76.   At a subsequent meeting on March 10, 1958, Heckscher was formally elected to both this position and the Council's Executive Committee.

77.   As noted on page 130, the "original" International Council held its First Annual Conference in May 1955; its Second Annual Meeting was held in May 1956. Following its Incorporation, the First Annual Meeting was held in San Francisco in November 1957—the first of what would become known as the Fall Meetings, now held annually in New York, while the Spring Meetings take place in other venues in this country and abroad.

78.   In response to an urgent request from the USIA, a second version of "Built in U.S.A.: Postwar Architecture" had been prepared for circulation in Romania—the first officially sponsored show of American art to be presented in that country since 1949. On April 12, 1958, John Crockett, Exhibits Officer for the American Legation in Bucharest, wrote to McCray: "The exhibit unquestionably had a great success not only with the masses that are traditionally interested in things from America, but also with the intellectual classes, many of whom, of course, are members of the Communist Party and active supporters of the regime's policies. . . . The exhibits . . . contributed to making quite a hole in the Romanian curtain." The Museum of Modern Art Archives: IC/IP Exh. Records (SP-ICE-20-57; Romania): Box 6.11.

79.   The Executive Committee subsequently voted to use this fund to cover costs of two catalogues for the U.S. representation at the IV Bienal de São Paulo—one on the representation as a whole, the other on the Pollock retrospective; an illustrated catalogue of the U.S. representation at the XXIX Biennale in Venice, 1958; an exceptionally full catalogue for "The New American Painting," with a number of color plates, as well as its translation into German, Italian, French, and Spanish for the various showings and its distribution to a large number of libraries and other cultural institutions in Europe and Latin America; and sharing with the Department of Education of the Berlin Senate and the USIA the expenses for transporting "The New American Painting" and "Jackson Pollock: 1912–1956" to Berlin in response to an unforeseen request that these shows might coincide with the Berlin Festival, 1958.

80.   In accordance with this agreement, on its return to New York the exhibition was shown at the Metropolitan Museum, February 3–March 15, 1959.

81.   See "Publicity: Press Clippings," "French Drawings from American Collections," Musée de l'Orangerie, Paris. The Museum of Modern Art Archives: IC/IP Exh. Records (SP-ICE-21-58; Paris): Box 108.1, 108.7.

82.   See also Kimmelman, "Revisiting the Revisionists," pp. 49–50 and p. 54 (n. 60). The exhibition's showing at The Museum of Modern Art in New York, May 28–September 8, following its return to the United States is discussed by Lynn Zelevansky in "Dorothy Miller's 'Americans,' 1942–63," pp. 86–89 of the present volume. The catalogue includes an introduction by Barr and a statement by each artist, as well as brief samplings of articles appearing in the foreign press of each of the countries on its European tour; see *The New American Painting: As Shown in 8 European Countries 1958–1959* (New York: Doubleday & Co., 1959), pp. 20–84.

83.   A translation of an article by Giovanni Russo, "Pollock Show at Rome Produces Discord Among Leftist Painters; Several Exponents of 'Social Realism' Become Converted to Abstraction," *Corriere d'Informazione,* March 26–27, 1958, is filed with the departmental records of the International Council, The Museum of Modern Art.

84.   On April 15, the opening of the exhibition, Miller and Rasmussen were horrified to learn of the fire at the Museum that day. They received a cable from McCray in New York: "Basel show remains only MoMA exhibition activity. Carry on!" International Program exhibition workfile (ICE-F-36-57; Basel), The Museum of Modern Art.

85.   All excerpts this paragraph, "Publicity: Press Clippings," "The New American Painting," Kunsthalle, Basel. The Museum of Modern Art Archives: IC/CP Exh. Records (ICE-F-36-57; Basel): Box 22.6.

86.   All excerpts this paragraph, "Summary of Press Reaction to 'The New American Painting,'" contained in a report submitted by Alfred V. Boernes, Public Affairs Officer, USIS, Rome, September 30, 1958, p. 5. The Museum of Modern Art Archives: IC/IP Exh. Records (ICE-F-36-57; Milan): Box 22.7.

87.   "Publicity: Press Reactions," "The New American Painting," Museo National d'Arte Contemporáneo, Madrid. The Museum of Modern Art Archives: IC/IP Exh. Records (ICE-F-36-57; Madrid): Box 22.8.

88.   "Publicity: Press Clippings," "The New American Painting," Hochschule für bildende Künste, Berlin. The Museum of Modern Art Archives: IC/IP Exh. Records (ICE-F-36-57; Berlin): Box 22.9.

89.   Giron to McCray, April 2, 1957. The Museum of Modern Art Archives: IC/IP Exh. Records (ICE-F-36-57; Brussels): Box 23.11.

90.   This and the following excerpt, "Publicity: Press Clippings," "The New American Painting," Palais des Beaux-Arts, Brussels. The Museum of Modern Art Archives: IC/IP Exh. Records (ICE-F-36-57; Brussels): Box 23.11. Translation by Richard Howard.

91.   All excerpts this paragraph, "Publicity: Press Clippings," "Jackson Pollock: 1912–1956," Whitechapel Art Gallery, London. The Museum of Modern Art Archives: IC/IP Exh. Records (ICE-F-35-57; London): Box 21.7.

92.   All excerpts this paragraph, "Publicity: Press Clippings" from "The New American Painting," Musée National d'Art Moderne, Paris. The Museum of Modern Art Archives: IC/CP Exh. Records (ICE-F-36-57; Paris): Box 23.12.

93.   "Publicity: Press Clippings," "The New American Painting," The Tate Gallery, London. The Museum of Modern Art Archives: IC/IP Exh. Records (ICE-F-36-57; London): Box 23.13.

94.   A list of these worldwide localities may be found in "Exhibitions Circulated by the International Program," issued quarterly beginning January 1957.

95.   It will be recalled that it was the Ford Foundation that had given the International Program a grant to select the U.S. representation at the III International Contemporary Art Exhibition of India in 1957 (see p. 130 of this essay).

96.   The National Small Industries Corporation

produced for distribution 20,000 copies of a fully illustrated catalogue prepared by the International Program, also designed by George Nelson & Company, and a twenty-two-page booklet, *Twelve Precepts of Modern Design.*

97.   Documenta had been initiated in 1955 by Arnold Bode, a painter and proprietor of a local art gallery, who succeeded in obtaining the enthusiastic support of a number of distinguished museum directors and art historians. They constituted the committee that determined the theme of the exhibition and selected the works to be shown.

98.   The works were lent by nine museums in the United States, sixteen galleries, and thirty-four private collectors, and nine collectors in England, Belgium, Italy, the Netherlands, and Switzerland. International Council departmental records, The Museum of Modern Art.

It seems extraordinary that with the exception of Pierre Restany in "Documenta II: Le plus colossal des témoignages du présent," *Art International* 3 (September 1959), the critics overlooked the three combines by Robert Rauschenberg, including *Bed* (1955), which at the first Festival of Two Worlds at Spoleto the year before had been considered so shocking that it was withdrawn from public exhibition and banished to a storeroom. Restany wrote: "Rauschenberg (35 years old) with his extraordinary assemblages, freely acknowledges his dadaist heritage. The only 'youth' among the grown-ups, his incongruous, unorthodox works display a fine intransigence, together with a sure instinct for the specific plastic possibilities of the materials he uses."

99.   As postludes, five paintings from the American section by Kline, Pollock, and Tobey were lent to the exhibition "Works from Documenta," held in November at the Louisiana Museum in Copenhagen, a museum of contemporary art newly founded in 1958. Three others by de Kooning, Pollock, and Tobey were included in "Tachism in Frankfurt: Quadriga 57," at the Historische Museum in Frankfurt-am-Main, October 16–November 7.

100.   See "Minutes of the Maine Conference, Northeast Harbor, August 14–17, 1959." The Museum of Modern Art Archives: Minutes of Committee Meetings, Box 3.2. The typewritten minutes are brief and carefully edited to omit details of some of the more heated discussions. The only published account, that of Lynes in *Good Old Modern* (pp. 388–90), was written some fourteen years later, and relied principally on statements by Eliza Bliss Parkinson and Elizabeth Shaw. Shaw, head of the Department of Public Information and a prime mover, with Arthur Drexler, of the "Young Turks," was hardly a disinterested informant.

Wheeler and Steichen were both out of the country at the time. Lynes's statement that the latter was among the disgruntled "in spirit if not in fact" (ibid., p. 389) seems unlikely, in view of the extraordinary assistance the International Program had rendered in producing the many copies of "The Family of Man" and the designer responsible was at that very moment in Moscow aiding him in the exhibi-

tion's installation and showing at the American Trade Fair.

101.   The zealous efforts of Council members on behalf of the Museum's fund-raising are documented in *The Museum of Modern Art, Thirtieth Anniversary: Contributors, Committees, Finance, Staff* (New York: The Museum of Modern Art, 1961). In addition to substantial monetary contributions, Council members helped organize and donated works of art to the benefit auction ("Fifty Modern Paintings and Sculptures," especially donated for the Benefit of the 30th Anniversary Fund of The Museum of Modern Art, New York, Parke-Bernet Galleries, Inc., April 27, 1960). Mrs. Bertram Smith served as Co-Chairman of the Auction Committee, and the catalogue acknowledges the assistance of collector Larry Aldrich and Junior Council member Walter Bareiss in obtaining works to be sold.

102.   McCray ultimately resigned in 1961 and was succeeded by the Program's Associate Director, Waldo Rasmussen.

103.   As previously noted, Toninelli had provided funds for the presentation of "The New American Painting" in Milan and published the Italian catalogue. Previously, he had served as Executive Secretary of the exhibition "Twentieth-Century Italian Art" held at The Museum of Modern Art in 1949.

104.   Eventually, "15 Polish Painters," the first comprehensive exhibition of postwar Polish painting to be seen in the United States, directed by Selz, was shown at The Museum of Modern Art August 1–October 11, 1961, under the auspices of the Department of Circulating Exhibitions, which then circulated it domestically in the United States and Canada. In the catalogue, Selz acknowledged the assistance of the Government of the Polish People's Republic in making arrangements for McCray and himself to see the artists' works. Aid was also provided by Polish museum directors, art critics, and artists, and the U.S. Embassy in Poland. The RBF and the International Council shared some of the preliminary costs of the exhibition, and the CBS Foundation, Inc., provided a subsidy underwriting its domestic tour.

105.   The Council subsequently voted an additional $5,000 grant to supplement the $10,700 raised by Adelyn Breeskin, Director of the Baltimore Museum.

106.   The Council sponsored the U.S. representation at the XXXI Biennale in Venice in 1962, for which d'Harnoncourt was Commissioner; it was organized by the staff of the International Program under the supervision of its Associate Director, Rasmussen. The selection included twenty-six paintings by MacIver, chosen by Soby; thirteen paintings by Jan Müller and three sculptures by Dmitri Hadzi, chosen by Selz; and one sculpture by Louise Nevelson, chosen by Miller. In his introduction to the catalogue, d'Harnoncourt pointed out that two of the four artists were women. This Biennale also included in the central pavilion a retrospective of forty-three paintings and drawings by Gorky selected by the joint Commissioners Umbro Apollonio of Italy and Lloyd Goodrich and Ethel K. Schwabacher of the United States.

It was not until the XXXII Biennale of 1964 that the government, through the USIA, for the first time assumed responsibility for organizing the U.S. representation. After both the Guggenheim Museum and the Los Angeles County Museum of Art bowed out, Alan Solomon of The Jewish Museum was appointed Commissioner and made the selection, which was divided into two sections. The first, "Four Germinal Painters," included Johns, Morris Louis, Kenneth Noland, and Rauschenberg. The second showed seventy-one works by four younger artists, John Chamberlain, Jim Dine, Claes Oldenburg, and Frank Stella. The inadequacies of the Pavilion were immediately apparent. The scale of the show exceeded the building's capacity, and while the large paintings of Louis and Noland occupied the galleries, a temporary structure had to be erected in the courtyard to house a token representation of works by each of the other artists, including four by Rauschenberg, who emerged the top prizewinner. See Alloway, *The Venice Biennale 1895–1968,* pp. 149–50.

107.   Members have been counted as coming from their primary residences, though several also maintained residences or offices in New York City. In 1955, there had been concern that the ratio of members was two-thirds women to one-third men, but it was decided that this should not be a factor in preventing a woman from joining the Council if she were qualified. By 1960, this disparity had disappeared, and there was an almost equal division between women (thirty-five) and men (thirty-two). International Council departmental records, The Museum of Modern Art.

108.   Major emphasis in this chronicle has been on exhibitions, and the Council's other activities have been referred to only briefly. In addition to the furnishing of the UNESCO Executive Board Room, mention has been made of book presentations, through which from 1955 to 1959 sets totaling more than 1,500 books and reproductions had been presented to twenty-five institutions in twenty-two cities in eight countries, including schools, universities, institutes of design, public libraries, museum libraries, etc. A Visitors Committee, formed in 1957, extended hospitality to foreign scholars, students, artists, critics, and other specialists when they visited the United States, and out-of-town members of the Council were aided in seeing exhibitions and private collections when they came to New York. In 1958, at the suggestion of Mrs. L. Corrin Strong, wife of the former U.S. Ambassador to Norway, the Council began discussions with the State Department about making loans of works of art to U.S. embassies and chancelleries. When, after two years of negotiations there was a stalemate over the question of control of the selections, a solution was reached by having the loans made to the ambassadors on a personal rather than on an official basis. Requests soon arrived from all over the world, and in the decade between 1960 and 1970, forty-one collections were assembled for embassies in Asia, Africa, Europe, and Latin America. The program was terminated in 1970, by which time the State Department had undertaken similar activity.

1. Lobby entrance to "Good Design," The Merchandise Mart, Chicago, 1950. Steel-mesh sign designed by Don Knorr

Between the Museum and the Marketplace: Selling Good Design

Terence Riley and Edward Eigen

In the final months of 1949, Edgar J. Kaufmann, Jr, was in the midst of preparing the most extensive exhibition program in the applied arts The Museum of Modern Art has ever undertaken. The program, called Good Design, was to be the realization of Kaufmann's vision of a broad collaboration between art and commerce—a vision that predated his 1946 appointment as Director of the Museum's Department of Industrial Design. In mid-1949 Kaufmann had noted, approvingly, that "In one season recently twelve American museums of art held exhibitions of applied design that served to guide the public toward good taste in objects available for purchase."[1] Of these exhibitions, he had been particularly impressed by the design exhibition "For Modern Living," staged earlier that year by his friend, the architect and designer Alexander Girard, for the Detroit Institute of Arts. But the projected scope of the Good Design program's intervention in the housewares industry—especially its ambition ultimately to influence the buying habits of American consumers and the selling practices of retailers—was without precedent in the United States, and was rivaled only by the activities of the Deutscher Werkbund in the 1920s. In its efforts to reform the applied arts in response to the rapid industrialization of society, the Werkbund had worked closely with museums, manufacturers, artists' guilds, and, particularly, retailers, who could directly affect consumer decisions.[2] A quarter-century later, The Museum of Modern Art would collaborate with The Merchandise Mart of Chicago, the nation's largest wholesale marketer, to realize a similar goal in the context of a newly prosperous postwar America. From 1950 to 1954, these two "national institutions"[3] would stage at the Mart semiannual exhibitions of readily available household goods of innovative design, publicizing the program through a far-reaching campaign in the print and broadcast media. At year's end, a "compendium" of design objects selected by Kaufmann from the January and June installations at the Mart would be shown in New York at the Museum.

By examining the extent and nature of Good Design's activism in the design field, this essay will explore the pragmatic relationship of the Museum to industry and commerce in its promotion of good modern design at mid-century.

•

The Museum of Modern Art's first exhibition of industrially-made products, "Machine Art," was held in 1934, and included furniture and objects designed for the home.[4] Its curator, Philip Johnson, sought not only to proselytize modern design but also to define for the American public what modern design was, just as the Museum's Founding Director, Alfred H. Barr, Jr., had sought to define modern painting and sculpture for a broad public.[5] Johnson's definition, stated in the catalogue of the exhibition, is notable for its canonical exclusions, which in effect also defined what modern design was not:

. . . the Paris Exposition of Decorative Arts of 1925, with its neo-classic trappings and bizarre ornament, made a strong impression on our designers. The problem in America has not been the conflict against a strong handicraft tradition but rather against a "modernistic" French machine-age aesthetic.

Besides the French Decorative movement in the '20's there developed in America a desire for "styling" objects for advertising. Styling a commercial object gives it more "eye-appeal" and therefore helps sales. Principles such as "streamlining" often receive homage out of all proportion to their applicability.

Conscious design and the development in machine building have fused and the twentieth century restores the art of making machines and useful objects to its place, as a technic of making rapidly, simply and well the useful objects of current life.[6]

Johnson placed his argument firmly within a fine-arts context, considering machined objects in purely aesthetic terms and prefacing his own words with quotations from Plato's *Philebus* and Saint Thomas Aquinas's *Summa Theologiae*, offered in classical Greek and Latin with English translations. The philosophers' speculations on the definition of beauty were followed by this imperative from Lawrence Pearsall Jacks: "Industrial civilization must either find a means of ending the divorce between its industry and its 'culture' or perish."[7] In its subsequent programs of exhibitions and publications, the Museum would attempt to play the role of matchmaker to Jacks's estranged couple. Of these programs, Good Design was undoubtedly the most ambitious.

"Good Design, A Joint Program to Stimulate the Best Modern Design of Home Furnishings" brought together the Museum and The Merchandise Mart in an effort to influence their respective audiences: the Museum's members and visitors, who may have been disposed toward modern design; and the Mart's wholesale buyers, who were instrumental in determining what goods appeared in retail stores throughout the country. The ultimate goals of this complex strategy—involving exhibitions, publications, symposia, advertising, consumer opinion polls, and other public programs—were to inform consumers and manufacturers about modern design products and to insure that these products were made widely available through retail markets. While many of the Museum's other programs toward these ends were educational in aspect—for instance, the circulation of exhibitions to schools, universities, and department stores—Good Design was unique in seeking to expand and transform the commercial design field in the United States.

As it took shape in late 1949, the program was to consist of three shows annually, the first two planned to coincide with the winter and summer housewares markets at the Mart, and the third, a year-end compilation shown at the Museum. Like most of the "Useful Objects" exhibitions—the logical successors to "Machine Art"—Good Design was clearly intended to influence not only what the public thought about modern design but also to encourage tasteful consumption. Both the "Useful Objects" and the Good Design exhibitions occurred at Christmastime and were accompanied by pamphlet-type catalogues listing the objects, their cost, and where they could be purchased. In a joint statement, René d'Harnoncourt, Director of the Museum, and Wallace O. Ollman, the general manager of The Merchandise Mart, declared, "Two national institutions . . . believe and hope than in combining their resources they will stimulate the appreciation of and creation of the best design among manufacturers, designers and retailers for good living in the American home."[8] Their mutual belief in the benefits of a collaboration among the participants in the housewares industry, and in the importance of the home and good living in the promotion of modern design, fueled their ambitions for the program. Equally vital to the success of Good Design was the institutional prestige that the two organizations brought to their alliance.

The guiding force of the Good Design program, and the person with whom the enterprise has become indelibly associated, was Edgar J. Kaufmann, Jr. (fig. 2), the son of the wealthy Pittsburgh merchant who had founded the prosperous department store that bore his name. His acumen as a curator and his enthusiasm for modern design owed much to his experience as a merchandiser in the home-furnishings department of his father's store and to his father's interest in modern design in relation to retailing. Kaufmann, like many proponents of modern design, had no formal educational degrees, although he had attended the Kunstgewerbeschule of the Oesterreichisches Museum für angewandte Kunst in Vienna during the late twenties and had studied painting and typography for three years with Victor Hammer in Florence. Kaufmann also had been a Fellow at Frank Lloyd Wright's Taliesin Foundation from 1933 to 1934 and was a keen promoter of the architect. Indeed, he strongly supported his father's decision to commission Wright to design the family's country home—the well-known masterpiece Fallingwater (1936), in Mill Run, Pennsylvania—as well as a number of unrealized civic projects. In addition, Wright designed the office of the senior Kaufmann in 1937.[9]

2. Edgar J. Kaufmann, Jr., 1951

Edgar J. Kaufmann, Sr., believed that the department store could play a progressive role in the cultural life of the community while conducting good business. He had retained the Viennese émigré architect Joseph Urban for an unrealized scheme to redesign the first floor of Kaufmann's department store and the Hungarian set designer Lazlo Gabor to arrange window displays. An advertisement for the store's eventual first-floor renovation in 1925 reads, "Our destiny as a creative nation which sponsors and encourages artistry is assured providing our power to appreciate continues to grow. . . . No modern organization is in a better position to observe this artistic evolution than a large department store."[10] Appropriately, along the walls of the store's first floor was a series of murals depicting the evolution of commerce by Boardman Robinson, who later painted the murals at Radio City Music Hall. Each year, the store's street windows housed displays called "Peaks of Progress" that illustrated the ten most important scientific, sociological, and historic events of the preceding year. Students in area schools wrote essays about the displays, underscoring the store's presence in the civic consciousness and demonstrating the windows' capacity for uses other than narrowly commercial ones.[11] The store also hosted traveling art exhibitions (some organized by The Museum of Modern Art) and shows of its own, including the 1926 International Exposition of Industrial Arts.[12]

In 1940, Edgar Kaufmann, Jr., representing his father's department store, wrote to Alfred Barr, then Director of The Museum of Modern Art, proposing a program that ultimately would be realized as the Organic Design in Home Furnishings Competition.[13] "Organic design," a catchphrase at the time,[14] no doubt referred to the current interest in Wright's theories of design, which Kaufmann played a large part in promoting. Kaufmann envisioned a collaboration in which the Museum would develop a competition brief, the department store would provide financing and space for "facilities for general living," and the designers would engage manufacturers to produce the winning designs. The plan was taken up in 1941 by the Director of the Museum's Department of Industrial Design, Eliot Noyes. The final brief states that, concurrent with the exhibition, twelve leading department stores—including Bloomingdale's in New York, Marshall Field's in Chicago, Gimbel's in Philadelphia, and Kaufmann's in Pittsburgh—would offer the prize-winning furniture for sale: "Through the cooperation of sponsoring department stores and manufacturers, the Museum has been able to eliminate the lag time between theory and application, a condition heretofore tending to discourage public interest in good design."[15] The jury, which included Barr, Marcel Breuer, Kaufmann, Noyes, Frank Parrish, and Edward Durell Stone, chose chairs and other furniture designed by Charles Eames and Eero Saarinen, among others (fig. 3).

Kaufmann formally joined the museum staff in 1946, following a tour of duty in the U.S. Air Force Intelligence Office. After returning briefly to the Museum after also serving in the Air Force, Noyes, who had been head of the design department since 1940, had left the Museum to work with the designer Norman Bel Geddes. By 1948, Kaufmann's ability to develop projects involving multiple constituencies was evident. The International Competition for Low-Cost Furniture Design of that year resulted from a collaboration between the Museum and the Museum Design Project, Inc., a group of prominent furniture retailers formed to promote the winning designs commercially. The competition, limited to storage units and seating units designed for one or more people, sought to apply mass-production techniques developed during the war to furniture "integrated to the needs of modern living, production, and merchandising."[16] In addition to publishing and exhibiting the designs at the Museum and promoting them with manufacturers and retailers, Kaufmann brought in technicians from major universities to advise the designers and industrialists on adapting prototypes for mass production. To secure designers a fair share of the profits, he even acted as their agent. The Museum Design Project, Inc., offered an exclusive franchise to the retailers who sold the prize-winning designs chosen by a selection committee that included Ludwig Mies van der Rohe and Gordon Russell. Like the goal of the Organic Design in Home Furnishings Competition—to reduce the "lag time" in the assimilation of modern design—the International Competition for Low-Cost Furniture Design provided technical and financial assistance to designers "who found it difficult to find ways to translate their ideas into reality."[17]

Kaufmann's place in the Museum became somewhat tenuous when the departments of Industrial Design and Architecture were consolidated under the direction of Philip Johnson in 1948. Until that time, the two departments had been under the respective direction of Kaufmann and Philip L. Goodwin, one of the architects of the Museum's 53rd Street building of 1939. Kaufmann subsequently carried out the

3. Charles Eames and Eero Saarinen. Drawing submitted for Organic Design in Home Furnishings Competition, 1941. Pencil on white posterboard, covered with cellophane, 30 x 20" (76.2 x 50.8 cm). The Museum of Modern Art, New York. Gift of the designers (861.42)

Good Design program largely independently of all other departmental activities. There was an unspoken but obvious antagonism between Kaufmann and Johnson, the two most visible proselytizers of modern design in the United States. Johnson had completed his architectural studies at Harvard University under Walter Gropius in 1943, and by 1949 had constructed his Glass House in New Canaan, Connecticut—a veritable salon for architectural theory—and he maintained a relatively elitist stance, focusing on design as an extension of the fine art of architecture. Kaufmann, though an astute organizer and patron of the arts, had been brought up in the practical world of commerce and had set his sights on converting the masses to a more populist, "domesticated" modernism.[18] By virtue of its popular appeal, the program was in stark contrast to Johnson's activities during these years, which were centered on formal interpretations of modern architecture and exhibitions geared toward the American establishment, including "Architecture for the State Department" (1953) and "Buildings for Business and Government" (1957).

D'Harnoncourt straddled the two positions, embracing Good Design as a way to define and guide popular taste even as he maintained the institution's ties to a wealthy and powerful elite. Mildred Constantine, then Assistant Curator in the Department of Architecture and Design, has stated that the reason d'Harnoncourt "was anxious to sponsor the Good Design shows, which were Edgar's baby, was because it did give [Kaufmann] a really strong position in an area he loved, with the Museum's support [and] without any interference from the department."[19] Toward this goal, d'Harnoncourt spent a week in St. Louis in 1950 promoting Good Design at the Scruggs, Vandevoort and Barney department store, where he gave lectures, radio interviews, and demonstrations. As he explained to local reporters, "Of every 100 persons who come to the Museum we estimate that no more than 10 actually accept a geometric abstraction by Piet Mondrian as valid art[,] . . . but when principles of good design permeate a home, the occupants tend to be more tolerant, more receptive to new ideas in art."[20] Whether or not Good Design ever effectively served to familiarize the public with modern art, it brought immense public attention to the Museum.

The Merchandise Mart, the Museum's collaborator, occupied a structure designed by the Chicago firm Graham, Anderson, Probst and White; built in 1928–31, it was the largest building in the world in floor area until the Pentagon was constructed in 1943. Though the complex originally had been constructed as the corporate warehouse and distribution center for Marshall Field's department store, the flamboyant entrepreneur Joseph P. Kennedy bought it during the Depression for a greatly compromised price, and by 1945 had expanded it into a national wholesale market for home furnishings. The Mart housed showrooms, manufacturers' offices, the Merchants & Manufacturers Club, and broadcast studios for the NBC and ABC networks. A publicity brochure stated that the complex made it easy for retailers to "do all their buying under one roof with a maximum of convenience and comfort"[21]—language now familiar from shopping-mall promotions. Beginning in 1948, the Mart opened its upper display floors to consumers, offering guided tours that attracted 80,000 visitors in the first year; 5,300 square feet of this public space would later be dedicated to the Good Design program. According to Kennedy, the Mart's interest in the program was related to consumer interest in specific goods seen in the manufacturers' showrooms.[22]

Good Design became a featured part of the Mart's semiannual home furnishing shows in January and June, which were attended by as many as 27,000 professional buyers. The Mart housed more than 2,000 lines of furniture for the home; as such, the prominent display of the items selected for Good Design exhibits at the Mart conferred a high degree of prestige. For the 3,200 manufacturers who displayed 1,209,000 separate items at the Mart, distinctiveness of any kind was a requirement of good business. Kaufmann was aware of the potential of The Merchandise Mart to influence manufacturers and distributors and, hence, popular taste and consumption. While Good Design was conceived to shape consumer buying habits, the public did not play an entirely passive role. An important function of the visitors was to rate the selections through polls taken at the door. At the inaugural exhibition in 1950, 8,130 ballots were cast by both buyers and consumers. Each person was asked to vote for five items, and 126 of the 250 objects in the Good Design exhibition were chosen. The results of the poll, essentially a marketing survey, were distributed to manufacturers, department stores, and the popular press.[23] The balloting not only prefigured the interactive information systems of today but also served as a useful guide to manufacturers and retailers, and to the Good Design selection committees as well. Items chosen in the polls were also featured in panel discussions organized by the Museum. These symposia were a way of directly involving design professionals and critics in the program while advancing the Museum's design values in the press and in critical discussions of specific items in the exhibitions.

Kaufmann's ability to manipulate commercial mechanisms to promote the Museum's goals is evident in the Museum and the Mart's joint statement of Good Design's objectives: "1. Greater consumer interest is to be focused on original design by taking advantage of its inherent news value. 2. To provide greater impetus for designers to produce good new products. 3. To encourage manufacturers to produce good design, and to draw their attention to the growing market by the wider consumer demand."[24] "Such effect," the brief continues, "would enhance the reputation of the Merchandise Mart and the Museum as leaders in sound design trends." This reputation was not an end in itself, but rather a means of influencing popular taste and consumption. Thus, the success of Good Design ultimately rested at the retail level, the nexus between the museum-going public and the wholesale housewares industry.

To encourage stores to install Good Design exhibits featuring the products they had purchased at The Merchandise Mart, the program's organizers employed overt marketing pitches: "Homemakers know GOOD DESIGN selections can be bought with confidence. GOOD DESIGN gives your store an unbiased choice of newly designed home furnishings most in keeping with modern living."[25] Kaufmann arranged for designers to create the department-store displays and offered stores Good Design tags so that the consumer could differentiate between the purportedly unbiased selections of the Museum's juries and those that were, by implication, unduly influenced by commercial concerns. Designed by Morton Goldsholl, a Chicago graphic designer who had studied with László Moholy-Nagy, the tags featured the Good Design logo: a white sans-serif typeface within a black circle against an orange background (fig. 4). True to Good Design's aspirations, the tag worked to the benefit of both the Museum and the Mart: As the Museum's seal of approval, it was an invaluable marketing device.

The Good Design program involved the participation of a wide range of

4. Good Design tags designed by Morton Goldsholl

designers, design professionals, and critics in staging and evaluating its activities, including the selection committee convened for each exhibition. These three-person juries were composed of prominent designers, critics, architects, and, in some cases, merchants, whose appointments as jurors resulted from the Mart's concern that "commercial vitality and acceptability of products be given some consideration . . . at least to the extent of having the judgment of one retailer at the selection committee level."[26] In addition, Kaufmann was a standing member of all the juries. Jurors for the first year included Meyric C. Rodgers, Curator of Decorative Arts at the Art Institute of Chicago; and Alexander Girard.[27] An effort was made to insure that the jurors who were designers did not have their works in the exhibitions of the same year as their jury service, though most of the judging designers' works were shown in the program at one time or another. According to Good Design literature, items for jury consideration were sought by "the Good Design research staff who shop wholesale and retail markets [and] scan trade and consumer publications."[28] One year into the program, Kaufmann hired Carolyn Rees of Los Angeles, a former Taliesin Fellow, as a scout to relay news of design activity on the West Coast. Solicitations in trade magazines created another source for a great number of goods; manufacturers were invited to send entries to the Mart for jury review two weeks prior to the show. Unlike furniture-design competitions, especially the International Competition for Low-Cost Furniture Design, which offered a $5,000 first prize in each of two design categories, the Good Design program brief states that there would be no awards category for "best" design. Instead, the program would seek to present a selection of high-quality, widely available wares that could be combined with one another according to shape, color, size, and function. Perhaps more importantly, by having no best-design category, Good Design sought to avoid the easy commercial appeal of designations like "better" and "best" even while actively promoting the longer-lasting value of "good" design in the same commercial venues that traditionally resorted to those catchwords. (D'Harnoncourt, concerned with the runaway promotional language of the Mart's publicity manager, Robert M. Johnson, asked that the word "exhibition" be substituted for "promotion" when referring to the Good Design program in publicity.[29])

Kaufmann also sought to promote design schools that were training the next generation of modern designers. As part of the fifth-anniversary exhibition of 1954–55, he invited universities—including the North Carolina State College School of Design, the Illinois Institute of Technology, the Massachusetts Institute of Technology, the University of Georgia, and the Cranbrook Academy of Art—to produce displays investigating materials, techniques, and design. The exhibition not only promoted these schools but also provided manufacturers valuable sources for new talent for their industries.

Unlike Johnson's pointed philosophical and aesthetic speculations in the "Machine Art" exhibition, Kaufmann's criteria for Good Design were relatively vague, allowing broad latitude for individual jurors' personal tastes concerning visual appeal, function, construction, and cost. George Nelson, whose work was frequently selected by the juries, characterized the nonideological basis of the program rather ungraciously: "Good Design, as popularized by the Museum of Modern Art and the Merchandise Mart, has come to mean a certain number of objects selected by Mr. Kaufmann and his juries . . . objects which may then carry a kind of label of approval when displayed for sale in stores."[30] Kaufmann's emphasis on "eye appeal," the very term Johnson derided in "Machine Art," reflected his experience as a retailer as much as his attitude toward design. Perhaps even more revealing of the program's market-responsive realism was the Mart's insistence that "the products selected be readily available and already in production"; yet Kaufmann, sympathetic to the concerns and travails of fledgling design studios, responded by suggesting that availability "is not a primary concern [because] an item may be *distributed better* after inclusion in the show. Availability[,] yes, [but] *wide* availability [is] not essential."[31] The Mart's concerns about the jury's selections were easy to understand. Lazette van Houten, an editor of *Retailing Daily* and a Good Design juror in 1954, wrote, "Maybe the Modern Museum is too arty to care about anything so vulgar as money (though some of its best enemies will chortle over that one) but no one can so basely accuse the Merchandise Mart."[32]

In his introduction to the first Good Design exhibition catalogue in 1950, Kaufmann emphasized the characteristic that would most distinguish the program from its predecessors at The Museum of Modern Art: "Twelve years ago the show (called Useful Objects) was limited in scope and modestly presented. Today, a comprehensive selection and fitting presentation have become possible."[33] Kaufmann's emphasis on a "comprehensive selection," combined with his belief in the validating forces of the marketplace, insured that the Good Design exhibitions would never be "limited in scope" (see, for example, fig. 5). The average number of items presented in each exhibition was 175 and during the height of the program approached 400 pieces, an array that emphasized comprehensiveness over selection in almost every aspect. Using a retailer's taxonomy, Kaufmann attempted to impose a degree of order

on what was at times an admittedly bewildering profusion of items (fig. 6). In the Good Design publications, the goods are arranged in a manner typically found in department stores: furniture, wallcoverings, kitchen and cleaning equipment, and so on. As such, a sugar bowl and a flower bowl, both designed by Glidden Parker, appeared in separate categories—the former in "tableware," the latter in "accessories"—emphasizing their roles in social rituals above any other characteristic. Similarly, distinctions rather than commonalities were made among sheer, drapery, and upholstery fabrics. The obvious synergy between education and consumption represented in the exhibition's taxonomy was, of course, at the heart of the Good Design program.

In contrast, the curator of the "Useful Objects" series, John McAndrew, delineated a group of functional criteria for selecting items for the exhibitions: suitability to purpose, materials and process of manufacture, and, only "after an object [had] been gauged in the first three standards, . . . aesthetic quality."[34] Central to the selection criteria was the price of the object. Each of the annual show titles included a maximum dollar amount for the items displayed, linking good design and good value while negating the assumption that design, like styling, was a surplus value that raised an item's price. "Useful Household Objects Under $5.00" was designed as a traveling exhibition; it was shown in stores and schools seventeen times over a four-year period beginning in 1938. In 1940, the show became "Useful Objects of Design Under $10," and in December 1942, "Useful Objects in Wartime Under $10." Elodie Courter, until 1947 the Museum's Director of Circulating Exhibitions, noted, "There are many fine examples of straightforward industrial design . . . which deserve exhibition in galleries devoted to the 'arts' of today."[35] However, McAndrew maintained a distinction between the fine and applied arts: "Fine art is that in which the intention of the artist is primarily aesthetic; this intention is usually conscious. 'Applied art' is that in which the intention of the artist is to make handsome an object which is primarily a useful one."[36] He added, "Between these are a few disputable border provinces and patches of no-man's land," suggesting that the antipode to good functional design was not art but styling—specifically, streamlining.

Left:
5. Installation view of "Good Design," The Merchandise Mart, Chicago, 1950. Installation design by Charles Eames

Right:
6. Installation view of "Good Design," The Merchandise Mart, Chicago, 1953. Installation design by Alexander Girard

An article in the Museum of Modern Art *Bulletin* (1942–43) compared a toaster shown in Johnson's "Machine Art" show of 1934 with one designed in 1940 that was "streamlined as if it were intended to hurtle through the air at 200 miles per hour."[37] Considering its function, this was an "unhappy use for a breakfast table utensil." But, while McAndrew placed aesthetic quality last and price first, Kaufmann had a distinct sensibility about the "look" of the objects chosen for inclusion in Good Design and a rather elastic definition of reasonable cost. When compared to Good Design's ambition to influence the housewares market and to survey the entire country for directions in sales and production, the "Useful Objects" series appeared limited in both size and reach.

Kaufmann's decision that each Good Design object be "new in the [U.S. market] since the previous show"[38] established an equivalence between the good and the new—a concept that became a characteristic of the optimism of the postwar years. Since the program coincided with one of the most prolific periods of design in the United States, when industrial capital and progressive design found a unique common ground, Kaufmann's policy was not a severe limitation, and it served to focus the program on the great stream of innovative products created in the early 1950s. Even so, since many Good Design products—from Venini glass (fig. 7) to Harry Bertoia's basketlike wire furniture (see fig. 21)—have become classics of twentieth-century design, the phenomenon has overshadowed the presence of more populist improvements in domestic life that might more appropriately be called novelties. As in the "Useful Objects" exhibition series, which in one instance included a revolving tie rack available at R. H. Macy's department store, the Good Design program featured a significant number of such objects, including the "Zipout" shrimp cleaner (fig. 8) and the "Susie Flipper" pancake turner, the principal virtues of which are plainspoken domestic ingenuity rather than aesthetic or technical virtuosity.

Unlike the Deutscher Werkbund exhibitions or the Festival of Britain exposition of 1951, Kaufmann's comprehensive survey had no nationalist definition. Items could be either domestic or foreign in origin, provided they were available in U.S. markets. In practice, a large percentage of the goods presented in the Good Design program were American-made. However, from the beginning of the program, the imported goods were almost all Scandinavian in origin—an indication of the extent to which northern European countries, largely neutral during World War II, had dominated the field of design and consumer production in the years when Allied governments were restructuring their manufacturing bases from a wartime to a peacetime economy. Among the Scandinavian designs in the inaugural exhibition were an armchair by Alvar Aalto for Artek, a ceiling lamp by Jørn Utzon for New Design, and ceramics by Stig Lindberg for Gustavsberg. The Danish designer Finn Juhl, of whose work Kaufmann had written in 1948,[39] was represented in the 1951 exhibition with a beechwood chair (fig. 9).

For the most part, the Scandinavian design products were mass-produced from relatively inexpensive materials and intended for a large middle-class market. Even so, they were appreciably more expensive (as were all the goods imported from Europe) than those mass-produced in the United States. For example, a simple tumbler designed by Freda Diamond for Libbey Glass sold for about fifteen cents, and similar glassware by Russel Wright sold for seventy cents; in contrast, tumblers designed by Kaj Franck for Wärtsilä cost twice as much as those by Wright.

7. Fulvio Bianconi. "Handkerchief" Vase, 1949. Glass, 13¼" (33.7 cm) high. The Museum of Modern Art, New York. Gift of Georg Jensen, Inc. (494.53.1) ("Good Design," 1952)

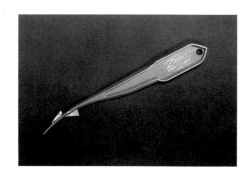

8. "Zipout" shrimp cleaner and deveiner by Stephen Paoli (Arthur Paoli & Son) ("Good Design," 1950)

9. Chair by Finn Juhl ("Good Design," 1951)

Left:
10. Sven G. Winquist. Self-aligning Ball Bearing, 1929. Steel and chrome-plated steel balls, 8½" (21.6 cm) diam. The Museum of Modern Art, New York. Gift of the manufacturer, SKF Industries, Inc. (211.34)

Right:
11. Marcel Breuer. Armchair, 1927–28. Chrome-plated tubular steel and canvas, 28⅛ x 30¼ x 27¾" (71.8 x 76.8 x 70.5 cm). The Museum of Modern Art, New York. Gift of Herbert Bayer (229.34)

Demonstrating the elasticity of Kaufmann's definition of reasonable cost, highball glasses manufactured by Baccarat were also included at a cost of $6.50 each, and a sterling-silver jug designed by Johan Rohde for the Georg Jensen Silversmithy was, at $210, equivalent in price to the washing machine designed by Henry Dreyfuss for the Hoover Company shown that same year.

This comprehensive approach is also evident in the materials and the manufacturing processes used to produce the Good Design products. In his "Machine Art" exhibition, Johnson had consciously attempted to make a direct connection between aesthetic form and machine processes and materials, illustrated by the pairing of a stainless-steel, self-aligning ball bearing produced by SKF Industries (fig. 10) and a chromium-finished, tubular-steel chair designed by Marcel Breuer for Thonet Bros. (fig. 11). Alfred Barr enthusiastically endorsed the exhibition, stating, "If, to use L. P. Jack's phrase, we are to 'end the divorce' between our industry and our culture we must assimilate the machine aesthetically as well as economically."[40] But Good Design demonstrated no such ideological position. It might even be said that, by the 1950s, such an approach was no longer possible. Considerably more materials, many developed in the war effort and few reflecting the machine imagery of tubular steel and polished chrome, were now being used in industrial production, including plywood, pressed wood, plastics, Lucite, rayon, nylon, fiberglass, spun metals, and synthetic rubber. Kaufmann also refused to make a distinction between the machine-made and the handcrafted in his selections. Thus, visitors to Good Design events encountered Plastic Productions' "Gray-N-Ware" mixing bowls as well as Chester Pfeiffer's hand-carved black-mahogany bowl; Russel Wright's designs for rayon-and-cotton casement cloth manufactured by Foster Textile Mills and Jack Lenor Larsen's handwoven, hand-painted linen; Harold Cohen and Davis J. Pratt's tubular-metal and red-nylon-mesh chair (fig. 12) and a solid hardwood chair, after an 1899 design by Richard Riemerschmid, manufactured by Dunbar Furniture Corp. Unsurprisingly, the machine-made items were less labor-intensive and thus less expensive than the handcrafted ones, though it should be noted that the items

12. Chair by Harold Cohen and Davis J. Pratt (Designers in Production) ("Good Design," 1954)

13. Dining chairs and table by William Katavolos, Ross Littell, and Douglas Kelley (Laverne Originals) ("Good Design," 1953)

mass-produced from newly-developed materials were normally more costly than those manufactured from traditional ones.

Kaufmann's nonpolemical stance toward the machine and handcraft is reflected in his statement that the Good Design program was to be staged "by people with no axes to grind,"[41] and, further, in his critical support of a number of new design studios that used neither machine- nor hand-production methods exclusively. Founded and directed by talented young designers, these firms produced furniture, fabrics, and housewares of exceptional quality on a limited mass-production basis. They included Design Unit New York (Ben Baldwin and William Machado), Designers in Production (Cohen and Pratt), Laverne Originals (Erwine and Estelle Laverne; fig. 13), Knoll Associates (Florence and Hans Knoll), and Gross Wood & Company (Gross and Esther Wood; fig. 14). While only Knoll Associates—a "little pip-squeak in terms of manufacturing" at the time[42]—would achieve tremendous commercial success, all of these studios had as a common goal the successful integration of design and manufacturing.

Very little current production seemed beyond Kaufmann's widely-cast net: "Modern design means design intended for present day life in regard to usefulness, to production methods and materials, and to the progressive taste of the day."[43] However, when considering the exhibitions' inclusions and exclusions, some interpretation of the "progressive taste of the day" can be discerned. Kaufmann's caveat against any "attempt to imitate the past"[44] has been at the heart of all progressive movements throughout the twentieth century, although his support of "comfort in every day living"[45] insured that the austerities of Johnson's machine aesthetic would surrender to the eye appeal of Good Design, with its emphasis on color, fluid linearity, and sensuous form. Historicist styles and applied ornament remained the principal dragons to be slain in the battle for good design.

14. Perforated metal bowls by Gross and Esther Wood (Gross Wood & Company); enamel-on-copper bowls by Harold Elberg; and black oxidized-metal-and-brass cigarette box by Paul Hagenaur ("Good Design," 1953)

Notably, the only non-Western products chosen for inclusion in the Good Design program were from Asia. Given Kaufmann's predilection for a tactile surface, it is predictable that the majority of these products were fabrics, including delicate silks and other handwoven cloths from Japan, Thailand, India, and the Philippines. Japan was also represented by a wide range of traditional handcrafts, such as papers, lacquerware, ceramics, and carved wood. Though he had assembled an exhibition of Mexican craftwork for Kaufmann's department store in 1940, and would direct the exhibition "Textiles U.S.A." for The Museum of Modern Art in 1956, Kaufmann was not the first to recognize the affinities between modern design and certain non-Western crafts. While the Good Design program presented America's revised, post-war perspective on Japan, a fascination with that country predates the twentieth century, stimulated in part by the presentation of traditional Japanese architecture and crafts at the 1876 Philadelphia Centennial and the 1893 World's Columbian Exposition in Chicago. Despite this history, it is striking to compare the formal, spatial, and textural relationships between the interiors of the Knoll Associates showroom of 1952 (fig. 15) and the Japanese Exhibition House constructed in the Museum's Abby Aldrich Rockefeller Sculpture Garden in 1954 (fig. 16).

•

The comprehensiveness with which Kaufmann approached Good Design has been noted at length; however, the fact that the program included nearly every important designer of the postwar period should not be seen simply as a result of Kaufmann's catholic taste. Indeed, many other broadly based surveys demonstrated a remarkable ability to overlook what now appears to have been the obvious talent of the day. The Good Design program represented an exceptional number of gifted young or mid-career designers and successfully identified the key figures in postwar design as well.

A few of the selected designers were born in the nineteenth century, and their continued presence as innovators in the 1950s attests to the root influences of Good

Left:
15. Showroom at Knoll Associates, New York, designed by Florence Knoll, 1951. Color photograph included in the exhibition "De Stijl" at The Museum of Modern Art, New York, 1952

Right:
16. Tea room of the Japanese Exhibition House, installed in the Abby Aldrich Rockefeller Sculpture Garden, The Museum of Modern Art, New York, 1954

17. Arne Jacobsen. "Ant" Stacking Side Chair, 1951. Molded plywood and steel, 30 x 16 x 15½" (76.2 x 40.6 x 39.4 cm). The Museum of Modern Art, New York. Gift of Richards Morgenthau Company (140.55) ("Good Design," 1954)

Design's vision of postwar American design. They included the Finnish architect Alvar Aalto (born 1898), whose plywood furniture had been exhibited at the Museum as early as 1938; Anni Albers (born 1899), who had been a weaving instructor at the Bauhaus before immigrating to the United States in 1933; Raymond Loewy (born 1893) and Walter Dorwin Teague, Sr. (born 1883), both of whom were instrumental in shaping modern industrial design in the United States. In contrast, the majority of those whose talents were featured in Good Design were born in the first two decades of the twentieth century; they included Arne Jacobsen (see fig. 17), Henry Dreyfuss, Kaj Franck, Finn Juhl, Boris Kroll, and Marianne Strengell. They, and figures such as Freda Diamond, Eszter Haraszty, Trudi and Harold Sitterle (see fig. 18), Russel Wright, and Eva Zeisel, primarily completed their education and apprenticeships after the Paris Exposition Internationale des Arts Décoratifs et Industriels Modernes in 1925 and before the outbreak of World War II in 1939. They had in common the experience of spending their early careers designing for societies conditioned by the privations of economic depression and wartime. In a keynote address at the opening of Good Design, the journalist Alfred Auerbach noted that President Calvin Coolidge had written a letter to the organizers of the 1925 exposition explaining that there was no American design in a modern enough vein to warrant the participation of the United States.[46] Good Design made clear that the shortage of design sophistication in the prewar period had been appreciably overcome.

The waves of immigration caused by the sociopolitical and economic crises of the 1930s brought a number of key European figures into direct contact with Good Design's golden generation. Marcel Breuer and Walter Gropius employed Eliot Noyes after he graduated from Harvard and before he began to work at the Museum as a design curator. Although George Nelson never worked for the Bauhaus émigrés, during his Prix de Rome travels in 1932 (following his studies at Yale University), he sought out and wrote about the International Style architects who had been featured that year in The Museum of Modern Art's "Modern Architecture: International Exhibition," organized by Henry-Russell Hitchcock and Philip Johnson. Nelson's elegantly proportioned and minimally detailed rolling table (fig. 19), presented in the 1952 edition of Good Design, attests to his self-selected influences. Florence Knoll, one of the few women of her generation trained as an architect, also worked for Breuer and Gropius in Cambridge, Massachusetts, following her studies at the Architectural Association in London and, under Ludwig Mies van der Rohe, at the Illinois Institute of Technology in Chicago. In addition to producing the work of a cadre of new young designers, Knoll and her husband, Hans, manufactured and ultimately popularized Breuer's and Mies's classic Bauhaus furniture designs in the United States. Her own work included upholstered chairs and sofas with profiles as linear and sleek as the metal and wood furniture of her peers. These trademark designs reflected not only the influence of the International Style but also her earlier experience at Cranbrook Academy in Bloomfield Hills, Michigan. In the thirties and forties, this seminal institution brought together the Finnish architect and president of the school, Eliel Saarinen, a dazzling circle of talented émigré teachers, and an equally talented group of students. In addition to Knoll (then Florence Schust), Benjamin Baldwin, Harry Bertoia, Charles and Ray Eames, Alexander Girard, Don Knorr, Jack Lenor Larsen, Eero Saarinen, and Harry Weese were all Cranbrook alumni whose works appeared in the Good Design program (see figs. 20, 21, 22).

18. Trudi and Harold Sitterle. Pepper Mill, 1949–50. Porcelain and steel, 4¾" (12.1 cm) high. The Museum of Modern Art, New York. Gift of the designers (21.SC.50) ("Good Design," 1950)

Left:
19. Mobile table by George Nelson ("Good Design," 1952)

Right:
20. Sideboard by Florence Knoll ("Good Design," 1950)

More than any other program at The Museum of Modern Art, Good Design featured a high percentage of women as designers, in symposia, and, by extension, in the media. The possibilities for women to work outside of the home had fluctuated with the needs of the war effort, increasing dramatically when they were called to fill factory jobs left vacant by departing servicemen, and ebbing when the same men returned to reclaim their jobs in peacetime. Nonetheless, the design field in the United States, as in Germany—specifically, at the Dessau Bauhaus—had been an area considered appropriate for, and therefore accepting of, women. Good Design, however, was not free of the types of limitations placed on women's roles that characterized the period—limitations that persist even today. In contrast to most other design categories in the program, furniture, which was always looked to as the most important area of design, was dominated by men. A further distinction between men and women lay in education, since the men best known for furniture design were trained as architects, a profession historically not open to women. Inevitably, it would be the trained architects—Eames, Jacobsen, Nelson, Saarinen, and others—who would have the broadest impact on design in the ensuing years. By virtue of their education, they were able to determine not only the design of objects but the environment as well, creating a more comprehensive context within which their work could be developed.

Left:
21. Harry Bertoia. Side Chair, 1952. Vinyl-coated steel, steel, and naugahyde seat pad, 30 x 21½ x 21" (76.2 x 54.6 x 53.3 cm). The Museum of Modern Art, New York. Purchase (449.56) ("Good Design," 1953)

Right:
22. Saddle stool by Don Knorr ("Good Design," 1952)

Although the historical barriers between the women designers and the men (and few women) trained as architects were quite arbitrary and unfair, the design work of the latter group must be recognized for its extraordinarily high distinction. Charles and Ray Eames's work consistently stood out, both in terms of the number of pieces selected by the juries and in the quality and originality of their designs. The "LTR" table, "ESU" storage unit (fig. 23), and model LAR fiberglass chair (fig. 24) are just a few of their many exceptional products that appeared in Good Design exhibitions.[47]

Predictably, then, all of the designers selected to direct the installations of the Good Design exhibitions were men trained as architects. Charles Eames, who had first achieved recognition at the Museum through his winning entry in the Organic Design in Home Furnishings Competition in 1941, provided the design for the inaugural installation in 1950 (see fig. 5). D. J. De Pree, President of the Herman Miller Furniture Company, whose first Los Angeles showroom the Eameses had designed a year earlier, donated $500 to cover part of their expenses for providing the Good Design installation.[48] The scheme included wood-laminate platforms, Marlite panels, simple screen partitions whose use Charles Eames had perfected in his Case Study House #8 (1945–49; fig. 25) in Santa Monica, California, sponsored by *Arts & Architecture* magazine. Also on display were whimsical wall-mounted photographs of eighteenth-century silverware, Constantin Brancusi's *Column Without End* (1937–38), and artworks by Pablo Picasso and Henry Moore. The fifteen objects on loan from the American Museum of Natural History, New York, included, despite the program's emphasis on the new, a Kava bowl and copper chisel. Don Knorr, winner of a first prize in the Museum's International Competition for Low-Cost Furniture Design, designed a large steel-mesh sign for the Mart's lobby (see fig. 1). In subsequent years, installations by Alexander Girard, Finn Juhl (see fig. 26), Paul Rudolph, and the partnership of Daniel Brennan and A. James Speyer featured innovative settings, space dividers, and formats for display.[49]

These installations reflected Kaufmann's attitude toward modern design and domestic interiors. In 1953, he published the booklet *What Is Modern Interior Design?*, which consolidated the material exhibited at the Museum in 1946–47 under the title "Modern Rooms of the Last Fifty Years."[50] The booklet proceeded region by region, showing how homes could become unified expressions of comfort, quality, lightness, and harmony with a distinctly modern, though not necessarily ideological, character. These formulations had predictably flexible parameters within which the modern home could be designed. The installations were not, however, simple approximations of residential spaces. Both the Museum and the Mart were concerned "that these exhibitions should present as high a level of progressive development of the art of display as they should in the art of product design."[51] This emphasis on the "art of display" as a way to contextualize the products confirmed Auerbach's observation that the Good Design retailers were "essentially merchants of environment, not just commodities."[52]

The conceptual complexity of Good Design is further reflected in the way Kaufmann disseminated information about the program. In addition to the traditional formats of exhibition display and printed catalogues, he assiduously sought to expand Good Design's sphere of influence through the print and broadcast media. For instance, in 1953 Kaufmann augmented the standard press releases and other

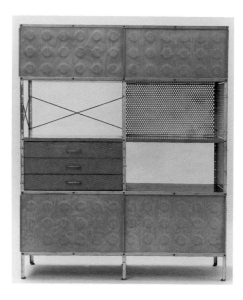

23. Charles and Ray Eames. "Eames" Storage Unit ("ESU"), 1950. Wood, plastic-coated plywood, lacquered Masonite, and chrome-plated steel, 58½ x 47 x 16¾" (148.6 x 119.4 x 42.5 cm). The Museum of Modern Art, New York. Gift of John C. Waddell (434.92) ("Good Design," 1951)

24. Charles and Ray Eames. Armchair, Model LAR, 1948–50. Fiberglass-reinforced polyester, steel wire, and rubber shock-mounts, 23 x 24¾ x 24½" (58.4 x 62.9 x 62.2 cm). The Museum of Modern Art, New York. Gift of the manufacturer, Herman Miller Furniture Company (348.50) ("Good Design," 1950)

Left:
25. Charles Eames, Case Study House #8 (living room), Santa Monica, California, 1945–49

Right:
26. Installation view of "Good Design," The Merchandise Mart, Chicago, 1951. Installation design by Finn Juhl

enticements to the print media by arranging for *Interiors* magazine to have its February, March, and September issues serve as visual catalogues of the year's Good Design selections. Other magazines also gave editorial coverage to the program, and Good Design used both paid and unpaid pages to present the jury's selections.

Recognizing the power of television, as well as its ability to show design objects "in the round," Kaufmann appeared daily on Margaret Arlen's "Morning Show" for a period of two weeks in early 1954 (fig. 27). At Arlen's prompting, Kaufmann described how the complementary arrangement of household objects according to scale and pattern could lead to an overall environment of good design similar to that found in the exhibitions themselves. Arlen commented, "I think the [Museum] and the organizers of 'Good Design' are doing a marvelous job of evaluating things which come from . . . manufacturers from all over the world and putting their stamp of Good Design upon them."[53] The exhibits were also shown on Dave Garroway's "Camel Caravan" news program.

A number of other, more ambitious programs were planned by a television production company hired by the Museum, among them, "Good Design at the Table," a game-show format that combined elements of promotion with expert opinion:

Every Tuesday night . . . we will show you beautiful table wares selected by MoMA. First dishes, then glasses, then accessories to dress the table up. In each program, you'll have the choice of three: one conservatively styled; one progressive, and one that represents a really unconventional but livable new idea. Remember, all three are endorsed for Good Design by MoMA. Your vote, and that of viewers all over the country, will decide the popular favorites.[54]

Another proposal involved Kaufmann's discussing selections from the exhibition with respected design specialists in thirteen half-hour programs broadcast weekly on a nationwide network. The program brief warns, "It is important that the programs be focused on products not personalities. The selection committee must remain the only, and clearly non-commercial, agency for determining the products for discussion."[55]

Kaufmann staged other events that were more in keeping with standard museological practice. Items selected by the polls were featured in panel discussions organized by the Museum, beginning in 1951 with "How Good Is Good Design?," with Christine Holbrook, editor of *Better Living;* Lazette van Houten, fashion editor of *Retailing Daily;* Eva Zeisel, ceramist; Paul McCobb, furniture designer; and Kaufmann. In the following year, the symposium "Good Design Can Be Better" included Edward Wormley and George Nakashima, furniture designers; Katherine Kinnane, floor-covering designer; and Fay Hines, executive editor of *House & Garden.* "Is Ornament Good Design?," in 1953, featured Paul Mayen, lamp designer; Suzanne Langer, author; Betty Pepis, furnishings editor of the *New York Times;* and Zeisel. Apart from his activities within the Museum, Kaufmann was also active in the Aspen Design Conferences, the first of which, "Design as a Function of Management," was held in 1951. The conference gave critical attention to the relationship of design, trade, and manufacture outside of the demands of sales and exhibitions, and was instrumental in the development of critical discourse on design in the postwar period.[56]

From a contemporary perspective, the Good Design program, both publicly and critically, is as notable for its widespread acceptance as for its unusually pragmatic conception. Pepis, reporting on the exhibit for the *New York Times* in 1954, revealed a certain level of skepticism in the subtitle of her article: "Home Can Be Outfitted from Chicago Exhibit, but a Sofa Would Be Lacking."[57] As a whole, however, the article accepted Good Design's premise and offered benign, straightforward reportage. That the nation's "newspaper of record" would print such an uncritical account with only slightly raised eyebrows indicates that its readers perceived Good Design in a similar light, despite its intricate and potentially controversial commingling of artistic and commercial interests. *House & Garden* was less cautious in endorsing the Museum and the Mart's joint efforts, observing, "Having watched these Good Design shows grow with increasing interest, *H&G* is happy to give you a preview in capsule form. We hope you will visit the show in New York and Chicago and have the fun of being your own judge, deciding for yourself why each item was chosen."[58]

The benevolent reception of Good Design's premise by general consumer publications is best understood in the immediate postwar context. During the war, companies like Revere Copper and Brass, Inc., General Electric, and American Gypsum launched intensive campaigns to keep their names in consumers' minds until commercial production resumed. The campaigns promised postwar plenty as a reward for enduring wartime shortages and hardship. In a Revere pamphlet of 1943, the architect William Lescaze wrote, "Today we are fighting to save our lives, our homes. Beyond this, we are fighting the never-ending battle to create better lives, better homes."[59] At war's end, these promises would be kept by the same means that fueled the war effort, such as massive industrial capacity and far-reaching advances in materials and techniques. The promotional images manufacturers proffered to consumers and servicemen were the harbinger of postwar wealth; even before domestic markets were open again, pictures in magazines provided views of the bounty soon to be served up by the quickly converted machines of war. The shift in the Museum's

27. Edgar Kaufmann, Jr., and Margaret Arlen during Mr. Kaufmann's guest appearance on Ms. Arlen's "Morning Show," 1954

"Useful Objects" exhibitions signaled the arrival of postwar prosperity. "Useful Objects in Wartime Under $10" in December 1942 featured objects meeting the standards of the Conservation and Substitution Branch of the War Protection Board, whereas "100 Useful Objects of Fine Design," organized by Philip Johnson in 1947, featured items "available under $100," including Limoges china.

The "fun" of Good Design, to use *House & Garden*'s word,[60] can thus be tied to the program's relationship to the kind of domestic pleasures deferred by the war effort. The taboos on consumption, conspicuous or otherwise, implied in "Useful Objects in Wartime" were lifted, heralding a new consumer era that would create and be characterized by rapid suburban expansion. The anticipated link between postwar economic expansion and the field of design can be seen in the 1951 advertisement announcing "the magazine that had to be"—*Better Design:* "Design is potentially the single most important selling factor in modern retailing. The creation of *Better Design* magazine was an inevitable reaction to the facts of business life in 1951."[61] Reflecting on the enormous growth in the demand for housewares, Alfred Auerbach had noted in his speech at the opening of Good Design in 1950 that there had been an unprecedented 900,000 housing starts in 1949, and a projected 10,000,000 new homes would be constructed by 1957—an expansion that presented a significant retailing problem for housewares manufacturers who lagged behind current design thinking. In addition, Auerbach had deplored the inconsequential innovations applied to mass-produced suburban houses: "Cape Cod houses and Georgian manor houses and low rambling ranch houses are all punctuated with picture windows . . . and presto, they are modern!"[62] Unsurprisingly, there is no mention of urban housing in the Good Design literature: Modern living was to be suburban living. The builder William Levitt conceived a plan for using mass-production techniques to provide suburban homes for returning veterans, who could purchase houses with loans from the Veterans' Administration and the Federal Housing Authority.[63] The first Levittown, in central Long Island, was opened to prospective buyers in October 1947 and sold out before construction had begun on many of its units.[64]

•

To the extent that the public identified its potential with The Museum of Modern Art, the Good Design program was as widely embraced by designers as by consumers. Recalling George Nelson's criticism that the program was too closely determined by Kaufmann's personal preferences rather than through any rigorous philosophical conceptions, Good Design was not without its skeptics. Even so, the wide acceptance among designers of Kaufmann's archly pragmatic alliance between the Museum and the Mart succeeded principally because of his perspicacity and earnestness in directing the program. From the program's inception, Kaufmann was concerned with the possibility that unscrupulous manufacturers might alter the specifications of the objects originally selected by the juries or make claims in their advertising that their products had been chosen for the Good Design exhibits. Perhaps his concerns reflected his experience as a housewares buyer who had to place large orders for goods based solely on the appearance of salesmen's samples. Obviously, the interests of the buyers were preserved by the retailers' insistence that the goods shipped would be identical to the approved samples. In a similar way, the Good Design tag was the main measure of assurance that goods selected by the

Museum based on Good Design criteria were the same goods available for purchase by the consumer. The tag reads:

The manufacturer guarantees that this article corresponds in every particular to the one chosen by The Museum of Modern Art, New York, for the Good Design Exhibition at the Merchandise Mart, Chicago. A registered description of this artifact is available for inspection at the Museum, at the Mart, and in the manufacturer's files.

In the process of labeling objects of good design, the Museum and the Mart became an archive for information on and examples of currently available wares. In 1951, Kaufmann wrote to Robert Johnson: "These descriptions of the articles should be extremely precise and thoroughly technical in order to make the manufacturer and retailer conscious of the care and precision with which the selection committee has used its power of approval. . . . This quasi-legal approach is absolutely necessary if we are to maintain any kind of standards of procedure."[65] The statement is notable for the displacement of consumer discrimination from the objects themselves onto their registered descriptions.

In February 1953, Kaufmann arranged with *Interiors* magazine to produce in its pages an illustrated catalogue of all the objects in the exhibition. "[The] advantage of this illustrated catalog," Kaufmann wrote, "is its authenticity. There can now be less confusion concerning what has been selected for Good Design; manufacturers' Good Design labels or tags can be more accurately applied, giving truer service to purchasers and trade buyers."[66] The authenticity of an object's being "of good design" came from its proper representation in the cycle of exhibition, retail display, and advertisement. Good Design, Inc., a nonprofit consortium, was set up by the Mart as a means to arrange advertising coverage in *Better Homes and Gardens* and *House & Garden*, in which participating manufacturers could share equally in the cost, and the prestige, of advertising their wares.[67] Stores sold the goods in areas designated solely for Good Design products and based their displays on plans supplied by designers of the installations at the Mart and the Museum, making the sales floor and the exhibition space remarkably similar. When they were not being used as paid venues, magazines such as John Entenza's progressive journal *Arts & Architecture* (an early promoter of the Eameses) were critically aware of design and lifestyles in the postwar era and gave a great deal of editorial coverage to the program.

The same year the Good Design program was instituted, the Swiss designer and architect Max Bill drafted plans for the Hochschule für Gestaltung, in Ulm, Germany, which would become an important center for European design education and critical discourse; concurrently, he organized the exhibition "Die gute Form" (translated by Bill as "Good Design"), which later traveled throughout Europe and the United States. In the accompanying catalogue, *Form: A Balance Sheet of Mid-Twentieth Century Trends in Design*—a title that evokes the reductivist reasoning of industrial-design practice—Bill raised the crucial question of public taste and the media:

The persistent cultivation of this myth (of public taste) is the unhappy hunting ground of unscrupulous manufacturers and middlemen who employ all the resources of publicity to persuade the consumer (which in such cases means everybody) that the myth is reality.

Now it has often been noticed that the consumer is, at bottom, far more responsive to good and pleasing form than might be supposed from his marked reluctance to accept them; the reluctance being due to his own uncertainty or ignorance, and the adroit commercial manner in which both are continually exploited. Thus what is sold is what is advertised, and what is advertised is what the consumer 'ought' to buy. . . . The barrier is really advertising, and the only way to counter such propaganda is by education.[68]

•

The Museum's direct and well-publicized alliance with the wholesale community represented a realistic and, in the end, highly successful approach to the task of promoting design appreciation, even if education was the product rather than the method of the program's activities. The correlation between advertising and consumption had been made quite clear before the war, but it was made more explicit in the years 1948 to 1955, a period during which half the homeowners in the United States acquired television sets.[69] Beginning in 1950, Levitt's basic house featured, along with a carport, an Admiral television set built into a living-room wall—all for $7,900. *Architectural Forum* reported that "there has yet been no report of a Levitt customer who balked at taking [a] built-in television."[70] And at The Museum of Modern Art, Breuer's House in the Garden, installed in 1949, was replete with a two-piece freestanding television set.

Yet, while Kaufmann was an ardent disciple of innovation, his artist's education tempered his merchandising skills. Kaufmann used Good Design to combat styling, which he called an "organized procedure to make some things appear 'out of date' after a season or a year."[71] He acknowledged that this might well "stimulate trade; but in design it affects only superficial details and is more likely to confuse or distort basic values than to forward them."[72] Stylists habitually advertised new and purportedly better versions of products, whereas Good Design avoided the label of "best" and advocated a relatively conservative notion of good design. In these years, stylists such as Raymond Loewy and Norman Bel Geddes were making signature design an important part of the corporate-product culture, pioneering, in Victor Margolin's words, "the image of [the] consultant designer as a celebrity."[73]

The commercial, chromium-plated, streamlined design that Kaufmann mockingly labeled "borax"[74] was featured in exhibitions of works by London's Independent Group, which ran concurrently with Good Design events. With their ironic appreciation of lavishly colored advertisements for home appliances and made-in-Detroit automobiles, Reyner Banham, Richard Hamilton, and Peter and Alison Smithson were instrumental in formulating a critique of America's disposable culture.[75] Despite the requirement that all items in the Good Design shows be new to the market, the objects had to embody design values that transcended frequently changing market biases. Through advertising, Kaufmann positioned Good Design to define those biases and to present the merchandise that best suited its goals. In an agreement between the Museum and the Mart over the terms of their collaboration, a list of benefits to accrue to each institution was made; five of the nine benefits for the Mart, and one of the two for the Modern, make explicit reference to media coverage and publicity.[76] As a result of the sponsoring institutions' abilities to take advantage of the media, the reputations of the two institutions, already strong in their respective fields, were also central beneficiaries of the program. The artists of the Independent Group wittingly manipulated the syntax of commercial imagery to underline the false expectations produced by it; conversely, Good Design sincerely sought to restore confidence in its governing role of fostering and supporting the truthfulness of the advertisements' claims. In this case, the advertiser was Good Design itself. With its continued references to the selection process, its product tag, and its design symposia, Good Design intended to create for the two institutions a reputation of unbiased advocacy.

•

Seen as an antidote to the emerging universality of consumer values created by a nascent mass-media culture, Good Design mirrored a number of concerns of postwar society's critics. A spate of sociological literature, including David Riesman's *The Lonely Crowd* (1950) and, later, Herbert Gan's *The Levittowners* (1967), had begun to describe the plight of uniformity in lifestyle and outlook of the new suburbs. Vance Packard's influential *The Hidden Persuaders* (1957) raised the specter of deep-motivational research used by advertisers to manipulate consumers' wants and needs. Also influential were the critiques of economists such as John Kenneth Galbraith, whose *Age of Affluence* (1958) revised Thorstein Veblen's "spectacle of inequality" by assessing the role of salesmanship and emulation in the product cycle: "The more that is produced the more that must be owned in order to maintain proper prestige."[77] An advertisement published by The Merchandise Mart reads, "People flock to see Good Design because they want their homes to be the epitome of good taste. . . ," and thereby demonstrates an acute awareness of consumer concerns.[78] Good Design in effect sought to mediate the production-consumption cycle: positive consumer response to the increased availability of newly designed products, manufactured to meet increasing consumer demand. Advertising simultaneously informed consumers about Good Design and enforced a de facto standardization by pre-selecting, through their inclusion in the Good Design program, the items consumers could choose. As such, Kaufmann attempted to traverse a slippery slope, agitating against the equalizing power of the media while using its structure to his own advantage. Furthermore, he strove to formulate high standards of popular taste even as he rejected standardization.

In his landmark study of 1954, *People of Plenty,* David Potter recognized that, in addition to the economic effects of increased sales, successful advertising was required "to make the purchaser like what he buys" and also "to like what he gets."[79] The confidence that Good Design tried to instill was not of the kind associated with the passing fortune of a designer or the waning of a style. Kaufmann's support for the undercapitalized design studios was critical in their respective successes. Furthermore, the patronage of the Museum lent to all the designers' works credibility and distinction beyond that which the marketplace might confer. Defining the autonomy of the designer, Kaufmann noted, "A frequent misconception is that the principal purpose of good modern design is to facilitate trade and that big sales are a proof of excellence in design. Not so. Use is the first consideration."[80] Indeed, the program was set up to encourage the long-term success of certain habits of design and manufacture so that both good design and good value would be widely available to the consumer, who could enjoy modern design as a matter of choice consistent with modern life, not dictated by it. Recalling Frank Lloyd Wright's lofty prose, Kaufmann asserted, "Modern design is intended to implement the lives of free individuals. Such an ideal leaves no room for the total standardization in the furnishings

of a home."[81] Nor is the search for good design "as difficult as it sounds; like any perception, it is sharpened by practice."[82]

•

As with almost all aspects of the Good Design program, the reasons for its demise
are somewhat complex and not entirely clear. There was apparent uneasiness with
the program within the Mart. Rent-paying tenants who were not included in the
Good Design program naturally would have been concerned about the attention
their competitors were receiving, subsidized by the Mart itself. Despite Kaufmann's
objections, a separate program, less elective in conception, was appended to Good
Design. The "Good Companions" rooms, arranged by six shelter magazines in cooperation with the Mart, "aimed to show that traditional and modern furnishings live
well together. Sources for the traditional pieces in the display were unlimited, the
modern exclusively from the 'Good Design' exhibition"[83] (see fig. 28). Though
Kaufmann despaired of the imitation of historic styles, he was aware of the commercial limits of his own program, and saw "Good Companions" as a way of
"encouraging consumers to use good modern design in their homes without completely revamping them."[84] The subsequent parting of the ways of Kaufmann and
the Mart was given its best face in a press release of 1955: "Now that the Good Design
project has so successfully fulfilled its original purpose, we are taking the opportunity presented by the necessary interruption due to the great demand for space at the
Mart to reevaluate the project in terms of the total program of both the Museum and
the Mart."[85]

Within The Museum of Modern Art, the Good Design program depended
almost exclusively on Kaufmann's personal efforts. Internal realignments had
increasingly marginalized his role within the institution; the end of the Good Design
program coincided with his departure from the Museum in 1955. According to
Arthur Drexler, who had come to the Museum from *Interiors* magazine in 1951 to
reorganize the Department of Architecture and Design, "The material was running
pretty thin, and they were big shows that took a lot of time and got on everybody's
nerves, and besides it had become a kind of shopper's service."[86] Despite Drexler's
tone, his attitude toward Good Design was not a simple case of personal antagonism
(although there were elements of that), but rather a matter of the different direction
in which Drexler wanted to take the department. One of the first major exhibitions
mounted during his tenure was "Olivetti: Design in Industry," of 1952. Directed by
Mildred Constantine, the exhibition dealt with Olivetti's integrated design philosophy, which encompassed architecture, product design, and graphics. In 1964, the
industrial-design firms Braun and Chemex would be similarly showcased.[87] In keeping with the growing professionalism of the Museum, all of Drexler's shows emphasized the design theories that motivated these corporations and shaped their
products— without, notably, the pricing and retailing information that had characterized Good Design and all of the Museum's previous design exhibitions.

Drexler's lack of enthusiasm for Good Design did not, however, include a negative assessment of the program's impact. Neither Drexler nor George Nelson, in crit-
icizing various aspects of Good Design, suggested that the program failed to
accomplish its stated objectives. Moreover, today—four decades later—the Good
Design concept retains its popular appeal, as illustrated by revivals of similar programs using Good Design's name in Chicago and Denver. Even so, it is difficult to

28. "Side by Side . . . Modern and Traditional." Page from *Retailing Daily,* April 27, 1951

gauge objectively its overall success relative to its stated goals. Inasmuch as Good Design sought to intervene in existing market structures, with an emphasis on design products readily available to the average consumer, an accurate assessment of its effects would require the use of highly sophisticated marketing models and analyses that are necessarily beyond the scope of this essay. For example, the Scandinavian presence as seen in the designs of Nanna and Jørgen Ditzel for the Dunbar Furniture Manufacturing Company, of Folke Ohlsson and Sten Hultberg for the Dux Company of San Francisco, and of others for various smaller U.S. enterprises in the third edition of Good Design, may have been influenced by the earlier success of Finn Juhl's furniture designs for the Baker Furniture Company. Nevertheless, the Good Design program coincided with the growth of the popularity of Scandinavian design in the United States, and the influence of one upon the other is not easily quantified. Similarly, the growth of industries such as Knoll Associates was undoubtedly related to the "greater consumer interest . . . focused on original design" that Kaufmann sought to foster. Even so, it is difficult to measure the degree to which the success of Knoll and others is indebted to the efforts of the Good Design program. A good indicator, albeit a relative one, might be to compare the square footage that Good Design installations occupied in The Merchandise Mart to the scale of the media attention it received. If the 3,000,000 square feet of floor space at the Mart is an indication of the size of the home furnishings industry, Good Design's claim to 5,300 square feet was small indeed. On the other hand, the national media attention the program received is thus indicative of its critical success rather than its size.

The items included in the last Good Design exhibition—the retrospective fifth-anniversary show of 1954–55—suggest further, if tentative, results of the program. The brochure that accompanied the event lists one hundred design products selected by the Museum's staff from all the previous Good Design exhibitions. The selection committee, consisting of Barr, d'Harnoncourt, Johnson, Kaufmann, and Porter A. McCray, Director of the Museum's International Program of Circulating Exhibitions, used visual excellence as its sole criterion. In addition to those items chosen by the staff, the brochure lists eighty-five items representing a more populist survey based on sales records.[88] There is a relatively narrow gap between the two groups—what might be called "the best of Good Design" and "Good Design's best-sellers." Both lists prominently feature Charles Eames, reflecting his dual status as a critical and a popular success. Numerous other best-selling designs are cited for visual excellence, including the metal-and-nylon lounge chair by Harold Cohen and Davis Pratt; the three-legged dining chair by William Katavolos, Ross Littell, and Douglas Kelley; glassware by Freda Diamond; and tableware by Kaj Franck, George Nelson, Gross Wood & Company, and Russel Wright. Yet even this popular and critical concordance must be qualified. While the public demonstrated its willingness to endorse the most innovative of the Good Design products, the best-seller list also reveals more quotidian concerns about utility and domestic comfort, as seen in Harold Elberg's enameled-copper lazy susan, Folke Ohlsson's easy chair, and Ole Wanscher's upholstered beechwood rocking chair (fig. 29).

A final estimation can be seen in the observations of one of the Good Design jurors. In her eulogy to the program, Lazette van Houten stated that "an Eames, a Wormley, a Robsjohn-Gibbings . . . can now be spotted by customers whose furniture designer knowledge five years ago probably consisted of Chippendale. . . . Perhaps when the record of 20th century design is written fifty years from now this fact will be pointed out as the program's greatest contribution."[89] With the benefit of nearly fifty years of hindsight, such an internal account of the program's success, and Kaufmann's efforts, is confirmed.

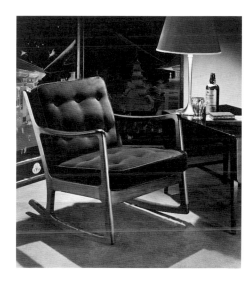

29. Rocking chair by Ole Wanscher ("Good Design," 1952)

Appendix

The following list provides names of the installation designer and selection committee members for each Good Design exhibition organized between 1950 and 1955. In addition to those members listed below, Edgar Kaufmann, Jr., was a standing member of all the committees. The installation designer was responsible for the design of the January and June exhibitions at The Merchandise Mart in Chicago as well as the year-end compilation, selected by Kaufmann, shown at The Museum of Modern Art. Each installation was accompanied by an illustrated, nonpaginated catalogue, with Morton Goldsholl's Good Design logo on the cover, that described each object exhibited, including its designer, its cost, and locations where it could be purchased.

1950 Installation design by Ray and Charles Eames

THE MERCHANDISE MART, CHICAGO. JANUARY: Selected by Meyric C. Rogers, Curator of Decorative Arts, Art Institute of Chicago; and Alexander Girard, architect and designer, Santa Fe. JUNE: Selected by Serge Chermayeff, formerly Director, Institute of Design, Chicago; and Berthold Strauss, President, Moss Rose Manufacturing Co., Philadelphia, and Trustee, Philadelphia Museum of Art
THE MUSEUM OF MODERN ART, NEW YORK. Exhibition no. 463, November 22, 1950–January 28, 1951

1951 Installation design by Finn Juhl

THE MERCHANDISE MART, CHICAGO. JANUARY: Selected by William Friedman, formerly Assistant Director, Walker Art Center, Minneapolis; and Hugh Lawson, formerly Divisional Merchandise Manager for Home Furnishings, Carson Pirie Scott & Co., Chicago. JUNE: Selected by Philip Johnson, Chairman, Department of Architecture and Design, The Museum of Modern Art, New York; Eero Saarinen, architect and designer, Bloomfield Hills, Michigan
THE MUSEUM OF MODERN ART, NEW YORK. Exhibition no. 494, November 27, 1951–January 27, 1952

1952 Installation design by Paul Rudolph

THE MERCHANDISE MART, CHICAGO. JANUARY: Selected by Harry Weese, architect and city planner, Chicago; and Charles Zadok, head, Gimbel Brothers, Milwaukee. JUNE: Selected by Gordon Fraser, President, Fraser's, Inc., Berkeley, California; and F. Carlton Ball, ceramist, silversmith, and Professor of Ceramics, University of Southern Illinois, Carbondale
THE MUSEUM OF MODERN ART, NEW YORK. Exhibition no. 520, September 23–November 30, 1952

1953   Installation design by Alexander Girard
THE MERCHANDISE MART, CHICAGO. JANUARY: Selected by D. J. De Pree, President, Herman Miller Furniture Co., Zeeland, Michigan; and Russel Wright, designer. JUNE: Selected by Florence Knoll, Director, Planning Unit, Knoll Associates, New York; and Harry Jackson, Executive Vice-President, Jackson Furniture Co., Oakland, California
THE MUSEUM OF MODERN ART, NEW YORK. Exhibition no. 542, September 22–November 29, 1953

1954   THE MERCHANDISE MART, CHICAGO. JANUARY: Installation design by Alexander Girard. Selected by Edward J. Wormley, Designer, Dunbar Furniture Corp., Berne, Indiana; and Lazette van Houten, formerly Fashion Editor, *Retailing Daily,* Fairchild Publications. JUNE: "Good Design: Fifth Anniversary." Installation design by Daniel Brennan and A. James Speyer. Selected by René d'Harnoncourt, Director, The Museum of Modern Art, New York; Alfred H. Barr, Jr., Director of Collections, The Museum of Modern Art; Porter McCray, Director, International Program, The Museum of Modern Art; and Philip Johnson, Director, Department of Architecture and Design, The Museum of Modern Art

1955   Installation design by Daniel Brennan and A. James Speyer
THE MERCHANDISE MART, CHICAGO. JANUARY: Selected by Arthur N. BecVar, industrial designer; and Just Lunning

1955   THE MUSEUM OF MODERN ART, NEW YORK. "Good Design: Fifth Anniversary." Exhibition no. 570, February 8–March 30, 1955

Notes

The authors acknowledge a debt of gratitude to Joan Ockman, who read an earlier draft of this essay and offered critical insights throughout its development.

The designation "Architecture and Design archive" refers to uncatalogued source material housed in the Department of Architecture and Design, The Museum of Modern Art.

1.   René d'Harnoncourt and Edgar Kaufmann, Jr., "Museums and Industrial Design," *Museums* 2 (May 1949), p. 35.
2.   See Joan Campbell's comprehensive study, *The German Werkbund: The Politics of Reform in the Applied Arts* (Princeton, N.J.: Princeton University Press, 1978).
3.   "Good Design, A Joint Program to Stimulate the Best Modern Design of Home Furnishings," brochure issued by The Museum of Modern Art, New York, and The Merchandise Mart, Chicago, 1950. The brochure stresses the institutional symmetry: "At the mid-point of the century, these two national institutions, whose very different careers began just 20 years ago, believe that in combining their resources they will further stimulate the growing appreciation of good living in the American home."
4.   In addition to furniture and objects designed for the home, Johnson's show also included scientific instruments, industrial precision parts—such as the self-aligning ball bearing produced by SKF Industries—and engineered objects. See Philip Johnson, *Machine Art* (New York: The Museum of Modern Art; Norton, 1934). See also Stanislaus von Moos, "The Visualized Machine Age or, Mumford and the European Avant-Garde," in Thomas P. Hughes and Agatha C. Hughes, eds., *Lewis Mumford, Public Intellectual* (New York: Oxford University Press, 1990), pp. 181–232.
5.   From its inception in 1929, the Museum, under the direction of Barr, sought to define for the public at large the meaning of modernism in the arts. In this vein, Barr instituted a series of expository exhibitions, lectures, and publications in the early forties; see, for example, Alfred H. Barr, Jr., *What Is Modern Painting?* (New York: The Museum of Modern Art, 1943).
6.   Philip Johnson, "History of Machine Art," in *Machine Art*, n.p.
7.   L[awrence] P[earsall] Jacks, *Responsibility and Culture: Yale Lectures on the Responsibility of Citizenship* (New Haven, Conn.: Yale University Press, 1924), p. 62.
8.   "Museum of Modern Art and The Merchandise Mart Announce Continuing Series of Exhibitions in a Joint Program: 'Good Design,'" MoMA press release no. 78, November 4, 1949. Department of Public Information, The Museum of Modern Art.
9.   For a detailed history of Wright's design, see Christopher Wilk, *Frank Lloyd Wright: The Kaufmann Office* (London: Victoria and Albert Museum, 1993).
10.   Quoted in ibid., p. 30.
11.   "Seller's Market," *Fortune* 28 (November 1944), pp. 123–31.
12.   Leon Harris, *Merchant Princes: An Intimate History of Jewish Families Who Built Great Department Stores* (New York: Harper & Row, 1979), p. 109. For a highly informative discussion of department stores and the culture of display, see William Leach, *Land of Desire: Merchants, Power, and the Rise of a New American Culture* (New York: Pantheon, 1993).
13.   Kaufmann to Barr, January 25, 1940. Architecture and Design archive. This was not Kaufmann's first contact with the Museum: In 1937, he had met John McAndrew, Curator of Architecture and Industrial Art, when McAndrew visited the Kaufmanns at Fallingwater.
14.   For example, in "Architects Design for Industry," *Architectural Record* 105 (June 1949), the author suggested, "In truth architects, as 'industrial designers,' are leading the way in organic design" (p. 102), without any further explanation of the term.
15.   "'Organic Design in Home Furnishings' Opens September 24," MoMA press release no. 69, September 9, 1941. Department of Public Information, The Museum of Modern Art. For a useful discussion of the activities of the Museum's design department during this period, see Kathryn B. Hiesinger, "Introduction: Design Since 1945," in Kathryn B. Hiesinger and George H. Marcus, eds., *Design Since 1945* (Philadelphia: Philadelphia Museum of Art, 1983), pp. IX–XXIV.
16.   "International Competition for Low-Cost Furniture Design," entry form and brochure issued by The Museum of Modern Art and the Museum Design Project, Inc., October 1948. Architecture and Design archive.
17.   Ibid. The jury consisted of Alfred Auerbach, Catherine Bauer, Luis de Florez, Hugh Lawson, Ludwig Mies van der Rohe, and Gordon Russell.
18.   For an inside account of the Kaufmann-Johnson relationship from a journalistic point of view, see Peter Blake, *No Place Like Utopia: Modern Architecture and the Company We Keep* (New York: Knopf, 1993).
19.   The Museum of Modern Art Archives: Mildred Constantine Oral History, The Museum of Modern Art Oral History Project; transcript, p. 61.
20.   Quoted in "Museum Director Explains Role of Art in Design of Today," *St. Louis Dispatch,* October 13, 1950.
21.   "Colossus of Chicago: The Merchandise Mart," brochure issued by The Merchandise Mart, Chicago, [c. 1950]. Architecture and Design archive.
22.   Ann Pringle, "Chicago Mart Joining Modern Museum Plan," *Herald Tribune*, November 10, 1949.
23.   "News from Good Design," press release issued by The Merchandise Mart, March 19, 1950. Architecture and Design archive.
24.   "Program of Home Furnishings Exhibitions to Be Held by the Merchandise Mart, Chicago, and The Museum of Modern Art, New York," typescript, [1950]. Architecture and Design archive.
25.   "Good Design Is the Label That Will Label Your Store as the Pace-Setter in Home Furnishing in Your Community," advertisement, *Retailing Daily*, August 6, 1951. Architecture and Design archive.
26.   Minutes of the meeting between representatives of the Museum and The Merchandise Mart regarding the Good Design program, July 26, 1951; typescript, [August 1951]. Architecture and Design archive. Present at the meeting were d'Harnoncourt and Kaufmann, and, representing the Mart, Robert M. Johnson, Donald Meade, Ollman, and Robert Sargent Shriver, Jr.
27.   For a listing of the installation designers and selection committee members for all of the Good Design exhibitions, see appendix, pp. 176–77.
28.   "How Good Design Works," typescript, [1950]. Architecture and Design archive. This document, produced by the Museum, was distributed to all those professionally involved with the Good Design program.
29.   D'Harnoncourt, memorandum to Kaufmann, March 5, 1951. Architecture and Design archive.
30.   George Nelson, "Good Design, What Is It for?," *Interiors* 113 (July 1954), pp. 72–75.
31.   Kaufmann, memorandum to d'Harnoncourt, [c. August 1951]. Architecture and Design archive. This handwritten note was written in response to an undated memorandum issued by Shriver after the meeting of representatives of the Museum and the Mart on July 26 (see n. 26 above).
32.   Lazette van Houten, "Five Years of Good Design," *Arts & Architecture* 71 (June 1954), p. 35.
33.   Edgar Kaufmann, Jr., Introduction to *Good Design* (New York: The Museum of Modern Art; Chicago: The Merchandise Mart, 1950).
34.   John McAndrew, "New Standards for Industrial Design," *The Bulletin of The Museum of Modern Art* 6 (January 1940), p. 6.
35.   Elodie Courter, "Notes on the Exhibition of Useful Objects," in ibid., p. 5.
36.   McAndrew, "New Standards for Industrial Design," p. 5.
37.   "Useful Objects in Wartime," *The Bulletin of The Museum of Modern Art* 10 (December 1942–January 1943), p. 9
38.   "How Good Design Works," typescript, [1950]. Architecture and Design archive.
39.   See Edgar Kaufmann, Jr., "Finn Juhl of Copenhagen," *Interiors* 108 (November 1948), pp. 96–99.
40.   Alfred H. Barr, Jr., Foreword to Johnson, *Machine Art*, n.p.
41.   Edgar Kaufmann, Jr., "Good Design '51, as Seen by Its Director," *Interiors* 110 (March 1951), p. 100
42.   Eric Larrabee and Massimo Vignelli, *Knoll Design* (New York: Abrams, 1981), p. 22.
43.   *Good Design* (New York: The Museum of

Modern Art; Chicago: The Merchandise Mart, 1952), n.p.

44. *Good Design* (New York: The Museum of Modern Art; Chicago: The Merchandise Mart, 1953), n.p.

45. *Good Design,* exhibition catalogue (New York: The Museum of Modern Art; Chicago: The Merchandise Mart, 1951), n.p.

46. Auerbach in speech given at the Good Design exhibition luncheon at the Merchants & Manufacturers Club, The Merchandise Mart, Chicago, January 16, 1950; typescript, n.d. Architecture and Design archive. The letter to which Auerbach referred was actually written by Herbert Hoover, then U.S. Secretary of Commerce.

47. See John Neuhart, Marilyn Neuhart, and Ray Eames, *Eames Design: The Work of the Office of Charles and Ray Eames* (New York: Abrams, 1989).

48. See Auerbach, letter to Kaufmann, September 25, 1950. Architecture and Design archive. De Pree would serve on a Good Design selection committee in January 1953. General Electric provided the lighting for the installation in return for promotional consideration.

49. For descriptions of the installations and their designers, see Arthur J. Pulos, "The 'Good Design' Syndrome," in *The American Design Adventure* (Cambridge, Mass., and London: MIT Press, 1988), pp. 110–21. The minutes of the July 26, 1951, meeting between the Museum and the Mart indicate the order of priorities in choosing an installation designer: "The architecture firm of Rudolph and Twitchell would be best qualified, first, because they, being a Florida concern, would bring geographical representation to the exhibits, second, because their work was not too well known and over publicized in the north, and third, because recent pictorial coverage of their work in magazines indicated they would do an outstanding job." Architecture and Design archive.

50. Edgar Kaufmann, Jr., *What Is Modern Interior Design?,* Introductory Series to the Modern Arts 4 (New York: The Museum of Modern Art, [1947]). The exhibition "Modern Rooms of the Last Fifty Years" was organized by Kaufmann.

51. The Merchandise Mart, draft letter to Eames, [November 1949]. Architecture and Design archive. The nature of the language in this draft leads one to believe it was written by Robert Johnson.

52. Auerbach in speech given at the Merchants & Manufacturers Club, Chicago, January 16, 1950; typescript, n.d. Architecture and Design archive.

53. See the transcript of Kaufmann's appearance on the Margaret Arlen "Morning Show," WCBS-TV, New York, March 17, 1954. The Museum of

Modern Art Archives: Early Museum History, Television Project, III.18.3.

54. "TV Proposal: Good Design at the Table: A Popular Vote on Favorite Table Settings from Good Design,' an Exhibition Selected by Museum of Modern Art, New York, and Merchandise Mart, Chicago," typescript, n.d. The Museum of Modern Art Archives: Early Museum History, Television Project, III.18.3.

55. Ibid.

56. See Reyner Banham, ed., *The Aspen Papers: Twenty Years of Design Theory from the International Design Conference in Aspen* (New York: Praeger, 1974).

57. Betty Pepis, "Furnishings Show Poses Challenge," *New York Times,* January 5, 1954.

58. Edgar Kaufmann, Jr., "Good Design Is a Lifelong Investment," *House & Garden* 122 (November 1951), p. 214.

59. William Lescaze, *A Country Club or Leisure Center,* Revere's Part in Better Living pamphlet series (New York: Revere Copper and Brass, 1943), p. 2.

60. Kaufmann, "Good Design Is a Lifelong Investment," p. 214.

61. Good Design advertisement, *Retailing Daily,* September 11, 1951.

62. Auerbach in speech given at the Merchants & Manufacturers Club, Chicago, January 16, 1950; typescript, n.d. Architecture and Design archive.

63. See Gwendolyn Wright, *Building the Dream: A Social History of Housing in America* (New York: Pantheon, 1981); and Kenneth T. Jackson, *Crabgrass Frontier: The Suburbanization of the United States* (New York: Oxford University Press, 1985).

64. See "The Builder's House," *Architectural Forum* 90 (April 1949), pp. 81–114.

65. Kaufmann to Johnson, January 31, 1951. Architecture and Design archive.

66. Edgar Kaufmann, Jr., "Good Design 1953," *Interiors* 112 (February 1953), p. 84.

67. The Merchandise Mart, memorandum to The Museum of Modern Art concerning the Good Design collaborative advertising program, [1951]. Architecture and Design archive.

68. Max Bill, *Form: A Balance Sheet of Mid-Twentieth-Century Trends in Design* (Basel: Karl Werner, 1952, in German, English, and French), p. 11.

69. See Lynn Spigel, "Installing the Television Set: Popular Discourses on Television and Domestic Space, 1948–1955," *Camera Obscura,* no. 16 (January 1988), pp. 11–46.

70. "Levitt's 1950 House," *Architectural Forum* 92 (April 1950), pp. 136–37.

71. Edgar Kaufmann, Jr., *What Is Modern*

Design?, Introductory Series to the Modern Arts 3 (New York: The Museum of Modern Art, 1950), p. 8.

72. Ibid.

73. Victor Margolin, "Postwar Design Literature: A Preliminary Mapping," in Margolin, ed., *Design Discourse* (Chicago: University of Chicago Press, 1989), p. 267.

74. Edgar Kaufmann, Jr., "Borax, or the Chromium-Plated Calf," *Architectural Review* 104 (August 1948), pp. 88–92.

75. See David Robbins, ed., *The Independent Group: Postwar Britain and the Aesthetics of Plenty* (Cambridge, Mass.: MIT Press, 1990).

76. "Program of Home Furnishings Exhibitions to Be Held by The Merchandise Mart, Chicago, and The Museum of Modern Art, New York," typescript, [December 1949].

77. John Kenneth Galbraith, *The Affluent Society* (Boston: Houghton Mifflin, 1958), p. 155.

78. Good Design advertisement, *Retailing Daily,* August 6, 1951. Architecture and Design archive.

79. David M. Potter, *People of Plenty: Economic Abundance and the American Character* (Chicago: University of Chicago Press, 1954), p. 188.

80. Edgar Kaufmann, Jr., "What Is Modern Industrial Design?," *The Museum of Modern Art Bulletin* 14 (Fall 1946), p. 3.

81. Kaufmann, *What Is Modern Design?,* p. 8.

82. Ibid., p. 9.

83. Hortense Herman, "Side by Side . . . Modern and Traditional," *Retailing Daily,* April 27, 1951.

84. Kaufmann, letter to Shriver, September 19, 1951. Architecture and Design archive.

85. MoMA press release no. 59, June 25, 1955. Department of Public Information, The Museum of Modern Art.

86. Russell Lynes, *Good Old Modern: An Intimate Portrait of the Museum of Modern Art* (New York: Atheneum, 1973), p. 319.

87. The exhibition "Two Design Programs: The Braun Company, Germany; The Chemex Corporation, USA," organized by the Department of Architecture and Design, was shown at the Museum May 27–August 23, 1964.

88. For this survey of "Popular Sellers from Good Design," *Retailing Daily,* the daily publication of the home furnishings industry, sent questionnaires to Good Design exhibitors, then compiled the sales information they provided. The brochure claimed, "The products represent tested public acceptance of Good Design 1950–1954" (quoted in *Good Design: Fifth Anniversary* [New York: The Museum of Modern Art; Chicago: The Merchandise Mart, 1954], n.p.).

89. Van Houten, "Five Years of Good Design," p. 35.

Appendix

The text that follows is excerpted from Alfred H. Barr, Jr.'s "Chronicle of the Collection of Painting and Sculpture" in his *Painting and Sculpture in The Museum of Modern Art, 1929–1967* (New York: The Museum of Modern Art, 1977). That original publication, from which we reprint pages 627–43, covered the period from the Museum's foundation in 1929 through Barr's retirement in June 1967, its author describing it (ibid., p. xiii) as "a Chronicle of the Collection of Painting and Sculpture, recounting its beginnings and growth year by year against the general background of the Museum. The Chronicle traces the early plans for forming a collection and records how and when works of art were acquired and purchase funds given, the work of various committees, statements of policy, special exhibitions of the collection, problems of space for continuous exhibition, studies of the collection in relation to those of other New York museums, and other problems and their solutions during the first thirty-eight years."

When Barr wrote his Chronicle, in the years following his retirement, he divided it into seven chapters, each covering in sequence some three to six years of the Museum's history, followed by summaries of such general issues as acquisitions, publications, space problems, and so on, insofar as they applied to the entire period of the particular chapter. This being so, it was not possible for us, in excerpting sections of his Chronicle for republication, simply to extract entries for those years around mid-century that are the focus of the present volume. We therefore reprint here, in their entirety, the third through sixth of Barr's seven chapters, which together cover the years 1940 through 1963. We have deleted Barr's numerical chapter headings and any cross-references to other materials within the volume where his Chronicle originally appeared. Otherwise, the text is exactly as Barr first published it; parentheses indicate Barr's own editorial comments and brackets and elisions his own emendations of the documents he quotes.

Although the 1977 publication containing the full version of Barr's Chronicle is still available, we felt that it would be useful to reprint this part of it here. Judging from existing studies of aspects of the Museum's history, the Chronicle is too little known. Additionally, since the articles in the present volume explore specialized aspects of the Museum's history at mid-century, Barr's overall view of the development of the collection of painting and sculpture in this period provides a broader context within which these articles might be read.

Reading this Chronicle, it will be observed that Barr's listing of loan exhibitions of paintings and sculptures is highly selective, comprising only those exhibitions from which acquisitions were made. We therefore have added a list compiled by Museum Archivist Rona Roob that includes all loan exhibitions of paintings and sculptures organized in the years covered here.   J.E.

CHRONICLE

OF THE COLLECTION OF PAINTING AND SCULPTURE [1940–63]

by Alfred H. Barr, Jr.

1940–1946

THE SEVEN YEARS from 1940 through 1946 were difficult. Although 1939 had been a grand year for the Museum, World War II had broken out before the first exhibition in the new building came to an end in September. During this "phony" war in Europe, the American "Defense Effort" got under way. Two years later Pearl Harbor changed the term to "War Effort."

In connection with World War II, the Museum executed thirty-eight contracts (valued at over $1,500,000) for various governmental agencies, including the Office of War Information, the Library of Congress, and the Office of the Coordinator of Inter-American Affairs; nineteen exhibitions were sent abroad and twenty-nine were shown in the Museum, all related to the war; in addition, the manifold Armed Services Program was carried on. A dozen members of the curatorial staff joined various services.

With its own program handicapped and diverted, the Museum faced "a challenge . . . to keep to its fundamental purpose, to maintain its standards, its integrity, its faith in the value of the arts of peace now that we too are at war" (from the Annual Report published at the end of 1941).

Many changes occurred: Nelson A. Rockefeller was called to Washington in 1940 and resigned as President early in 1941 when he became the Government's Coordinator of Inter-American Affairs; John Hay Whitney was then elected President but soon left to enter the Air Force; Stephen C. Clark, Chairman of the Board, took on the arduous obligations of President, as well.

In November 1943 Alfred H. Barr, Jr., was asked to resign as Director of the Museum and Curator of Painting and Sculpture, but he continued to install the collection under the title Director of Research. James Thrall Soby was appointed Director of the Department of Painting and Sculpture, and Dorothy C. Miller was appointed Curator.

Mr. Soby resigned as Director of Painting and Sculpture on January 1, 1945, but continued to serve on various committees and remained Director of the Museum's Armed Services Program. James Johnson Sweeney was then appointed Director of Painting and Sculpture, serving from January 1945 until autumn 1946.

Edward M. M. Warburg, Chairman of the Acquisitions Committee, was succeeded by Mr. Soby in 1941 followed by Mr. Clark in 1943.

The Acquisitions Committee was replaced in May 1944 by the Committee on the Museum Collections. Mr. Soby was Trustee Chairman and Mr. Sweeney, Vice Chairman; other members were William A. M. Burden, Mr. Clark, Mrs. Simon Guggenheim, Bartlett H. Hayes, Jr., Mrs. Sam A. Lewisohn, Miss Agnes Rindge, Mrs. George H. Warren, Jr., and Mr. Barr. From 1946 until the autumn of 1947, Mr. Clark was again Chairman.

A departmental Committee on Painting and Sculpture, in existence from May 1944 through 1946, comprised Messrs. Sweeney (Chairman 1945–46), Soby, and Barr, and, briefly, Miss Rindge.

With the two young Presidents gone, one after the other, the older Trustees, founders of the Museum, resumed responsibility. The staff was a generation younger, and so were the active members of the Advisory Committee; all were stimulated by the new building and eager to give advice.

Many of the proposals and policies effected between 1929 and 1939 were reconsidered and debated during the period from 1940 to 1946, particularly since certain intentions of the previous decade had gone unfulfilled. There were new approaches, too. Much talk and more writing resulted in a score of reports and statements, some published, some private. Three Trustees, Chairman of the Board Clark, Vice President Sam A. Lewisohn, and former President Goodyear, all great collectors, had a deep interest in the Museum and a particular concern for the Department of Painting and Sculpture, but they issued no reports. (They eventually bequeathed the best of their collections to other museums.)

Henry Allen Moe, First Vice Chairman of the Board, on the other hand, wrote a sagacious report late in 1944 as Chairman of the Committee on Policy.

The Advisory Committee produced two elaborate studies, one in 1941, under the chairmanship of William A. M. Burden, and another in 1943, under Mr. Sweeney. Messrs. Soby, Sweeney, and Barr, singly or together, wrote ten or more special reports during the 1941–46 period.

1941

MARCH 12: Alfred H. Barr, Jr., prepared a report for the Advisory Committee on the Collection of the Museum. A brief excerpt follows:

We need more works of real quality and historic importance. Probably only half our collection of oils would prove really useful for exhibition in the Museum even if there were plenty of space, and perhaps only one-eighth could be considered as worthy of an ideal collection. There are still many serious gaps to be filled. . . .

No permanent exhibition of the modern arts, such as the Museum plans, exists anywhere in the world. Other collections have finer or more numerous works of particular schools or countries but no other museum is in a position to present so comprehensive a collection in such a way that it would combine recreation, education and challenging esthetic adventure. The Museum has a unique opportunity—and responsibility.

APRIL: The comprehensive, painstaking "Advisory Committee Report on the Museum Collections" was issued by William A. M. Burden, Chairman, and his committee, Lincoln Kirstein, Mrs. Duncan H. Read, James T. Soby, and Monroe Wheeler. Begun in July 1940, the study was prepared with the assistance of Charles H. Sawyer, Winslow Ames, and Michael M. Hare. The Director worked with the Committee and was in general agreement with the report. At his suggestion, the term "Permanent Collection" was replaced by the more flexible "Museum Collection." Some of the principal recommendations in the forty-eight page report are excerpted here, but many are omitted, having been considered or confirmed in reports, publications, and resolutions referred to under the dates 1929, 1931, 1933, 1935, 1936, and 1938.

The Advisory Committee considered all departments, but gave most space to Painting and Sculpture:

The American section . . . should cover more of the country and be more representative of advanced . . . American painting and sculpture. The French section needs more major works and more works by the younger generation. The 19th century is over-represented. . . .

Gaps in the representation of certain schools of modern art should be filled. Futurism, German Expressionism, Fauvism and Analytical Cubism are the schools least adequately represented. [*Note:* Futurism, by early 1950, was represented by the best collection assembled anywhere, including Italy; the representation of German Expressionism by 1955 was outstanding but was later surpassed by German museums;

Fauvism was still inadequately represented as late as 1967; and Analytical Cubism, only adequate by 1945, improved in the 1950s.]

Future development of the Collection can be financed almost entirely by sales from the existing Collection. A large proportion of the 19th century pictures, particularly the Cézannes . . . should be sold. . . .

The Collection should be properly catalogued. A detailed outline of the ideal museum collection should be made at once.

The Acquisitions Committee should represent more points of view than at present . . . and should keep in touch with the art market and the current work of artists more thoroughly. Our relations with collectors and artists should be handled with more care and tact.

The Committee concurs with the Trustees' decision to show the Collection at all times. A new building for the Collection is needed, but in the present crisis [war in Europe] it is more important to build up the Collection itself.

Some statistics listed in the Advisory Committee report:

INSURANCE VALUE OF ACQUISITIONS OF PAINTING AND SCULPTURE, 1929–1940 (condensed)

Paintings	Sculpture	Total	Gifts	Purchases
$624,610*	$83,054†	$707,664	$645,268	$62,396‡

*The Lillie P. Bliss Bequest, acquired in 1934, accounts for more than half the value of the paintings.

†The Abby Aldrich Rockefeller Collection, given in 1939, accounts for about a third of the value of the sculpture.

‡There were no purchase funds until 1935. The insurance value of 1939 purchases was greater than the total of the purchases of all the previous years, thanks largely to Mrs. Simon Guggenheim's gifts.

DATES BY DECADE OF 713 OBJECTS, INCLUDING OIL PAINTINGS, WATERCOLORS, PASTELS, COLLAGES, DRAWINGS, SCULPTURE, CONSTRUCTIONS, ETC.

Date produced	Number	Percentage
Unknown (Folk Art)	24	3.4
Before 1900	48*	6.7
1900–10	27	3.8
1910–20	118	16.6
1920–30	249	34.9
1930–40	247	34.6
	713	100.0

*It is significant, however, that the forty-eight 19th-century works, valued at $319,525, account for about 45 per cent of the total value of the collection.

BREAKDOWN OF THE COLLECTION BY NATIONALITY OF ARTISTS, 1940

Nationality	Number of paintings*	Number of sculptures	Total	Insurance valuation	Percentage of total valuation
American	288 (75)	36	324	$103,476	14.7
French 19th Century	44 (19)	1	45	317,525	44.9
School of Paris	171 (81)	43	214	241,943	34.2
German	30 (9)	15	45	25,590	3.6
Russian	29 (8)	2	31	1,508	0.2
Mexican	35 (18)	0	35	15,049	2.1
English	5 (3)	5	10	1,663	0.2
Other	8 (4)	1	9	910	0.1
	610 (217)	103	713	$707,664	100.0

*Including drawings, watercolors, gouaches, collages, etc. Figures in parentheses indicate number of oil paintings.

Though the French and School of Paris works constitute the overwhelming majority of the value of the Collection, it is clear that American artists have by no means been neglected either in number of works or in total expenditures.

1942

THE FIRST GENERAL CATALOG of the collection, *Painting and Sculpture in the Museum of Modern Art,* was published. In the Foreword the President, John Hay Whitney, defended the international scope of the Museum, and in the Introduction, Alfred H. Barr, Jr., Director, wrote:

Even though the collection may seem transitory in comparison with those of other museums it takes on a certain air of permanence in relation to the Museum's kaleidoscopic program of temporary and circulating exhibitions. . . . It is one of the functions of the Museum Collection to give a core, a spine, a background for study and comparison, a sense of relative stability and continuity to an institution dedicated to the changing art of our unstable world.

1943

DECEMBER 8: The Advisory Committee received the "Report of the Subcommittee on the Museum Collection," James Johnson Sweeney, Chairman. Some excerpts follow:

It is important to define the direction of the Museum's interest in making acquisitions. Is it to acquire a collection of outstanding pieces of contemporary art—"high spots," as it were—or to acquire a well-rounded educational unit? The Committee feels that the latter should be true . . . Private collectors can be more limited and personal in their choice. A museum has its duty toward a wide public and the general education of that public.

The building up of a museum collection . . . should be given system. It should not be left to chance. Lack of system can only lead to lack of balance in the collection, such as exists today.

From reading over the previous report and studying the Collection through the published checklist, the Committee assumes that there have been five major reasons for the unbalanced, spotty condition of the Museum Collection today.

1. Lack of funds in the past;
2. The unwillingness of the Acquisitions Committee to make certain purchases because of personal dislikes for certain forms of contemporary expression, which nevertheless have a historical place;
3. The feeling that even though the gap in the Collection was serious, the works available were not good enough examples; . . .
4. The feeling that the price asked was disproportionate; . . .
5. The failure to learn that a desirable item was available . . . through the Committee members' lack of acquaintance with the market, the lack of time for such work in the case of staff members, and finally the lack of a specially deputed investigator in this field.

1944

JANUARY 15: From "The Museum Collections: A Brief Report," by Alfred H. Barr, Jr.:

1. *The Museum's Purpose: A Suggested Restatement.*

Fourteen years ago in applying for a charter . . . the Museum stated that its purpose was "to encourage and develop the study of the modern arts and the application of such arts to manufacture and practical life." In this sentence the word "study" is conspicuous. Doubtless it was used to reassure the Board of Regents as to the Museum's serious educational intentions. . . . I should like to propose a new statement based upon a deeper and more active meaning of education than is implied by the word "study." This statement would be:

The primary purpose of the Museum is to help people enjoy, understand and use the visual arts of our time.

By *enjoyment* I mean the pleasure and recreation offered by the direct experience of works of art.

By *helping to understand* I mean answering the questions raised by works of art such as: why? how? who? when? where? what for?—but not so much to add to the questioner's store of information as to increase his comprehension.

By *helping to use* I mean showing how the arts may take a more important place in everyday life, both spiritual and practical.

Obviously, these three activities—enjoying, understanding, using—should be thought of as interdependent. Each confirms, enriches and supports the others. Together they indicate the Museum's primary function, which is educational in the broadest, least academic sense.

2. *Purpose and Value of the Museum Collections.*

The value of the Museum collections can perhaps be most clearly understood if they are compared to the loan exhibitions in quality, concentration, comprehensiveness, continuity, authority, educational value and general public interest.

a. Quality: The Museum collections in so far as they are exhibited in the Museum should be superior in quality to the more hastily assembled, experimental and inclusive temporary shows.

b. Concentration: Temporary exhibitions, especially during the war years, have tended to include almost anything interesting that comes along. The Museum collections should by contrast keep strictly to the Museum's essential program of the modern visual arts. . . .

c. Comprehensiveness: Though each of its sections would have to be highly concentrated and selective, the collections as a whole would be far more comprehensive than any loan exhibition.

d. Continuity: Owned or controlled by the Museum, the Museum collections make possible exhibitions which are comparatively permanent or, to be more exact, continuous. . . .

e. Authority: The Museum collections as exhibited should be for the public the authoritative indication of what the Museum stands for in each of its departments. They should constitute a permanent visible demonstration of the Museum's essential program, its scope, its canons of judgment, taste and value, its statements of principle, its declarations of faith. From this central base or core the temporary loan exhibitions could then set out on adventurous (and adventitious) sorties without too gravely bewildering the public.

f. Educational Value: Each of the above factors contributes obviously and specifically to the educational values of the Museum collections both for the general public and the schools and colleges. The temporary loan exhibitions, however brilliant and exciting they may be, are too transitory and often too specialized to be of consistent use to schools and colleges. The hundreds of teachers in greater New York need comparatively permanent exhibits which they can count on using in relation to their courses. . . .

g. Public Interest: Of course, semi-permanent or recurring exhibitions lack the publicity value of the big temporary shows, but if the Museum collections are fine enough in quality, interesting enough in installation and varied enough in scope, they should hold their own in the public eye. . . .

In a discussion as to whether the collection should be primarily an assemblage of fine paintings or an historical survey, there need be in my opinion no serious conflict. To acquire and exhibit works of the finest possible quality is imperative. This should be the chief objective of the Museum in this department of its collection, because the excellence of the works of art contributes not only to the public's enjoyment but also to the educational effectiveness of the Museum.

MAY 11: The Trustees of the Museum sold at auction at the Parke-Bernet Galleries, New York, "certain of its nineteenth century works of art to provide funds for the purchase of twentieth century works" (from the catalog of the sale). Further, "the proceeds . . . will be spent with the utmost care. . . . It is our intention to perpetuate the generosity of donors to the Museum Collection by making sure that their names are applied only to works comparable in importance to those originally given us."

Included were four Cézanne oils and four watercolors, two Seurat drawings, a Matisse—all from the Lillie P. Bliss

Collection; in addition there were a Matisse and two large Picassos given by Stephen C. Clark. Financially the sale was not satisfactory. Furthermore, publicity surrounding a public auction created grave doubts about the Museum's acquisitions policy.

JUNE: The Museum received a letter from Sam A. Lewisohn, an older Trustee with a great collection. The Museum had not only sold some of its nineteenth-century paintings at auction the month before, it had recently purchased important paintings by Pollock, Motherwell, and Matta. Further, there had been recurrent discussions about the Museum as a center of study and education. Excerpts from the letter follow:

1. We should encourage collectors of the latter part of the 19th century, as well as of the 20th century, to bequeath [the] best examples [of their collections to the Museum]. . . .

2. It would be too bad completely to ignore all the Impressionists who might have something to say to contemporary painters; and perhaps it would revive interest in the beauty of pigment. . . .

3. After all, the Museum's purpose is not just classifying and pigeon-holing—it has a more profound educational intent. . . .

4. The Museum should not only be a classroom—it should also be a sanctuary where people can get a sort of sensual and mystical pleasure. Art appreciation is created, it seems to me, by exposing people to the best rather than merely to examples that are useful to the intensive student.

OCTOBER: From the minutes of the Committee on the Museum Collections:

IMPORTANT EUROPEAN WORKS OF ART RECOMMENDED FOR CONSIDERATION BY THE DEPARTMENTAL COMMITTEE ON PAINTING AND SCULPTURE

Artist	Work	Owner	Insurance valuation	Price
Brancusi	*The Miracle (Seal)* (1938)	Artist	$6,000	$7,000 (1939)
Braque	*L'Homme à la guitare* (1911)	Collector	6,732	?
Chagall	*I and the Village* (1911) $1,500 (1936)	Coll.		2,500 (1939)
Duchamp	*The Large Glass* (1915–23)	Coll.	20,000	?
La Fresnaye	*The Conquest of the Air* (1913) $6,000 (1936)	Coll.		16,666 (1939)
Lipchitz	*Mother and Child* (1941) $3,600 (1941)	Artist		4,500 (1944)
Matisse	*Women at the Spring* (1917?)	Dealer		6,000 (1940)

Modigliani	Portrait of Jean Cocteau (1917)	Coll.	7,500	7,500
Picasso	Woman Ironing (1904)	Dealer	25,000	?
Picasso	Girl with a Mandolin (1910)	Coll.	5,000	12,000 (1940)
Picasso	"Ma Jolie" (1912 ?)	Coll.	8,976	?
Picasso	The Race (1922)	Artist	5,000	?
Picasso	Three Dancers (1925)	Artist	20,000	?
Picasso	Guernica and at least 20 drawings and studies (1937)	Artist	25,000	?

Here is the list of important works which we might consider for acquisition. We now have a good deal of money which is restricted to purchase of works in the "masterpiece" class. Not all the works listed belong in this class, but I think they do include a good number of the best things *now on the market*. A good many of them are works which I have had in mind for years and many of them are actually in our possession and might well have been purchased during the past few years had not the war cut us off from the owners.

Most of the prices are problematical: those given before the war started would doubtless have been raised.

Six days ago it became possible to write to Paris even though on postcards only. We could write Picasso and shortly, I suppose, Gaffé [a collector] in Brussels. . . . Already color reproductions reveal a number of works painted during the war which the Museum might soon consider. A[lfred] H. B[arr], Jr.

After some discussion Mr. Soby was authorized to send letters to the owners of the above pictures asking for an opportunity to buy without committing the Museum to any definite purchases. . . . Mr. Clark questioned whether some of the new pictures in Europe might not be better than the ones on the list. Mr. Clark also suggested that a possible drop in prices within the next 12 months should be taken into consideration.

The Braque, Chagall, and Picasso "*Ma Jolie*" were bought in 1945; the La Fresnaye, in 1947; the Lipchitz, in 1951; the Picasso *Girl with a Mandolin* was bought by a private collector, who, in 1958, promised to give it to the Museum.

OCTOBER: The "Report of the Committee on Policy" was presented to the Board of Trustees. Henry Allen Moe, Chairman of the Committee, wrote the report; other members of the Committee were J. E. Abbott, Stephen C. Clark, Adele R. Levy, James T. Soby, James J. Sweeney, and Monroe Wheeler. Some of the statements on acquisitions were of particular significance:

In the matter of purchases, your Committee is of [the] opinion that especially in view of the Museum's limitations of exhibition space and of purchase funds, the present policy guiding purchases for the Museum's collections is much too indefinite. We think it is necessary to adopt a clearly-stated policy in reference to purchases and we recommend that the Committee on Museum Collections be directed to formulate such a statement and report it for the consideration of the Board of Trustees.

The issue to be resolved by the Trustees, as the issue developed in this Committee, is the following: If the Museum collections are limited to major works, the collections will be deficient as teaching instruments by reason of the lack of supplementary minor works. If the collections be developed with emphasis on work primarily historical in character, the collections will be deficient in major works of quality. What is the Museum's best policy in this situation?

The members of this Committee have views upon the matter but agreement has not been arrived at, and, in view of the importance of the question to the present and future of the Museum, have thought it best to put it up to the Committee on Museum Collections for an all-aspect study and report to the Board.

However, here we firmly suggest that the Museum's Permanent Collections—our acquisitions—should be shown once each year for an extended period, a showing in the nature of a report to the Trustees and to the public upon our stewardship. What the collections of the Museum contain is largely unknown, even to the Trustees, and this is an unhealthy condition in that we do not get the benefit of advice and criticism upon them; it provides fuel for charges of cultism and preciousness, and omits fulfillment of one of our primary functions.

1945

James T. Soby's resignation as Director of Painting and Sculpture became effective January 1. He was succeeded by James Johnson Sweeney. In January Mr. Soby wrote a five-page response to the Policy Committee, his document headed "Report to the Trustees in Connection with a Review of the Museum Collection." Mr. Barr also responded to the Policy Committee report with "Notes on Museum Collection Policy." The third member of the departmental Committee on Painting and Sculpture, Mr. Sweeney, did not write an individual response, but joined with Messrs. Soby and Barr in signing a statement of policy, dated January 25. This statement, sent to each member of the Board of Trustees for study before the February meeting, follows:

The Chairman of the Board has asked the Committee on Painting and Sculpture to consider a problem previously discussed by the Policy Committee, and to submit their suggestions to the Trustees during the present review of the Museum's collection of painting.

"The issue to be resolved by the Trustees, as the issue developed in this Committee, is the following: If the Museum collections are limited to major works, the collections will be deficient as teaching instruments by reason of the lack of supplementary minor works. If the collections be developed with emphasis on work primarily historical in character, the collections will be deficient in major works of quality. What is the Museum's best policy in this situation? . . . From the Report of the Committee on Policy to the Board of Trustees."

Mr. Moe has described this issue accurately as it developed in the Policy Committee. Yet we feel it need not be carried to such black and white extremes. Possibly (as Mr. Lewisohn has suggested) the semantic difficulties produced a dilemma which we believe tolerant and thoughtful study would resolve.

It is generally agreed that quality is of primary importance; that quality is to be found in a great variety of works, large and small, in different media and of different, even diametrically opposed schools. Quality, for practical purposes, is a problem of finding the best of its kind. It is quality, too, that is the primary factor in making a work of art historically important or educationally valuable.

A reasonably balanced policy is desirable. As heretofore, the great proportion of the Museum purchase funds should be spent on works of importance; a much smaller proportion on minor works of quality by established artists, and on the exploration of new talent.—J. T. Soby, J. J. Sweeney, A. H. Barr, Jr.

JANUARY 24–30: A private exhibition of paintings from the collection of the Museum was arranged for the Trustees in explicit and firm response to the "Report of the Committee on Policy." For lack of space in the Museum, half of the 650 paintings, watercolors, pastels, color collages, and other works were on view January 24 and 25 at the Museum and the other half on January 30 at a nearby warehouse. The more valuable works were shown in the galleries on the second and third floors of the Museum and the less valuable in the warehouse, this disparity suggested by the Chairman, Mr. Clark. The division was made with some difficulty by Messrs. Soby and Barr and curator Dorothy C. Miller. Since the exhibition was arranged on short notice, many of the paintings were missing—about ninety of them on tour and thirty on loan to other museums. The sixty paintings on public view prior to the private showing were taken down and arranged against the walls with the others brought out from "study storage."

The Trustees were given a ten-page guide to the show with analysis and explanation:

What factors make a painting "valuable for exhibition in Museum Collection galleries"?

This question of course raises a general problem of Museum policy, which is currently in debate. The staff, however, having to act before this debate is settled, proceeded on the principle that the Museum as in the past has broad cultural and educational responsibilities.

In the light of these responsibilities judging the value of a work of art is a complex problem.

In the minds of the staff *quality* was as always the primary factor but the staff believes that quality *is a relative and variable criterion which differs radically in different kinds of painting. . . .*

There is . . . room for at most 90 of these paintings in the gallery space now allocated to the Museum Collection on the third floor. (The current installation, of October 1944, includes only 60.)

Of the 90 perhaps *30 or 40 might be valuable enough*—"classic" enough—to keep on view at all times leaving the balance to be changed

from time to time either singly or by galleries. . . .

Section A [shown in the Museum] includes not only minor works of quality . . . but, in addition, [works of]:

a) *historical importance* such as the Burchfield (no. 70)* or the Braque (no. 703, supplement)

b) *documentary interest:* Lawrence (360)

c) *technical originality:* Dove (179), Arp (7)

d) *esthetic originality:* Ernst (195), MacIver (383)

e) *importance as the only example in the collection:* Awa Tsireh (15), Bellows (26), Duchamp (182), Dufy (185)

f) *interest as the work of exceptionally talented young Americans:* Bloom (44), Graves (256), Greene (257), Pickens (766), Pollock (767), Sharrer (775). Several of these paintings by younger Americans ought scarcely to be called minor—except in fame.

*Numbers refer to *Painting and Sculpture in the Museum of Modern Art,* 1942, and its supplement, 1945.

The Trustees were interested and their opinions interesting: many had definite feelings about certain artists and their works, but few agreed. When they did it was often for different reasons. The best-known masters were taken for granted and scarcely mentioned. Some polarity of attitudes remained but was less acute than before. The curators learned a great deal. This exchange was typical: Trustee: "Do you think that the exhibition of the Permanent Collection in its entirety will make clear the policy behind it?" Curator: "No. There will be no automatic conclusion from looking at the pictures. You must also understand why each piece was acquired."

Mr. Soby referred to the difference in approach between the private collector and the museum curator in his January "Report to the Trustees in Connection with a Review of the Museum Collection":

The Collector and Museum Acquisitions: As Professor Sachs so eloquently pointed out at the Trustees' meeting of January 11, 1945, there is a great natural difference between the collector's viewpoint on acquisitions and the museum curator's. . . .

It is not always easy to keep these problems in mind—I know that it was often difficult for me to do so, as Director of Painting and Sculpture, after fifteen years of private collecting in the Museum's own modern field. For that reason I would like to list here some of the contrasts in approach:

1. Collector: The gratification of private taste and love of the arts.
    Curator: The broad educational program of a public institution.

2. Collector: Absolute freedom of choice within financial limits.
    Curator: The necessity for covering all significant aspects of a given field.

3. Collector: Expenditure of one's own money.
    Curator: Expenditure of somebody else's money, given in faith and confidence to a public institution.

4. Collector: A free hand in changing the contents of a collection through sale, disposal or trade, following the dictates of personal taste.

Curator: A professional responsibility in making sure that personal changes in taste do not lead to eliminations which will:

a) be hasty and perhaps a mistake

b) break the continuity of a public collection which should *illustrate* changes in taste within reasonable limits, rather than be reconstituted entirely according to these changes.

5.   Collector: Freedom from public pressure and from responsibility toward living artists.

Curator: *a)* The need to consider carefully pressure from public groups, to refute it if ill-founded, to weigh it if it appears fair.

b) A tremendous moral responsibility toward living artists whose careers and fortunes can be drastically affected by the Museum's support or lack of it.

JUNE: The exhibition *The Museum Collection of Painting and Sculpture* opened with 355 works on the second and third floors. About one-third of the collection was on view for seven months.

The news release was headed "Museum of Modern Art opens Large Exhibition of Its Own Painting and Sculpture." Toward the end of the release are the following remarks:

Finally, though without intending to exaggerate the sculptor's importance, two of Lehmbruck's large figures are allotted a gallery to themselves in order to give the visitor a sense of how effective sculpture can be when shown in ample, well proportioned space. . . .

A museum exhibition of this size requires more than a purely esthetic or decorative arrangement, yet categories and sequences inevitably lead to certain errors of emphasis. Only a few works of art are conveniently simple enough to fit into classifications. Many of the categories suggested by the installation are therefore tentative and inexact. Critics, scholars and the public are cordially invited to offer suggestions.

No comprehensive collection of modern art, however, can possibly assume a rigid or final character. And this was never the intention of the men and women who have given so generously of their money and faith to make the collection possible. . . .—A.H.B., Jr.

NOVEMBER 15: Stephen C. Clark, Chairman of the Board, referred to the exhibition in his address to the Sixteenth Annual Meeting of The Museum of Modern Art (his remarks were quoted in the *Museum Bulletin,* February 1946):

The principal exhibition of the year was the presentation for the first time of the Museum's Collection of Painting and Sculpture, by which the Museum's acquisition policy was strikingly vindicated. Both the general public and the critics responded to it with enthusiasm. Without much question the Museum possesses the outstanding collection of contemporary art in the world, although due to lack of space only part of it can be shown and much of it remains in storage.

American Art and Artists 1940–1946

In 1940 a number of American abstract painters picketed the Museum because they felt it paid too little attention to their work. (Later, in 1958, and again in 1960, realist painters protested.)

At that time, three other New York museums were more or less interested in twentieth-century American art: the Whitney Museum of American Art, The Metropolitan Museum of Art, and the Museum of Non-Objective Painting (renamed the Solomon R. Guggenheim Museum in 1952). The Museum of Modern Art was involved in showing the best in contemporary art whether national or international; in addition to painting and sculpture, it was also seriously concerned with other arts, such as architecture, photography, and film. (In 1938 the Trustees had approved an informal policy on purchasing American art. Earlier, in 1933, the same matter had been discussed in the Director's "Report on the Permanent Collection.")

The *Museum Bulletin* of November 1940 was devoted to "American Art and the Museum," not so much, it said, "to answer these occasional criticisms as to present to the members a report of the extent and variety of what the Museum has done in the field of American art." Most of the *Bulletin* concerns temporary exhibitions in the Museum and elsewhere, notably *Trois Siècles d'art aux États-Unis* organized by the Museum for the Musée du Jeu de Paume, Paris, in 1938, a grand effort with all departments well represented.

Twentieth-century American paintings, drawings, and sculpture in the Museum Collection were listed by comparative numbers in the same issue of the *Bulletin*:

	Paintings, etc.	Sculptures	Totals
United States	274	33	307
Latin America	38	0	38
School of Paris	181	45	226
All other countries	72	25	97

In the Museum's 1942 catalog, *Painting and Sculpture in the Museum of Modern Art,* 142 American artists were listed, by comparison with seventy-nine French and international School of Paris artists, sixteen Germans, seven Mexicans, and twelve Russians.

In the Foreword of the same 1942 catalog, John Hay Whitney, President, wrote:

There is one aspect of the Collection which seems to me to have a special meaning. . . . This is its catholicity and tolerance. It is natural and proper that American artists should be included in greater numbers than those of any other country. But it is equally important in a period when Hitler has made a lurid fetish of nationalism that no fewer than twenty-four nations other than our own should also be represented in the Museum Collection.

James T. Soby, Director of the Department of Painting and Sculpture in 1944, wrote an article for *Museum News* (June 15, 1944) entitled "Acquisitions Policy of The Museum of Modern Art," in which he forcefully defended the Museum's policy:

In recent years the Museum has sometimes been berated for not buying more painting and sculpture by American abstract and Expressionist artists. . . .

But it should be remembered that the Museum does not exist for the direct benefit and patronage of artists. . . . And viewed purely in terms of dollars and cents, the Museum has made a far more important contribution to the support of living painters and sculptors through its educational program than it could possibly have done through direct patronage. . . .

Standards of selection have been purposefully broad, and bias in favor of any one school has been avoided—always admitting that prejudice cannot be totally disabled by any force of detachment. In a word, we try to buy representative examples of work by those modern artists whom we consider to be among the best of a good kind.

We do not consider it our job to force contemporary art in one direction or another through propaganda or patronage, much as enthusiasts for a particular dogma would like to have us do so. For in the final analysis it is not our job to lead artists, but to follow them—at a close, yet respectful distance.

In the first large exhibition of the Museum's painting and sculpture collection, from June 1945 to February 1946, American works numbered 134, and foreign works, 221.

Space Problem 1940–1946

The tripled gallery space in the new building brightened hope for showing continuously some part of the Collection of Painting and Sculpture; but in the first two years after the building's opening, the collection was on view for only eighteen weeks. Four great exhibitions had occupied almost the whole Museum: *Art in Our Time* and *Picasso: Forty Years of His Art* in 1939; *Twenty Centuries of Mexican Art* in 1940; and *Indian Art of the United States* in 1941.

From the Director's March 12, 1941, report on the collection to the Advisory Committee:

The Museum . . . now has a large and valuable collection but at the present moment [with the installation throughout the Museum of *Indian Art of the United States*], . . . the casual visitor would not be aware of it. But all have agreed that the Indian exhibition should be the last huge show to occupy all three gallery floors of the Museum. After it closes, plans have been made to give over half the gallery space to curatorial departments primarily for the purpose of showing the Museum collection. . . .

To be really useful the essential part of such a collection would have to be on view at all times. Teachers, students, amateurs as well as the general public should be able to count on seeing it, the most significant works in public galleries, the less important things in easily accessible study storage rooms with trolley racks for pictures, sliding shelves for models, etc.

Even with half the Museum gallery space there are still far too few galleries to show adequately the collections of painting, sculpture and graphic arts and at the same time give a modicum of exhibition space to the departments of Photography, Architecture and Industrial Design as well as the Film Library, Education Project and Dance Archives. Nor is there any space for accessible study storage unless the very limited and crowded permanent storage is moved elsewhere. . . .

Of the 225 oil paintings . . . in the collection less than 50 could be properly hung in the space now allotted.—A.H.B., Jr.

The Museum Collection fared somewhat better in the next five years. The exhibition *Painting and Sculpture from the Museum Collection* was on view on most of one floor from May 1941 through the end of April 1944. Thereafter the 15th Anniversary Exhibition, *Art in Progress,* occupied the whole building until mid-October. After that, only fifty paintings from the collection were again shown.

From June 1945 to February 1946, however, *The Museum Collection of Painting and Sculpture* filled the entire second- and third-floor galleries with 355 works—the first comprehensive showing of the collection since 1933, when twelve paintings and ten sculptures comprised all the Museum owned.

To further dramatize the space problem, statistics were prepared in December 1946 in anticipation of a fund-raising drive the following year:

Collection	Number in Collection	Number on view
Paintings	702	105 (15%)
Sculptures	155	77 (50%)
Drawings	278	11
Prints	2,034	None
Photographs	1,933	29
Architecture	Models and enlarged photographs	None
Industrial Design	394 objects	None
Theatre and Dance	c. 300	None

The report concluded: "Lack of space has proved a more serious handicap to the Museum's collections than lack of funds."

Purchase Funds 1940–1946

By 1940–41 the ample purchase funds of the previous years were no longer available. The decline was caused partly by unforeseen maintenance expenses of the new building but also by the Defense Effort and the entry of the United States into the war late in 1941. The suggestion that five per cent of the budget be allocated for acquisitions was turned down.

At the beginning of 1942, purchase funds stood as follows:
Mrs. Simon Guggenheim Fund (restricted to major purchases), about $45,000

Inter-American Purchase Fund (restricted), about $25,000

Mrs. John D. Rockefeller, Jr., Fund (not restricted), $5,000

Anonymous Fund (not restricted), $5,000

Lillie P. Bliss Fund (residue), $680

Previously, in 1938 and 1939, Mrs. Guggenheim had given funds for specific gifts, Picasso's *Girl before a Mirror* and Rousseau's *Sleeping Gypsy*.

Subsequently other purchase funds were made available, as the lists of purchases imply. (Many acquisitions listed as gifts were actually purchases made with funds purposely solicited by the Museum or offered by a donor for the acquisition of a given work.)

The auction held on May 11, 1944, at Parke-Bernet Galleries provided additional funds for purchase of twentieth-century works.

Publications on the Collections 1940–1946

"Except for the Bliss catalogue, film program notes and occasional notes in the Bulletin, the collection has not received either scholarly or popular publication, a neglect at least as serious as our inability to give it adequate exhibition. It is essential that other members of the curatorial staff, in addition to the director, should have time to work upon their sections of the collection."—A. H. Barr, Jr., March 1941, Director's Report.

Between 1942 and 1945, four major publications on the painting and sculpture collection appeared:

1942   *Painting and Sculpture in the Museum of Modern Art*, Foreword by John Hay Whitney, President, edited by Alfred H. Barr, Jr.; indexes of artists by medium and nationality and by movement or school; 690 entries, 136 reproductions.

1943   *The Latin-American Collection of the Museum of Modern Art*, by Lincoln Kirstein, Foreword by Alfred H. Barr, Jr.; 267 entries, 112 reproductions; Bibliography by Bernard Karpel.

1943   *What Is Modern Painting?* by Alfred H. Barr, Jr.; 51 reproductions, 38 from the Museum Collection.

1945   *Painting and Sculpture in the Museum of Modern Art: Supplementary List, July 1942–April 1945*, edited by James J. Sweeney; 136 entries, 33 reproductions.

Acquisitions 1940–1946

Of exceptional interest were Orozco's *Dive Bomber and Tank*, a fresco in six interchangeable panels painted in the Museum in late June 1940 just after the fall of France; van Gogh's *The Starry Night*, acquired by exchanging three minor works from the Lillie P. Bliss Bequest; Beckmann's *Departure*, the first of his series of triptychs; and Mondrian's last completed work, *Broadway Boogie Woogie*.

Five extraordinary paintings were bought with the Mrs.

Simon Guggenheim Fund: Léger's *Three Women*, Chagall's *I and the Village*, Matisse's *Piano Lesson*, and two elaborate allegories: Blume's *Eternal City* and Tchelitchew's *Hide-and-Seek*.

As the war came to an end several important paintings became available and were purchased: Braque's *Man with a Guitar* (1911), Picasso's *"Ma Jolie"* (1911–12) and his brilliant *Card Player* (1913–14).

The Inter-American Fund, provided by a Trustee in 1942, made possible the acquisition of fifty-eight paintings and sculptures selected in Argentina, Brazil, Chile, Colombia, Cuba, Ecuador, Mexico, Peru, and Uruguay. Lincoln Kirstein, appointed Consultant in Latin-American Art, made the purchases in South America, and Alfred H. Barr, Jr., with Edgar Kaufmann, Jr., made selections in Mexico and Cuba. To quote from the 1943 Latin-American Collection catalog cited above: "Thanks to the second World War and to certain men of good will throughout our Western Hemisphere, we are dropping those blinders in cultural understanding which have kept the eyes of all the American republics fixed on Europe with scarcely a side glance at each other during the past century and a half. In the field of art we are beginning to look each other full in the face with interest and some comprehension. . . ."—A.H.B., Jr.

With the many paintings by the Mexican masters already in the Museum, the works acquired in nine countries in 1942 made possible the "most important collection of contemporary Latin-American art in the United States, or for that matter in the world (including our sister republics to the south)."

Acquisitions year by year, represented by selective lists of artists' names and some titles of works:

1940   *Purchases:* Bérard's *Jean Cocteau*, Stuart Davis's *Summer Landscape*, Ensor's *Tribulations of St. Anthony*, Kokoschka's *Self-Portrait*, MacIver's *Hopscotch*, Rivera's *Agrarian Leader Zapata* (fresco commissioned for Museum exhibition, 1931).
Commission: Orozco's *Dive Bomber and Tank*.
Gifts: a La Fresnaye, a Nicholson, Stanley Spencer's *The Nursery*.

1941   *By Exchange:* van Gogh's *The Starry Night*.
Purchases: Braque's *The Table* (1928), a de Chirico, a Gris (1911).
Gifts: a Barlach, Bonnard's *The Breakfast Room*, Degas's *Dancers* (c. 1899), a Gorky, Hopper's *New York Movie*, a Mondrian (1925), Noguchi's *Capital*, Rouault's *Christ Mocked by Soldiers*.

1942   *Purchases:* Blume's *The Eternal City*, Braque's *Soda* (1911), Gorky's *Garden in Sochi*, ten Graves gouaches, a Lam, a Matta, a Mérida, Orozco's *Self-Portrait*, Tamayo's *Animals*, Tchelitchew's *Hide-and-Seek*.

By Exchange: Ernst's *Napoleon in the Wilderness.*

Gifts: Beckmann's *Departure,* a Portinari (mural), Schlemmer's *Bauhaus Stairway,* a Torres-García.

1943   *Purchases:* an Archipenko, Brancusi's *The Newborn,* Calder's *The Horse,* Feininger's *The Steamer Odin, II,* Hartley's *Evening Storm,* Hopper's *Gas,* Joseph Stella's *Factories,* a Tunnard.

By Exchange: a Braque (1908).

Gifts: Chagall's *Time Is a River without Banks,* a Figari, Lipchitz's *Blossoming,* a Masson, Mondrian's *Broadway Boogie Woogie,* a David Smith (1938), a Tanguy.

1944   *Purchases:* Balthus's *André Derain,* Feininger's *Viaduct,* two Klees, a Kuniyoshi, Motherwell's *Pancho Villa, Dead and Alive,* Matta's *Le Vertige d'Éros,* Picasso's *Fruit Dish* (1909), Pollock's *The She-Wolf,* Weber's *The Geranium* and *The Two Musicians.*

1945   *Purchases:* Braque's *Man with a Guita*r (1911), Chagall's *I and the Village,* Stuart Davis's *Egg Beater,* Duchamp's *The Passage from Virgin to Bride,* Lam's *The Jungle,* Léger's *Big Julie,* Marin's *Lower Manhattan (Composing Derived from Top of Woolworth),* Miró's *Dutch Interior, I,* O'Keeffe's *Lake George Window,* Picasso's *"Ma Jolie"* (1911–12) and *Card Player* (1913–14), Prendergast's *Acadia.*

1946   *Purchases:* van Doesburg's *Rhythm of a Russian Dance,* Grosz's *Metropolis,* Matisse's *Piano Lesson,* Sutherland's *Horned Forms.*

Gifts: Gottlieb's *Voyager's Return.*

Museum exhibitions from which acquisitions were purchased or given (exhibition directors' names are in parentheses):
1942   *Americans 1942* (Dorothy C. Miller)
1943   *Alexander Calder* (James J. Sweeney)
1946   *Fourteen Americans* (Dorothy C. Miller)

1947–1952

JOHN HAY WHITNEY, who had been elected Chairman of the Board of Trustees on June 6, 1946, was in office throughout this period, serving until December 1956; Nelson A. Rockefeller was re-elected President on June 6, 1946, and remained in that position until June 1953.

René d'Harnoncourt was appointed Director of the Museum in October 1949. During the previous five years he had been Director of the Curatorial Departments and later Chairman of the Coordinating Committee.

William A. M. Burden was appointed Chairman of the Committee on Museum Collections in 1947, serving until 1950, when James Thrall Soby succeeded him.

In February 1947, Alfred H. Barr, Jr., was appointed Director of the Museum Collections, and Dorothy C. Miller, Curator, both in special charge of painting and sculpture. Appointed Advisers to the Museum Collections were Andrew Carnduff Ritchie, Director of Painting and Sculpture, in 1948 (serving until 1957), and René d'Harnoncourt, in 1951 (serving until 1968).

1947

SEPTEMBER 15: After much discussion, an inter-museum agreement was signed by the Whitney, the Metropolitan, and the Modern museums. Under the terms of the agreement, The Museum of Modern Art agreed to "sell to the Metropolitan Museum of Art paintings and sculptures which the two museums agree have passed from the category of modern to that of 'classic.'" Twenty-six European works were sold, including Cézanne's *Man in a Blue Cap,* Maillol's *Île de France* (torso), and Picasso's *Woman in White;* fourteen examples of American folk art were also sold. The proceeds were used to buy contemporary works for the Museum Collection.

The Metropolitan Museum agreed that whenever a work bought from The Museum of Modern Art was exhibited, cataloged, or reproduced, appropriate reference would be made to the name of The Museum of Modern Art and the name of the original donor.

As part of the same agreement, The Museum of Modern Art received as extended loans Maillol's *Chained Action* and Picasso's *Gertrude Stein,* which the Metropolitan Museum did "not consider inappropriate for lending." (The agreement with the Metropolitan Museum was terminated in February 1953.)

1948

EARLY IN THE YEAR, some older members of the Committee on the Museum Collections, encouraged by adverse newspaper criticism, vigorously questioned the validity of certain acquisitions, including paintings called "abstract expressionist." Purchase was difficult. (Later, in 1952, a member of the Committee "reluctantly" resigned when a Rothko was acquired; another member had resigned when Giacometti's *Chariot* was purchased in 1951; it was "not a work of art," he wrote. Both men, however, remained on the Board of Trustees.)

The second edition of *Painting and Sculpture in the Museum of Modern Art* was published, the Preface by John Hay Whitney, Chairman of the Board, and Introduction by Alfred H. Barr, Jr. Listed were 797 paintings and sculptures with 384 reproductions; 96 per cent of the works were twentieth-century; thirty-three countries and ninety-nine donors were represented.

Mr. Whitney wrote in his Preface:

The art of our fantastically various world cannot be homogeneous. Two works of art completed yesterday in one and the same city may have nothing more in common than their date and the fact that they are both painted on rectangular canvases. One may present a transforming rediscovery of ancient values too long neglected; the other may be a courageous sortie into unexplored territory. So different will the paintings be that the two artists, and their supporters, may regard each other with contempt. Yet, if the pictures seem superior in quality, both, it is to be hoped, may find their way into the Museum collection, whether they happened to be painted in an American city or somewhere on the other side of this shrinking globe.

In the course of trying to make wise, fair and discriminating choices from the vast panorama of contemporary art there will inevitably be many errors. The Trustees are fully aware of this danger. Yet they believe that it is only by taking such risks that this living, changing collection can best serve the living present and, with the helpful editing of time, the present yet to come.

The Museum's aim of making the collection accessible was explained in the Introduction:

Exhibition in the Museum galleries is, of course, the primary use made of the collection. . . . However, the collection has other uses. Much of it is currently out on loan to special exhibitions in museums throughout the country or abroad. A larger proportion is lent to the Museum's Department of Circulating Exhibitions for its touring shows. The balance is kept in accessible storerooms adjacent to the galleries. Visitors may see any works of art in the storerooms by applying to the office of the Museum Collections. Students, teachers, writers and the interested public are urged to make use of the collection.—A.H.B., Jr.

1949

NOVEMBER: Alfred H. Barr, Jr., compiled a list headed "Gaps in Collection: European Painting 1900–1920" for the Committee on the Museum Collections. (Asterisks were added in the list below to indicate acquisitions made after 1949: a single asterisk signifies a promised or remainder-interest gift, and a double asterisk, a work actually purchased or received):

France and School of Paris

Cézanne, a landscape, 1900–1906**. *Renoir,* a nude, 1915–1916. *Signac* or *Cross,* a painting, 1900–1905**. *Bonnard,* a nude; a flower piece or still life.

Matisse, a fauve painting, 1904–1907*; a still life, 1908–1910. *Rouault,* a nude, 1905–1910; a courtroom or clown picture, 1905–1920**. *Derain,* a fauve oil, 1904–1906**. *Vlaminck,* a fauve oil, 1904–1907**; a landscape, 1910–1914. *Utrillo,* a street scene, 1910–1914. *Modigliani,* a nude**.

Picasso, an early painting, blue period or before, 1900–1904; a circus period painting or pastel, 1905*; a rose period painting, 1906; an early cubist painting, 1908–1909**; a collage, 1912–1914**; an important cubist painting, 1915–1920**; a neo-classic figure, 1918–1921**. *Léger,* an early cubist painting, 1912–1915**; a "machine" painting, 1918–1920**. *Braque,* a cubist painting, 1915–1920. *Delaunay,* an early cubist painting, 1910–1912*; an orphist painting, 1912–1915**.

Outside France

Kandinsky, a painting, 1908–1910**; a painting, 1910–1916**. *Boccioni,* a painting, 1910–1914**. *Carrà,* a metaphysical painting, 1916–1920. *Marc,* a painting, 1910–1914. *Nolde,* a painting, 1910–1915**. *Schmidt-Rottluff,* a painting, 1910–1920**. *Kokoschka,* a composition, 1915–1920. *Klee,* watercolors, 1912–1920**.

Acquisitions 1947–1952

"Exceptionally generous contributions by Mrs. Simon Guggenheim to her purchase fund for masterworks, and the recurring income from the sale to the Metropolitan Museum of older European works of art, particularly those from the Lillie P. Bliss Bequest, gave the Museum resources with which to seize a number of extraordinary opportunities," according to the *Museum Bulletin* (vol. 17, no. 2–3) in 1950.

Mrs. Guggenheim made possible the purchase of Matisse's *The Red Studio* and his variations in bronze of *The Back, I, III,* and *IV* (the "lost" variation *II* was to be acquired in 1956); Picasso's *Three Musicians* (long sought for the collection) and *Night Fishing at Antibes;* La Fresnaye's *The Conquest of the Air;* and Lachaise's *Standing Woman.*

Through funds from the Lillie P. Bliss Bequest, the Museum bought Chagall's *Calvary* and *Birthday,* and Brancusi's great marble *Fish.* Mr. and Mrs. Allan D. Emil gave Picasso's *Three Women at the Spring.*

Preparations for the exhibition *Twentieth Century Italian Art,* 1949, led to several purchases, notably seven Futurist works of 1910 to 1913, including four capital pieces: Boccioni's *The City Rises,* bought with the Guggenheim Fund, and the same artist's bronze striding figure, *Unique Forms of Continuity in Space,* Carrà's *Funeral of the Anarchist Galli,* and Severini's *Dynamic Hieroglyphic of the Bal Tabarin,* the last three purchased with the Bliss fund.

Twelve paintings by New York abstract expressionists were acquired between 1947 and 1952; the artists were Baziotes, Gorky, Kline, de Kooning, Motherwell, Pollock (*Number 1, 1948,* his most important work until then, was purchased in 1950 and two others in 1952), Pousette-Dart, Rothko, Stamos, and Tomlin. Earlier, between 1941 and 1946, paintings by Gorky (two), Gottlieb, Motherwell, and Pollock had been acquired.

Acquisitions year by year, represented by selective lists of artists' names and some titles of works:

1947   *Bequest:* Anna Erickson Levene in memory of her husband, Dr. Phoebus Aaron Theodor Levene: three by Gris (1912, 1913, 1913).
Gift: Stamos's *Sounds in the Rock.*
Purchases: Baziotes's *Dwarf,* a Gabo (1941), La Fresnaye's *The Conquest of the Air,* Moore's *The Bride.*

1948   *Bequest:* Abby Aldrich Rockefeller: van Gogh's *Hospital Corridor at Saint Rémy.*
Gifts: Albright's *Woman,* Nadelman's *Man in the Open Air.*
Purchases: a Bacon (1946), two Boccioni bronzes, a Braque (1937), Carrà's *Funeral of the Anarchist Galli,* van Doesburg's *Composition (The Cow),* a Gris (1914), a de Kooning (1948), Lachaise's *Standing Woman.*

1949   *Purchases:* Balla's *Speeding Automobile* and *Swifts: Paths of Movement + Dynamic Sequences,* Brancusi's *Fish,* Chagall's *Birthday* and *Calvary,* de Chirico's *Sacred Fish,* a Ferber, Giacometti's *Woman with Her Throat Cut,* a Guttuso, Maillol's *The River,* Matisse's *The Red Studio,* a Morandi (1916), Picasso's *Three Musicians,* Severini's *Dynamic Hieroglyphic of the Bal Tabarin,* Wyeth's *Christina's World.*

1950   *Gifts:* Calder's *Whale,* Corinth's *Self-Portrait,* Masson's *Meditation on an Oak Leaf,* Shahn's *Pacific Landscape.*
Purchases: a de Chirico, Gorky's *Agony* (1947), Klee's *Equals Infinity,* Lippold's *Variation Number 7: Full Moon,* Modigliani's *Reclining Nude,* two Mondrians (1913–14, 1914?), Motherwell's *Western Air,* a Pevsner (1942), Picasso's *Harlequin* (1915) and *Seated Bather* (1930), Pollock's *Number 1, 1948,* Roszak's *Spectre of Kitty Hawk,* Schwitters's *Picture with Light Center* (1919).

1951   *Gifts:* Davis's *Lucky Strike,* Magritte's *Empire of Light, II.*
Purchases: Boccioni's *The City Rises,* Ensor's *Masks Confronting Death,* Giacometti's *Chariot,* Kirchner's *Street, Dresden* (1908), a Kupka (1911–12), Lipchitz's *Mother and Child, II,* Modigliani's *Caryatid* (stone), Picasso's *Still Life with Liqueur Bottle* (1909) and *Sleeping Peasants* (1919).

1952   *Bequest:* Sam A. Lewisohn: Picasso's *Pierrot* (1918), Rouault's *Three Judges* (1913), Ben Shahn's *Violin Player.*
Gifts: Derain's *London Bridge* (1906), Edwin Dickinson's *Composition with Still Life,* Dubuffet's *Work Table with Letter,* Kline's *Chief* (1950), Picasso's *Three Women at the Spring,* Pollock's *Full Fathom Five* (1947) and *Number 12* (1949), a Rothko (1950), a Tomlin (1949).
Purchases: Gauguin's *Still Life with Three Puppies,* two Légers (1919, 1925), eight Matisse bronzes (including three of *The Back* series and four of the five *Jeannette* portraits), Picasso's *Night Fishing at Antibes* (1939).

Museum exhibitions from which acquisitions were purchased or given (exhibition directors' names are in parentheses):

1947   *Ben Shahn* (James Thrall Soby)
1948   *Elie Nadelman* (Lincoln Kirstein)
1949   *Twentieth Century Italian Art* (James Thrall Soby and Alfred H. Barr, Jr.)
1950   *Chaim Soutine* (Monroe Wheeler)
1951   *Abstract Painting and Sculpture in America* (Andrew Carnduff Ritchie)
1952   *15 Americans* (Dorothy C. Miller)

1953–1958

1953

FEBRUARY 15: A radical change of policy was announced by the Board of Trustees. A permanent nucleus of "masterworks" was to be selected under the supervision of the Board. In accordance with this new policy, the 1947 agreement with the Metropolitan Museum was terminated; The Museum of Modern Art would no longer sell to the other institutions its "classical" paintings in order to purchase more "modern" works. Instead it would permanently place on public view masterpieces of the modern movement beginning with the latter half of the nineteenth century.

APRIL 7: The Policy Committee for the Museum's Permanent Collection of Masterworks was appointed; it was to draw up a statement of policy for ratification by the Board. (Their resolution was not presented until three years later.)

SPRING: The Abby Aldrich Rockefeller Sculpture Garden, designed by Philip Johnson, replaced the ingenious but necessarily modest garden of 1939. The new and superb area opened with the exhibition *Sculpture of the Twentieth Century,* directed by Andrew Carnduff Ritchie. Afterwards the Museum's own collection usually occupied the Sculpture Garden.

The Katherine S. Dreier Bequest came to the Museum during this year. Miss Dreier had died on March 29, 1952, and bequeathed ninety-nine works to the Museum, among them fifty-two paintings and sculptures. They included valuable and needed works by Archipenko, Baumeister, Brancusi, Campendonk, Covert, Duchamp, Ernst, Kandinsky, Klee, Léger, Lissitzky, Marcoussis, Miró, Mondrian, Péri, Pevsner, Ribemont-Dessaignes, Schwitters, and Villon.

Miss Dreier was co-founder with Marcel Duchamp and Man Ray of the Société Anonyme: Museum of Modern Art 1920. Together they had collected avant-garde works that were expressionist, post-cubist, and dada and surrealist for the Société

Anonyme as well as for Miss Dreier's personal collection. The Société Anonyme collection was presented to Yale University in 1941, at which time both she and Duchamp were appointed trustees. Works from her personal collection came to The Museum of Modern Art through the kind offices of Marcel Duchamp, her old friend and colleague.

Miss Dreier was a painter and had shown at the Armory Show in 1913, where Duchamp's *Nude Descending a Staircase* had shocked the New York art world. One of her best pictures, the *Abstract Portrait of Marcel Duchamp,* painted in 1918, was purchased for the Museum in 1959.

1954

JUNE: The Trustees of the Museum established the Patrons of the Museum Collections to honor the donors of the principal purchase funds and works of art, their names to be listed in publications about the collections and inscribed on a plaque at the entrance to the collection galleries.

OCTOBER 19: The Museum's *25th Anniversary Exhibition* opened with 495 paintings and sculptures from the Museum Collection on view on all three floors and in the new Abby Aldrich Rockefeller Sculpture Garden. Dag Hammarskjöld, Secretary-General of the United Nations, made the inaugural address, in which he said in part:

The art collected here is not modern in the sense that it has the vain ambition of expressing the latest shifting fashions of a mass civilization which long ago lost its anchorage in a firm scale of values, inspired by a generally accepted faith. Nor is it modern in the sense of the comic strips or similar attempts to use the techniques of art to cater for broad emotional needs through a cheap representation of a sentimentalized reality. It is a Museum for "modern art"—that is, for you and for me, a museum for the art which reflects the inner problems of our generation and is created in the hope of meeting some of its basic needs.

FALL: *Masters of Modern Art,* a book on the Museum Collections, was published. It comprised 240 pages and 356 reproductions, seventy-seven of them in color. Edited by Alfred H. Barr, Jr., it encompassed all the collections. A list of contents reveals its scope:
FOREWORD: The Collections of the Museum of Modern Art by John
  Hay Whitney, Chairman of the Board of Trustees
PREFACE by René d'Harnoncourt, Director
INTRODUCTION by A. H. Barr, Jr., Director of the Museum Collections
PAINTING, SCULPTURE, DRAWING, PRINT COLLECTIONS by A. H. Barr, Jr.,
  and William S. Lieberman
PHOTOGRAPHY COLLECTION by Edward Steichen
THE FILM LIBRARY by Richard Griffith
ARCHITECTURE AND DESIGN COLLECTIONS by Philip C. Johnson
THE MUSEUM COLLECTIONS: COMMITTEES AND DEPARTMENTS

DONORS TO THE COLLECTIONS
BIBLIOGRAPHY AND INDEX OF ARTISTS
From the Preface:

Within the Museum's structure the collection is an intrinsic and important factor. It contributes constantly to all the Museum's varied and far-flung activities. As it grew in scope and excellence it became more and more capable of setting standards and providing a sense of continuity to the activities of the various departments of the Museum. By demonstrating the vast variety of styles and concepts so characteristic of modern art in the recent past, it makes for an open mind and helps keep the institution receptive to new trends.

On the other hand, nearly all departmental activities contributed to the development of the collection. Not only did many works of art come to the Museum's attention through these activities, but the very existence of these activities has created a non-academic climate and kept the Museum close to the realities of today's art life.—René d'Harnoncourt, Director of the Museum

From the Introduction:

The words "best" or "most characteristic" immediately raise certain fundamental questions not only about this volume but about the collection it represents and, indeed, about the Museum itself. The Museum collects works radically different in purpose, medium, school and generation. Who is to say what is really important? The public is often slow to comprehend; critics and museum people are notoriously blind.

Even the artist is no guide. Whistler's contempt for Cézanne was equalled only by Cézanne's contempt for Gauguin. Frank Lloyd Wright assails Le Corbusier. A leading authority on cubism still insists that a Mondrian is not a work of art at all; a devotee of Mondrian denounces the surrealism of Ernst and Dali as perversion of true art; a dadaist of 1920 finds the abstract expressionist of 1950 tedious; and the socialist realist cries a plague on all their bourgeois-bohemian houses.

Artists and their champions may indeed seem a squabbling banderlog of isms. But, actually, they are not; their differences are real and significant, slowly developed, passionately believed in, and expressive not simply of artistic convictions but often of deeply-felt philosophies of life.

Even granting that the Museum should collect works of many kinds, there is still the problem of choosing the best of each. Quality, of course, should be and has been the first criterion. Yet the matter is not so simple. Picasso's *Three Musicians* may be superior in quality to Picasso's *Demoiselles d'Avignon,* but the latter, with all its coarseness and experimental changes of mind may be equally important to the Museum: whatever its esthetic quality, it is a dramatic record of agonistic effort and the first detonation of a great historic movement. —Alfred H. Barr, Jr.

1955

LOANS FROM THE COLLECTION increased to a somewhat disquieting degree. During the two years from July 1, 1953, to June 30, 1955, "the Museum made no less than 783 loans of painting and sculpture to touring exhibitions, television, et cetera, and to 155 special shows in the museums of the United States, Brazil, Canada, England, France, Germany, Israel, Italy, Japan, The Netherlands, Norway, Scotland, Switzerland, and Venezuela" (*Museum Bulletin*, vol. 23, no. 3, 1956).

In addition, 130 American paintings and sculptures were included in the exhibition *50 Ans d'Art aux États-Unis: Collections du Museum of Modern Art de New York*, opening in Paris in April of 1955 and later shown in Zurich, Frankfurt, Barcelona, London, The Hague, Vienna, and Belgrade. The show was important particularly because it included twenty American abstract-expressionist paintings, then little known in Europe. Aside from the risks involved in allowing so many works to travel in one group, the Museum was deprived of most of its best American paintings for eighteen months.

Loans to the United States embassies had begun informally in Oslo in 1953 and then officially in Bonn in 1960 through the Museum's International Program; loans to foreign consulates and United Nations embassies in New York had begun earlier. President Dwight D. Eisenhower borrowed a landscape by Fausett and a seascape by Sterne for the White House. Secretary-General Dag Hammarskjöld carefully chose paintings by Braque, Glarner, Gris, Kane, La Fresnaye, Léger, Picasso, and others for his office and reception rooms at the United Nations.

1956

MAY 2: The Policy Committee for the Museum's Permanent Collection of Masterworks presented a resolution to the Board of Trustees for its approval. The resolution, with part of its preamble, follows:

In its early years the Museum of Modern Art, primarily devoted to loan exhibitions, planned its Collections with the stated policy of eventually passing on the works of art to other institutions or otherwise disposing of them as they matured or no longer seemed useful.

However, the Trustees have recently determined, as a radically new departure, to establish a collection of works of art, limited in number and of the highest quality, which shall remain permanently in the Museum's possession. . . .

After discussion, it was, on motion made and seconded, unanimously resolved that:

1. The Trustees of the Museum of Modern Art herewith confirm the establishment of a Permanent Collection of Masterworks of Modern Art.
2. The Permanent Collection of Masterworks shall comprise works of art selected from the Museum's general Collection together with such additions as may be approved from time to time by the Trustees.
3. In general, the Permanent Collection of Masterworks shall not include works of art executed prior to the mid-nineteenth century.
4. The Collection of Masterworks shall have the same degree of per-

manence as the collections of the other great museums of this country. No work of art accepted as a gift for the Permanent Collection of Masterworks shall be eliminated from it except in accordance with the conditions, if any, originally stipulated by the donor.

5. No works of art shall be eliminated from the Permanent Collection of Masterworks, and no material change shall be made in the policies governing the Permanent Collection of Masterworks, unless approved by three quarters of the Trustees of the Museum then in office. (Quoted in *Painting and Sculpture in The Museum of Modern Art*, 3rd ed., 1958, pp. 5–6.)

DECEMBER 13: Nelson A. Rockefeller was named Chairman of the Board of Trustees, succeeding John Hay Whitney, who was appointed United States Ambassador to Great Britain.

1957

MAY 22: The *Picasso: 75th Anniversary Exhibition* opened. A birthday tribute to Picasso, organized by the Museum with the support of the Art Institute of Chicago and the Philadelphia Museum of Art, the exhibition surveyed sixty years of the artist's work. Shown were over 300 paintings, sculptures, and drawings from ninety-eight public and private collections. A catalog of the exhibition, edited by Alfred H. Barr, Jr., and the biographical record *Portrait of Picasso*, by Roland Penrose, were published in conjunction with the exhibition. Acquired from the show was the *Studio in a Painted Frame* of 1956.

1958

APRIL 15: A fire in the southwest area of the second floor during reconstruction caused total loss of a large mural painting by Monet, a smaller Monet, and a mural by Portinari; damaged but later restored were Boccioni's *The City Rises* and Rivers's *Washington Crossing the Delaware*. The restoration of *The City Rises* was a tour de force by Jean Volkmer, the Museum's conservator.

Although the fire was confined to the second floor, the entire Museum was closed, the gallery walls were dismantled, and improved fireproofing measures were begun. The ground floor was reopened on May 1 to enable visitors to see the two temporary exhibitions on view before the fire, first the *Seurat Paintings and Drawings*, which ran until May 11, and then *Juan Gris*, from May 12 until June 1. The Museum remained closed for the rest of the summer to undertake a reconstruction program. A conservation laboratory was added and the Library was enlarged.

JUNE: The third edition of *Painting and Sculpture in the Museum of Modern Art: A Catalog* was published. The listing included 1,360 works by artists of some forty different nationalities.

OCTOBER 7: The Museum formally reopened with the exhibition *Works of Art: Given or Promised.* From the Preface to the catalog:

On this, the occasion of its reopening, the Museum of Modern Art is proud indeed to present to the public a truly extraordinary exhibition of works of art recently added to its collections or promised as future gifts. The objects from the excellent collection of the late Philip L. Goodwin; the admirable paintings given by the late Nate B. Spingold and his wife, Frances Spingold; the four superb pictures from the collection of Mrs. David M. Levy; the notable works presented by LeRay W. Berdeau, David Rockefeller and G. David Thompson; the purchases made through the generosity of Mrs. Simon Guggenheim, the great patron of the Museum Collections, and Mr. and Mrs. Peter A. Rübel; all these, taken together, form the most important treasure of new accessions since the Lillie P. Bliss Bequest was received by the Museum in 1934.

Together with the exhibition of these gifts are shown some twenty-five more works of art which occupy a status perhaps unprecedented in American museum history. Several trustees and other friends of the Museum have in the past declared their definite intention to give or bequeath to the Museum a number of the finest works in their collections. Wishing at this time in the Museum's history to make some special gesture of support, they have consulted with the Museum in selecting for the current exhibition a number of works of art, which though not yet presented to the Museum are lent with the promise that they will eventually come into its possession through gift or bequest. These patrons include Mr. and Mrs. William B. Jaffe, William S. Paley, Mrs. John D. Rockefeller, 3rd, Mr. and Mrs. Herbert M. Rothschild, Mrs. Louise R. Smith, James Thrall Soby, the Honorable and Mrs. John Hay Whitney and the two undersigned. Very likely there are others who have similar but hitherto undisclosed intentions and may indicate their willingness to join in future exhibitions of a similar character. Their participation will be very welcome. Meanwhile, the present exhibition of works of art, given or promised, attests to the devotion of the Museum's friends and their particular concern with the future of its Collections.

Nelson A. Rockefeller
Chairman of the Board

William A. M. Burden
President

From the Introduction:

The importance of these works of art to the Museum's collection is very great. Their extraordinary quality is obvious. Their enormous value makes them, practically speaking, irreplaceable. Furthermore, and to a remarkable extent, they will strengthen the collection often where it is weakest.—Alfred H. Barr, Jr.

The artists represented included Arp, Brancusi, Boccioni, Braque, Cézanne (represented by two works), de Chirico (two), Degas, Delaunay, Gauguin, Klee, Léger (two), Lipchitz, Matisse, Miró (two), Mondrian, Monet, Picasso (nine), Renoir (two), Rouault, Seurat (two), Toulouse-Lautrec (two), Vuillard (three). (Within the next ten years, ten of the thirty-nine works were given to the Museum outright; nine were given with the donors retaining a life interest; eighteen were promised by letter.)

On the same date, October 7, the Museum opened the exhibition of works given by the late Philip L. Goodwin—a small collection but one of exceptional quality. Mr. Goodwin was the first architect of the Museum and Vice Chairman of the Board. His generosity to the architecture and design as well as to the painting and sculpture collections was indeed significant (see 1958 painting and sculpture acquisitions).

The Fall 1958 issue of the *Museum Bulletin* served as an illustrated catalog of the two exhibitions.

Acquisitions 1953–1958

Some major gifts included Rodin's *Balzac,* presented in memory of Curt Valentin by his friends; Matisse's *The Moroccans,* given by Mr. and Mrs. Samuel A. Marx; and Rousseau's *The Dream,* given by Nelson A. Rockefeller. The Katherine S. Dreier Bequest was particularly rich in works by Marcel Duchamp.

Acquisitions year by year, represented by selective lists of artists' names and some titles of works:

1953   *Bequest:* Katherine S. Dreier: Brancusi's *Magic Bird,* Duchamp's *To Be Looked At (From the Other Side of the Glass) with One Eye, Close To, For Almost an Hour, Fresh Widow,* and *3 Stoppages étalon;* Ernst's *Birds above the Forest;* Kandinsky's *Blue (Number 393)* and three watercolors (1913); eight Klees; Léger's *Propellers;* Lissitzky's *Proun 19D;* a Mondrian (1926); Pevsner's *Torso;* nineteen works by Schwitters.
Gifts: Stuart Davis's *Visa,* Dufy's *Sailboat at Sainte-Adresse* (1912), a Heckel (1912), Maillol's *The Mediterranean,* a Picasso, a Vantongerloo (1921).
Purchases: Bacon's *Dog,* Brancusi's *Mlle Pogany,* Butler's *The Unknown Political Prisoner* (international first-prize project for a monument), Giacometti's *Artist's Mother,* Gonzalez's *Woman Combing Her Hair,* de Kooning's *Woman, I,* Renoir's *Washerwoman* (bronze).

1954   *Bequest:* Mrs. Sam A. Lewisohn: Cézanne's *L'Estaque,* Soutine's *Maria Lani,* Maurice Sterne's *After the Rain.*
Gifts: Stuart Davis's *Salt Shaker,* Giacometti's *Man Pointing,* Man Ray's *The Rope Dancer,* Redon's *Vase of Flowers,* Rousseau's *The Dream.*
Purchases: Balla's *Street Light,* Delaunay's *Simultaneous Contrasts: Sun and Moon,* two Kandinskys (mural compositions, 1914), a Lipton, Picabia's *I See Again in Memory My Dear Udnie,* a Soutine, a Still (1951), Tanguy's *Multiplication of the Arcs,* Tobey's *Edge of August.*

1955   *Bequest:* Curt Valentin: Beckmann's *Descent from the Cross.*
Gifts: van Dongen's *Modjesko, Soprano Singer,* Ernst's *The King Playing with the Queen,* Matisse's *Goldfish and Sculpture, Jeanette, II,* and *The Moroccans,* Motherwell's

The Voyage, Nolde's *Christ among the Children,* Rivers's *Washington Crossing the Delaware,* Rodin's *Monument to Balzac,* Tamayo's *Girl Attacked by a Strange Bird,* Tomlin's *Number 9: In Praise of Gertrude Stein.*

Purchases: a Baziotes, a Sam Francis, Léger's *The Divers, II* and *Three Musicians,* Monet's *Water Lilies* (mural), a Nolan, a Picasso, Rodin's *St. John the Baptist Preaching,* a Sickert, a Sutherland.

1956   *Gifts:* a Bacon, a Baumeister, Beckmann's *Self-Portrait with a Cigarette,* Gonzalez's *Torso,* Kirchner's *Artillerymen,* Lachaise's *Knees* (marble), a Macke, Magritte's *Portrait,* a Nolde, five Picassos (including the bronzes *Glass of Absinth* and *Pregnant Woman*), a Renoir, Stettheimer's *Family Portrait, II.*

Purchases: Brancusi's *Socrates,* a Butler, Dubuffet's *The Cow with the Subtile Nose,* Kokoschka's *Tiglon* and *Port of Hamburg,* four Kupkas (including *The First Step*), a Manzù, Matisse's *The Serf, The Back, II,* and *The Rose Marble Table,* two Monets, five Picassos (including the bronzes *Baboon and Young* and *Goat Skull and Bottle),* a Wols.

1957   *Gifts:* a Bazaine, Cézanne's *Le Château Noir,* Degas's *At the Milliner's,* Kirchner's *Emmy Frisch,* Klee's *Still Life with Four Apples* (1909), two Mondrians (1913–14, 1921), a Motherwell, Picasso's *Studio in a Painted Frame* (1956), two Pollocks (1950, 1953–54), Schmidt-Rottluff's *Houses at Night,* Seurat's *Evening, Honfleur,* Shahn's *Father and Child,* Toulouse-Lautrec's *La Goulue at the Moulin Rouge.* *Purchases:* Klimt's *The Park,* Picasso's *Woman by a Window,* David Smith's *History of LeRoy Borton,* a Wotruba.

1958   *Bequest:* The collection of Philip L. Goodwin, given by members of his family following the wish of the deceased: Brancusi's *Blond Negress,* de Chirico's *The Great Metaphysician,* a Demuth, a Derain (1905), Dove's *The Intellectual,* a Klee, a Léger (1913), Marin's *Lower Manhattan,* Nadelman's *Woman at the Piano,* a Noguchi, Picasso's *The Rape* (1920).

Gifts: Francis's *Big Red,* Johns's *Target with Four Faces,* Léger's *Exit the Ballets Russes,* Nevelson's *Sky Cathedral,* Rivers's *The Pool.*

Purchases: Giacometti's *Dog,* Gottlieb's *Blast, I,* Heiliger's *Ernst Reuter,* a Gwen John, Johns's *White Numbers* and *Green Target,* a Pollock (1945), a Popova, a Vasarely.

Museum exhibitions from which acquisitions were purchased or given (exhibition directors' names are in parentheses):
1955   *The New Decade* (Andrew Carnduff Ritchie)
1956   *Julio Gonzalez* (Andrew Carnduff Ritchie)

1956   *Twelve Americans* (Dorothy C. Miller)
1957   *David Smith* (Sam Hunter)
       Picasso: 75th Anniversary Exhibition (Alfred H. Barr, Jr., and William S. Lieberman)˙

1959–1963

1959

NOVEMBER: The Thirtieth Anniversary Drive to raise twenty-five million dollars began. A section of the Drive brochure was headed: "The Museum's Invisible Collections":

The collections of the Museum of Modern Art are in crisis—collections which owe their existence to many hundreds of donors whose generosity has been so extraordinary that the Museum has never drawn on its endowment or its annual budget for purchase funds. Nor is it asking for such funds now, much as it needs them, because its collections face an acute predicament: *invisibility.* The collections must have space for exhibition and accessible storerooms, or the Museum will have failed to meet its obligations toward the public, the artists represented, and the donors—past, present and future—of works of art. . . .

A modern museum must have storage spaces that are conveniently accessible. People with specialized interests—collectors, scholars, foreign visitors—they must be served as well as the general public.

Simultaneously, the special exhibition *Toward the "New" Museum of Modern Art* opened. To dramatize further the need for gallery space, paintings from the collection were hung two or three deep in a densely crowded installation. Some visitors sympathetically disapproved; others unexpectedly liked the rich, traditional effect of "skying."

The collector Larry Aldrich offered the Museum a fund of $10,000 a year for a five-year period to buy works by American artists not yet represented in the painting and sculpture collection. Each work was to cost no more than $1,000. At the end of the first five years, Mr. Aldrich renewed his fund for another such period. With this fund the Museum was able to acquire works by many young artists whose later achievement confirmed their early promise.

1961

FEBRUARY: An exhibition consisting of works pledged or given to the Museum by James Thrall Soby and comprising sixty-nine paintings, sculptures, and drawings was shown at the galleries of M. Knoedler and Company for the benefit of the Museum Library. Works of exceptional interest were Bacon's *Study of a Baboon;* Balthus's *The Street* (1933); eight paintings by de Chirico (1914–17), unmatched in any other collection—among them

Gare Montparnasse (The Melancholy of Departure), The Enigma of a Day, The Duo, The Seer, and *Grand Metaphysical Interior;* three by Miró: his *Self-Portrait, Portrait of Mistress Mills in 1750,* and the unique *Still Life with Old Shoe;* Picasso's famous *Seated Woman* (1927), *The Sigh* (1923), and the grand *Nude Seated on a Rock* (1921, only 6 1/4 x 4 3/8 inches); Dubuffet's *My Cart, My Garden;* and Shahn's *Liberation.* Also included were paintings by Berman (two), Blume, Bérard, Bonnard, Dali, Ernst, Hartigan, Johns, Klee (two), Leonid (two), MacIver (two), Matta (two), Morandi, Kay Sage, Sutherland, Tanguy (two), and Tchelitchew (three).

Sculptures included Reg Butler's *Figure in Space,* Calder's *Swizzle Sticks,* Cornell's *Taglioni's Jewel Casket,* Giacometti's *Tall Figure,* and works by Chadwick, Lehmbruck (two), Maillol (two), and Marini (two).

A fully illustrated catalog was published, with Preface by Blanchette H. Rockefeller, President of the Board of Trustees, and notes by James T. Soby and Alfred H. Barr, Jr.

1962

MAY–SEPTEMBER: *Picasso in the Museum of Modern Art: 80th Birthday Exhibition* was the most important show based on the Museum Collections during the period from 1959 to 1963. Included were seven sculptures and thirty-four paintings owned by the Museum, along with eighteen promised or fractional gifts; drawings and prints were also included. Picasso's extended loan of the *Guernica* and fifty-three of its studies enhanced the exhibition.

Other exhibitions drawn from the collection during the five-year period included *Fernand Léger* (1960–61; fifteen paintings); *America Seen: Between the Wars* (1961); *Modern Allegories* (1961–63); *André Derain in the Museum Collection* (1963; sixteen paintings).

OCTOBER 22: The Cuban crisis broke; two days later twenty-eight of the Museum's best paintings were sent to prepared vaults over a hundred miles from the city. Soon seventy-four others, almost as valuable, followed—and then still more, including drawings and prints. Other works were substituted on the gallery walls. The crisis was terrible but short.

NOVEMBER–DECEMBER: The fund-raising drive begun in 1959 came to an end, by far the largest and most successful in the Museum's history. Ground-breaking for the new building was celebrated on November 25. The building would house the East Wing Galleries (Fifty-third Street), the East Garden terrace, and beneath it, the Garden Wing (Fifty-fourth Street), with its large gallery; the West Wing would contain accessible Study Storage and the Conservation Laboratory.

1963

MRS. YVES TANGUY (Kay Sage), through the efforts of a Museum Trustee, her close friend James Thrall Soby, left the Museum $104,785.52, the largest purchase fund for painting and sculpture thus far bequeathed. In addition, her bequest included works by Breton, Calder, Delvaux, Hélion, Miró, and others, as well as a large group by her late husband, Tanguy. During her lifetime she had given the Museum a number of other works, notably Magritte's *Portrait.*

JUNE: The Museum's operating expenses for the year ending in June were $2,367,468, compared with about $78,000 in 1933. The Collection of Painting and Sculpture comprised 2,223 works in 1963; there had been nineteen works in 1933. The spaces planned for both public and study galleries were far greater than thirty years before—but they were still not great enough.

DECEMBER: At last the major part of the program of enlarging and remodeling the building could be undertaken. The Museum had to be closed for six months, and during this time none of its contents was accessible to the New York public. However, works of art from the collection were lent to leading museums in the United States and Canada.

DECEMBER 16: The National Gallery of Art in Washington, D.C., opened an exhibition of 153 paintings from the Museum Collections, carefully selected to represent the various modern movements. The choice ranged from Cézanne, van Gogh, and Prendergast to Vasarely, Jasper Johns, and Ellsworth Kelly. The exhibition was enthusiastically welcomed and was attended by 181,153 visitors in a little more than three months.

A catalog of the exhibition *Paintings from the Museum of Modern Art, New York,* was published by the National Gallery. It contained a preface by John Walker, Director of the National Gallery, a foreword by René d'Harnoncourt, and an introduction by Alfred H. Barr, Jr. One hundred pages in length, the catalog reproduced every painting, fourteen of them in color.

From the Preface:

The Museum of Modern Art has played a remarkable role both in America and abroad. Opened to the public in 1929 in several rented rooms in a New York office building, it has grown until it now occupies a complex of buildings of its own. But even these quarters have proved too small. Its enlargement this year, necessitating a temporary closing, has provided an opportunity for the National Gallery of Art to show a part of what is probably the most distinguished and representative international collection of modern art to have been assembled anywhere.

The physical growth of The Museum of Modern Art is, to be sure, impressive. But far more significant is the impact it has had on a generation of taste in America. One is apt to forget that forty years ago painters of the School of Paris, artists such as Matisse, Braque and Picasso, were so controversial that for a time their work was considered too radical for many museums. . . .

John Walker, *Director*
National Gallery of Art

From the Foreword:

The Museum of Modern Art was not conceived solely as a repository for works of art; neither has it been limited to the traditional fields of painting, sculpture and the graphic arts but has included besides these architecture, design, photography and the film. Its concern has been to present the interplay among *all* the visual art forms of our time. In setting forth its future goals in its first prospectus of 1929, the Museum states: "The ultimate purpose of the Museum will be to acquire (either by gift or purchase) a collection of the best modern works of art."

René d'Harnoncourt, *Director*
The Museum of Modern Art

From the Introduction:

Art lovers are passionate—and even those who have little interest in art sometimes descend to fury in the presence of paintings they have never sought to understand, especially paintings produced by their contemporaries. Living artists create problems. Working in freedom, they can be exasperating to the individual, and even an embarrassment to the state, if we are to believe such political philosophers as Plato and Stalin. Neither truth nor poetry is often welcomed by society.

The sense of continuity, of tradition, of history is of the greatest importance in our democratic culture. This awareness of the valuable past is well served by the National Gallery collection even when visitors take it for granted. The Museum of Modern Art's period lies in the past, too, but it is a far shorter past: it begins with yesterday and looks back not a few centuries but a few decades. Yet during those few decades the art of painting appears to have widened its horizons more often and more radically than during the previous half millennium. As the expressionist Franz Marc declared, a bit defiantly, "traditions are beautiful—to create—not to follow."

Alfred H. Barr, Jr.
Director of the Museum Collections
The Museum of Modern Art

Acquisitions 1959–1963

Among major works acquired were two mural paintings by Monet from his Water Lilies series, one 19 1/2 feet wide, the other a triptych 42 feet wide, unmatched elsewhere except in Paris. Added to the collection in 1959, they were later installed in the new building in a gallery dedicated to the donor, Mrs. Simon Guggenheim. Thanks to her, another 19 1/2 foot mural, Miró's *Mural Painting,* was bought in 1963.

Also acquired in 1959 were two extraordinary works by Picasso, the bronze *She-Goat* (1950), purchased with the Mrs. Guggenheim Fund, and the *Two Nudes* (1906), the gift of G. David Thompson. In 1961, Henry Moore's *Reclining Figure,*

II (1960), was also given by Mr. Thompson.

In 1963 Governor Nelson A. Rockefeller gave Matisse's *Dance (first version,* 1909), a mural about the same size as the second version (1910), now in Leningrad. Cézanne's *Le Château Noir,* Degas's *At the Milliner's,* Seurat's *Evening, Honfleur,* and Toulouse-Lautrec's *La Goulue at the Moulin Rouge* had been given in 1957 by Mrs. David M. Levy, the donor retaining a life interest. Upon her death in 1960, these invaluable works came to the Museum. In addition, she bequeathed Picasso's *Violin and Grapes,* reserving for her husband a life interest, which Dr. Levy most generously relinquished so that the painting might immediately join the four nineteenth-century pictures.

Analysis of the 1960 acquisitions as an example of the period: The year's harvest was richer than average in late-nineteenth-century works, sparse in works from the 1940s, and abundant in those of the last few years. Included, as usual, were pastels, watercolors, color collages, assemblages, constructions, as well as painting and sculpture:

Number of acquisitions: 94 (including an extended loan).

Number of older works acquired: 27, dating from a Degas of 1882 to a Torres-García of 1940; one dating from the period 1941 to 1951.

Number of more recent works acquired: 65, dating from 1952 to 1960.

Number of gifts: 59.

Number of purchases: 34, including four dated 1892, 1904, 1905, and 1917, and 28 dating from the last four years: 1956 (2), 1957 (2), 1958 (4), 1959 (12), 1960 (8).

Number of artists: 81. Number of nations represented: 16. Australia 1, Belgium 1, Cuba 1, France 15, Germany 3, Great Britain 3, Italy 8, Japan 1, Poland 2, Spain 2, Switzerland 3, Tanzania 1, Uruguay 1, U.S.A. 37, U.S.S.R. 1, Venezuela 1.

The acquisitions for 1960 were published in the *Museum Bulletin* (vol. 28, nos. 2–4, June 30, 1961), with introduction and eighty-eight illustrations. These checklists of new acquisitions were published regularly in the *Museum Bulletin* from 1950 to 1963.

Acquisitions year by year, represented by selective lists of artists' names and some titles of works:

1959   *Gifts:* an Avery, Boccioni's *The Laugh,* a Guston, Kandinsky's *Picture with an Archer* (1909), Picasso's *Two Nudes* (1906), a Tinguely.
    Purchases: a Léger (1926), Monet's *Water Lilies* (two murals), Newman's *Abraham,* Picasso's *She-Goat,* Rosso's *The Concierge* and *The Bookmaker,* a Rothko (1958), a Frank Stella (1958).

1960   *Bequests:* Mrs. David M. Levy: Cézanne's *Le Château Noir,* Degas's *At the Milliner's,* Seurat's *Evening, Honfleur,*

Toulouse-Lautrec's *La Goulue at the Moulin Rouge,* and Picasso's *Violin and Grapes* (1912). (The first four were accessioned in 1957.) Alexander M. Bing: Duchamp-Villon's *Baudelaire* (bronze), a Klee.

Gifts: works by Balla, Bérard, Bontecou, Burchfield, Frankenthaler, Gottlieb, Hartigan, Hepworth, Jensen, Klee (two), Matisse, Metzinger, Nakian, Noguchi, Richier.

Purchases: works by Anuszkiewicz, César, Fontana, Kelly, Nevelson (two), Ntiro, Sickert, Tinguely.

1961 *Bequest:* Loula D. Lasker: Matisse's *Lemons against a Fleur-de-lis Background* (1943).

Gifts: Chamberlain's *Essex,* an Ernst, a Kjarval, a Klee, a Liberman, Moore's *Reclining Figure, II* (1960), Motherwell's *Elegy to the Spanish Republic, 54,* an Oldenburg, a Tajiri, a Tàpies, a Vasarely.

Purchases: an Albers, Arp's *Floral Nude,* a Botero, Bourdelle's *Beethoven, Tragic Mask,* a Brecht, an Edwin Dickinson, Dubuffet's *Joë Bousquet in Bed* and *Beard of Uncertain Returns,* Indiana's *The American Dream,* a Landuyt, a Latham, a Samaras.

1962 *Gifts:* Lindner's *The Meeting,* Matisse's *Music* (1907), Warhol's *Gold Marilyn Monroe.*

Purchases: a Bernard (1887), Dubuffet's *Business Prospers,* Epstein's *The Rock Drill,* Marisol's *The Family,* Oldenburg's *Two Cheeseburgers . . . ,* a Reinhardt (1960–61).

1963 *Bequest:* Mrs. Yves Tanguy (Kay Sage): works by Calder, Delvaux, Hélion, Miró, Tanguy, and others.

Gifts: Ferber's *Homage to Piranesi, I,* Grosz's *Explosion,* Hofmann's *Memoria in Aeternum,* Matisse's *Dance (first version,* 1909), Ortiz's *Archeological Find.*

Purchases: a Bontecou, Calder's *Black Widow,* Ipousteguy's *David and Goliath,* two Morris Louis works, a Miró (large mural, 1951), a Poons, a Wesselmann.

Museum exhibitions from which acquisitions were purchased or given (exhibition directors' names are in parentheses):

1959 *New Images of Man* (Peter Selz)
  16 Americans (Dorothy C. Miller)
1960 *New Spanish Painting and Sculpture* (Frank O'Hara)
1961 *Mark Rothko* (Peter Selz)
  Max Ernst (William S. Lieberman)
  15 Polish Painters (Peter Selz)
  The Art of Assemblage (William C. Seitz)
1962 *Jean Dubuffet* (Peter Selz)
  Recent Painting USA: The Figure (staff committee)
  Mark Tobey (William C. Seitz)
1963 *Americans 1963* (Dorothy C. Miller)
  Hans Hofmann (William C. Seitz)

THE MUSEUM OF MODERN ART
PAINTING AND SCULPTURE LOAN EXHIBITIONS, 1940–63

Compiled by Rona Roob

This list comprises all loan exhibitions of paintings and sculptures that were held at the Museum from 1940 through 1963. It is intended to supplement the exhibition lists in Alfred H. Barr, Jr.'s "Chronicle of the Collection of Painting and Sculpture," which includes only exhibitions from which acquisitions were made. (These exhibitions are preceded by an asterisk [*] in the present list.) Preceding each entry is the number assigned to the exhibition by the Museum's Department of Registration; when no such number has been assigned to an exhibition, the number of the exhibition preceding it in the Museum's records is given in brackets. Titles correspond either to the publication that accompanied the exhibition or, when there was no publication, to that given on the exhibition checklist. Names in parentheses following the title refer to the directors of the exhibition. When a director is associated with a department other than a curatorial one, the department is noted. When the author of an important exhibition publication differs from the exhibition director, the author is noted.

1940

[93.] *Picasso's* Seated Nude, *1911: A Visual Analysis of a Cubist Painting* (Advisory Committee/Sidney Janis; installation by Frederick Kiesler)

97. *Modern Masters from European and American Collections* (Dorothy C. Miller)

98. *Italian Masters* (Alfred H. Barr, Jr.)

99. *Four American Travelling Shows: The Face of America; 35 Under 35; Mystery and Sentiment; Prints by Jennie Lewis* (Dorothy C. Miller)

105. *The Artist as Reporter: P.M. [New York evening newspaper] Competition* (Holger Cahill)

106. *Twenty Centuries of Mexican Art* (Catalogue by Dr. Alfonso Caso, Prof. Manuel Toussaint, Roberto Montenegro, Miguel Covarrubias)

108. *Portinari of Brazil* (Alfred H. Barr, Jr.)

1941

123. *Indian Art of the United States* (Frederic H. Douglas, René d'Harnoncourt)

130. *Britain at War* (Sir Kenneth Clark; catalogue by E. J. Carter, Carlos Dyer, T. S. Eliot, Herbert Read, Monroe Wheeler)

135. *Paul Klee* (Department of Circulating Exhibitions/Elodie Courter)

138. *Masterpieces of Picasso* (Alfred H. Barr, Jr., in collaboration with Daniel Catton Rich)

[141.] *Techniques of Painting* (Advisory Committee/Jean Charlot)

150. *George Grosz* (Department of Circulating Exhibitions/ Lenore Browning, Elodie Courter)

157. *Joan Miró* (James Johnson Sweeney)

158. *Salvador Dali* (James Thrall Soby)

1942

*168. *Americans 1942: 18 Artists from 9 States* (Dorothy C. Miller)

170. *U.S. Army Illustrators of Fort Custer, Michigan* (Monroe Wheeler)

174. *Art in War: OEM [Office for Emergency Management] Purchases from a National Competition* (Public Buildings

Administration: Section of Fine Arts; installation by Monroe Wheeler)

175. *Henri Rousseau* (Daniel Catton Rich)

185. *Josephine Joy: Romantic Painter* (Dorothy C. Miller)

199. *20th Century Sculpture and Constructions* (Department of Circulating Exhibitions)

203. *Tchelitchew* (James Thrall Soby)

204. *The Sculpture of John B. Flannagan* (Dorothy C. Miller)

205. *Art from Fighting China* (Dr. Chang Tao-fan)

209. *20th Century Portraits* (Monroe Wheeler)

212. *Joe Milone's Shoe Shine Stand* (Alfred H. Barr, Jr.)

1943

217. *American Realists and Magic Realists* (Dorothy C. Miller)

226. *Religious Folk Art of the Southwest* (Dorothy C. Miller)

234. *The Paintings of Morris Hirschfield* (Sidney Janis)

*242. *Alexander Calder* (James Johnson Sweeney)

245. *Marines Under Fire* (Armed Services Program/James Thrall Soby)

246. *Romantic Painting in America* (Dorothy C. Miller, James Thrall Soby)

1944

255. *Modern Cuban Painters* (Margaret Miller)

258. *Art in Progress: Fifteenth Anniversary Exhibition*
258a. *Painting and Sculpture* (James Thrall Soby)

261. *American Battle Painting 1776–1918* (Lincoln Kirstein)

262. *Paintings by Jacob Lawrence* (James Thrall Soby, Monroe Wheeler)

263. *Marsden Hartley* (Hudson D. Walker)

264. *Lyonel Feininger* (Dorothy C. Miller)

1945

282. *Piet Mondrian* (James Johnson Sweeney)

284. *Georges Rouault* (James Thrall Soby)

293. *Fourteen Paintings by Vincent van Gogh* (Loan exhibition from Netherlands Government)

298. *Stuart Davis* (James Johnson Sweeney)

1946

306. *Arts of the South Seas* (René d'Harnoncourt, Ralph Linton, Paul S. Wingert)

316. *Marc Chagall* (James Johnson Sweeney)

319. *Georgia O'Keeffe* (James Johnson Sweeney)

325. *Paintings from New York Private Collections* (Monroe Wheeler)

*329. *Fourteen Americans* (Dorothy C. Miller)

332. *Florine Stettheimer* (Marcel Duchamp; catalogue by Henry McBride)

335. Le Tricorne *by Picasso* (George Amberg)

339. *Henry Moore* (James Johnson Sweeney)

1947

346. *Large Scale Modern Paintings* (Margaret Miller)

351b. *Alfred Stieglitz Exhibition: His Collection* (James Johnson Sweeney, in consultation with Georgia O'Keeffe)

*358. *Ben Shahn* (James Thrall Soby)

1948

365b. Portrait of Gertrude Stein *by Picasso* (Alfred H. Barr, Jr.)

369. *Gabo–Pevsner* (Monroe Wheeler)

370. *Miró* Mural (James Thrall Soby)

376. *Pierre Bonnard* (John Rewald)

380. *Loren MacIver Mural Paintings* (Monroe Wheeler)

381. *New York Private Collections* (James Thrall Soby)

385. *Collage* (Margaret Miller)

*388. *The Sculpture of Elie Nadelman* (Lincoln Kirstein; installation by René d'Harnoncourt)

393. *Timeless Aspects of Modern Art* (René d'Harnoncourt)

1949

403. *Georges Braque* (Henry R. Hope)

*413. *Twentieth-Century Italian Art* (Alfred H. Barr, Jr., James Thrall Soby)

415. *Oskar Kokoschka* (James S. Plaut)

418. *Sculpture by Painters* (Department of Circulating Exhibitions/Jane Sabersky)

423. *Modern Art in Your Life* (Robert Goldwater in collaboration with René d'Harnoncourt)

433. *Paul Klee* (James Thrall Soby)

1950

434. *Percival Goodman War Memorial Model* (Philip Johnson)

439. *Charles Demuth* (Andrew Carnduff Ritchie)

440. *Franklin C. Watkins* (Andrew Carnduff Ritchie)

444. *New Talent Exhibition [I]: Seymour Drumlevitch, William D. King, Raymond Parker* (Andrew Carnduff Ritchie)

450. *Edvard Munch* (Frederick B. Deknatel, Johan H. Langaard, James S. Plaut)

452. *Three Modern Styles* (Department of Circulating Exhibitions/Libby Tannenbaum)

455. *Carvers, Modelers, Welders: A Selection of Recent American Sculpture* (Department of Circulating Exhibitions/Jane Sabersky)

*462. *Soutine* (Monroe Wheeler)

464. *New Talent Exhibition [II]: Louis Bunce, Ynez Johnston and Ernest Mundt* (Andrew Carnduff Ritchie)

1951

*466. *Abstract Painting and Sculpture in America* (Andrew Carnduff Ritchie)

471. *Lebrun:* Crucifixion (Andrew Carnduff Ritchie)

474. *Modigliani* (William S. Lieberman, Margaret Miller, Andrew Carnduff. Ritchie, Jane Sabersky; catalogue by James Thrall Soby)

477. *New Talent Exhibition [III]: Henry Di Spirito, Irving Kriesberg, Raymond August Mintz* (Andrew Carnduff Ritchie)

478. *Selections from the Alfred Stieglitz Collection*

479. *Modern Relief* (Department of Circulating Exhibitions/Jane Sabersky)

480. *Selections from Five New York Private Collections* (Andrew Carnduff Ritchie)

485. *Lipchitz:* Birth of the Muses (Andrew Carnduff Ritchie)

491. *James Ensor* (James S. Plaut)

492. *Henri Matisse* (Alfred H. Barr, Jr.)

1952

*507. *15 Americans* (Dorothy C. Miller)

510. *New Talent Exhibition [IV]: Philip C. Elliott, Gorman Powers, Walter R. Rogalski, Carol Summers* (Andrew Carnduff Ritchie)

514. *French Paintings from the Molyneux Collection* (John Rewald)

515. *Understanding African Negro Sculpture* (Department of Circulating Exhibitions)

521. *Les Fauves* (John Rewald)

524. *New Talent Exhibition [V]: Byron Goto, John Hultberg, Louise Kruger* (Andrew Carnduff Ritchie)

527. *De Stijl* (Alfred H. Barr, Jr.)

1953

529. *International Sculpture Competition: The Unknown Political Prisoner* (U.S. jury directed by Andrew Carnduff Ritchie; installation by Carlos Dyer)

533. *Forty Paintings from the Edward G. Robinson Collection* (Andrew Carnduff Ritchie)

535. *Rouault* (Monroe Wheeler)

536. *Sculpture of the Twentieth Century* (Andrew Carnduff Ritchie)

545. *Léger* (Katharine Kuh)

546. *New Talent Exhibition [VI]: Keith Monroe, Ira Schwartz, Robert Sowers* (Andrew Carnduff Ritchie)

1954

550. *Ancient Arts of the Andes* (René d'Harnoncourt)

555. *Edouard Vuillard* (Andrew Carnduff Ritchie)

558. *The Sculpture of Jacques Lipchitz* (Henry R. Hope)

560. *Niles Spencer* (Department of Circulating Exhibitions/ Dorothy C. Miller)

561. *Japanese Calligraphy* (Arthur Drexler)

1955

572. *15 Paintings by French Masters of the Nineteenth Century lent by the Louvre and the Museums of Albi and Lyon*

577. *New Talent Exhibition [VII]: Tom Benrimo, Hugh R. Townley, Richard O. Tyler* (Andrew Carnduff Ritchie)

*579. *The New Decade: 22 European Painters and Sculptors* (Andrew Carnduff Ritchie)

580. *Paintings from Private Collections* (Alfred H. Barr, Jr.)

583. *Giorgio de Chirico* (James Thrall Soby)

584. *Yves Tanguy* (James Thrall Soby)

592. *New Talent Exhibition [VIII]: Martin Craig, Leander Fornas, Nora Speyer* (Andrew Carnduff Ritchie)

1956

*597. *Julio Gonzalez* (Andrew Carnduff Ritchie)

598. *Toulouse-Lautrec* (Andrew Carnduff Ritchie)

602. *New Talent Exhibition [IX]: Pierre Clerk, Dimitri Hadzi, Robert Kabak* (Andrew Carnduff Ritchie)

603. *Kandinsky Murals* (Letitia Howe)

*604. *12 Americans* (Dorothy C. Miller)

607. *Masters of British Painting 1800–1950* (Andrew Carnduff Ritchie)

611. *Balthus* (James Thrall Soby)

612. *Jackson Pollock* (Sam Hunter)

1957

618. *New Talent Exhibition [X]: George M. Cohen, Gabriel Kohn, Miriam Schapiro* (Andrew Carnduff Ritchie)

*619. *Picasso: 75th Anniversary Exhibition* (Alfred H. Barr, Jr.)

620. *Matta* (William Rubin)

*621. *David Smith* (Sam Hunter)

622. *German Art of the 20th Century* (Andrew Carnduff Ritchie; catalogue by Werner Haftmann, Alfred Hentzen, William S. Lieberman)

1958

629. *Seurat: Paintings and Drawings* (Daniel Catton Rich)

630. *Juan Gris* (James Thrall Soby)

631. *Arp* (James Thrall Soby)

1959

641. *Joan Miró* (William S. Lieberman, James Thrall Soby)

642. *New Talent Exhibition [XI]: David V. Hayes* (Peter Selz)

644. *Recent Sculpture U.S.A.* (Dorothy C. Miller, James Thrall Soby)

645. *The New American Painting: As Shown in 8 European Countries 1958–1959* (International Program/Dorothy C. Miller)

648. *New Talent Exhibition [XII]: Ronni Solbert* (Peter Selz)

*651. *New Images of Man* (Peter Selz)

*656. *Sixteen Americans* (Dorothy C. Miller)

1960

658. *New Talent Exhibition [XIII]: Peter Voulkos* (James E. Elliott, Peter Selz)

660. *Claude Monet: Seasons and Moments* (William C. Seitz)

661. Homage to New York: *a self-constructing and self-destroying work of art conceived and built by Jean Tinguely*

666. *Art Nouveau* (Peter Selz)

*668. *New Spanish Painting and Sculpture* (Frank O'Hara)

669. *New Talent Exhibition [XIV]: Mowry Baden, Walter Gaudnek, Leo Rabkin* (Peter Selz)

1961

*679. *Mark Rothko* (Peter Selz)

*680. *Max Ernst* (William S. Lieberman)

681. *Norbert Kricke* (Peter Selz)

685. *Futurism* (Peter Selz; catalogue by Joshua C. Taylor)

689. *The Adele R. Levy Collection: A Memorial Exhibition* (Alfred H. Barr, Jr.)

*690. *15 Polish Painters* (Peter Selz)

*695. *The Art of Assemblage* (William C. Seitz)

696. *The Last Works of Henri Matisse: Large Cut Gouaches* (Monroe Wheeler)

697. *Chagall: The Jerusalem Windows* (Peter Selz)

698. *Orozco: Studies for the Dartmouth Murals* (Elaine Johnson)

699. *Odilon Redon, Gustave Moreau, Rodolphe Bresdin* (John Rewald)

1962

*702. *The Work of Jean Dubuffet* (Peter Selz)

*707. *Recent Painting USA: The Figure* (Alfred H. Barr, Jr. with William S. Lieberman, Dorothy C. Miller, Frank O'Hara)

[709.] *Art of the Asmat—The Collection of Michael C. Rockefeller* (Museum of Primitive Art exhibition held in The Museum of Modern Art Sculpture Garden)

*710. *Mark Tobey* (William C. Seitz)

716. *Arshile Gorky* (William C. Seitz)

1963

717. *The Intimate World of Lyonel Feininger* (William S. Lieberman)

719. *Emil Nolde* (Peter Selz)

721. *Rodin* (Peter Selz)

*722. *Americans 1963* (Dorothy C. Miller)

*727. *Hans Hofmann* (William C. Seitz)

729. *Medardo Rosso* (Peter Selz; monograph by Margaret Scolari Barr)

Photo Credits

The photographs reproduced in this publication were provided in most cases by The Museum of Modern Art. The following list, keyed to page numbers, applies to photographs for which an additional acknowledgment is due.

Contributors

Edward Eigen is a doctoral candidate in the department of architecture at the Massachusetts Institute of Technology

Helen M. Franc is a former Editor-in-Chief of the Department of Publications

Michael Kimmelman is chief art critic of the *New York Times*

Terence Riley is Chief Curator of the Department of Architecture and Design

Rona Roob is Museum Archivist

John Szarkowski is Director Emeritus of the Department of Photography

Lynn Zelevansky is Curatorial Assistant in the Department of Painting and Sculpture

A Note to Contributors

Studies in Modern Art publishes scholarly articles focusing on works of art in the collection of The Museum of Modern Art and on the Museum's programs. It is issued annually, although additional special numbers may be published from time to time. Each number deals with a particular topic. A list of future topics may be obtained from the journal office.

Contributors should submit proposals to the Editorial Committee of the journal by January 1 of the year preceding publication. Proposals should include the title of the article; a 500-word description of the subject; a critical appraisal of the current state of scholarship on the subject; and a list of works in the Museum's collection or details of the Museum's program that will be discussed. A working draft of the article may be submitted as a proposal. The Editorial Committee will evaluate all proposals and invite selected authors to submit finished manuscripts. (Such an invitation will not constitute acceptance of the article for publication.) Authors of articles published in the journal receive an honorarium and complimentary copies of the issue.

Please address all inquiries to:

Studies in Modern Art
The Museum of Modern Art
11 West 53 Street
New York, New York 10019

Trustees of The Museum of Modern Art